Mentoring for the Professions:
Orienting Toward the Future

A Volume in:
Mentoring Perspectives

Series Editor
Frances K. Kochan

Mentoring Perspectives

Series Editor

Frances K. Kochan
Auburn University

Mentoring for the Professions: Orienting Toward the Future

Aimee A. Howley
Mary Barbara Trube

INFORMATION AGE PUBLISHING, INC.
Charlotte, NC • www.infoagepub.com

Library of Congress Cataloging-in-Publication Data

The CIP data for this book can be found on the Library of Congress website (loc.gov).

Paperback: 978-1-62396-835-9
Hardcover: 978-1-62396-836-6
eBook: 978-1-62396-837-3

Copyright © 2015 Information Age Publishing Inc.

Printed in the United States of America

CONTENTS

PART II

MENTORING IN PROFESSIONAL FIELDS & THROUGH PROFESSIONAL ORGANIZATIONS

PART III

MENTORING WITH DIFFERENT POPULATIONS

DEDICATION

Collectively the authors of the chapters wish to dedicate their work in this book to the following mentors and mentees who are no longer among us: Catherine Brown, Robert B. Cairns, William T. Eaton, Bill Fox, W. A. Gray, Jr., Grace Iriagbonse Idemudia, Jean Meadows, Najee Muhammad, Alan Osborne, John Petelle, Timothy Robertson, H. T. "Ted" Salzman, Ray Skinner, Michael Thomas, and Eleanor P. Vinet.

PREFACE

When a combination of more and less experienced employees find themselves in the same office suite, department, division, unit, college, corporation, or profession, they sometimes self-organize into mentor–mentee dyads. Far more often, though, the less experienced people do not find ways to connect with good mentors, and the more experienced people hesitate to volunteer to play this role. In organizations where collaboration, sharing, and mutual support are not well-established norms, structured mentoring programs can fill in the gap. But norms of autonomy, interpersonal competition, defensiveness, and invidiousness tend to minimize the benefits of formal programs and keep informal arrangements from developing spontaneously.

We would all like to hope that our organizations nurture rather than devour their young. This volume came into being out of that hope and out of the belief that productive mentoring arrangements are more likely to take place when mentors and mentees are knowledgeable about the benefits and pitfalls of mentoring as well as strategies for using mentoring to good advantage: when they have models, tools to support mentor–mentee relationships, and assurance that mentoring is a practice with a well-established track record.

Another reason for assembling these chapters was that, for us, mentoring began to look like a meme. In conversations with colleagues, we asked what they were studying, and they asked us what we were studying: "Mentoring" was the

Mentoring for the Professions: Orienting Toward the Future, pages xi–xii.
Copyright © 2015 by Information Age Publishing

response we often gave and heard. Mentoring seemed important to our colleagues who were advising doctoral students, working in teacher preparation programs, helping businesses become more productive, providing guidance to newly hired employees, and engaging in networking and many other enterprises for which teamwork was a necessary ingredient. Along with our colleagues, mentoring also seemed important to us as a way to grow professionally and give back to our professions—both at the same time.

Discussions of mentoring often elicit fond and not so fond memories. Graduates of master's and doctoral programs may have received generative mentoring from advisors, or they may have had less productive (and sometimes quite counterproductive) experiences. Professionals may recall receiving assistance from knowledgeable and generous coworkers, or they may recollect inattention or even betrayal from those more senior employees who might have given them help. Because of our experiences, we all view mentoring through both an intellectual and an emotional lens. The chapters in this book acknowledge and strive to make sense of both perspectives. What they present is varied, but there are common themes running across them all. Both the themes and the variations offer relevant insights, in our view.

This edited volume would not have been possible without assistance from our peer reviewers and copyeditors. We offer sincere thanks to Tanis Furst, Xiaodan Huang, Edwina Pendarvis, and Pamela K. Scheurer. We also have been extremely fortunate to work with outstanding staff at IAP: Many thanks to Amanda Uriarte and all others on the editorial and publication team as well. Finally, we want to express our deep appreciation to the Patton College of Education for giving us opportunities to receive mentoring and to become mentors. We thank the college also for providing the funds that enabled us to obtain three peer reviews for each chapter and to employ professional copyeditors to assist with final manuscript preparation.

PART I

CONCEPTUALIZING MENTORING

CHAPTER 1

MENTORING

Its Nature and Practices across the Professions

Mary Barbara Trube

ABSTRACT

The chapter provides introductory remarks establishing a context for the exploration of mentoring undertaken in the chapters in this volume. It offers a brief review of the extensive body of literature on the nature of mentorships, the characteristics and experiences of mentors, and the practice of mentoring. Throughout the discussion in the chapter, mentoring is positioned as a collaborative, reciprocal learning relationship with potential benefits for both mentees and mentors. When mentoring relationships work well, they enable employees to establish, sustain, and enrich personal growth and professional learning. Increasingly, moreover, employers across fields as diverse as education and industry encourage informal mentoring arrangements or implement formal mentoring programs with the aim of helping new employees and employees in new roles learn about their work environments and acquire job-specific competencies—learnings that help assure the effective performance and job satisfaction of these employees.

INTRODUCTION

During the past quarter-century, an increasing number of scholars have turned their attention to mentoring—its characteristics, practices, and outcomes. By identifying different types of mentors and contexts for mentoring, personal and professional dimensions of mentoring, approaches and behaviors associated with effective mentorships, and qualities of productive mentor–protégé relationships, these scholars are contributing to a broader and deeper understanding of both formal and informal mentoring (Allen, Eby, O'Brien, & Lentz, 2008). As their work reveals, the principles underlying the practice of mentoring have applicability to a range of discussions and debates about learning, especially those concerning adult learning, professional development, and team learning. Today, mentoring is recognized not only as a highly active field of practice and research (Ragins & Kram, 2007), but often as an essential strategy for sustaining effective organizations (Rothwell, 2000) by building the capacities of the individuals within them (Zachary, 2000).

In this second decade of the 21st century, many research and development efforts focus on investigating the processes, styles, dimensions, and functions of mentors and the relative benefits of mentoring relationships for mentors and protégés alike. Some of these efforts also design and offer mentoring resources and tools. The introductory remarks presented here provide a brief review of the literature related to mentorships, mentors, and mentoring in order to establish a context for the deeper exploration of mentoring that chapter authors provide. With a similar perspective to the one offered by these scholars, we position mentoring as a collaborative, reciprocal learning relationship with potential benefits for both mentees and mentors. Other recent work on mentoring favors this perspective as well.

THEMES FROM THE LITERATURE
ON MENTORING

The concept of mentoring as an important practice for the cultivation of knowledge is ancient, as reflected in Homer's account of the mythological figure of Mentor, friend and retainer of Telemachus, the son of Ulysses. Mentor educated and shaped the character of his youthful charge while Ulysses was away at war. According to legend, when Telemachus confronted critical decisions, Athena, goddess of wisdom, took on Mentor's form to offer "good counsel, prudent restraint and practical insight" (Barondess, 1995, p. 4). The ancient Greek tale illustrates that, to be an effective mentor, one must possess certain knowledge, skills, and values and, in the most demanding circumstances, be able to offer counsel of the wisest nature for the good of the individual protégé and the community to which the protégé and mentor belong.

Mentorships in modern organizations and institutions can enhance novices' launching of their careers, negotiation of social networks, development of professional identity, and performance in the workplace (Zey, 1988). A meta-analysis conducted by Allen, Eby, Poteet, Lentz, and Lima (2004) revealed that mentoring contributes to the career success of protégés both in terms of objective measures (e.g., monetary compensation, promotion) and in terms of subjective ones (e.g., satisfaction, commitment). Additionally, mentorships support a mentee's induction and promote opportunities for networking in professional associations.

This chapter will explore these ideas in greater detail by focusing on the mentoring role and functions, mentoring relationships, and characteristics of effective mentors. First, however, it considers definitions of terms related to these topics.

Definitions

Interesting in its link to the ancient concept of mentoring is the National Aeronautics and Space Administration's (NASA, n.d.) definition of mentor: "an experienced individual that serves as a trusted counselor, loyal adviser and coach who helps and guides another individual's development" (p. 4). NASA defines the mentor's protégé or "mentee" as "a self-motivated individual seeking to continuously promote personal development" (NASA, n.d., p. 6). Reflecting a similar perspective, Noe, Greenberger, and Wang (2002) define a mentoring relationship as "an intense interpersonal exchange between mentor and protégé" (p. 129). Also viewing mentoring in this way, Barker and Pitts (1997) define it as a "relationship-driven, personal concept showing reciprocity between two or more individuals that facilitates goal accomplishment, provides emotional and psychological support, assists with professional development, and offers role-modeling" (p. 222).

Whereas these definitions are quite broad, encompassing practices such as coaching and providing emotional support, others are narrower. Some definitions explicitly distinguish between coaching and mentoring. Stone (2004), for example, suggests that coaching involves one-on-one guidance or training—tending to be more "hands-on" than mentoring. For Stone, "Mentoring...is a process by which a wise and helpful guide or advisor uses experience to...help the individual advance in her career" (2004, p. v). This author also suggests that mentors draw on their own experiences to help mentees steer clear of common mistakes and to skirt organizational roadblocks.

An exhaustive review of definitions of terms related to mentoring is well beyond the scope of this chapter. But one important aim is to point out some differences across definitions. As noted above, some definitions of mentoring include coaching and some do not. Other distinctions are listed below:

- Some definitions focus on the benefits of mentoring primarily for the mentee, while others focus on the benefits for both mentors and mentees.

- Some definitions treat mentoring as a temporary type of support—for example, when an employee is newly hired by a company, agency, or school; but others talk about mentorships that last for years.
- Some definitions construe mentor–mentee relationships as fitting within the structure and culture of a particular organization, but other definitions talk about such relationships as taking place across as well as within organizations.

As these variations illustrate, mentoring is a constellation of loosely defined practices. No one definition of this constellation prevails. Moreover, the fuzzy boundaries around the concept allow for considerable variability in practice—encouraging creative and intensive efforts in some organizations but permitting "lip-service" efforts in others. Whatever their actual level of engagement with mentoring approaches, organizations often use the term "mentoring" to label initiatives for linking new employees or employees in new roles with more experienced colleagues.

The Mentoring Role and Function

Considering the variability in definitions, it is not surprising that characterizations of the role and function of mentoring differ among those who study it, as well as among those who put it into practice. According to some researchers (e.g., Levinson, 1978), for example, supporting and facilitating a protégé's dream is the most important function of the mentor. This individualistic focus is, however, less in keeping with the perspective that had been dominant from ancient to modern times of viewing mentoring as a practice that links the success of the mentee with the success of the community to which the mentee belongs.

Some studies (e.g., Clutterbuck, 2004; Kram, 1985; Ragins & Kram, 2007; Scandura & Ragins, 1993; Zey, 1988) identify three major functions of mentoring: refining career skills, furthering psychosocial skills, and modeling desirable behaviors. In her seminal book, *Mentoring at Work*, Kram (1985) detailed the psychosocial functions of a mentor as role modeling, acceptance and confirmation, counseling, and friendship.

These functions are recognized in a variety of vocational and professional organizations (Murray & Owen, 1991). Further, child- and youth-serving agencies, including academic institutions at all levels, rely on mentoring relationships and networks with career, psychosocial, and modeling functions to sustain their somewhat diverse missions. Zelditch (1990) described the various functions of mentors as follows:

- Mentors are advisors with career experience who are willing to share their knowledge.
- Mentors are supporters who give emotional and moral encouragement.
- Mentors are tutors who give specific feedback on one's performance.

- Mentors are supervisors or employers to whom one is apprenticed.
- Mentors are sponsors who aid in obtaining opportunities and funds.
- Mentors are role models who the mentee aspires to be like in terms of knowledge, skills, and talents.

Mentoring Relationships

As these descriptions, particularly the broader ones, suggest, a mentor may take on the role of supervisor, administrator, coach, role model, teacher, or friend (see also Holmes, Hodgson, Simari, & Nishimura, 2010). Performance of the functions associated with these roles entails a certain level of expert knowledge coupled with the ability to foster a trusting and supportive relationship with the mentee. Both the mentor's and the mentee's ability and willingness to assume responsibility for establishing and maintaining such a relationship influence the extent to which the mentorship will promote learning (Lankau & Scandura, 2007).

That mentorships always have and always will offer an important method of teaching and learning is suggested by educational theorist Jerome Bruner, who argues that knowledge and skills develop through dynamic social interactions between people and, as such, are "participatory, proactive, communal, collaborative, and given over to the construction of meanings rather than receiving them" (Bruner, 1996, p. 84).

Generally, in the workplace, the mentor counsels the mentee about career-related issues, providing career guidance and developmental support to the less-experienced protégé, or induction to the novice. Research findings on mentoring further suggest, as Bullis and Bach (1989) contend, that mentor–mentee relationships impact the organization and profession as a whole by reaching beyond the individuals directly involved in the mentoring relationship.

Four phases of mentoring relationships have been identified by Kram (1985, cited in Turban & Lee, 2007)—initiation, cultivation, separation, and redefinition. The initiation phase typically lasts from 6 to 12 months, during which time expectations for the mentoring relationship are set. The cultivation phase provides "mentoring assistance" in career and psychosocial functions for from 2 to 5 years (Turban & Lee, 2007, p. 23). The separation phase results in autonomy-seeking behaviors by the protégé that are generally due to his or her growing confidence and self-efficacy. Lastly, during the redefinition phase, the mentor and mentee come to recognize one another as peers (Kram, 1985, cited in Turban & Lee, 2007).

In the same vein, Zachary (2000) suggests that stages of mentoring commonly enact preparation, negotiation, enabling, and ending. Preparation is a time of readying for the processes of mentoring and being mentored; followed by negotiation, a period for defining goals, expectations, and benchmarks while gaining a clearer understanding of the functions each individual involved in the mentorship will perform. Next is the enabling stage—a stage at which the mentorship is fully underway—with the mentor providing opportunities for growth through monitoring, evaluating, negotiating, supporting, and encouraging behaviors. Finally, the ending stage brings the mentoring relationship to closure, allowing the mentor and mentee to move on to another phase of their relationship and, in many cases, to focus less attention on training and more attention on performance.

At its best, according to many writers on the subject, mentoring is grounded in a reciprocal relationship that offers benefits to both the mentor and the protégé (Ragins, Cotton, & Miller, 2000). The National Academy of Sciences (1997) characterizes an effective mentoring relationship as one in which there is "mutual respect, trust, understanding, and empathy" (p. 2). Mutuality in a high-quality mentoring relationship is viewed as a perspective that "promotes mutual growth, learning, and development within the career context" for the mentor and protégé (Fletcher & Ragins, 2007, p. 374).

Some scholars who write about mentoring claim that having a constellation of mentoring relationships via a developmental network (Higgins & Kram, 2001), in which different individuals offer a range of viewpoints, provides a "mutuality perspective" that is particularly helpful to the mentee (Dobrow, Chandler, Murphey, & Kram, 2012, p. 211). Others also favor a network approach rather than an individualistic one. According to Holmes and associates (2010), "Mentoring can and should facilitate the development of personal learning networks. Such networks can be lifelong resources for continued career development, collaboration, and personal and professional growth.... Depending on the stage of the mentor-mentee relationship, the description of the role will differ" (p. 337). According to Le Cornu (2005), mentorships enacted through co-mentoring, collaborative groups, or peer mentoring promote "professional dialogue...so that learning outcomes are maximized for all" (p. 356).

Regardless of role and function, however, the mentor's approach to a protégé is often "defined by his [sic] perception of the protégé's personal qualities, skills, and the expected need for help" (Holmes et al., 2010, p. 7). In general, according to Allen (2007), when mentors have the option of selecting their mentees, they tend to prefer those whom they view as most promising. Whether or not this tendency benefits an organization is certainly arguable because the organization's less promising new employees may actually need and benefit from mentorships more than its more competent ones.

Characteristics of Effective Mentors

NASA (n.d.) describes effective mentors as dedicated and ethical professionals who are experts in their fields and who are people-oriented—good motivators, good teachers, humanists in outlook, and thoughtful listeners who respect differences in perspectives and opinions. Related to this latter quality are findings from many studies that recognize the importance of a mentor's openness to the mentee's concerns and questions. These studies also show that effective mentors are cognizant of and insightful about their own roles as learners, supporters, facilitators, and guides.

As Abiddin and Hassan (2012) point out, the essential mentoring practices include listening, asking questions, and enabling. With these practices at the core of their efforts, effective mentors tend either to be (1) permissive, finding ways to help mentees set and accomplish goals that both mentor and mentee regard as worthwhile through their mutual construction of a sense of purpose, or (2) authoritative, finding ways to use the tools of formal mentorships provided in institutions and organizations in order to provide mentees with structured experiences directed toward learning and reflection. As a result, mentors with the predisposition to be authoritarian (rather than either permissive or authoritative) need to work hard to keep from intimidating their mentees and affording them too little agency.

Because support from an effective mentor may make or break a new professional's career, the characteristics, knowledge, skills, and dispositions required for effective mentors have been topics of much study. Glenn (2006) describes effective mentors in education as individuals who "collaborate rather than dictate, relinquish an appropriate level of control, allow for personal relationships, share constructive feedback, and accept differences" (p. 88). Being an effective mentor demands an understanding of the importance of dependability, engagement, authenticity, and the ability to tune into the needs of the mentee.

Cohen (1999) developed a behavioral profile of an effective mentee. In *The Mentee's Guide to Mentoring* (1999, p. 28), Cohen suggests the following specific considerations: When a mentor is building a *relationship* by asking questions, sharing reflections on experiences, and listening empathetically, the mentee reciprocates by offering detailed answers and explanations. When the mentor is seeking *information* in his or her effort to offer strategic advice, the mentee provides facts and records or whatever else might be needed. When the mentor is taking on a *facilitative* role by offering alternatives to the mentee, the protégé explains the basis for his or her choices and, by doing so, reveals something about his or her interests, abilities, and motivations. When the mentor is *confrontational* in order to investigate the mentee's counterproductive strategies and behaviors, the mentee reflects on his or her behaviors and examines the need and capacity to change. When the mentor is acting as a *model* to increase motivation, the mentee exerts effort, takes risks, and works to overcome difficulties. When the mentor is sharing the *employer's vision* with the intention of fostering initiative and the ability to think critically about a practice or step in the mentee's career, the mentee constructs an image of his or her own future and professional potential. Such relational behaviors appear to promote productive outcomes for the mentor, mentee, and the organization or institution for which they work.

Adding to the Existing Literature

As the discussion above illustrates, diverse mentoring models arise out of individual and organizational needs for one-on-one, peer, team, and group mentoring. Whatever mentoring approach is used (e.g., formal or informal; one-on-one, group, or network), its coherence and success are dependent on the characteristics of mentors and mentees and the characteristics of the relationship they build. The success of mentoring, moreover, requires the support of the organizations that sponsor (and ultimately benefit from) mentoring arrangements.

In fact, recent efforts to investigate mentoring processes and outcomes reflect growing awareness of the value of mentoring—awareness that spans the traditional theory-to-practice gap. In fact, scholarship on mentoring depends on partnerships between the community of researchers with an interest in mentoring and their hosts—executives in corporations, educational institutions, and other agencies that stand to benefit from mentoring. Whereas efforts thus far have provided many useful insights, deeper understanding of mentoring is still needed. The collection of chapters presented in this volume explores some of the emerging questions by offering theoretical interpretations, reporting on empirical studies, and detailing specific mentoring programs.

EXPLORATION OF MENTORING
IN THE PROFESSIONS

Before readers turn to the chapters themselves, they may find it helpful to consider an editor's-eye view of what the chapters contribute. This synoptic perspective on the book as a whole presents it as themes and variations across two domains—the definitional and descriptive domain ("what is mentoring?" "what does it look like?") and the domain focusing on diversity of needs across different types of mentees and mentoring contexts ("who needs what?" "who benefits from what?" "where does mentoring take place?" "how does a particular place help foster a contextually useful form of mentoring?"). Turning from this thematic approach, the chapter ends with a sequential one that explains the commonalities that prompted our arrangement of the book's chapters into five sections.

Themes and Variations

As readers will see, the chapters represent diverse perspectives offered from a variety of vantage points. In fact, the overarching aim of the book is to represent mentoring as a diverse set of related practices that to some degree cross organizational barriers (i.e., constitute themes) and to some degree reflect the particular character and missions of specific organizations or organizational types (i.e., represent variations).

Definitions and Descriptions

Although many chapters start with definitions and description of mentoring, the primary purpose of several of them is to define mentoring and clarify what is involved in being a mentor, offering mentoring, and establishing an effective mentoring relationship. Moreover, these chapters illustrate the definitions they present by using examples from different fields (adult basic education, counseling, higher education, retail merchandizing).

Reynolds, Smith, and Johnson focus on adult basic education (ABE) to illustrate how mentoring functions as an intentional relationship, between more- and less-experienced professionals, for the purpose of promoting learning and growth. The authors use examples of the variations of mentoring in different ABE contexts.

In their chapter, Pillay, Fulton, and Robertson use Bernard's Discrimination Model of Supervision to describe mentoring as a particular approach to supervision. They ground their discussion in their collective experiences with supervision in mental health organizations.

Ovando offers a definition borrowed from research on mentoring graduate researchers of color, and identifies the importance of acquiring both practical skills and social-emotional insights in the course of a dynamic mentorship experience. She positions mentoring as a journey of mutual discovery that may result in a professional relationship that lasts a lifetime. Similarly, Foley's definition and illustrations from his experience mentoring doctoral students in mathematics education draws attention to the stewardship that mentoring entails and the lifelong learning that effective mentoring relationships promote.

Trube and Wan use their interviews with experienced mentors to induce a definition of a *mentor* as an individual with professional knowledge, experience, and skills who provides support, nurture, and advice within a wider constellation of relationships across more and less experienced professionals. Grounded in their study of faculty's experiences as mentors and mentees, Osa, Oliver, and Walker propose a view of mentoring suggesting that it functions best (at least within the context of higher education) when mentors share lessons from their own experience, provide support, and challenge mentees to become productive members of the institution. Drawing on data from a study of employees in the retail industry, Thornburgh and Paulins present a description of mentorships that focuses on the leadership characteristics and behaviors of mentees' first bosses.

Taking the definition of mentoring beyond the conceptual to the operational level, Howley, Dudek, Williams, and Trube describe work to develop an instrument for measuring the mentoring styles of the experienced teachers in K–12 schools who provide mentoring to the student teachers placed in their classrooms. Their work categorizes mentoring styles along four continua: directive to nondirective mentoring, collaborative to noncollaborative mentoring, convergent to divergent mentoring, and mentoring that is more or less open to instructional experimentation.

Responding to Diverse Needs and Contexts

Several authors discuss mentoring as a response to the complex needs of individuals, programs, organizations, or society as a whole. According to chapter authors and the works they cite, these needs result from demographic changes, economic challenges, and human capital demands of a postindustrial world. Viewing mentoring primarily in terms of the needs it serves, several chapters consider mentoring that supports different types of novices (e.g., students, faculty members, newly appointed or practicing administrators, and so on).

Mahaffey and Mares focus on the needs of nontraditional (what they term "new-traditional") undergraduates, and present evidence suggesting that peer-mentoring programs promote student retention. Mather, Marvel, and Nelson suggest that mentoring environments can incorporate activities such as service learning that encourage students in colleges and universities to make meaning by dedicating themselves to the well-being of others.

Two chapters draw attention to the use of mentoring to meet the needs of candidates in teacher preparation programs. Gut and Beam describe a study that demonstrated the powerful support that co-teaching and co-mentoring in preservice education provided to individuals preparing to teach secondary level STEM (science, technology, engineering, and math) disciplines. Gray and Gray offer situational mentoring as a response to the needs of society to produce STEM-prepared professionals. Their model teaches preservice teachers how to function effectively as STEM mentors of adolescents who are enrolled in STEM courses.

Considering the needs of faculty members, Maybee turns to the question of mentoring adjunct faculty. He suggests a learning-outcomes model as a way to support these faculty members through one-to-one mentoring—an approach that could also be adapted to meet the needs of small groups of faculty. Reflecting insights from her own experience, Middleton's chapter explores the needs of more experienced faculty members who are beginning to think about taking on leadership roles. Her version of "educative mentoring" draws on three models of leadership—powerful models that help meet the needs of diverse individuals whose paths to leadership positions are often impeded by institutionalized forms of prejudice.

Other needs of higher education institutions are addressed by several authors who recommend mentoring as an especially effective form of professional development. VanDerveer, Howard, and VanDerveer discuss the mentoring of female coaches. Doyle-Scharff and Conley draw attention to the mentoring of female faculty members in STEM disciplines. Moore and Colorado talk about the benefits of a mentoring program that provides mentoring to emerging scholars in a way that transcends institutional boundaries.

Shifting the focus from higher education institutions to K–12 schools, Larson's chapter describes the Leadership Project, which began as a grassroots initiative in response to school superintendents' need for help in dealing with increasingly complex roles and responsibilities. With school improvement in view, Salzman and Boch's chapter discusses a three-year school–university partnership that uses mentor educators to provide guidance to teachers that is based on feedback gathered during "instructional rounds."

THE ARRANGEMENT OF CHAPTERS

The discussion of themes and variations shows the network of ideas explored in the chapters that are included in the collection. This perspective is useful for synoptic purposes, but my co-editor and I found it less useful as a basis for organizing the chapters into a meaningful sequence. For that purpose, we chose a five-part organizational scheme. Part 1 focuses on theories undergirding mentoring. Part 2 includes chapters that report empirical studies of mentoring. Parts 3 and 4 focus on mentoring with different aims—to support learning in higher education institutions on the one hand, and to promote professional development on the other. Part 5 concludes the book with chapters that push the idea of mentoring beyond its more commonly accepted borders. Perhaps it might be called "mentoring with a new twist."

Part 1: Theoretical Perspectives

Chapters 1 and 2 begin with a theoretical overview that grounds discussions throughout the chapters in *Mentoring for the Professions: Orienting toward the Future*. My initial chapter provides a brief review of relevant literature and introduces the rest of the book. It is followed by a chapter by Renée Middleton that contextualizes mentoring within the theoretical literature on leadership.

Part 2: Empirical Studies

Chapters 3 through 6 report findings from recent empirical studies about mentoring. Chapter 3, contributed by Barbara Trube and Guofang Wan, presents an exploratory study to identify experienced mentors' perceptions of the essential knowledge, skills, and dispositions that effective mentors use in various contexts. In Chapter 4, Aimee Howley, Marged Dudek, Natalie Williams, and Barbara Trube report on the process of developing an instrument for measuring mentoring style and the data supporting the validity and reliability of the instrument. Chapter 5, provided by Dianne Gut and Pam Beam, investigates the processes and outcomes associated with using models of co-mentoring and peer coaching to enhance clinical experiences for preservice teachers. In Chapter 6, Barbara Mahaffey and Alvin Mares present a case study of peer tutoring for nontraditional college students. Focusing on the mentoring experiences of faculty in higher education Chapter 7, written by Justina Osa, Andrean Oliver, and Tracy Walker, presents the results of survey research conducted at one institution.

And in Chapter 8, Allison Thornburgh and Ann Paulins report on a study exploring the lived experiences of early career women in the fashion merchandising and retail industry.

Part 3: Mentoring in Higher Education

The overarching focus of Chapters 9 through 12 is mentoring for higher education. Chapter 9 presents *The Stanford Way*, by authors Tara VanDerveer, Vicki Howard, and Beth VanDerveer; it examines the history of coaching and the role mentoring of coaches has contributed to the increasing prominence of women's basketball. In Chapter 10, Richard Maybee proposes a mentoring model that offers five communication tools as vehicles for promoting positive learning outcomes for adjunct faculty. In Chapter 11, Gregory Foley addresses the development of scholars through doctoral education.

His particular focus is on doctoral programs in mathematics education, but his guidance applies more generally across disciplines. Also considering doctoral-level preparation, Chapter 12 focuses on how author Martha Ovando uses four essential mentoring practices to facilitate the dissertation research of students from diverse backgrounds. Chapter 13, written by Maureen Doyle-Scharff and Valerie Martin Conley, presents information suggesting that females enrolled in various National Science Foundation programs benefit from programs using mentoring models to expand career opportunities in science, technology, engineering, and mathematics (STEM) fields. Numerous mentoring programs are featured in the chapter.

Part 4: Mentoring for Professional Development

Chapters 14 through 18 explore mentoring for professional development in a variety of contexts for different populations. In Chapter 14, James Salzman and Karen Boch describe a rural school district's experience of embedding mentoring practices into a broad-based strategy for school improvement. Contributed by William Gray and Marilynne Miles Gray, Chapter 15 explores "Mentor-Assisted Enrichment Projects" that have demonstrated promising results in improving teacher preparation, increasing adolescents' learning of STEM, and creating a pipeline for preparing STEM professionals. In Chapter 16, Sharon Reynolds, Cristine Smith, and Kimberly Johnson discuss the transformation that occurs for adult basic education (ABE) teachers who receive mentoring and coaching as a form of professional learning. Models in Minnesota, Massachusetts, and Ohio are highlighted.

Chapter 17, contributed by William Larson, highlights the Leadership Project (LP), which has existed for more than 20 years to provide mentoring and other forms of support to school administrators and central office personnel in rural Appalachian districts in southern Ohio.

Part 5: Mentoring with a New Twist

The final section of the volume, incorporating Chapters 19 and 20, focuses on stretching the concept of mentoring to applications beyond those that are typical. In Chapter 19, Yegan Pillay, Bethany Fulton, and Timothy Robertson position mentoring as an extremely powerful approach to professional supervision. In Chapter 20, Peter Mather, Diana Marvel, and Lisa Nelson explore the idea of mentoring environments—a concept that goes beyond the traditional view of mentoring as inherent to relationships and instead locates mentoring within a wider set of educative experiences. Interestingly, this idea harks back to linkages between mentoring and leadership that Renée Middleton explores in the first section—what she calls "educative mentoring."

FINAL THOUGHTS

The chapters in this volume offer a range of perspectives on mentoring, reflect a variety of different scholarly methods for studying it, and offer persuasive arguments for using it. Both my co-editor and I have learned a great deal about mentoring by reading multiple versions of the chapters: when they arrived as first drafts, then came back again with revisions that responded to reviewers' comments, and finally returned to us bearing the helpful editing suggestions of the copyeditors.

The perspectives offered by chapter authors, varied as they are, nevertheless all point to the promise that mentoring offers as a practice for helping employees and employers, novices and experts, schools and businesses, individuals and society as a whole. I find this promise heartening: It is not a technical "fix" to the problems that we face, but something far more significant and far better grounded: a scaffold to improvement that gains traction and grows in power because it resides in the networks of mutually supportive relationships among colleagues.

REFERENCES

Abiddin, N. Z., & Hassan, A. (2012). A review of effective mentoring practices for mentees' development. *Journal of Studies in Education, 2*(1), 72–89.

Allen, T. D. (2007). Mentoring relationships from the perspective of the mentor. In B. R. Ragins & K. E. Kram (Eds.), *The handbook of mentoring at work: Theory, research, and practice* (pp. 123–147). Thousand Oaks, CA: SAGE Publications, Inc.

Allen, T. D., Eby, L. T., O'Brien, K. E., & Lenz, E. (2008). The state of mentoring research: A qualitative review of current research methods and future research implications. *Journal of Vocational Behavior, 73*, 343–357.

Allen, T. D., Eby, L. T., Poteet, M. L., Lentz, E., & Lima, L. (2004). Career benefits associated with mentoring for protégés: A meta-analytic review. *Journal of Applied Psychology, 89*, 127–136.

Barker, R. T., & Pitts, M. W. (1997). Graduate students as mentors: An approach for the undergraduate class project. *Journal of Management Education, 21*(2), 221–231.

Barondess, J.A. (1995). A brief history of mentoring. *Transactions of the American Clinical Climatological Association, 106*, 1–12.

Bruner, J. (1996). *The culture of education.* Cambridge, MA: Harvard University Press.

Bullis, C., & Bach, B. W. (1989). Are mentor relationships helping organizations? An exploration of developing mentee-mentor-organizational identifications using turning point analysis. *Communication Quarterly, 13*(3), 199–213.

Cohen, N. (1999). *The mentee's guide to mentoring.* Amherst, MA: HRD Press.

Clutterbuck, D. (2004). *Everyone needs a mentor: Fostering talent at work* (4th ed.). London, England: Chartered Institute of Personnel & Development.

Dobrow, S. R., Chandler, D. E., Murphy, W. M., & Kram, K. E. (2012). A review of developmental networks: Incorporating a mutuality perspective. *Journal of Management, 38*(1), 210–242.

Fletcher, J., & Ragins, B. R. (2007). Stone center relational cultural theory: A window on relational mentoring. In B. R. Ragins & K. E. Kram (Eds.), *The handbook of mentoring at work: Theory, practice and research* (pp. 373–400). Thousand Oaks, CA: Sage.

Glenn, W. J. (2006). Model versus mentor: Defining the necessary qualities of the effective cooperating teacher. *Teacher Education Quarterly, 33*(1), 85–95.

Higgins, M. C., & Kram, K. E. (2001). Reconceptualizing mentoring at work: A developmental network perspective. *Academy of Management Review, 26*(2), 264–288.

Holmes, D. R., Hodgson, P. K., Simari, R. D., & Nishimura, R. A. (2010). Mentoring: Making the transition from mentee to mentor. *Careers in Cardiovascular Research, 121*, 336–340.

Kram, K. E. (1985). *Mentoring at work.* Glenview, IL: Scott Foresman.

Lankau, M. J., & Scandura, T. A. (2007). Mentoring as a forum for personal learning in organizations. In B. R. Ragins & K. E. Kram (Eds.), *The handbook of mentoring at work: Theory, research, and practice* (pp. 95–122). Thousand Oaks, CA: Sage.

Le Cornu, R. (2005). Peer mentoring: Engaging pre-service teachers in mentoring one another. *Mentoring and Tutoring: Partnership in Learning, 13*(3), 355–366.

Levinson, D. J. (1978). *The seasons of a man's life.* New York, NY: Knopf.

Murray, M., & Owen, M. A. (1991). *Beyond the myths and magic of mentoring: How to facilitate an effective mentoring program.* San Francisco, CA: Jossey-Bass.

NASA Training and Leadership Development. (n.d.). *Mentoring program handbook: A guide for NASA first mentors.* Washington, DC: NASA. Retrieved from http://leadership.nasa.gov/nasa_first/Mentoring_Handbook.doc

National Academy of Sciences; National Academy of Engineering; & Institute of Medicine. (1997). *Adviser, teacher, role model, friend: On being a mentor to students in science and engineering.* Washington, DC: The National Academies Press.

Noe, R., Greenberger, D. B., & Wang, S. (2002). Mentoring: What do we know and where do we go from here. In G. Ferris (ed.), *Research in Personnel and Human Resources, 21*, 129–173.

Ragins, B. R., Cotton, J. L., & Miller, J. S. (2000). Marginal mentoring: The effects of type of mentor, quality of relationship, and program design on work and career attitudes. *Academy of Management Journal, 43*(6), 1177–1194.

Ragins, B. R., & Kram, K. E. (2007). *The handbook of mentoring at work: Theory, research & practice.* Thousand Oaks, CA: Sage.

Rothwell, W. M. (2000). *Effective succession planning: Ensuring leadership continuity and building talent from within* (2nd ed.). New York, NY: Amacom.

Scandura, T. A., & Ragins, B. R. (1993). The effects of gender and role orientation on mentorship in male-dominated occupations. *Journal of Vocational Behavior, 43,* 251–265.

Stone, F. M. (2004). *The mentoring advantage: Creating the next generation of leaders.* Chicago, IL: Dearborn Trade Publishers.

Turban, D. B., & Lee, F. K. (2007). The role of personality in mentoring relationships. In B. R. Ragins & K. E. Kram (Eds.), *The handbook of mentoring at work: Theory, research, and practice* (pp. 21–50). Thousand Oaks, CA: Sage.

Zachary, L. J. (2000). *The mentor's guide: Facilitating effective learning relationships.* San Francisco, CA: Jossey Bass.

Zelditch, M. (1990). *Mentor roles.* Proceedings of the 32nd Annual Meeting of the Western Association of Graduate Schools. Tempe, AZ. 16–18 March, 1990. Conference Presentation.

Zey, M. G. (1988). A mentor for all reasons. *Personnel Journal, 67,* 46–51.

CHAPTER 2

MENTORING FOR EFFECTIVE LEADERSHIP IN HIGHER EDUCATION ORGANIZATIONS

Renée A. Middleton

ABSTRACT

Leadership has always been a significant organizational function in institutions of higher education, and with increasing pressures on such institutions it may be even more critical now. Not all leadership is effective, however. Arguably, practices that draw on key insights from theories of transformational, distributed, and situational leadership offer a strong basis for leadership in contemporary colleges and universities. Cultivating leadership of this type requires mentoring—an undertaking to which practicing leaders need to commit their time and energy. This chapter draws on the personal experiences of one university dean to elaborate a model of transformational mentoring that links the interests and career plans of new and aspiring leaders to institutions' needs for succession planning and innovation. Meeting these needs will depend on institutions' ability to nurture leaders from diverse backgrounds who bring vision and expertise to bear on the executive functions they perform.

Mentoring for the Professions: Orienting Toward the Future, pages 19–43.

INTRODUCTION

The critical function of leadership in organizations has been well established (e.g., Hersey, Blanchard, & Johnson, 2008), and leadership is especially important in difficult times—when organizations are under stress or need to change in response to changing circumstances (e.g., Kotter, 1996). Arguably, with pressures for increased accountability, more efficient management, and more responsive programs, institutions of higher education are currently experiencing tremendous stress (Bolton, 1996; Morrill, 2013; van Ameijde, Nelson, Billsberry, & van Meurs, 2009). According to numerous observers, the need for effective leadership in such organizations is, therefore, acute (e.g., Bolton, 1996; Bowen & Shapiro, 1998; Rowley & Sherman, 2001; van Ameijde et al., 2009).

Institutions of higher education, moreover, employ both academic and non-academic leaders. Whereas leaders in the latter group may come to their positions with some formal leadership training, those in the former group typically do not (e.g., Gmelch, 2000; Raines & Alberg, 2003). Rather, they move through the ranks as faculty—in some cases developing leadership skills along the way (Bolton, 1996; Wolverton, Ackerman, & Holt, 2005)—but their acquisition of the full range of leadership skills they will need for roles as chairpersons, deans, or provosts often depends on the support they receive from formal and informal mentors (Raines & Alberg, 2003).

What is known about mentoring support for academic leaders in higher education and the types of relationships between mentors and mentees that make it effective? A relatively limited number of studies actually explore these questions empirically, but those that do suggest that (1) effective mentors provide opportunities and remove barriers (e.g., Gibson, 2006; Rheineck & Roland, 2008; Tolar, 2012); (2) they support mentees by serving in the role of "sounding board" (e.g., Stowers & Barker, 2010; Tolar, 2012); and (3) a team approach to leadership may work best to provide an organic type of leadership mentoring (e.g., Bensimon & Neumann, 1993). Studies of mentoring for leadership roles in higher education also show that not all new and aspiring higher education leaders appreciate mentoring, and some even find it intrusive (Tolar, 2012).

In the current chapter, I expand on the extant empirical literature to provide a theoretical rationale for a particular approach to mentoring in higher education institutions. Grounding for this approach comes from a commitment to distributing leadership in organizations for the purpose of fostering transformation (e.g., Spillane, 2006; van Ameijde et al., 2009). This commitment fits well with a social justice perspective and a progressive view of organizational development. My approach also draws on insights from situational leadership pertaining in particular to the synergistic possibilities of a good fit between a leader's style and the specific challenges that his or her organization is facing (e.g., Hersey et al., 2008). Following a discussion of my leadership framework, I consider the nature of productive mentor–mentee relationships and briefly review various types of mentorships. I then examine the tenets of developmental mentoring and next look at the special challenges and opportunities associated with mentoring women and people of color for roles as academic leaders in colleges and universities. I conclude the chapter with a vignette and list of insights drawn from my experiences mentoring new and aspiring leaders in my role as dean of a college of education in a large, public, research-intensive university.

A LEADERSHIP FRAMEWORK

In this section of the chapter, I elaborate an approach to higher education leadership that combines features of three recognized theories of leadership from literature on business management and education—transformational leadership (e.g., Bass & Avolio, 1994), distributed leadership (e.g., Spillane, 2006), and situational leadership (e.g., Hersey et al., 2008). These theories are not the only ones contributing to successful outcomes, nor are they always fully compatible with one another. But a personal approach to leadership can combine features of different theories in meaningful and practical ways. In this case, whereas each theory alone contributes important guidance to academic leaders, I believe that none of the theories are powerful enough on their own to enable academic leaders to confront all of the challenges they face in the contemporary university.

Leading for Change: Transformative Leadership

For good or ill, universities have been required in the last 20 years to make major changes, and commentators believe the process is ongoing (e.g., Christensen & Eyring, 2011; Rowley & Sherman, 2001). I use the word *required* intentionally here in order to point out that the changes universities need to make appear to respond to forces that are beyond the control of universities themselves—political shifts, changes in the developmental trajectory from adolescence to adulthood, economic imperatives. Universities play a role in shaping their own responses, but the conditions causing them to change are often external. Arguably, as well, the rhetoric calling for change—a rhetoric fueled by these same external forces—limits the terms of the debate about why and how universities ought to change (Hotho, 2013).

Because these external forces are so powerful and their rhetoric so insistent, wise leadership for change entails visionary thinking—thinking that is neither reactive nor impetuous. Transformational leaders, particularly those who are willing and able to place the needs of the wider community above their own personal needs, and sometimes even above the purported "needs" of their own organizations, bring significant strengths to the change process. Such leaders do not give in to the immediate pressures of students for credentials or faculty for resources or research offices for expanding "indirects" (i.e., facilities and administration charges to grants) (e.g., Keeling & Hersh, 2012; Saltmarsh, Sutherland-Smith, & Randell-Moon, 2011). Rather, such leaders determine when it is appropriate to place the mission of the organization, the needs of the organization, and the needs of the community, above their own needs.

Furthermore, they play an active role in executing the mission of the organization so that it aligns with their fundamental ethical principles. By doing so, these leaders assure that the changes that the organization makes will advance an ethical agenda (e.g., Ehrich, Cranston, Kimber, & Starr, 2012). In my own practice, for example, I have emphasized social justice on behalf of diverse populations and communities. Advocacy for students from diverse backgrounds and students from low-income homes, appreciation for the Appalachian culture that surrounds my university, and work on behalf of the fair treatment of local schools have all been central to my vision for shifting the college's mission away from conventional preparation of professionals and toward the preparation of professionals whose practice promotes social justice.

Interestingly, a leader's efforts to embrace an ethical mission or promote social justice are sometimes misinterpreted by, or alienating to, people in the university whose aims tend to be more conventional. For example, politicians in the state where my university is located often seek to pit the interests of K–12 education against those of higher education. When I come out in support of the K–12 schools—a position that the university's president understood was within my sphere of autonomous action—it makes some faculty and administrators uncomfortable. Some would prefer I remain quiet about my support for our K–12 partners. Because I could not ethically separate the interests of K–12 schools from those of higher education, a position that I had made clear when I interviewed for the position, I risked losing support from some colleagues within the state. This experience led me to realize that leaders can sometimes become so engrossed in the internal politics of their institutions that they cease to be effective externally, ultimately forgetting about the deeper ethical imperative that ought to guide what we do. Institutions have a responsibility to serve their communities, as does their leadership.

Distributed Leadership

Recent scholarship on leadership for K–12 schools has emphasized the need to cultivate the leadership potential of all professionals within school systems (e.g., Spillane, 2006). With this perspective in view, professional development, including mentorships and other intensive forms of professional development, focuses attention not just on academic content and pedagogy, but also on leadership preparation (e.g., Koellner, Jacobs, & Borko, 2011). The benefits of collaboration and critical decision making among all professionals in a school system justify this approach.

Although the literature on distributed leadership has devoted less attention to the higher education than to the K–12 context (but cf. Burke, 2010), evidence about shared governance suggests that institutions of higher education might benefit by deploying this approach to leadership. According to Crellin (2010), for example, older models of shared governance no longer work well, given the challenges that institutions of higher education are facing. The literature on shared governance in higher education, in fact, reveals a kind of tug-of-war between the interests of faculty and those of trustees and administrators (Crellin, 2010).

By contrast, efforts in the K–12 community to create collaborative professional cultures tend to break down *unproductive* norms of autonomy and promote shared accountability (Louis, Leithwood, Wahlstrom, & Anderson, 2010; McNulty & Besser, 2011). Arguably, autonomy norms are even stronger among faculty members in higher education institutions than among K–12 teachers, and these norms may, in some cases, contribute to dysfunctional systems of shared governance in which faculty call for increased levels of participation but, at times, refuse to accept much responsibility for the consequences of organizational decisions (e.g., del Favero & Bray, 2005).

Of course, as numerous studies show, professionals, including academics, require a certain amount of autonomy in order to function effectively (Katz & Coleman, 2005). Norms of autonomy become a problem, however, when they interfere with the kinds of cooperation and accountability that enable organizations to accomplish their most important aims (e.g., Donaldson, Johnson, Kirkpatrick, Marinell, Steele, & Szczesiul, 2008). Distributed leadership theory supports an approach in which autonomy aligns with and supports, rather than defies or supplants agreed-upon aims and practices (Burke, 2010). This approach enables a leader to formulate and share a vision to guide the work of the organization, while at the same time it gives considerable control over implementation to other professionals within the organization (i.e., teachers in K–12 schools or faculty in institutions of higher education) (e.g., DuFour & Mattos, 2013).

Sometimes in institutions of higher education, faculty perspectives cannot readily accommodate the vision of the leader. For example, when a leader needs to intervene to change an unproductive or toxic culture,[1] he or she cannot work from the assumption that faculty members will follow his or her lead (Dad, 2010). Indeed, under some circumstances, faculty members will subvert efforts to share leadership in productive ways because they have a vested interest in maintaining a toxic culture. Toxic cultures breed practices that cause organizations to underperform or underachieve. Consequently, the leader must persist in maintaining the high ground, distributing leadership to those with similar commitments to the wider community and the good of the organization and restricting the influence of those whose interests run counter to a vision of organizational effectiveness and community engagement (e.g., Barth, 2002; Bolman & Deal, 2013; Dad, 2010). Changing toxic cultures into healthy ones is an arduous, long-term project fraught with considerable risks (Barth, 2002; Bolman & Deal, 2013), but as Barth (2002) noted, this effort is perhaps the single most important one that educational leaders will ever undertake.

Situational Leadership: Addressing Emerging Challenges

The third leadership theory that undergirds my approach relates to the situational nature of leadership challenges. Not all leaders, in my view, work well in all organizations or at all times in the life of the same organization. For example, a faculty primarily comprising tenured, senior professors requires leadership of a different sort from that required by a faculty primarily comprising probationary faculty (Hersey et al., 2008).

Flexibility in the use of different leadership practices ensures a certain amount of adaptability, but leaders seem to be flexible only to some extent and under certain conditions (e.g., Sumner-Armstrong, Newcombe, & Martin, 2008). Nevertheless, one important goal of leadership development is to expand the range of leadership practices and styles with which leaders feel comfortable, and to help them analyze organizational contexts in order to determine which approaches to leadership will be most likely to work effectively in consideration of particular conditions and constraints (Hersey et al., 2008).

Situational leadership, moreover, allows the leader to establish a functional balance between a transformational and a distributed approach, depending on the organization's needs at a particular point in time. As noted above, for example, distributing leadership to a faction whose aim is to perpetuate a toxic culture is not a wise strategy. Nor is it helpful to persist in touting a vision—that is, using an overt transformational approach—with employees who already are deeply committed to that vision (e.g., Collins, 2001). Arguably, leaders who are able to regulate their practices in response to organizational needs and conditions will be more likely to foster positive change than those who are constrained by their devotion to or capacity to use just one approach to leadership (see e.g., Johnson & Wallace, 2011).

WHY HIGHER EDUCATION LEADERS OUGHT TO BE MENTORS

As a broad literature on leadership reveals, the practice of this craft is neither intuitive nor easy. In some arenas—higher education for one—various and sometimes competing pressures from the external environment make the need for competent leadership particularly acute. Furthermore, the academic leadership needs of higher education institutions—needs for department chairs, deans, and provosts—are rarely met through the employment of individuals who have received formal preparation for leadership responsibilities. Rather, faculties often move their willing colleagues onto the first rung of the leadership ladder (i.e., program coordinator or department chair positions), and those who find the work interesting propel themselves forward.

This circumstance points to a gap that higher education institutions might want to fill—namely a gap in the guidance provided to new and aspiring academic leaders. Mentorship arrangements of a formal or informal nature sometimes fill this gap. My experience suggests that higher education institutions would benefit from expanded efforts to provide mentoring to emerging academic leaders. Arguably, of course, not every senior academic leader makes a good mentor, but leaders in higher education institutions ought to do what they can to become effective mentors. This perspective gains support from a view of leadership that looks beyond the present circumstances in an organization (e.g., a college or university) toward its future.

Leading for the Future: Transformational Mentoring

According to various commentators, effective leaders do not think only about their organization's needs at the present time (e.g., Marx, 2006; Penney & Neilson, 2010). Based on formal and intuitive assessments, such leaders make judgments about what is likely to happen in the near and even more distant future, and how their organizations ought to position themselves in the present for the purpose of achieving success in the future. For example, institutions of higher education rely on environmental scans, analyses of market trends, and occupational projections in order to plan in forward-looking ways. "Strategic thinking" is the term often applied to this approach (e.g., Stacey, 1993).

As part of strategic thinking, future-oriented leaders also consider the capacities of current members of their organizations (or new recruits) who are likely to assume leadership positions in the future. And they realize that the competencies that future leaders will need are different from those valued in the present. Van Velsor and Wright (2012), for example, conducted an online survey of current leaders from the business, government, nonprofit, and education sectors to identify their views about the knowledge, skills, and dispositions that would be required of leaders in the future. Their findings indicated that the following characteristics are most likely to be valued by organizations in the next generation:

- Comfort and skill with technology and social networks
- Creativity, openness, and innovativeness
- Multicultural and global awareness and tolerance of difference
- Adaptability, orientation toward learning, and receptivity to a rapid pace of change
- Confidence and a willingness to take a stand or challenge the status quo
- Energy, enthusiasm, dedication, and work ethic
- Collaborative ethos and team-oriented approach, and the willingness to work across boundaries
- A strong sense of ethics, commitment to service-oriented leadership, and desire to make a difference (p. 9)

Succession Planning: Distributed Mentoring

Concern for cultivating a new generation of leaders for an organization often fuels the decision to plan succession intentionally and provide training and mentoring opportunities to individuals earmarked for leadership positions in the future (e.g., Fink, 2010). Interestingly, even though this approach has been considered in the human resources literature since the 1980s and intentionally used in business and industry for several decades before that time, many organizations still prefer didactic leadership training to more job-embedded approaches such as mentoring (Kim, 2010). In a recent interview study of high-level human resource executives from multinational companies, for example, Kim (2010) found that 86% reported that their companies used didactic training methods whereas only 29% reported that their companies used mentoring.

From my perspective, however, mentoring is the far more potent approach. I do, of course, also encourage new and prospective leaders to participate in relevant training workshops, including intensive ones such as the Higher Education Resource Services (HERS) summer institute at Bryn Mawr College. But mentoring allows me to take personal responsibility for helping nurture another individual's capacities and influence his or her thinking about the organization, the community it serves, and its longer-term needs.

This role is particularly important because it offers the possibility for extending one's vision for organizational improvement into a future beyond one's own employment in the university in which they currently work. Taking explicit steps is particularly important when social justice is the focus of the transformation that a leader intends to accomplish because, without continuing support for social justice, an organization can move back to the status quo once a transformational leader leaves.

Mentoring, from this vantage, might be seen as selfish. However, a leader must be concerned with who follows them. I do not want my work to be for naught. I want to be sure there will be people to build on the groundwork completed during my tenure, thereby extending the progress that has already been made. In an important sense, this selfishness reflects one's commitment to stewardship of the institution, not wanting the institution to lose ground when you leave it, but instead to become better and stronger.

WHAT HIGHER EDUCATION MENTORING ENTAILS

Mentoring for leadership in higher education makes use of many of the skills required for mentoring in other types of organizations and involves many of the same practices. These skills and practices manifest in different ways depending on the organizational context, the already evolving skill set of the mentee, and the personal histories of both the mentor and the mentee.

As with other organizations, colleges and universities vary based on a number of contextual features—size, organizational type (e.g., public/private, two-year/four-year, religious/nonsectarian), selectivity, funding, clientele, and so on. Not only do these contextual features have an impact on the types of leadership that would advance the mission of the college or university, but they also have an impact on the type of mentoring that is useful. For example, a new department chair in a very small, private university might not feel comfortable sharing his or her worries with another administrator from that same institution. Perhaps a department chair from another institution would be a better mentor under the circumstances.

Not only do new and emerging leaders in higher education institutions differ because of the characteristics of their institutions, but their own backgrounds, knowledge, and skills also vary considerably. In some disciplines, practical leadership experience in another type of organization is a requirement for employment as a faculty member. For example, faculty members in business administration, public administration, health administration, educational administration, higher education, and sports administration typically come into higher education faculty positions with a well-established set of leadership skills. Assistant professors in other fields—often traditional academic fields such as philosophy, English, and physics—are not likely to bring a similar skill set with them from their previous employment. Often scholars in these fields move directly from being students to being faculty members.

The Mentoring Process: Mentoring Skills and Relationships

Recent scholarship about the process of new teacher induction has contributed a perspective on mentoring that I find particularly generative (e.g., Feiman-Nemser, 2001; McDonald & Flint, 2011; Norman & Feiman-Nemser, 2005). What these scholars call "educative mentoring" involves mentoring toward a particular vision of professional practice, not just mentoring for the cultivation of a particular set of decontextualized skills. It fits closely with the model of "transformative mentoring" proposed by Gerber and Nyanjom (2009). According to these authors, the transformative approach "involves the establishing of learning alliances for professional development and a commitment to social and organizational change" (p. 896).

Educative mentoring occurs within the context of a collaborative relationship between mentor and mentee. The description below relates specifically to the mentoring of new teachers, but by substituting a few words, one can see its applicability to the mentoring of new and aspiring leaders.

> Educative mentoring can be distinguished from other forms of mentoring (primarily about technical advice and emotional support) in that it responds to the present needs of the teacher, assisting them in their own learning and the learning of the students.... It can be concluded, then, that educative mentoring is based on experiences that promote future growth and lead to richer subsequent experiences.... It can be further argued that educative mentoring rests on an explicit vision of good teaching, and that mentors who share this vision address beginning teachers' concerns and questions about their teaching and progress. (McDonald & Flint, 2011, p. 35)

This approach to mentoring requires the mentor to possess (1) relevant knowledge of professional practice that conforms to a vision of excellence, and (2) the skills to help another person put that knowledge to use. For me, the relevant knowledge concerns tenets of the three approaches to leadership discussed above (transformational leadership, distributed leadership, and situational leadership). And the educative mentoring I provide to new and aspiring leaders involves three critical skills: the ability to communicate well, the ability to demonstrate care and understanding (see also McDonald & Flint, 2011), and the capacity to identify and address the mentee's evolving needs.

The context for this type of mentoring is a relationship of mutual trust (e.g., Cull, 2006; Watt, 2004). Building such a relationship involves care for the mentee, openness to the mentee's perspectives and emotional responses, and the willingness to fit learning experiences to a timetable that corresponds with the mentee's developmental trajectory. It also entails willingness to participate openly with the mentee in reflecting on organizational events and practices (e.g., Gerber & Nyanjom, 2009; Stowers & Barker, 2010). Notably, mentors can use their rich and nuanced understanding of organizational dynamics—formal structures and processes as well as informal politics—to guide the mentee's deepening awareness of the leadership challenges and opportunities present in a particular college or university.

As the discussion thus far suggests, the work of being an engaged and responsive mentor takes a great deal of time. For me, it has been helpful to dovetail mentoring discussions with other meetings with the individuals whom I am mentoring. This approach has worked well with individuals employed in my institution; it is less workable, of course, for those who work elsewhere. My mentoring of those individuals has taken place through phone conversations, on the tennis court or golf course, at social gatherings, at informal office meetings, and at get-togethers at conferences and other similar events.

Even though mentoring takes considerable time, it is not thankless work. Rather, the benefits to the organization or to the field more broadly become evident at some point in the future when the mentee assumes a leadership role and performs effectively in that role. This benefit is quite different from expecting something in return from a mentee. A mentoring relationship does not work well if either party tries to organize it on *a quid pro quo* basis. Mentoring is a form of teaching—and teaching works best when it is a generous contribution to the well-being of another or the advancement of the organization.

Choosing Not to Mentor

Because mentoring involves a commitment of time and a good fit between the mentor and mentee, organizational leaders may choose not to mentor a particular individual or they may refrain from mentoring anyone for a certain period of time. In fact, the choice not to mentor often is deliberate and situational. Perhaps refraining from mentoring during stressful times in the life of an organization may be wise. Choosing not to provide mentoring to a particular junior colleague, for example one with whom the leader has difficulty communicating, may turn out to be a more supportive approach than taking the risk of providing a negative experience (see e.g., Duck, 1994).

Some leaders also may believe that mentoring is not something they do well, and therefore they choose not to take on the role. From my perspective, this approach is unacceptable over the long term. Leadership entails teaching—so taking on the role of mentor is an inevitable and necessary consequence of the decision to accept a leadership position. Higher education administrators—department chairs, deans, provosts, and others—who lack confidence in their mentoring skills should seek training to improve their mentoring skill set. Some research (e.g., Gordon & Brobeck, 2010) shows that formal mentors do improve their mentoring skills through job-embedded learning experiences. Opting out of mentoring is not a reasonable alternative, in my opinion.

In fact, when higher education administrators think about what mentoring for leadership contributes, they will likely realize that preparing someone else to be an effective leader can be an exciting part of their own careers, especially if they value the organization with which they are aligned. If an administrator truly values that organization, mentoring is something that he or she will do. When I'm looking for people to surround myself with, I want people who view mentoring as positive, right, and good. That tells me they really do value the organization.

Types of Mentoring

Mentoring can involve various strategies, depending on the needs of the mentee and the opportunities available in the organization. A detailed discussion of each of these strategies is beyond the scope of this chapter, but a brief overview may provide a useful starting point for understanding these approaches.

Coaching

Although some writers use the terms "coaching" and "mentoring" interchangeably, I do not believe they are the same thing. Others agree, but not exactly for the reasons I will mention. According to Stowers and Barker (2010), for example,

> The essential difference between a coach and a mentor is that the coach does not give advice or answers but asks effective questions to help reveal the individual's current reality and vision for themselves. Ultimately, a coaching relationship has the objective to change or improve something about the person being coached. (p. 364)

While the distinction between telling mentees what to do and helping them discover how to perform is a good one, it does not seem to distinguish the two processes. I know many coaches who tell people what to do, just as I know many mentors who facilitate learning rather than giving advice. Moreover, both coaching and mentoring focus on changing the person who participates as the learner.

Rather than making the distinction on these terms, I have found it helpful to view mentoring as the educative relationship and coaching as one of the strategies that can make the educative relationship productive. In other words, coaching is one of the strategies that can be deployed within a mentoring relationship. Coaching entails particular types of teaching practices that offer a support structure to professionals as they are learning new skills. Defining coaching in this way has enabled various authors to offer guidance—more and less evidence-based—to leaders who want to make use of this approach. For example, Tschannen-Moran and Tschannen-Moran (2011) have suggested the following effective coaching practices:

- Effective coaches respect the people whom they are coaching and offer them understanding, choice, and responsibility.
- They understand what their mentees are experiencing by showing concern and appreciation.
- They recognize the vitality of the people they are coaching and build on their strengths.
- They emphasize competence by building on well-established skills and scaffolding to new skills.
- They create a no-fault experience. (pp. 14–17)

Job-Shadowing

Sometimes used with secondary school and college students to expand their awareness of what various occupations entail, job shadowing is a strategy that has also been used in higher education institutions to help aspiring leaders learn about what leadership practice is like (e.g., Reille & Kezar, 2010). Although job shadowing works well in the early stages of leadership preparation, I have found it helpful later on as well. For example, I recently asked a new department chair to accompany me to a meeting at which I was engaging in a difficult negotiation. My aims in inviting her were (1) to show her some strategies and techniques that were effective in high-level negotiations and (2) to give her an insider's view of the stress involved in the leadership work of deans and provosts. Nothing I could have told this colleague would have achieved these aims nearly so well as actually bringing her into the room as the negotiation was taking place.

Structured Mentoring Conversations

With this approach, mentors use guiding questions as the basis for conversations with mentees. Perhaps the best known example of this approach is the GROW model (Whitmore, 2002). Using this model, the mentor structures conversations at each stage of interaction with the mentee to identify and then continue to reflect on (1) the mentee's goals, (2) the mentee's current view of the opportunities and impediments to achieving his or her goals, (3) alternatives for achieving the goals, (4) the best option among the alternatives, and (5) the plan of action for moving forward with the best option. An objective observer often records what takes place at the mentoring session in order to give feedback to the mentor in particular. Information that the observer records can also assist the mentee to remember what was discussed.

Although mentors who are providing support to aspiring and newly employed higher education leaders may find this approach too confining (Gerber & Nyanjom, 2009), they can modify it to fit their circumstances. According to Gerber and Nyanjom (2009), moreover, structured mentoring conversations (either those using the GROW protocol or those relying on other protocols) work best for mentors who have strong listening skills, productive insights about how to frame useful questions, and the ability to offer constructive feedback in ways that the mentee can understand and accept.

Formal Mentoring Programs

A number of formal programs—seminar programs and summer institutes, for example—offer to prepare professionals for leadership positions in colleges and universities. The HERS program, mentioned earlier, is one of the most well known, as are programs offered through the National Education Association (NEA), the American Council on Education (ACE), and the American Association for Colleges of Teacher Education (AACTE).

Formal mentoring arrangements can also be organized by a college or university. Often such arrangements involve the creation of documents (e.g., memoranda of understanding) that specify the character of and expectations for the mentorship: goals, activities, anticipated outcomes, roles and responsibilities of the mentor and mentee, and timetables. In my college, for example, new tenure-track faculty members have the option of participating in a mentoring program for three of their six probationary years. Not only can they select their own mentors, the college also provides an honorarium to show appreciation to the mentor and signal the importance of the arrangement. In this program, moreover, each probationary faculty member can select an intensive college-related mentorship—what Feldman, Arean, Marshall, Lovett, and O'Sullivan (2010, p. 6) refer to as a "career mentorship," an intensive research-related mentorship—what Feldman and associates refer to as a "scholarly mentorship," or a combined mentorship focusing on both college-related matters (e.g., developing syllabi, tenure and promotion procedures, service work) and research-related matters.

Informal Mentoring

Professionals tend to have many mentors throughout their careers. Most of these mentors play an informal role. Sometimes such relationships are transitory. For example, when an individual accepts a new position, he or she may find an individual with more experience in the organization to provide guidance regarding policies, procedures, organizational culture, and so on. But sometimes, informal mentoring relationships last for a long time—over the course of a long career. Whether transitory or long-lasting, informal mentorships tend not to involve remuneration, they are not structured through formal plans, times for getting together are often impromptu, and telephone or email often substitute for face-to-face meetings.

Sometimes informal mentoring arrangements cross organizational boundaries. Newly employed school principals, for example, often seek mentors from other schools or even other districts in order to enable a more open and candid exchange of ideas. Similar circumstances may encourage higher education leaders to look for mentors in other colleges or universities. Sometimes retired administrators can provide helpful mentoring. One of my most trusted mentors is retired.

Situational (or Developmental) Mentoring

Several authors conceptualize mentoring in and of itself as a developmental process (e.g., Gilbert & Rossman, 1992; Shea, 1994) because it is directed toward the professional development of a protégé, early career professional, newly employed leader, or other mentee. Furthermore, some theorists and researchers maintain that effective mentoring relationships adjust to the developmental needs of mentees by proceeding in well-delineated stages (e.g., Kram, 1983, 1985). Kram, in particular, has defined four stages in the mentoring process: initiation, cultivation, separation, and redefinition.

Another way to conceptualize the developmental character of mentoring is to think of it in terms of Hersey and Blanchard's (1969) situational approach to providing guidance to employees who are at different levels of "maturity" with respect to learning a particular skill or performing a particular scope of work. This is one of the approaches I often rely on in my work as a dean—for example, with newly employed faculty members and administrators.

Using a mentoring strategy that draws on Hersey and Blanchard's insights, one might choose to be more directive with aspiring or recently employed leaders who have the least experience, and collaborative with those who are more confident and competent with the new leadership role. Ultimately, using this model, the mentor lets go once the mentee has reached a certain level of mastery—a process that Kram views as part of the separation and redefinition phases of a mentorship. Offering a similar perspective, Glickman, Gordon, and Ross-Gordon (2013) outlined a developmental supervisory strategy for use by instructional coaches and mentors that specifies three levels of support—directive, collaborative, and nondirective.

In my experiences as a mentee and a mentor, I have found that one of the most important tools for developmental mentoring is the professional development plan. Such a plan allows the mentee to set goals for increased competence and comfort with a new role, identify applicable learning strategies, and establish a sequence of steps (and related benchmarks) for accomplishing each goal. Even before individuals seek informal mentors or begin working with formal mentors, they might ask themselves the question, "Over the next three to five years, where do I want to be in my career?" The answer that a person gives to the question can help him or her determine what kind of mentor would be most helpful and what activities would be most productive during the term of the mentorship. From a developmental perspective, these activities (and sometimes even the mentor) ought to change over time to match up with the mentee's emerging skill sets and reframed needs.

The Mentee's Prerogatives

According to various writers, one of the most important tenets of an effective mentoring relationship is that it should serve the self-identified needs of the mentee (e.g., Zachary & Fischler, 2009). As a result, these writers suggest that many of the important decisions regarding the focus and direction of the mentorship should be made by the mentee. With this said, most theorists of mentoring emphasize the reciprocal nature of effective mentoring relationships, and they operationalize reciprocity by giving responsibility for structuring activities (e.g., goal-setting, setting up meetings, and so on) to mentors and responsibility for the direction and focus of the mentorship to the mentee. As Zachary and Fischler (2013) note,

> Although both mentor and mentee must play active roles in the goal-setting process, the responsibility for facilitating it lies with the mentor. The mentor's role is to ensure that the mentee's goals fit within the framework of workplace reality, as well as the mentee's capability and talent. Goal setting [i.e., the focus of the mentorship] should be driven by the mentee. (p. 76)

With a reciprocal perspective in view, I have found that certain mentee dispositions are productive of an effective mentorship relationship. Notably, the mentee needs to be willing to hear guidance and suggestions, but he or she does not necessarily need to accept the mentor's advice. Whether or not the mentee agrees with the mentor's specific recommendations, the mentor's guidance nevertheless offers a framework through which the mentee can construct thoughts and actions. The mentor thus offers a perspective on the organization and the actions that will likely result in a particular outcome. Reflection on what the mentor offers might prompt the mentee to accept the course of action as the best way to achieve the outcome, cause the mentee to question the value of the outcome, or encourage the mentee to think about alternative approaches for achieving the outcome. All a mentor wants to know is that the mentee thinks things out in response to his or her suggestions. An effective mentor might even say, "This is not a decision I can make for you."

Another important disposition of mentees is the willingness to establish their own identity separate from the identity of the mentor. Sometimes a mentee desires to emulate the personal characteristics and attributes of the mentor. Within limits, this desire can provide benefits. But the mentee is a different person from the mentor, with a different personal history, different strengths, and different perspectives. Viewing the mentorship as a path to *self*-discovery is a useful way for the mentee to acknowledge the salutary characteristics of the mentor without feeling bound to copy them exactly.

The Mentor's Stance

Caring is an essential skill: An effective mentor needs to be people-focused. More effective mentors understand human behavior and possess an understanding of organizational behavior.

For example, I have found it useful when I mentor aspiring and new leaders to be willing to take or share blame even when it might properly belong to the mentee. I believe it is important during the duration of the mentorship to free up the mentee to make mistakes. By taking or sharing blame for the mentee's mistakes, I accomplish two purposes. First, I give the mentee the freedom to explore the new role and to be experimental and creative in that role. Second, I model the important leadership practice of assuming responsibility for whatever happens in one's unit, whether or not one is personally at fault. When something happens "on my watch," I am responsible. I want the mentee to see what this practice looks like and to observe its consequences. Rather than weakening a leader, this approach enhances the leader's trustworthiness and builds his or her base of support.

As is the case with supervised or managed employees in any hierarchical institution, the faculties of many higher education institutions take a certain pride in dismissing leaders as unnecessary and criticizing them unfairly. A leadership mentee needs to understand this feature of many higher-education cultures and learn to adjust. Such adjustment involves openness and receptivity to helpful criticism, coupled with the ability to shrug off complaints that are ill-founded or designed simply to provoke a reaction. One gets blamed for a lot of things as a leader that have nothing to do with one's performance, and a wise leader is willing to take it. At the same time, I think, a wise leader learns neither *to take it personally nor to become a reactionary leader.*

MENTORING WOMEN AND INDIVIDUALS
FROM DIVERSE BACKGROUNDS

My experience in higher education leadership has convinced me that a range of challenges confront women and people of color who seek administrative advancement. A fairly robust literature also supports this perspective, suggesting that leadership in colleges and universities, as well as in other professional occupations, continues to be dominated by white men (Buttner, Lowe, & Billings-Harris, 2009; Flowers & Moore, 2008). Women and people of color who do obtain leadership positions, moreover, often find that they are placed in less prominent positions than their white, male counterparts (Flowers & Moore, 2008) or are offered positions that are undesirable or beset with problems (e.g., Tallerico & Burstyn, 1996). Furthermore, women and individuals from diverse backgrounds often know fewer of the unwritten rules for navigating mainstream culture (e.g., Gibson, 2006), and they receive less guidance from supervisors and colleagues (Otto, 1994).

Of course, the ample literature on mentoring suggests that all people, including white men, benefit from mentoring. With respect to a variety of professional roles including leadership positions, individual characteristics and experiences rather than group differences determine gaps in knowledge and skills (and therefore employees' needs for preparation and support). In other words, women and people of color are no less competent for these positions than white men. Nevertheless, aspiring and practicing leaders from these groups do confront circumstances that offer fewer affordances and more impediments to success. For this reason, mentoring may be particularly helpful (see e.g., Rheineck & Roland, 2008).

Despite their needs for and openness to mentoring, women and people of color are less likely than white men to find mentors (Cole, as cited in Wenniger & Farrington, 2000). White men may indeed be willing to mentor these aspiring and new leaders, but they often feel uncomfortable interacting with people whose backgrounds and experiences differ significantly from their own. Furthermore, because white men have not themselves experienced the difficulties typically encountered by people of color and women, their knowledge about how to handle such difficulties is limited. And there is a paucity of diverse leaders to provide mentorships to women and people of color who are assuming professional and leadership roles in the academy (Gibson, 2006).

For these reasons, I believe formal structures are required in order to provide women and people of color with productive mentorships. This circumstance is inherently unfair; nevertheless, it is the reality. What white men can readily obtain informally, women and people of color typically receive only through a formal arrangement. Institutional racism and sexism work this way—and rather than deny guidance to aspiring and new leaders from diverse backgrounds, it is certainly better to cultivate adequate formal structures to support their professional development.

As an African American woman who has served as a professor, director, and upper-level college administrator in large research-intensive universities, I have had numerous opportunities to mentor aspiring and new leaders from both mainstream and diverse backgrounds. This work has been extremely rewarding. I draw on this experience in the two sections that conclude the chapter—a vignette describing interactions with a faculty member who begins to take on leadership responsibilities, and the chapter "take-away"—a list of key insights I offer to mentees in general, and female mentees and mentees from racially and/or ethnically diverse backgrounds in particular.

PERSONAL EXPERIENCES AS A MENTOR:
A CASE STUDY

In order to show how mentoring for higher education leadership works in practice, I will end this chapter with a case study drawn from my own experience mentoring less-experienced leaders in the college of education in which I currently serve as dean. The case represents a composite: not a real individual, but an exemplar incorporating the characteristics and experiences of several different individuals whom I currently mentor or have mentored in the past.

Stuart

A senior faculty member in one of the departments of the college, Stuart had been at the university for several years before I arrived. He was soft-spoken, but his direct (and seemingly penetrating) way of looking at people made him seem intense. When I first encountered Stuart, he was chairing the faculty research committee and sought a consultation about a particularly sensitive funding application. Our conversation revealed that Stuart had a strong commitment to research excellence and an abiding care for the well-being of colleagues. In fact, the issue that he raised with me concerned a tension between caring for a colleague and upholding high standards of scholarship.

My conversation with Stuart suggested to me that his role as the chair of a university committee was providing him with opportunities to learn some leadership skills and to get a broad picture of how the university functioned. In a subsequent discussion with Stuart, I asked him whether or not he had any plans to assume a leadership role in the college. Laughing, he said that he preferred friends to enemies and had little interest, therefore, in taking on a leadership position.

Nevertheless, Stuart's department experienced upheaval over the next several years. The longtime department chair retired, several faculty members left for positions at other universities, and a once-profitable institute started to lose money. Several influential faculty members came to talk with me about the situation and suggested that Stuart might provide effective departmental leadership at least during what seemed like a transition period. I indicated that I would support his nomination from the faculty if Stuart agreed to serve and if the faculty elected him.

Soon thereafter, I received word that Stuart had been elected as the department's choice for chair, and I enthusiastically accepted the recommendation. Stuart and I met several weeks later and began what was to be a three-year mentorship.

Goals for Stuart's Leadership Development

In our initial discussion, I talked with Stuart about his goals for the department. I suggested that, in consideration of these goals, he make a list of the department's assets and challenges, noting how each asset might help the department meet each of the goals in turn and how each challenge might get in the way. This assignment represented a kind of coaching because the assignment was intended to teach Stuart a simplified version of SWOT (strengths, weaknesses, opportunities, threats) analysis by asking him to perform one.

My second assignment was for Stuart to develop a list of mid- to long-term goals for his own development as a leader. I speculated that such a list would be helpful as a basis for structuring our next discussion, which I thought might be most effective if we were to conduct it in an off-campus location. As it turned out, both Stuart and I soon needed to be in attendance at a meeting on another campus—a two-hour's drive each way. I invited him to travel with me and to bring along his list of goals. After a brief discussion about the meeting we were travelling to attend, we turned attention to Stuart's goals.

His list showed considerable self-knowledge and a few blind spots. For example, Stuart indicated that he needed to learn to listen more than talk. As a long-time faculty member, he realized that talking was a large part of what his job entailed. Listening to faculty in the department, however, would give him valuable information about department dynamics. I agreed with his assessment of the value of cultivating careful listening skills, and talked with him about some tools that might be helpful. Curiously, though, Stuart mentioned nothing about problems that might result from his need for the approval of faculty colleagues. I suspected, however, that his strong affiliation needs would get in the way when he was required to make difficult and/or unpopular decisions. Because Stuart did not mention this issue, I raised it. He laughed, a bit nervously, when I attributed this personality characteristic to him, but he seemed open to my thoughts about the way affiliation needs sometimes get in the way of effective leadership. He agreed that developing greater independence from the judgment of colleagues would be a good skill to work on.

After our talk in the car, I asked Stuart to write up a professional development plan that might address the goals we had surfaced. He and I met twice thereafter to refine the document and identify sources of support for the learning experiences it specified.

The Big Investment

By mid-year, Stuart and I had met on three or four more occasions, during which time I provided coaching to help him learn particular leadership skills, used reflective listening as a way to help him analyze organizational dynamics, and engaged with him in direct conversations about his work to improve listening skills and increase his tolerance for negative reactions from faculty colleagues. At our meeting in January, Stuart asked if I would support his application to participate in a national program for aspiring and new higher education administrators. The program offered an intensive summer experience and relied on the expertise of some of the nation's most prestigious academic leaders. Needless to say, the program also carried a hefty price tag.

I indicated to Stuart that I would be supportive, first by counting his time at the summer institute as work time, and second by writing a strong letter of support to accompany his application for university professional development funds that would enable him to participate in the summer program. Our college did not have the resources to send Stuart to the summer institute, so funding it directly was not an option. Moreover, my approach had hidden benefits. As dean, I wanted to let the provost know that mentoring Stuart was worth our effort and investment and that I desired the university's help in providing financial support for that investment. In other words, one benefit of my approach was to engage the provost in my efforts to build my college's leadership capacity. It was important for the provost to see that this was also an investment in the institution. In addition, I wanted Stuart to take ownership for the proposal—not only by applying to the institute but also by putting in the application for university funds. Stuart ended up receiving the funds and attending the institute, which he found helpful on several fronts.

Letting Go

One of the bittersweet consequences of giving Stuart support that enabled him to participate in the institute related to the network of colleagues that he met during the summer. One of these colleagues turned out to become a provost several years after participating. Remembering Stuart as both caring and competent, she invited him to apply for a deanship that had opened up at her university. Stuart, who by then had become a good listener and was somewhat better at handling the disapproval of faculty colleagues, applied for, was selected, and eventually accepted the position.

Selfishly, I would have liked Stuart to stay at my university, to complete a few more years as department chair and to become my associate dean. But good mentoring means letting go, particularly when the mentee is ready to take on new challenges and is given the opportunity to do so.

Stuart and I remain in contact, and in some senses I am still his mentor. In some senses, though, we have become mutually supportive colleagues. Our conversations now focus primarily on being an effective dean—we now offer each other insights that are useful to both of us in our practice as college leaders. I hope he and I stay in contact across our careers. I, for one, rely on my experiences as the mentee of a now-retired university dean to shape my expectations for what a career-long mentor–mentee relationship with Stuart can offer us both.

TAKE-AWAY: ESSENTIAL INSIGHTS FOR LEADERSHIP MENTEES FROM DIVERSE BACKGROUNDS

- If you lack knowledge or skills, it's because of lack of experience and exposure, not because of lack of intelligence or ability. If you had the opportunities to learn this knowledge or these skills, you would have learned them to a high level. You would be "walking circles" around your mainstream counterparts.
- Accept the opportunities that come your way so long as they advance your career and do not distract you from achieving your ultimate goals. Committee work in your department or college, participation on writing teams to address accreditation standards, involvement with state-level policy or advisory groups—all of these types of activities can provide valuable expe-

riences. Treating these activities seriously, as service to the profession and the wider community, is also critical. Election to an office or service on a committee should not be treated primarily for its vitae-building potential. You will become known for the work you contribute, not for the list of accomplishments on your curriculum vitae.

- Women and people of color often take different career pathways from those taken by white men. In particular, their ascent through the various levels of leadership tends to be more gradual—in part because they are offered fewer opportunities. So while a white male may become department chair and then dean, a person who is considered culturally diverse may first be a program coordinator, then a department chair, then an assistant dean, an associate dean, and finally a dean. Of course, the opposite may also sometimes be the case. Notably, some female leaders and leaders of color are promoted too quickly without having had the relevant and necessary experiences to ensure their success. Overall, it is far better to be over-prepared than under-prepared. So the more gradual path, even if it results from unfair circumstances, can actual provide benefits to a leader from a diverse background. Once such a leader reaches the deanship or above, he or she will have acquired a lot of skill and a lot of savvy.

- Throughout your career, constantly look for opportunities to develop yourself as an academic leader. It's important to recognize that such opportunities may not come in the form of official positions of authority. Rather, various kinds of leadership participation are available on campuses because of the tradition of shared governance. So you might look for those committees that have an influence on policy, for example, as a way to extend your leadership abilities and impact. First participating on such a committee and later becoming its chair is a trajectory that offers you an insider perspective on important institutional matters such as budgets, administrative structures, tenure and promotion policies and procedures, and administrator–governing board relationships.

- It's important for an aspiring leader to achieve full-professor status before becoming a formal leader. An early move into leadership is likely to limit one's eventual trajectory in leadership positions. Even though organizations, including colleges and universities, may have a vested interest in promoting you to leadership early (i.e., to improve their diversity statistics), such a move is not likely to be in your best interests.

- It is important for you to give back by providing mentorship opportunities to other women and people of color. That process, moreover, ought to begin now. Someone in your organization always can benefit from your experience and from ways that you reflect on those experience. Lead and mentor from your current position and sphere of influence. It is not too soon. If is not a value you hold dear now, it will not become one later. If we don't give back in this way, we will restrict leadership opportunities for others from groups that have traditionally been excluded or marginalized.

NOTE

1. I use this term to refer to a culture that does not build or develop talent— one where participants rarely see the good in anyone or anything and show malice toward anything positive that does not advance their own interests or elevate their own stature.

REFERENCES

Bass, B. M., & Avolio, B. J. (Eds.). (1994). *Improving organizational effectiveness through transformational leadership.* Thousand Oaks, CA: Sage Publications.

Barth, R. S. (2002). The culture builder. *Educational Leadership, 59*(8), 6–11.

Bensimon, E. M., & Neumann, A. (1993). *Redesigning collegiate leadership.* Baltimore. MD: Johns Hopkins University Press.

Bolton, A. (1996). The leadership challenge in universities: The case of business schools. *Higher Education, 31*(4), 491–506.

Bolman, L. G., & Deal, T. E. (2013). *Reframing organizations: Artistry, choice, and leadership* (5th ed.). San Francisco, CA: Jossey-Bass/John Wiley.

Bowen, W., & Shapiro, H. (1998). *Universities and their leadership.* Princeton, NJ: Princeton University Press.

Burke, K. M. (2010). Distributed leadership and shared governance in post-secondary education. *Management in Education, 24*(2), 51–54. doi:10.1177/0892020610363088

Buttner, E., Lowe, K. B., & Billings-Harris, L. (2009). The challenge of increasing minority-group professional representation in the United States: Intriguing findings. *International Journal of Human Resource Management, 20*(4), 771–789. doi:10.1080/09585190902770604

Christensen, C. M., & Eyring, H. J. (2011). *The innovative university: Changing the DNA of higher education from the inside out.* San Francisco, CA: Jossey-Bass.

Collins, J. (2001). *Good to great: Why some companies make the leap ... and others don't.* New York, NY: HarperCollins Publishers.

Crellin, M. A. (2010). The future of shared governance. *New Directions for Higher Education,* (151), 71–81. doi:10.1002/he.402

Cull, J. (2006). Mentoring young entrepreneurs: What leads to success? *International Journal of Evidence Based Coaching and Mentoring, 4*(2), 8–18.

Dad, D. (2010). The toxic workplace test. *Department Chair, 21*(3), 27–28.

del Favero, M., & Bray, N. (2005). The faculty–administrator relationship: Partners in prospective governance? *Scholar-Practitioner Quarterly, 3*(1), 53–72.

Donaldson, M., Johnson, S. M., Kirkpatrick, C. L., Marinell, W. H., Steele, J. L., & Szcesiul, S. A. (2008). Angling for access, bartering for change: How second stage teachers experience differentiated roles in schools. *Teachers College Record, 110*(5), 1088–1114.

Duck, S. (1994). Stratagems, spoils, and a serpent's tooth: On the delights and dilemmas of personal relationships. In W. R. Cupach & B. H. Spitzberg (Eds.), *The dark side of interpersonal relationships* (pp. 3–24). Hillsdale, NJ: Erlbaum.

DuFour, R., & Mattos, M. (2013). How do principals really improve schools? *Educational Leadership, 70*(7), 34–40.

Ehrich, L., Cranston, N., Kimber, M., & Starr, K. (2012). (Un)ethical Practices and ethical dilemmas in universities: Academic leaders' perceptions. *International Studies in Educational Administration, 40*(2), 99–114.

Feiman-Nemser, S. (2001). Helping novices learn to teach: Lessons from an exemplary support teacher. *Journal of Teacher Education, 52*(1), 17–30.

Feldman, M. D., Arean, P. A., Marshall, S. J., Lovett, M., & O'Sullivan, P. (2010). Does mentoring matter: results from a survey of faculty mentees at a large health sciences university. *Medical Education Online, 15*(1), 1–8. doi:10.3402/meo.v15i0.5063

Fink, D. (2010). *The succession challenge: Building and sustaining leadership capacity through succession management.* Thousand Oaks, CA: Sage.

Flowers, L. A., & Moore, J. L. III (2008). Unraveling the composition of academic leadership in higher education: Exploring administrative diversity at 2-year and 4-year institutions. *Journal of Thought, 43*(3/4), 71–81.

Gerber, H., & Nyanjom, J. A. (2009). Mentor development in higher education in Botswana: How important is reflective practice? *South African Journal of Higher Education, 23*(5), 894–911.

Gibson, S. K. (2006). Mentoring of women faculty: The role of organizational politics and culture. *Innovative Higher Education, 31*(1), 63–79.

Gilbert, L. A., & Rossman, K. M. (1992). Gender and the mentoring process for women: Implications for professional development. *Professional Psychology: Research and Practice, 2,* 233–238.

Glickman, C. D., Gordon, S. P., & Ross-Gordon, J. M. (2013). *Supervision and instructional leadership: A developmental approach* (9th ed.). Boston, MA: Allyn & Bacon.

Gmelch, W. H. (2000, February). *Rites of passage: Transition to the deanship.* Paper presented at the American Association of Colleges for Teacher Education Conference, Chicago, IL.

Gordon, S. P., & Brobeck, S. R. (2010). Coaching the mentor: Facilitating reflection and change. *Mentoring & Tutoring: Partnership in Learning, 18*(4), 427–447. doi:10.1080/13611267.2010.511851

Hersey, P., & Blanchard, K. H. (1969). Life cycle theory of leadership. *Training and Development Journal, 23*(5), 26–34.

Hersey, P., Blanchard, K. H., & Johnson, D. E. (2008). *Management of organizational behavior: Leading human resources* (9th ed.). Upper Saddle River, NJ: Pearson/Prentice Hall.

Hotho, S. (2013). Higher education change and its managers: Alternative constructions. *Educational Management Administration & Leadership, 41*(3), 352–371. doi:10.1177/1741143212474806

Johnson, P., & Wallace, C. (2011). Increasing individual and team performance in an organizational setting through the situational adaptation of regulatory focus. *Consulting Psychology Journal: Practice & Research, 63*(3), 190–201. doi:10.1037/a0025622

Katz, E., & Coleman, M. (2005). Autonomy and accountability of teacher-educator researchers at a college of education in Israel. *Innovations in Education & Teaching International, 42*(1), 5–13. doi:10.1080/14703290500048754

Keeling, R. P., & Hersh, R. H. (2012). *We're losing our minds: Rethinking American higher education.* New York, NY: Palgrave Macmillan.

Kim, Y. (2010). Measuring the value of succession planning and management: A qualitative study of multinational companies. *Performance Improvement Quarterly, 23*(2), 5–31. doi:10.1002/piq.20079

Koellner, K., Jacobs, J., & Borko, H. (2011). Mathematics professional development: Critical features for developing leadership skills and building teachers' capacity. Mathematics *Teacher Education & Development, 13*(2), 115–136.

Kotter, J. P. (1996). *Leading change*. Boston, MA: Harvard Business School Press.

Kram, K. E. (1983). Phases of the mentor relationship. *Academy of Management Journal, 23*(4), 608–625.

Kram, K. E. (1985). *Mentoring at work*. Glenview, IL: Scott, Foresman.

Louis, K., Leithwood, K., Wahlstrom, K., & Anderson, S. (2010). *Learning from leadership: Investigating the links to improved student learning*. New York, NY: Wallace Foundation.

Marx, G. (2006). *Future-focused leadership: Preparing schools, students, and communities for tomorrow's realities*. Alexandria, VA: Association for Supervision and Curriculum Development.

McDonald, L., & Flint, A. (2011). Effective educative mentoring skills: A collaborative effort. *New Zealand Journal of Teachers' Work, 8*(1), 33–46.

McNulty, B. A., & Besser, L. (2011). *Leaders make it happen! An administrator's guide to data teams*. Englewood, CO: Lead + Learn Press.

Morrill, R. (2013). Collaborative strategic leadership and planning in an era of structural change: Highlighting the role of the governing board. *Peer Review, 15*(1), 12–16.

Norman, P. J., & Feiman-Nemser, S. (2005). Mind activity in teaching and mentoring. *Teacher and Teacher Education, 21*, 679–697.

Otto, M. L. (1994). Mentoring: An adult developmental perspective. *New Directions for Teaching & Learning, 57*, 15–24.

Penney, S. H., & Neilson, P. A. (2010). *Next generation leadership: Insights from emerging leaders*. New York, NY: Palgrave MacMillan.

Raines, S. C., & Alberg, M. (2003). The role of professional development in preparing academic leaders. *New Directions for Higher Education, 124*, 33–39.

Reille, A., & Kezar, A. (2010). Balancing the pros and cons of community college "grow-your-own" leadership programs. *Community College Review, 38*(1), 59–81. doi:10.1177/1069397110375597

Rheineck, J. E., & Roland, C. B. (2008). The developmental mentoring relationship between academic women. *Adultspan Journal, 7*(2), 80–93.

Rowley, D. J., & Sherman, H. (2001). *From strategy to change: Implementing the plan in higher education*. San Francisco, CA: Jossey-Bass.

Saltmarsh, S., Sutherland-Smith, W., & Randell-Moon, H. (2011). 'Inspired and assisted', or 'berated and destroyed'? Research leadership, management and performativity in troubled times. *Ethics & Education, 6*(3), 293–306. doi:10.1080/17449642.2011.632722

Shea, G. E. (1994). *Mentoring: Helping employees reach their full potential*. New York, NY: American Management Association.

Spillane, J. P. (2006). *Distributed leadership*. San Francisco, CA: Jossey Bass.

Stacey, R. D. (1993). *Strategic thinking and the management of change*. London, England: Kogan Page.

Stowers, R. H., & Barker, R. T. (2010). The coaching and mentoring process: The obvious knowledge and skill set for organizational communication professors. *Journal of Technical Writing & Communication, 40*(3), 363–371. doi:10.2190/TW.40.3.g

Sumner-Armstrong, C., Newcombe, P., & Martin, R. (2008). A qualitative investigation into leader behavioural flexibility. *Journal of Management Development, 27*(8), 843–857.

Tallerico, M., & Burstyn, J. (1996). Retaining women in the superintendency: The location matters. *Educational Administration Quarterly, 32*, 642–664.

Tolar, M. H. (2012). Mentoring experiences of high-achieving women. *Advances in Developing Human Resources, 14*(2), 172–187.

Tschannen-Moran, B., & Tschannen-Moran, M. (2011). The coach and the evaluator. *Educational Leadership, 69*(2), 10–16.

van Ameijde, J. J., Nelson, P. C., Billsberry, J., & van Meurs, N. (2009). Improving leadership in higher education institutions: A distributed perspective. *Higher Education, 58*(6), 763–779. doi:10.1007/s10734-009-9224-y

Van Velsor, E., & Wright, J. (2012). *Expanding the leadership equation: Developing next-generation leaders* (A White Paper). Greensboro, NC: Center for Creative Leadership

Watt, L. (2004). Mentoring and coaching in the workplace. *The Canadian Manager, 29*(3), 14–17.

Wenniger, M.D., & Farrington, L. (Eds.). (2000). Social change requires academic women's leadership. *Women in Higher Education, 9*(6), 1–2.

Whitmore, J. (2002). *Coaching for performance.* London, England: Nicholas Brealey.

Wolverton, M., Ackerman, R., & Holt, S. (2005). Preparing for leadership: What academic department chairs need to know. *Journal of Higher Education Policy & Management, 27*(2), 227–238. doi:10.1080/13600800500120126

Zachary, L. J., & Fischler, L. A. (2009). *The mentee's guide: Making mentoring work for you.* San Francisco, CA: Jossey-Bass.

Zachary, L. J. & Fischler, L. A. (2013). Facilitating mentee-driven goal setting. *T+D, 67*(5), 76–77.

CHAPTER 3

MENTORS' PERSPECTIVES ON MENTORING FOR THE PROFESSIONS

Barbara Trube and Guofang Wan

ABSTRACT

This chapter presents data from an exploratory qualitative study conducted in a comprehensive college of education and human services for the purpose of identifying experienced mentors' perceptions of the knowledge, skills, and dispositions that effective mentors use in various contexts. The participants all of whom had experiences as mentors and as mentees identified the profile of a mentor as a content expert engaged in building relationships, gathering information, facilitating reflection, challenging perspectives, and creating and supporting opportunities for networking. Further, participants identified common mentoring skills and practices across academic disciplines, practices that should be emphasized in professional development programs for prospective mentors. Analysis of data from interviews reveals mentoring to be a developmental process dependent on an evolving network of colleagues in the work place as well as others who belong to the communities of practice with which an individual is affiliated.

Mentoring for the Professions: Orienting Toward the Future, pages 45–66.

INTRODUCTION

Colleges of education and human services within academic institutions of higher learning are organizations that depend upon mentoring relationships to discover, invent, reinvent, and sustain their specific missions. Within comprehensive colleges that include diverse departments, common mentoring practices may be used to support the mission of the college and sustain the quality of its programs.

This chapter reports on a study that helped one professional development team learn about the characteristics of effective mentors from eight individuals who mentor in diverse contexts within a comprehensive college of education and human services in a Midwestern state in the United States. The motive for the study was to seek input from experienced mentors in order to inform intentional determinations about the content to include in an online workshop composed of a series of professional development modules. Their input helped module developers ensure that those who enrolled in this online workshop would acquire knowledge, gain understanding, and sharpen skills toward the goal of becoming effective mentors for work undertaken in formal or informal mentoring relationships with novice educators and other professionals.

The college includes departments that prepare undergraduate and graduate students for careers in business, industry, human service, and education. Each of the eight participating mentors in the study, identified hereafter as "participants," shared his or her perspectives about mentoring in an individual interview, conducted by one of the investigators and videotaped. These participants self-identified as both mentors of others and as recipients of ongoing mentoring within a constellation or network of mentors. In response to interview questions, the participants described what they believed to be essential knowledge, skills, and dispositions needed for mentoring others. Further, participants communicated their views about the content that would be important to include in professional development training designed to prepare mentors for work in diverse contexts.

BRIEF REVIEW OF RELATED LITERATURE

The benefits of effective mentoring have been realized for decades. However, understandings about what makes mentoring effective are somewhat more elusive. In order to be purposeful in creating a program that addresses the needs of novice educators and other professionals from diverse populations, it is important to identify traits, capabilities, and dispositions of effective mentors across academic disciplines.

Attuned to this perspective, a wide body of practical and empirical literature from several fields recognizes mentoring as an essential part of professional preparation (Ragins & Kram, 2007). This literature suggests that mentorship activities within organizations contribute to their effective functioning and long-term sustainability (Bullis & Bach, 1989; Rothwell, 2000). Various features of mentoring   processes, styles, dimensions, and functions have been investigated for the purpose of developing mentoring resources and tools and making them available to support the training of mentors (Dougherty & Dreher, 2007). Additional efforts to identify and reflect on the knowledge, skills, and dispositions from the perspective of those who mentor others contribute to a broad understanding about what is needed to design professional development for those who wish to sponsor mentorships in diverse contexts.

Various studies have identified the roles of mentors as well as the characteristics, knowledge, skills, and dispositions of individuals who have been successful in their roles as mentors. These studies have revealed that mentors are primarily supporters of less experienced colleagues, serving as guides and facilitators who listen and question (Abiddin & Hassan, 2012; Brown & Krager, 1985; Carter & Lewis, 1994) thereby encouraging reciprocity (Parsloe, 1999) and mutuality (Dobrow, Chandler, Murphy, & Kram, 2012) in the mentor–mentee relationship. Zelditch (1990), frequently quoted in the literature, describes roles such as advisor, supporter, tutor, master, sponsor, and model. Hogue and Pringle (2005) suggest a set of guiding principles as a framework for individuals getting started with mentoring, as follows:

1. Strive for mutual benefits
2. Agree on confidentiality
3. Commit to honesty
4. Listen and learn
5. Build a working partnership
6. Lead by example
7. Be flexible (pp. 51–52).

Other scholars have described successful mentors as being people-oriented, good motivators, effective teachers, excellent with technological knowledge and skills, and prideful in their profession (e.g., Glenn, 2006). Further, scholars suggest that the successful mentor understands the mission, vision, and values of his or her profession, supports the profession's initiatives, and maintains mutual respect with mentees (Aldisert, 2001). Effective mentors are viewed as individuals who are good at time management and communication and who are successful because they are well-educated and well-organized (Abiddin & Hassan, 2012). Hart (2010) listed seven key tasks of an effective mentor, as follows:

1. Develop and manage the mentoring relationship.
2. Sponsor the mentee by opening doors and advocating for the mentee.
3. Survey the environment for positive opportunities and threats to the mentee.
4. Guide and counsel the mentee as a confidant, sounding-board, or advisor.
5. Teach and impart knowledge, share experiences, make recommendations.
6. Model and lead.
7. Motivate and inspire the mentee through validation and encouragement.

Several authors focus attention on the ways mentors help shape a culture of mentoring. According to Zachary (2005), mentors who know and understand the benefits of mentoring, despite the challenges and drawbacks, seek to create a culture of mentoring within their organizations. Also focusing on how mentors themselves encourage broad use of the practice, Johnson (2007) suggests that deliberate mentoring has a wide range of benefits such as employee retention, satisfaction, and commitment. From Johnson's perspective, to wait for a culture of mentoring to develop on its own is a mistake. Tailoring a program of mentoring to fit the context of an organization is recommended. Such a program, according to Johnson, ought to track mentoring connections and evaluate mentoring outcomes. Johnson, who writes about mentoring in academic institutions says, "When administrators are serious about mentoring, faculty are serious about mentoring" (2007, p. 234). This insight applies to mentoring in other types of institutions as well.

Despite a fairly robust empirical literature describing mentoring and examining correlates of effective mentoring, a limited body of empirical literature directly records the perspectives of mentors regarding the role and the capabilities it requires. Some notable exceptions include Hudson's (2013) recent mixed-methods study in which mentors revealed the fact that the role both requires and helps them to develop communication, leadership, and problem-solving skills. Hudson's findings mirror those of several earlier studies of experienced educators who mentor student teachers and/or novice teachers (e.g., McDonald & Flint, 2011; Peterson, Valk, Baker, Brugger, & Hightower, 2010). Peterson and colleagues' study, moreover, emphasized the social and emotional insights needed by mentors as they navigate relationships with different mentees.

Another study this one involving faculty mentors from underrepresented groups revealed that mentoring graduate students involves the skills needed for serving in three roles: ally, ambassador, and master-teacher (Lechuga, 2011). Whereas the roles of ally and ambassador call upon the types of skills cited in the studies reported above, the role of master-teacher also requires a high level of professional expertise. Drawing attention as well to the master-teacher role, a study conducted by Mutton, Mills, and McNicholl (2006) emphasized the critical need for mentors to have and be able to share expert knowledge. Unlike many of the studies that have used interview methods to investigate the knowledge, skills, and dispositions that mentoring requires, our study asked participants to take a retrospective look at their own mentoring over the duration of relatively long careers. Furthermore, it asked participants to share what they learned about mentoring both from their own experiences as mentors and from their recollections of those professionals who have provided mentoring to them.

RESEARCH DESIGN AND METHODOLOGY

The purpose of this study was to explore mentoring, broadly construed, by investigating the perspectives of highly experienced mentors in a college of education and human services. Data from interviews with these mentors allowed the researchers to identify similarities and differences in the perspectives of the participants regarding what is essential for effective mentors to know and be able to do. Further, the study sought to determine if and how participants' experiences and perspectives matched up with common characteristics described in recent scholarship on mentoring.

The study took place in a comprehensive college of education and human services in a Midwestern state in the United States of America. The research was part of a larger professional development effort. Notably, findings from the study informed the development of a set of online modules designed for individuals interested in mentoring others. The college planned to encourage its cooperating teachers (i.e., practicing teachers who mentor preservice teachers) to make use of the online modules. Eventually, the college planned to package the modules as a professional development workshop that would be widely available to educators and other professionals within its region of the state.

The study was exploratory in nature, using a qualitative approach that allowed for extensive and forthright dialog between researchers and participants dialog of the sort that promotes deep understanding of the participants' frames of reference and social realities (Blaxter, Hughes, & Tight, 2006). One researcher conducted all of the interviews, asking mentors to share their perspectives about mentoring based on their own experiences.

Participants

An invitation was issued to 24 people representing a variety of academic units (e.g., centers, departments, and programs of study) within the college. The invitation asked potential participants to share information that would help the researchers identify common perspectives about mentoring and the knowledge, skills, and dispositions contributing to effective mentoring relationships and experiences.

Eight of the individuals who were invited to participate agreed to do so. These individuals had long histories of performing either formal or informal mentoring roles in diverse higher education departments and centers as well as mentoring individuals in the local community or in professional associations. Among the fields represented by the participating mentors are the following: early care and education, youth leadership, business and industry, P–20 education, teacher preparation, recreation and sport pedagogy, counseling, and service learning.

Participants volunteered to be interviewed and videotaped. The interviewer kept written anecdotal records of what transpired in each interview. She also transcribed the audio portions of each video recording.

Interviews

During an introduction to the videotaped interview, participants were given the following probe: From your perspective, what is the essential set of knowledge, skills, and dispositions needed for individuals who want to mentor others? Further, they were informed that their perceptions about mentoring could be addressed by discussing any of the following:

- In your own words, what is mentoring?
- Have you ever had a mentor?
- What are the benefits of a mentoring relationship?
- Are resources, including training, important for mentors?

During the video recording phase of the interviews, the researcher did not use the probes as a sequential set of interview questions. Rather she allowed participants to talk about mentoring in whatever ways made sense to them. When the interviewer sensed that more information could be elicited from a participant, she inserted one or more probes in an effort to obtain a more extensive response from the participant. Recommendations from Blaxter et al. (2006) informed this approach to qualitative interviewing.

Data Analysis

Using the set of transcripts as the primary source of data and following recommendations from Thomas (2006) and Strauss and Corbin (2000), one of the researchers along with a research assistant used inductive methods to code and categorize the data. As they worked with the data, the researcher and her assistant discussed emerging codes and categories. Through frequent discussion during the data analysis phase, they reached consensus about which categories and subcategories would represent the final set to be used. With this list of categories and subcategories in mind, they revisited the data in order to organize it in a way that would support a clear interpretation.

The trustworthiness of the data analysis was assured by consistency checks (having the two coders compare and discuss the categories that seemed to emerge) and stakeholder checks (sharing each participant's video and transcript with him or her) (Thomas, 2006). These approaches resulted in an interpretive analysis that made sense to the interviewer, the second researcher, and the research assistant.

FINDINGS

This section begins with a brief description of the characteristics of the eight participating faculty members. It then proceeds to a discussion of the data in each of four interpretative categories: (1) participants' understanding of the terms *mentor* and *mentee*, (2) mentoring constellations, (3) tie strength, and (4) developmental mentoring.

Participant Characteristics

Participants included six current faculty members and two former faculty members whose experience as mentors incorporated the activities of advising, coaching, problem-solving, and encouraging mentees' self-reflection. Through these activities, they had helped a wide variety of mentees access resources, expand professional networks, and acquire relevant knowledge and skills. Two of the participants were males and six were females; one was African American, and seven were European Americans. Two mentors were directors of programs that served children, youth, and families from the local region as well as other countries; two directed centers that support local, state, national, and international outreach initiatives; two were chairs of academic departments offering undergraduate and graduate programs; one was a senior college administrator; and three were faculty in P–20 academic programs offering informal and formal mentoring support to statewide organizations. Four had previously received training in formal career mentoring, and each of these four had provided professional development in cross-disciplinary mentoring programs associated with internship placements. One co-coordinated a program for training mentors who were alumni of one university department. Participants brought diverse types of expertise to their mentoring roles, and, as participants in the study, they all contributed unique perspectives grounded in professional practice over relatively long careers.

Participants' Understanding of the Terms Mentor and Mentee

Interviews revealed that the participating mentors all subscribed to the classical definition of a mentor, characterizing a person who fills this role as an individual who imparts wisdom, knowledge, and guidance based on his or her experience. As one participant shared:

> In my opinion, it's really valuable to have mentors who are experienced, who've done things that take education, time, application, progression in a career. (Participant A, December 28, 2011)

Participants also understood the term *mentor* primarily in relation to a set of roles and responsibilities. The following quotes show how several participants characterized the knowledge, skills, and dispositions of mentors:

> I believe a mentor is really anybody that's there, that is going to be able to help, and is willing to help you with your goal…help you define your goals, help you make your goals…and help you realize your goals…and they'll track you along the way and help you out in any way they possibly can. (Participant C, December 21, 2011)

> A mentor's a troubleshooter, somebody I go to…to help troubleshoot whatever's going on in my life, be it personal or be it professional. So that's basically what a mentor is to me, a troubleshooter, who helps me troubleshoot my way through life. (Participant A, December 28, 2011)

My mentor was a good sounding board for me, and if I had a problem, I would just call her and say, "This is what's going on." We would talk it through and she would say, "Okay what do you think we should do?" ...I always felt that she helped me build more confidence in myself. (Participant H, December 13, 2011)

Participants also saw the classical definition of a mentee (or protégé) as useful. This definition describes a mentee as an individual who needs nurturing, council, direction, and advice from an experienced individual. Participants with primarily teaching/faculty responsibilities were more likely to use the term *mentee* than were faculty with outreach and administrative responsibilities. The participant who most often used the term *protégé* was from a department linked to business, industry, and service. The participant said:

Mentoring is important for both the protégé and the mentor. The mentor often wishes to give back to his or her profession, and supporting the protégé during the internship phase can be a valued part of the faculty role. (Participant D, December 28, 2011)

Characteristics and Dispositions

According to study participants, effective mentors should demonstrate characteristics and dispositions that will encourage mentees to form positive relationships with them and take their advice seriously. In particular, mentors should be honest, trustworthy, kind, approachable, open, dependable, empathetic, caring, responsive, and aware.

For several participants, moral virtues such as honesty and trustworthiness were extremely important characteristics of effective mentors. As one of them noted about her own mentor,

I felt very comfortable with her. I had a lot of respect for her, as well. I really trusted her, too...so that's what made for it being one of the more formal relationships that I have had and yet the most effective. (Participant G, December 13, 2011)

A second participant commented,

I mentioned being honest. I think that another important thing is that a mentor can't be someone who tells you what you want to hear. It's not someone who...will stroke your ego, but is someone who you really know is going to be constructive about whatever topic is at hand...if you're seeking advice or seeking just a conversation about ideas, thinking, brain-storming. (Participant D, December 28, 2011)

A similar perspective about the need for forthrightness was offered by another participant:

You can be their friend as a mentor but you also have to be able to say, "Hey look, this is what you need to work on, and we'll figure out how to work on it together. We'll try this and if it doesn't work, we'll try something else." (Participant C, December 21, 2011)

That participant went on explicitly to talk about the linkage between trustworthiness and the ability to deliver both positive and negative feedback:

> On the whole I think mentors have to develop some trust. I think that's very, very key. Mentors are going to be giving feedback, positive and negative, and if they need to give the negative feedback, they need to be able to be trustworthy so that the feedback will be used. (Participant C, December 21, 2011)

A similar perspective was voiced in a comment from another participant:

> I think that if you're able to show that you're respectful of the mentee, then your words that you use when it's time to do corrective action will hit more home. I think it will be much more effective, that they'll take that word more to heart and learn from the situation.... There's got to be a system of mutual trust there between a mentor and a mentee and I think it has to develop early for that relationship to be effective...and lasting. (Participant F, December 28, 2011)

Some participants focused attention on the affective characteristics of strong mentors, such as their ability to show caring or empathy. According to one participant,

> A mentor is someone who cares about me and who seeks to be open enough in his or her own work...someone who is approachable if I really need someone to listen to an idea or give me some feedback. (Participant B, December 21, 2011)

That participant also talked at a bit more length about what he meant by "approachability":

> Approachable...the demeanor that I try to emulate now. I think that the more I'm approachable, the better I can help and the more feedback I'm able to give...the more receptive they are. (Participant B, December 21, 2011)

Kindness was the affective quality that seemed most salient to another participant. Speaking about a previous mentor, she commented,

> She was very kind with me 'cause there were times that...I probably was at her door every single day and with all the other responsibilities she had, she took the time and would tell me, "This is the time when we can talk about this; this is when we can figure this out." (Participant H, December 13, 2011)

That same participant also noted, this time referring to several of her mentors, "I think they were very empathetic, and empathy is, I think very important rather than sympathy. They didn't indulge me" (Participant H, December 13, 2011).

In addition to relevant moral virtues and affective responses, certain cognitive and communicative skills also seemed, from the vantage of participants, to characterize effective mentors. The two passages below illustrate the types of mentoring capabilities that participants discussed   the first focusing on the mentor's communication skill (in this case the ability to be a good listener) and the second on the mentor's perspicacity:

> She was always very much open to listening to me. I took a management class and they were speaking a language (business management)…I had no clue what they were talking about. (Participant H, December 13, 2011)

> Mentors need to have…an awareness…if you aren't aware of the world around you, if you aren't aware of the way people are perceiving you or aren't able to respond to an environment, to be responsive to a person who's confiding in you, then you're going to have a hard time being a mentor or being a leader because of the inability to relate and to pick up on those cues. (Participant A, December 28, 2011)

Mentoring Functions

Participants provided insights into the functions performed by mentors as they help mentees improve professional performance and psychosocial interactions. In addition to modeling and teaching, mentors seem to use reflective conversations as a way to assist mentees with the difficulties they are encountering. As one participant noted, "He or she will share with me strategies…ways of navigating difficult situations… accomplishments" (Participant D, December 28, 2011).

Another participant focused on the way that a mentor helped her think about problems in the workplace:

> They're just like, "Well, let's talk about what's going on and let's see what your next step should be." So, it's kind of like breaking it down instead of seeing the whole black "Eeyore" cloud. It was like, "Okay, let's see, what is the next thing to do?" And it was just, you know, little steps. (Participant H, December 13, 2011)

According to several participants, active listening followed by questioning can help the mentee identify problems that underlie surface difficulties. As Participant H put it,

> I think…being a good listener. Sometimes, it's not what you're saying; sometimes it's what you're not saying. And so sometimes it would be they could say, "Okay, so what's really bothering you?" (December 13, 2011)

Another participant emphasized the way conversations between mentors and mentees helped contextualize events in the workplace:

> When I talk to her about being a supervisor now, we talk about…all the stresses of being a supervisor…all the excitement of being a supervisor, the joys of seeing people you supervise…grow and achieve, and also the disappointments that also come with it, being that we're in a human institution. (Participant A, December 28, 2011)

Several participants shared their belief that mentors serve as models that their mentees often strive to emulate. According to one such participant,

You have to be honest and to remember to say in that relationship, "I have a philosophy. I strive to do a certain thing. I'm not necessarily going to always be the best example, but I'm going to be aware that I'm an example, and when I make mistakes or hit difficult situations, I'm going to try and model or to share that I have mentors, I have confidantes, I have people that are just good to talk things out, and having a trusted person is the way that you work through difficult situations." Mentors need to model that. (Participant C, December 21, 2011)

In part because mentees emulate them, participants stated the need to hold high standards for themselves as mentors, as well as for their protégés. As one participant put it:

I'm kind of a stickler about getting work done and having high-quality work, so I expect a lot out of people in my environment. I try to be a role model and not expect other people to do things I wouldn't myself. I think that when you're a mentor you're a role model, and when you're a leader, you have a target on you.... If you're setting the bar and you're sharing ways to be strategic about being effective in the workplace or at home or to balance your life, or to lead in whatever capacity, then people are watching the way you do that, and you have to be aware that you're a role model. (Participant D, December 28, 2011)

Recognizing the fact that needs vary across different protégés appears to guide the work of many mentors. Part of their work, therefore, is to find ways to help each protégé address his or her needs. One example of this approach involves work to help mentees establish balance in their lives. As one participant noted,

My area of study is in family and consumer sciences so I always figure, if we can't recognize the value of family and balance that in the workplace, then who can? And we should, at least, set a good example. So, recognizing that people are more than employees or more than students and that there are many other things that complicate their lives…and helping people balance that, I think becomes part of mentoring. To recognize that a student may be a husband and a father, and a student and a son, and an employee, and will continue to be those things and more as he moves through his career; and a student may be a sister and a daughter, and a mother and that she will continue to be those things as she moves through her career. Understanding how to balance that and really recognizing that and having discussions and working that into… "How can I be a better employee?" [The question for the mentee/protégé becomes…] "Well, are you making sure that you are taking care of things away from the workplace so that you can give attention to the workplace as needed?" (Participant D, December 28, 2011)

Mentoring Constellations

According to most participants, mentoring involves a constellation of relationships and experiences. In its simplest form, the mentor–mentee dyad provides both professionals with opportunities to learn. The mentor learns by interacting with and observing the mentee, and the mentee learns by engaging in the experiences that the mentor makes available to him or her. Those experiences often allow the mentee to connect to (and learn from) a wider network of professionals than those available to him or her in the workplace on a daily basis. According to one participant, such experiences represent a critical part of the mentoring constellation:

> The people that you're able to connect with, and then how those connections are made and the windows of opportunity that open from taking advantage of those situations, make it possible to move forward in a positive way…it's making those contributions and then moving forward. (Participant E, December 28, 2011)

In fact, the network of other professionals to which an effective mentor introduces the mentee includes some professionals who will also offer mentoring to the novice. This outcome reflects the tendency for mentoring to exist in many different forms   in other words, for there to be many different types of mentors. According to one participant, for instance, a network of mentors might include "informational mentors, intellectual guides, [and] mentors for professional careers" (Participant G, December 13, 2011). According to another, "I have different people for different purposes. Even though I speak to them about the same thing, I may speak to them about it from different angles" (Participant E, December 28, 2011).

Not only do many professionals find value in interacting with several different mentors, they also report the benefits of a career-long involvement with a constellation of mentoring relationships and experiences. Most participants, for example, said that they had themselves received guidance from several mentors, some of whom became long-time colleagues, friends, and/or associates in an ongoing community of practice. As one participant explained,

> I have had a couple of mentors in my life. I didn't necessarily call them mentors when I started out but as I have progressed, personally and professionally, I have come to realize they played great mentoring roles and they still play great mentoring roles in my life. I'm still in touch with some of them. (Participant A, December 28, 2011)

Tie Strength

Within networks of mentor–mentee relationships, some connections are inevitably stronger than others. Tie strength refers to the power of the bond between a mentor and a mentee. The strength of the bond does not necessarily depend on the location of the mentor   that is, whether he or she is part of an inner or an outer network. It does, however, influence the career or other benefits that a mentoring relationship provides (Higgins & Kram, 2001). Stronger ties increase the salience of the mentoring relationship   enhancing its benefits when mentoring is functioning effectively and constraining the mentee when it is working badly. A mentor who has strong influence over a mentee, therefore, plays a decisive role in what the mentee learns and how well he or she flourishes within his or her organization.

When a strong tie between a mentor and mentee promotes positive interactions (e.g., appropriate communication and lack of competition), it enables a productive mentoring relationship to ensue (Reagans, 2005). Such a relationship is characterized by commitment and follow-through, mutual respect in a climate of trust, and the provision of appropriate resources to support the mentee's learning.

Study participants' comments about effective mentoring reinforced what others have said about how strong mentoring relationships contribute to positive mentoring outcomes. For example, one participant focused on the importance of communication, follow-through, and commitment:

> Most effective were just the fact that from the very beginning, we had very, very good communication.... [W]e followed through on our commitments to the mentoring relationship. (Participant B, December 21, 2011)

Another talked about the ways that various resources work to strengthen the mentor's skill set, enabling him or her to provide effective guidance to protégés:

> I think resources are critical and I think that there are different types of resources. I think people, of course, become a very instrumental resource. I think it's the people you interact with in the profession who can help. So I think the resources can be people. Of course, there are multiple books written about mentoring, mentoring in the milieu. It goes way back to Homer...anyone who studies mentoring knows where we're from   the place from where it originated. I think that it's important to... read information that is available with the literature... [to] know where mentoring has taken us and then what the future is. I think there are a variety of different resources that are available for people, and I think opening up to a lot of different ways to capitalize on those resources is important. (Participant E, December 28, 2011)

Developmental Mentoring

According to various scholars, mentors respond to mentees' need to acquire institutional knowledge, understand local politics and organizational power, manage conflict, respond to acceptable norms of behavior, and set short- and long-term goals (e.g., Johnson & Ridley, 2008). Attentiveness to these concerns allows mentors to support not only the evolving practices of their mentees but also their evolving use of self-reflection as an ongoing approach to self-evaluation and planning. As one participant explained,

> When I was a first-year teacher and a second- and a third-year teacher, a teacher in my building took me under her wing. And it was a very informal situation 'cause there wasn't a formal mentoring program. But, as I look back, this was 20-something years ago, that was such an important piece of my growth and development. It was informal but it was very important. There were things that I learned that aren't

textbook things, just simply who important people were in the community and in the building, how to get along, the expectations, the unwritten things were an important part of this mentoring relationship, as well as a reflective piece. This person asked me a lot of questions and had me reflect on my teaching practices and gave me pointers, practical things of how to motivate and engage 28 first-graders. (Participant G, December 13, 2011)

Because each mentee's proficiency and reflectiveness increases over time, moreover, successful mentors use scaffolding methods to provide and then withdraw support. One participant recalled her experience as a mentee to describe what this approach felt like from the protégé's vantage:

She gave me opportunities to kind of figure things out, but yet I could still go to her when I really had no idea what I was doing or what I needed to be doing. And she helped me kind of learn new structures and learn new systems within the university. (Participant B, December 21, 2011)

Reflecting the insights shared in published works about mentoring, participants in the current study expressed the belief that successful mentoring requires mentors to embrace a collaborative and developmental model. Developmental mentoring is attuned to the learning needs and trajectory of each mentee as well as to the learning needs of the mentor, and it emerges only when the mentor and mentee inhabit a safe environment in which both can develop personally and professionally (Lankau & Scandura, 2007). As comments from one participant suggest, developmental mentoring emphasizes *lifelong learning* for the mentor and the mentee:

I think that you have to showcase…model and show the value [and] the accountability…given for mentoring. And it is lifelong learning…the education process… that the more we educate others about the importance of the mentoring [process] and bringing new ideas for change, that it is going to happen and is happening. (Participant E, December 28, 2011)

Another provided a strong rationale for matching mentoring support to the evolving needs of the protégé.

Professional development is essential in order for formal mentoring to be effective. The state looks at four distinct phases and prepares mentors to meet the developmental needs of educators. Without the training, mentors aren't even aware of the developmental levels at the first, second, third or even fourth year of mentoring. We seek to mentor them not overwhelm them; we want to retain them not send them running! (Participant F, December 28, 2011)

For several of the participants, the effectiveness of mentoring in part depends on the extent to which the mentor continually seeks to learn from his or her own mentors. As one participant commented,

Mentors need mentors. We're always learning, growing, developing, honing in on our skills as leaders in organizations. It's often the personal learning   s e l f - knowledge   that powerfully impacts one's next steps. Having that mentor that trusted, wise person   available to you to acquire that self-knowledge is something mentors themselves need. (Participant D, December 28, 2011)

For another, mentoring offered so many organizational benefits that those who practiced it needed not only to refine their craft but also to advocate explicitly on its behalf. The participant noted:

I think we have to be spokespeople about it…about the importance of mentoring. Is there always a dollar sign with it? No. Some things you can't pay a price for. I think as a citizen [of the organization] that you know the importance of it, and that's your investment. (Participant E, December 28, 2011)

DISCUSSION AND CONCLUSIONS

The results of this study not only support major findings from previous research on mentoring, but also support some important theories about the nature of teaching and learning. Notably, study participants described a mentor as an individual with professional knowledge, experience, and skills who provides support, nurture, and advice to a less experienced professional. This description is similar to the description of mentors provided in some of the scholarly and practical literature about mentoring (e.g., NASA, n.d., p. 6).

Previous literature, moreover, had suggested that effective mentors must demonstrate the appropriate dispositions to engage in mutually beneficial relationships with mentees. This perspective was also confirmed by the participants in the current study who described effective mentors as experienced professionals who value and demonstrate characteristics such as being honest, kind, approachable, open, trustworthy, dependable, empathetic, caring, and responsive. In addition, findings from previous literature and from the current study indicate that mentors must have the time and interest to mentor others and the ability to work well with mentees.

One disposition of particular importance to participants in the current study was caring. Other studies have supported this disposition as a critical part of any process in which one person seeks to help another person learn. Arguing for the fundamental importance of caring and its role in promoting social, intellectual, and personal development, Nel Noddings (1984) claims that authentic human liberation and social justice can only be achieved by caring people in caring communities (Berman, 2004). For Noddings, among others, teaching of all sorts (including mentoring) is an ethical act, dependent on care, empathy, and genuine interest in the learning experiences of others.

This perspective is reiterated in Brookfield's theory (1995) of adult learning, which adds to an understanding of how positive attitudes contribute to a positive teaching and learning environment for both mentees and mentors. According to

Brookfield, participation in any learning experience is voluntary, and adults seek learning experiences that will be effective for them. Such experiences typically share certain characteristics: (1) they foster the self-direction and empowerment of adult learners; (2) they cultivate respect among participants for each other's self-worth and contributions to the learning experience overall; (3) they view adult learning as a collaboration between the mentor and the mentee; (4) they make explicit linkages between theory and practice; and (4) they help adults use critical reflection to make sense of what they are learning (Brookfield, 1995).

The current study as well as earlier research has found that mentors not only care for mentees and deploy principles of adult learning in their interaction with them, but that mentors also fill a variety of roles and perform a variety of functions in their relationships with mentees. Among the functions that were most salient for participants in the current study are nurturing mentees' career development (Kram, 1985), providing support for mentees' psychosocial development (Kram, 1985), modeling professional performance and demeanor (Scandura & Ragins, 1993), and teaching relevant knowledge and skills.

Similar to findings from the current study, other scholarship on mentoring suggests that both mentees and mentors benefit from a network or "constellation" of mentoring relationships that is attentive to their developmental needs (Higgins & Kram, 2001; Higgins & Thomas, 2001). Such a constellation, moreover, helps to nurture a "mutuality perspective" because it introduces multiple viewpoints into the dialog between mentor and mentee (Dobrow et al., 2012, p. 211). According to some scholars, mutuality of this sort "promotes mutual growth, learning and development within the career context" for the mentor and protégé (Fletcher & Ragins, 2007, p. 374).

This perspective gains strong theoretical support from Vygotsky's (1978) work on the social foundations of learning as well as Bruner's (1996) insights about its cultural foundations. Whereas these theories draw on similar insights, they differ in important ways.

According to Vygotsky, learning occurs within the context of a particular type of social interaction. Among the features of such an interaction are: (1) intersubjectivity, whereby two participants begin a task with different understandings but arrive at a shared understanding; (2) scaffolding, whereby social support, assistance, and guidance enable the learner gradually to acquire new knowledge or a new skill and gain increasing independence and competence; and (3) guided participation, whereby learners and guides engage in ongoing and critical dialog about what is being learned.

According to Bruner, learning occurs as a result of social interactions but not necessarily interactions with particular characteristics. As a cultural learning theorist, Bruner (1996) maintains that knowledge is a cultural construct and that therefore learning takes place whenever social interactions are "participatory, proactive, communal, [and] collaborative" (p. 15).

Taken together, these theories suggest that novice professionals will inevitably learn what the cultures of their organizations present as salient but that mentors can help them distinguish between more and less functional skills, knowledge, practices, and dispositions. In other words, organizations present many opportunities for novice professionals to learn, but certain of those opportunities will invariably offer more benefits than others. The mentor's work, then, involves (1) helping the mentee identify the learning opportunities with the greatest potential benefits, (2) helping the mentee navigate an organizational culture in ways that emphasize its positive features and downplay its negative ones, and (3) assisting the mentee in his or her reflections about the most salient (negative or positive) organizational experiences that he or she confronts.

The ethical character of the mentoring role becomes obvious in this formulation, as does its complexity. We therefore encourage potential mentors to make informed decisions regarding their ability and willingness to take on the role. The questions in the following list can help experienced professionals decide if they are ready to take on the role: (1) Do I possess the expertise in my field and have the willingness to share my knowledge and/or skills with another? (2) Do I have access to or insight related to networking opportunities and resources that would create mentoring constellations that would benefit a mentee? (3) Do I have the time to devote to a responsive mentoring relationship in order to help the mentee identify, work toward, and meet personal and professional goals? (4) Do I model professional characteristics and ethical behaviors through my words and actions with the ability to provide feedback, guidance, and support to a diverse population of mentees? (5) Do I enjoy a climate of mutual respect and value creative dialogue and critical inquiry that have the potential to result in reciprocal learning, growth, and change?

Although we offer these questions as a way to help experienced professionals decide whether or not they are ready to mentor, we also strongly encourage such professionals to augment their own skills, modify their own dispositions, and organize their own work lives in ways that will enable them to answer the above questions in the affirmative. After all, experienced professionals did not themselves become competent and seasoned practitioners without the assistance of others. As Aldisert (2001) suggests, one of the best ways one can pay back the favor of having a mentor is to mentor someone else oneself. The cycle of mentoring is about learning from someone and passing the wisdom along to someone else.

To summarize the specific wisdom about mentoring that participants in this study shared, we have developed Appendix A. In the Appendix, Figure 3.1 presents essential mentoring knowledge, Figure 3.2 presents essential mentoring skills, and Figure 3.3 presents essential mentoring dispositions.

REFERENCES

Abiddin, N. Z., & Hassan, A. (2012). A review of effective mentoring practices for mentees development. *Journal of Studies in Education, 2*(1), 72–89.

Aldisert, L. (2001). The value of mentoring. *Bank Marketing, 33*(3), 40.

Berman, R. (2004). Caring for the ethical ideal: Nel Noddings on moral education. *Journal of Moral Education, 33*(2), 149–162.

Blaxter, L., Hughes, C., & Tight, M. (2006). *How to research* (3rd ed.). London, England: Open University Press.

Brookfield, S. (1995). Adult learning: An overview. In A. Tuinjman (Ed.), *International encyclopedia of education* (pp. 1–16). Oxford, UK: Pergamon Press.

Brown, R. D., & Krager, L. (1985). Ethical issues in graduate education: Faculty and student responsibilities. *The Journal of Higher Education 56*(4), 403–491.

Bruner, J. (1996). *The culture of education.* London, England: Harvard University Press.

Bullis, C., & Bach, B. W. (1989). Are mentor relationships helping organizations? An exploration of developing mentee-mentor-organizational identifications using turning point analysis. *Communication Quarterly, 13*(3), 199–213.

Carter, S., & Lewis, G. (1994). *Successful mentoring in a week.* London: Headway.

Dobrow, S. R., Chandler, D. E., Murphy, W. M., & Kram, K. E. (2012). A review of developmental networks: Incorporating a mutuality perspective. *Journal of Management, 38*, 210–242. doi:10.1177/0149206311415858.

Dougherty, T. W., & Dreher, G. F. (2007). Mentoring and career outcomes: Conceptual and methodological issues in emerging literature. In B. R. Ragins & K. E. Kram (Eds.), *The handbook of mentoring at work: Theory, research, and practice* (pp. 51–93). Thousand Oaks, CA: Sage.

Fletcher, J. K., & Ragins, B. R. (2007). Stone center relational cultural theory: A window on relational mentoring. In B. R. Ragins & K. E. Kram (Eds.), *The handbook of mentoring at work: Theory, research, and practice* (pp. 373–400). Thousand Oaks, CA: Sage.

Glenn, W. J. (2006). Model versus mentor: Defining the necessary qualities of the effective cooperating teacher. *Teacher Education Quarterly, 33*(1), 85–95.

Hart, E. W. (2010, June 30). Seven ways to be an effective mentor. *Forbes.com.* Retrieved from http://www.forbes.com/2010/06/30/mentor-coach-executive-training-leadership-managing-ccl.html

Higgins, M. C., & Kram, K. E. (2001). Reconceptualizing mentoring at work: A developmental network perspective. *Academy of Management Review, 26*(2), 264–288.

Higgins, M. C., & Thomas, D. A. (2001). Constellations and careers: Toward understanding the effects of multiple developmental relationships. *Journal of Organizational Behavior, 22*, 22–247.

Hogue, W. F., & Pringle, E. M. (2005). What's next after you say hello: First steps in mentoring. *Educause Quarterly, 2*, 50–52.

Hudson, P. (2013). Mentoring as professional development: 'Growth for both' mentor and mentee. *Professional Development in Education, 39*(5), 771–783. doi:10.1080/19415257.2012.749415

Johnson, W. B. (2007). *On being a mentor: A guide for higher education faculty.* Mahwah, NJ: Lawrence Erlbaum Associates.

Johnson, W. B., & Ridley, C. R. (2008). *The elements of mentoring.* New York, NY: Palgrave Macmillan.

Lechuga, V. (2011). Faculty–graduate student mentoring relationships: Mentors' perceived roles and responsibilities. *Higher Education, 62*(6), 757–771. doi:10.1007/s10734-011-9416-0

Lankau, M. J., & Scandura, T. A. (2007). Mentoring as a forum for personal learning in organizations. In B. R. Ragins & K. E. Kram (Eds.), *The handbook of mentoring at work: Theory, research, and practice* (pp. 95–122). Thousand Oaks, CA: Sage.

McDonald, L., & Flint, A. (2011). Effective educative mentoring skills: A collaborative effort. *New Zealand Journal of Teachers' Work, 8*(1), 33–46.

Mutton, T. T., Mills, G. G., & McNicholl, J. J. (2006). Mentor skills in a new context: Working with trainee teachers to develop the use of information and communications technology in their subject teaching. *Technology, Pedagogy & Education, 15*(3), 337–352. doi:10.1080/14759390600923840

NASA Training and Leadership Development. (n.d.). *Mentoring program handbook: A guide for NASA first mentors.* Washington, DC: NASA. Retrieved from http://leadership.nasa.gov/nasa_first/MentoringHandbook.doc

Noddings, N. (1984). *Caring: A feminine approach to ethics and moral education.* Berkeley, CA: University of California Press.

Parsloe, E. (1999). *The manager as a mentor.* London: The Guernsey Press.

Peterson, S. M., Valk, C., Baker, A. C., Brugger, L., & Hightower, A. (2010). "We're not just interested in the work": Social and emotional aspects of early educator mentoring relationships. *Mentoring & Tutoring: Partnership in Learning, 18*(2), 155–175. doi:10.1080/13611261003678895

Ragins, B. R., & Kram, K. E. (2007). *The handbook of mentoring at work: Theory, research, and practice.* Thousand Oaks, CA: Sage.

Reagans, R. (2005). Preferences, identity, and competition: Predicting tie strength from demographic data. *Management Science, 51*(9). Retrieved from http://pubsonline.informs.org/doi/abs/10.1287/mnsc.1050.0389.

Rothwell, W. M. (2000). *Effective succession planning: Ensuring leadership continuity and building talent from within* (2nd ed.). New York, NY: Amacom.

Scandura, T. A., & Ragins, B. R. (1993). The effects of sex and gender role orientation on mentorship in male-dominated occupations. *Journal of Vocational Behavior, 43,* 251–265.

Strauss, A. L., & Corbin, J. (2008). *Basics of qualitative research: Techniques and procedures for developing grounded theory* (3rd ed.). Thousand Oaks, CA: Sage Publications, Inc.

Thomas, D. R. (2006) A general inductive approach for analyzing qualitative evaluation data. *American Journal of Evaluation, 27*(2), 237–246. Retrieved from http://flexiblelearning.auckland.ac.nz/poplhlth701/8/files/general_inductive_approach.pdf

Turban, D. B., & Lee, F. K. (2007). The role of personality in mentoring relationships. In B. R. Ragins & K. E. Kram (Eds.), *The handbook of mentoring at work: Theory, research, and practice* (pp. 21–50). Thousand Oaks, CA: Sage.

Vygotsky, L. S. (1978). *Mind in society: The development of higher psychological processes* (14th ed.; M. Cole, V. John-Steiner, S. Scribner, & E. Suoberman, Eds.). Cambridge, MA: Harvard University Press.

Zachary, L. J. (2005). *Creating a mentoring culture.* San Francisco, CA: Wiley.

Zelditch, M. (1990). *Mentor roles.* Proceedings of the 32nd Annual Meeting, Western Association of Graduate Schools (2–12). Tempe, AZ, 16–18 March 1990, Conference Presentation.

APPENDIX A

Exemplifying high standards	being willing to model adherence to high standards
Content experts	acquiring high level scholarship
Experience in the field	considering both learned information and observations
Strategic	sharing and demonstrating acquired information effectively
Resourceful	creating opportunities to make connections and go deeper
Ways of navigating	being able to discuss learned information in various contexts
Situational	ascertaining whether or not information is communicated appropriately
Responsible	possessing clear and strong knowledge of a field or discipline as a foundation
Reflecting	being able to evaluate incoming information with existing knowledge and engage in critical thinking to arrive at a concise description of the issue
Accomplished	demonstrating learned information
Lifelong learning	acquiring information throughout the tenure of one's profession
Big-picture overview	recognizing and understanding concepts, foundation of field and relatedness across disciplines

FIGURE 3.1.   Perceptions of essential knowledge

Listener	demonstrating active communication skills
Sounding board	providing a receptive environment for the expression of another
Troubleshooter	providing a responsive environment for the expression of another
Critical thinker	displaying ability to analyze, synthesize, or evaluate information in a given area
Interacter	communicating ideas and learned knowledge while engaging with another
Showcaser	demonstrating use of tools to present competencies
Model	demonstrating competencies in field
Spokesperson	expressing ideas related to an organization, a field of study, or a profession
Feedback provider	knowing what, when, and how to share observations with another
Adviser	providing access to skills in overt ways
Counselor	giving counsel based on tried and true strategies for success
Consoler	making suggestions on what is known and what is yet to be learned or experienced
Recognizer	being astute at recognizing and knowing what, when, and how to activate skill set
Nurturer	recognizing and meeting the needs of another to promote confidence
Decision maker	making decisions and following through
Guide	providing guidance
Tracker	having the necessary skills to follow another and determine measures of success
Translator	being able to hear and understand the motivation behind the questions of another
Manager of time	managing timelines by meeting deadlines and addressing issues incrementally
Questioner	tuning in to the actions and expressions of another and asking questions or providing prompts to stimulate thinking or action
Motivator/Self-motivator	recognizing the potential in another and providing the quality of feedback that motivates performance without overwhelming another
Engager	encouraging mutual or co-participation to arrive at a successful outcome
Collaborator	possessing the ability to synthesize information and work in a team

FIGURE 3.2.   Perceptions of essential skills

Accessible	being available to serve another when it is convenient for the other
Honest	being truthful and objective in reporting or giving feedback
Open	being willing to share and communicate
Approachable	balancing intellect and emotion with consideration of another person
Caring	being able to display concern for another person openly and honestly
Dependable	possessing willingness to respond as appropriate from the vantage of commitment
Appropriate	knowing when to speak and when to refrain from speaking
Respectful	demonstrating care, concern, or empathy for another
Kind	treating another in a manner that communicates care and thoughtfulness
Trustworthy	demonstrating that one has the capacity to be honest
Understanding	putting oneself in the position of another to relate to his/her ideas or issues
Receptive to others' values	accepting the cultural values of another
Compassionate	being concerned about the success and/or welfare of another
Accountable	responding to the ethical obligations inherent in mentoring another
Generous	giving credit to another without reservation
Discreet	keeping shared information confidential
Willing	demonstrating they have the will to do what is necessary to mentor another
Friendly	acting in a way that is nonthreatening, respectful, and agreeable
Positive	willing to view and approach a situation from a strength's perspective

FIGURE 3.3.   Perceptions of essential dispositions

CHAPTER 4

MENTORING STYLE

Insights from the Development of an Instrument for Cooperating Teachers[1]

Aimee Howley, Marged H. Dudek,
Natalie Williams, and Barbara Trube[2]

ABSTRACT

This chapter reports on a research project with the aim of producing an instrument for measuring the mentoring styles of cooperating teachers. Such an instrument can be used by cooperating teachers as a basis for reflecting on their dominant mentoring styles. Efforts to change mentoring styles—perhaps expanding the use of a preferred style, for instance—can also be monitored using the instrument. The chapter describes the multistage process by which the research team tested the validity and reliability of the evolving instrument. The final version of the instrument measures four distinct styles represented by the following continua: directive to nondirective mentoring, collaborative to noncollaborative mentoring, convergent to divergent mentoring, and mentoring that is more or less open to instructional experimentation. Whereas theory suggests that some styles (e.g., collaborative mentoring) might be more helpful than others, additional empirical research is now needed in order to establish the connection between particular mentoring styles and desired mentoring outcomes.

Mentoring for the Professions: Orienting Toward the Future, pages 67–84.

INTRODUCTION

To improve the quality of mentoring provided to teacher interns[3] by enabling co-operating teachers to use systematic evidence as a basis for self-reflection, our research team designed and pilot tested a mentoring style inventory. According to research about the clinical experiences included in teacher preparation programs, mentors' self-reflection about mentoring styles—both those they prefer and those associated with beneficial outcomes—can help them become better mentors (e.g., Arnold, 2002; Harrison, Lawson, & Wortley, 2005). As some researchers note, moreover, such self-reflection is an important component of programs that focus explicitly on preparing cooperating teachers for the mentoring role (Iancu-Haddad & Oplatka, 2009; Russell & Russell, 2011). Furthermore, the use of valid and reliable measures of cooperating teachers' mentoring styles, coupled with similarly adequate measures of student teachers' learning styles, can support the efforts of teacher preparation programs to match interns and mentors as a way to increase the effectiveness of the culminating clinical experience (Tripp & Eick, 2008).

LITERATURE REVIEW

Recent research on the contribution of cooperating teachers to the learning of teacher interns suggests that certain characteristics of mentors—characteristics that correspond to particular "mentoring styles"—play a role in determining the effectiveness of the internship phase of teacher candidates' preparation. These features of mentoring style are different from and may either augment or detract from the modeling of effective teaching practice that the cooperating teacher provides (e.g., Osunde, 1996). In other words, even when cooperating teachers model effective instructional practice, they do not necessarily contribute positively to the learning of interns because their styles of mentoring may or may not match up with the learning needs and learning styles of their teacher interns (Lesley, Hamman, Olivarez, Button, & Griffith, 2009).

As this insight suggests, cooperating teachers' modeling of effective teaching practice constitutes one basis for interns' professional learning—learning acquired through observation—but other forms of learning may be more significant. Lesley and associates (2009), for example, found that cooperating teachers' efforts to promote the active engagement of interns, expressed through their work in guiding and providing scaffolding to their interns, were more helpful for interns' learning than their efforts to oversee the more passive processes of observation and imitation. Glenn's (2006) qualitative study of intern-cooperating teacher dyads also showed that mentoring tended to be effective when the cooperating teacher guided and provided scaffolding to the intern by "collaborat[ing] rather than dictat[ing], relinquish[ing] an appropriate level of control, allow[ing] for personal relationships, shar[ing] constructive feedback, and accept[ing] differences" (p. 94). Reaching similar conclusions, Rhoads, Radu, and Weber (2011) reported that, even if cooperating teachers and teacher interns differed in their educational philosophies, interns felt supported when their mentors were open to their experimentation with different teaching approaches, worked to build close rapport with their interns, and provided ongoing feedback.

Despite insights from these and other small-scale studies on mentoring perspectives and practices that contribute to productive clinical experiences for teacher interns, little work has focused on the development and field testing of instruments to identify the mentoring styles of cooperating teachers. Moreover, few studies in other professional fields have addressed the systematic specification and measurement of mentoring styles. Before reporting on the few relevant initiatives in the field of education, we turn to related work in other fields.

One of the professional development services that a consulting firm named Mentoring Solutions (*http://www.mentoring-solutions.com/*) provides is the administration and scoring of an instrument intended to measure the mentoring styles of managers in various fields. The instrument, which has been modified to match the needs of mentors in organizations of various types, has four scales relating to different mentoring styles: informational, guiding, collaborative, and confirming (Buros Center for Testing, 2012; W. Gray, personal communication, September 10, 2012). Scores on these scales help categorize mentors as preferring a single dominant mentoring style, a mixed mentoring style, or a balanced mentoring style. According to Gray (personal communication, September 10, 2012), the four styles support a repertoire of practices from which experienced mentors choose in order to meet the needs of particular mentees. Two reviews from the Buros Center for Testing (Areola's and Carney's reviews) indicate that the instrument's validity and reliability have not been tested empirically. Conversation with Gray, however, revealed a theoretical basis for each of the scales, an approach to scale development that tends to promote construct validity.

Focusing on the mentoring of novice entrepreneurs, St-Jean and Audet (2011) developed items to measure a nondirective form of mentoring, which they termed "maieutic" mentoring (p. 1). Using just three items to measure this style, the authors reported a relatively low alpha reliability of .69 but, nevertheless, correlated a scale comprised of these items with other scales purporting to measure mentoring outcomes. Based on their analysis of these associations, the researchers concluded that the maieutic style was a more productive approach than more directive alternatives. Although their insight about the potential value of nondirective mentoring does fit with some theoretical literature (e.g., Glickman, 1981), additional work on their instrument seems warranted. Nevertheless, as the discussion below suggests, our research team also decided that the distinction between directive and nondirective mentoring was a promising way to conceptualize one aspect of mentoring style.

In the education literature, research pertinent to the measurement of mentoring style has thus far focused on the mentoring that cooperating teachers provide to teacher interns. Our study builds directly on this work. A study conducted by Kahan (2002), for example, involved the construction of an instrument to assess physical education cooperating teachers' "beliefs about supervisory behavior, perceptions of conditions that facilitate or inhibit supervision, and supervisory styles and preferences" (p. 65). Despite the very small sample used to pilot test the instrument (n = 11), the author claimed that it had adequate internal consistency and test-retest reliability. Unfortunately, Kahan did *not* use data from a larger second sample (n = 76) either to compute reliability a second time or to examine the discreteness of the different scales. He did use these data to conduct mean comparisons, however, one of which revealed that teaching level (i.e., elementary, middle, high school) was associated significantly with scores on the supervisory behavior scale. Nevertheless, for a reader of the study, interpretation of the higher scores of elementary and middle school teachers in comparison to those of high school teachers was problematic, because the published article did not include a copy of the instrument. A reader, therefore, could not tell which behaviors were more evident among mentors in elementary and middle schools than among mentors in high schools. Whereas this study did offer an interesting justification for exploring salient mentoring characteristics of cooperating teachers, namely to help teacher education programs identify mentors whose perspectives fit with the program's assumptions, it did not undertake a sufficiently rigorous or extensive data collection and analysis effort. Its limitations clearly demonstrate the need for more research on the mentoring styles of cooperating teachers.

Another study, which focused on the development of an instrument to discern cooperating teachers' motivators and challenges, used a far more systematic and rigorous method of instrument construction (Clarke et al., 2012). The research entailed collaboration between teacher educators at the University of British Columbia and cooperating teachers in an ongoing professional development network. The cooperating teachers generated statements regarding their motivators and challenges—a set of statements that the researchers then used to validate the scales. The motivators scale listed incentives such as "Renewing the profession" and "Improving my own teaching practices," and the challenges scale listed issues such as "Concerns about [student teachers'] pre-practicum preparation" and "Uncertain feedback and communication practices" (p. 189). The authors positioned the final version of the scale as a tool that cooperating teachers could use either independently or in collaboration with others to reflect on their practice, examining and problematizing their perspective on the mentoring role by exploring the balance between its motivators and challenges. The careful instrument development methods used by this research team provided an excellent model to guide our work, but its conceptual focus—on mentoring motivators and challenges—differed markedly from the sorts of mentoring styles we investigated.

Studies of the mentoring provided by cooperating teachers to teacher interns suggest that instruments measuring mentoring style might have a range of applications. They might assist mentors in thinking about their own practice; provide a common language to promote collaborative discussions among mentors; and help employers (e.g., faculty and administrators in teacher preparation programs) select mentors with beliefs, dispositions, and propensities that fit well with organizational or programmatic aims and perspectives. Nevertheless, as our review of the literature shows, few efforts have been made to develop valid and reliable instruments for use with cooperating teachers or other mentors to guide self- or employer assessment of their characteristics, styles, or beliefs.

INSTRUMENT DEVELOPMENT

Our research team developed a mentoring style instrument by first reviewing extant literature from a variety of fields as the basis for constructing a concept map. Team members then conducted two focus group interviews to evaluate the salience of the ideas reflected in the concept map. Data from the focus group interviews informed development of a pilot instrument, which the team tested with a convenience sample of educators from across the United States. After modifying the instrument in response to findings from the first pilot test, the team conducted a second pilot test of the revised instrument. The discussion below details these procedures and their outcomes.

Construction of a Concept Map from Extant Literature

The research team began the instrument development process with a search of relevant empirical literature. The few extant studies that offered guidance revealed that mentoring style is not a unitary construct, but that various characteristics of mentors describe discrete parts of their mentoring style (Hudson, 1966; Riding & Cheema, 1991; Stahlhut & Hawkes, 1987; Vonk, 1996). Moreover, the literature suggested that these *mentoring styles* reflect more generalized preferences for particular modes of cognitive processing, social interaction, and problem-solving.

The literature, in fact, pointed to four domains that seemed to define salient differences in mentoring style: (1) cognitive style, which corresponded to an analytic/intuitive continuum (Armstrong, Allinson, & Hayes, 2002; Riding & Cheema, 1991); (2) one-on-one interaction style, which corresponded to a directive/collaborative/nondirective continuum (Glickman, 1981); (3) general interaction style, which linked to a broadly construed set of personality traits (e.g., Keirsey, 1998); and (4) problem-solving style, which corresponded to a continuum from convergent to divergent thinking (Hudson, 1966). The team created a concept map distinguishing the characteristics associated with the four domains and used this map as the basis for developing a first draft of the *mentoring style inventory*. The initial concept map is presented in Figure 4.1.

Focus Group Interviews

The team used this preliminary version of the *mentoring style inventory* as a prompt to stimulate focus group discussions of the domains representing mentoring style and items that might measure individual variation across those domains. The preliminary instrument contained a total of 16 items, four from the cognitive

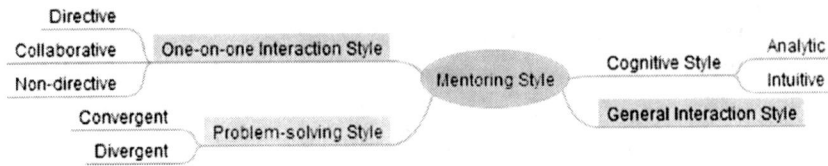

FIGURE 4.1. Initial concept map

style domain, two from the one-on-one interaction style domain, seven from the general interaction style domain, and three from the problem-solving domain.

The first focus group included 21 participating educators, most of whom were currently working as teachers or administrators in K–12 schools and all of whom were enrolled in a graduate workshop on mentoring conducted by faculty from a large university located in a Midwestern state in the United States. One member of the research team conducted the interview by first asking the participants to complete the instrument and then leading a discussion to elicit feedback about the items and their relevance to the four mentoring style domains. The researcher audio-recorded and transcribed the interview, and another of the team's researchers analyzed the transcripts to identify recurring themes and specific recommendations for improving the instrument. Overall, the participants agreed that the domains were relevant to the work of mentoring teacher interns, but they had concerns about the degree to which items on the preliminary instrument would actually distinguish among cooperating teachers with different mentoring styles.

Based on data from the first focus group interview, the research team revised the instrument with the aim of producing an improved version for use with the second focus group. Using the revised version of the instrument to prompt discussion, one member of the research team conducted the second focus group interview with 15 participants who were members of an advisory council that gave guidance to the teacher preparation program at a small university also in the Midwestern United States. Participants included one K–12 educator, two principals, one Head Start administrator, 10 higher education faculty members, and one higher education staff member. The processes used with the second focus group mirrored those used with the first.

Participants' critical comments related to the definition of terms, clarity of certain items, and the number of response choices made available to respondents. Addressing these concerns, the research team further refined the instrument. In addition to making minor changes in wording and in the number of response choices provided for each item, the team created additional items to provide adequate coverage of each of the four mentoring style domains that the instrument intended to measure.

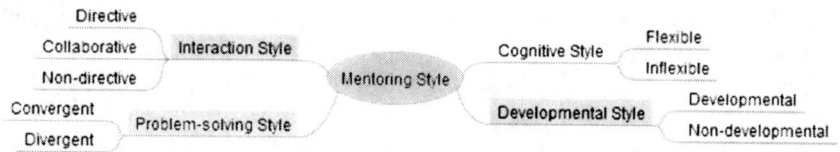

FIGURE 4.2.   Concept map guiding development of the first pilot test

Pilot Testing: The First Pilot Test

The third version of the instrument contained 67 items: 42 directly measuring mentoring styles in the *interaction style* and *problem-solving* domains and indirectly measuring mentoring styles in the *cognitive style* and the *developmental* domains. Figure 4.2 depicts the concepts used as the basis for the items included on the first pilot test.

The team also included a number of items, 25 in all, to serve as validity measures. These items elicited specific self-disclosures about preferred mentoring styles. The team reasoned that a correlation between responses to an explicit item and its comparable scale might help establish the content validity of the scale. For example, the scale measuring problem-solving style (i.e., the continuum between convergence and divergence) might gain credibility if people who had convergent scores on the scale also self-identified as having a preference for seeking convergent solutions to problems. This approach, while recommended by some researchers (e.g., Basadur, Graen, & Wakabayashi, 1990; Heppner & Petersen, 1982), also poses challenges. As Lohman (2004) and Atkins and Wood (2002) noted, for example, scales and rating systems for measuring domains like problem-solving style and interaction style are often developed precisely because people are not very effective at categorizing their own preferred styles. As the discussion below shows, the research team may have encountered this difficulty with many of the validity items.

In order to measure two domains directly and two indirectly, the team developed different schemes for scoring the 42 items. One scoring guide described a direct scheme for scoring the items in the *problem-solving style* domain, and another described a direct scheme for scoring the items in the *interaction style* domain. The remaining two scoring guides described different ways of scoring some of the 42 items to reflect differences in respondents' *developmental mentoring style* and *cognitive mentoring style* (conceptualized along the continuum from flexible to inflexible). The extant literature on mentoring style supported this approach through results showing that (1) developmental mentors tend to exhibit variation in their interactive styles, especially the use of directive, collaborative, and nondirective strategies (e.g., Glickman, 1981; Vonk, 1996) and (2) flexible mentors, in contrast to their inflexible counterparts, tend to give mentees more room for self-determination and to allow them to solve problems in divergent ways (e.g., Greyling & du Toit, 2008; Grisham, Ferguson, & Brink, 2004).

The first pilot test of the instrument entailed an online survey of a convenience sample of teachers and principals from districts in various states across the U.S. Using email addresses obtained from web sites, the team sent invitations to approximately 3,000 educators nationwide. In response to a single mailing to these educators, the team received a total of 267 responses, 247 of which were complete.

To determine whether or not the domains that the instrument intended to measure actually matched a coherent factor structure, the team performed a principal components analysis with varimax rotation using all scored items (i.e., items scored multiple times using different scoring guides). The results of this analysis were inconclusive, however. Without restricting the number of factors, the analysis yielded a structure with 14 factors, none of which clearly met Stevens's (2002) criteria for factor reliability. Forcing a two-factor solution, a second analysis yielded one reliable factor on which 14 items loaded at the .4 or above level. Examination of the content of the items suggested that this scale measured *developmental mentoring*. The internal consistency reliability (i.e., Cronbach's alpha) of this 14-item scale was .75. As a result of this analysis, the research team decided to make minor revisions to the response choices and scoring procedures for the 14 items on the scale and then to pilot test the scale again with another sample of educators.

Although the items on the *cognitive style* scale (i.e., those representing the flexibility-to-inflexibility continuum) did not form a coherent factor, the team decided to retain the construct by identifying the subset of *cognitive style* items with the highest alpha reliability. Using a sequential process, the team found five items that could be combined to form a scale with an alpha reliability of .77. The team used the same approach for selecting items to constitute a *problem-solving* scale representing the continuum from convergent to divergent. In this case, six conceptually related items represented the subset with the highest reliability—a reliability estimate of .87. Analysis of both the *developmental* and the *cognitive style* scales suggested that a simple additive approach to scoring would work better than a more complicated one.

The analysis of items that had been developed to measure *interaction style* yielded surprising results. First, by inspecting correlations among the items, the team noticed two sets of empirically discrete items—one set relating to the continuum between directive and nondirective mentoring and the other relating to the continuum between collaborative and noncollaborative mentoring. Counter to what theory had suggested, collaborativeness did not appear to represent a midpoint between directiveness and nondirectiveness but, rather, to represent an unrelated construct.[4] With this interpretation in mind, the team separated the two sets of items and examined their internal consistency. The first set of items (i.e., the eight items relating to the *directive–nondirective interaction style*) combined to produce a scale with an alpha reliability of .77. The second set of items (*collaborative–noncollaborative interaction style*), however, produced a scale with an unacceptable level of internal consistency (alpha = .62). For this reason, the team did not sum the items to produce a scale but rather determined that additional items relating to a collaborative scale would be needed for the next version of the instrument.

A final step was to examine correlations between the four scales and the individual items developed to investigate their content validity. First, the team correlated the 14-item *developmental* scale with the explicit items that had been created to test the content validity of that scale. None of the Spearman Rho rank order correlations, however, turned out to be significant—a finding that suggested the need for caution in linking the scale to the construct, *developmental mentoring*. Similarly, the *flexibility scale* did not correlate significantly with any of the relevant content validity items. By contrast, the *directive/nondirective interaction scale* correlated significantly with two of the relevant validity items, but both correlations were relatively weak (−.19 and −.13 respectively), and one of the applicable validity items had a low correlation with the *problem-solving (i.e., convergent/ divergent) scale* (r = −.18).

Based on these analyses, the research team developed a fourth version of the instrument to be used in a second pilot test of the instrument. This version contained five scales: the *directive/nondirective interaction style scale*, which included 8 items; the *collaborative/noncollaborative interaction style scale*, which included 6 items (3 of which were new); the *divergent/convergent problem-solving scale*, with 7 items (1 of which was new); the *developmental scale*, which included 13 items; and the *flexibility scale*, which included 10 items.

Pilot Testing: The Second Pilot Test

The team pilot tested the fourth version of the instrument in January, 2012. With help from principals and superintendents, the team contacted teachers from approximately 300 school districts from one Midwestern state, asking each teacher to complete the online questionnaire. The team received 832 responses to the instrument, 793 of which were usable.

To analyze these responses, the team performed a principal components analysis with varimax rotation. With one exception, the factor structure fit the pattern that had been predicted based on interpretation of the findings from the first pilot test. With the factor solution limited to a total of five factors, the analysis yielded four factors that met Stevens's (2002) criteria for factor reliability and exhibited conceptual coherence. The one exception involved the items that had originally been considered to form a separate *developmental scale*. Rather than constituting a discrete factor, these items loaded on the same factor as the items from the *directive/nondirective interaction scale*. Their factor loadings on this scale, however, were lower than those for the items measuring *directive/nondirective interaction*. For this reason, the team decided to eliminate these items and the construct, *de-*

FIGURE 4.3. Final concept map

velopmental mentoring style, from the final set of scales. In other words, because the items on the *developmental scale* failed to produce a factor that could be differentiated empirically from the *directive/nondirective interaction* scale, the team surmised that the construct *developmental mentoring style* would also be difficult to disentangle conceptually from the construct *directive/nondirective interaction style*.

Following the sequential approach described above to identify items for each scale that contributed to the greatest possible internal consistency, the team produced a final 7-item version of the *directive/nondirective interaction scale* with an alpha reliability of .80. To facilitate discussion of the scale with teacher educators as well as with cooperating teachers, the team simplified the name of this scale to the *directiveness scale*. Similarly, using a simplified title for the second scale, the *collaborativeness scale*, the team identified a final set of five items measuring that subdomain of interaction style. The alpha reliability for the *collaborativeness scale* was .93. With a somewhat less robust reliability of .84, the final *convergence scale* included 6 items. The one other scale in the final version of the instrument consisted of half of the items from the *flexibility scale* that had been included in the second pilot. The team removed the other items because they interfered with overall scale reliability. With those items removed, the Cronbach alpha reliability of .79 represented adequate internal consistency. A review of the semantic content of the items suggested that *openness to experimentation* (*openness*, for short) represented a better name for the construct than *flexibility*. A copy of the final *Mentoring Style Inventory* is provided in Appendix A. The concept map supported by work to develop a final version of the instrument is presented in Figure 4.3.

Following the same procedure for investigating the content validity of the scales as had been used with data from the first pilot test, the team computed correlation coefficients between each scale and single items that elicited direct self-reports of respondents' approaches to mentoring. For the *directiveness scale*, the two items were:

- It is important that student teachers create their own lesson plans during most of the student teaching experience.
- I prefer to be highly structured.

TABLE 4.1.   Conceptual Definitions of Four Scales Measuring Mentoring Style

Scale	Conceptual Domain	Definition
Directiveness	One-on-one Interaction Style	The directiveness scale measures the continuum between a nondirective and a directive mentoring style. More directive mentors provide explicit guidance to teacher interns for a longer period of time during the internship experience. Less directive mentors encourage teacher interns to assume greater responsibilities from an early stage in the student teaching experience.
Collaborativeness	Collaborative Style	The collaborativeness scale measures the continuum between a more and less collaborative mentoring style. Collaborative mentors share tasks and responsibilities with teacher interns more often and earlier in the internship experience than do less collaborative mentors.
Convergence	Problem-solving Style	The convergence scale measures the extent to which mentors give teacher interns opportunities to solve problems either in "tried and true" ways or in more novel ways.
Openness	Openness to Experimentation	The openness scale measures the willingness of the mentor to allow the teacher intern to experiment in the classroom with progressive or constructivist pedagogical methods.

Whereas the correlation between the *directiveness scale* and the latter item was nonsignificant, the moderate negative correlation between the scale and the first item was significant ($r = -.31$).

The team correlated the *collaborativeness scale* with one item, "I prefer collaboration to working independently," and obtained a significant positive correlation of .18. One of the two correlations between relevant content validity items and the *convergence scale* was also significant, but weak ($r = .13$). The item was "A problem is best solved by breaking it into smaller components and analyzing those components one at a time." Finally, the *openness scale* correlated significantly (though weakly) with both of the items used to investigate its content validity:

- In working with a student teacher, my goal is to provide a climate that encourages experimentation. ($r = .24$)
- In general, I see myself as highly flexible. ($r = .20$)

In combination with the clear factor structure obtained for four of the five scales on the second pilot test of the instrument, these correlation coefficients lent support to the conclusion that the instrument was able to measure four distinct mentoring styles. Alpha reliabilities of .80, .93, .84, and .79, respectively, suggested that the four scales had adequate reliability, especially for use in future research and as a basis for giving feedback to cooperating teachers about their preferred approaches to the mentoring of teacher interns. Further research to establish the instrument's reliability and validity across different populations of cooperating teachers is, of course, recommended.

Following the construction and pilot testing of the instrument and its four sub-scales, the research team wrote conceptual definitions of the four scales as well as developing preliminary norms that teacher educators could use in comparing a particular cooperating teachers' scores with scores from the sample of 793 teachers responding to the second pilot test. The norms include the means and standard deviations for responses to each scale. The conceptual definitions are included in Table 4.1. The norms are provided in Appendix B.

DISCUSSION

For the research team, this instrument development effort led to several insights—perspectives that will inform our continuing work and may contribute to the work of other researchers with an interest in studying mentoring style. These insights relate to the process of instrument development, conceptual and empirical alignments and distinctions within the mentoring style domain, and the applicability of instruments measuring the mentoring style of cooperating teachers.

With respect to process, we found the focus group interviews particularly illuminating. These interviews gave us a chance to hear the perspectives of experienced K–12 teachers who had provided guidance to teacher interns as well as teacher educators from several institutions of higher education. Their candid commentary about the process of mentoring clarified our thinking about mentoring style, helping us see the somewhat limited applicability of general interaction style and cognitive style and the salience of the specific interaction style characterized by the directive-to-nondirective continuum. In addition to these benefits for the work of instrument development, comments from participants in the focus groups suggested that they appreciated having a voice in processes for improving the clinical preparation of teacher interns. This perspective, namely the view that improvement of teacher education ought to represent collaboration between teacher educators and K–12 partners, corresponds to insights reported by Clarke and his research team (2012).

Not only did the focus group interviews lead to new understandings, but the pilot tests also offered insights, helping to clarify the importance of particular associations and distinctions. In particular, we were able to conceptualize collaborativeness, not as a midpoint between directive and nondirective mentoring as Glickman's (1981) work had suggested, but as a separate dimension of mentoring style. This finding suggested that highly collaborative mentors might be either directive or nondirective in terms of interaction style, and that less collaborative mentors might similarly be either directive or nondirective.

The pilot tests further implied that "developmental mentoring" might best be conceptualized not as a style unto itself but rather as an intentional use of different styles under different circumstances. Nevertheless, the loading of items designed to measure developmental mentoring on the same factor as items designed to measure the continuum between directive and nondirective mentoring provided some empirical support for Glickman's (1981) claims about the value of using directive mentoring with less experienced teachers (or in this case, teacher interns), on the one hand, and nondirective mentoring with more experienced teachers (or teacher interns), on the other.

Although the pilot tests seemed to show that the convergence–divergence factor and the openness to experimentation factor (Rhoads et al., 2011) represented dimensions of mentoring style, an alternate explanation might be that these apparent dimensions of style actually represent responses to external conditions. Notably, the press in some schools for teachers to focus on standards and associated accountability tests might restrain divergence and openness to experimentation even among teachers whose natural inclinations fit with those styles. Further research is needed to determine the degree to which these two mentoring styles in particular vary in response to the restrictiveness of the conditions under which mentor teachers work.

As our discussion thus far has shown, additional work is still needed in order to establish the construct validity of the four mentoring styles we identified. In addition, studies of the association between the different styles and mentoring efficacy are critical if the instrument is to gain wide use in professional development programs that aim to improve mentoring. Notably, without information about whether convergence (or collaborativeness or directiveness or openness) has positive or negative influences on mentoring outcomes, teacher educators and cooperating teachers will not know how to think about and respond to high or low scores on the scale. Should they treat a high score on the scale as an encouraging indicator or as a cause for concern?

Researchers, moreover, will need to learn more about the interaction between different mentoring styles and teacher interns' characteristics and capabilities. For instance, Glickman's model suggests that nondirective and directive mentoring will *work better* with interns who have more and less experience, respectively. Nevertheless, at present, empirical work does not definitively support the use of his developmental model despite the seemingly self-evident nature of its theoretical claims. Furthermore, with four (or possibly more) different dimensions of mentoring style, interactions among the dimensions will inevitably support different mentoring personas. And determining the fit between an intern's pattern of characteristics and the needs and persona of the mentor might be so complicated as to render unworkable the intentional matching of teacher interns and cooperating teachers.

Whatever the actual circumstances, however, perspicacious use of the instrument depends on deeper understanding of what its scale scores mean and how the instrument functions as a tool for professional development or for matching teacher interns with mentors whose styles fit with their needs. We hope that recent interest in expanding the clinical model of teacher education will encourage other teacher educators to join us in taking up these issues through a focused program of empirical research into the character and impact of various mentoring styles.

In the meantime, cautious use of the scale in its current form seems like a reasonable recommendation. In particular, we believe that cooperating teachers will learn about themselves by completing the instrument and reflecting on the results. They can use the published norms, moreover, to compare their scores with those from the large sample of teachers who participated in the second pilot test. In addition, groups of cooperating teachers might gain valuable insights from professional development activities involving completion of the scale followed by discussion of the potential benefits and possible drawbacks of mentoring styles represented by the poles of the continua that the four scales on the instrument measure: namely, the continuum from directiveness to nondirectiveness, the continuum from collaborativeness to noncollaborativeness, the continuum from convergence to divergence, and continuum from greater to lesser openness to experimentation.

NOTES

1. This work was supported through funding from the Martha Holden Jennings Foundation.
2. The research team wishes to thank Christine Crumbacher for her assistance with data analysis.
3. We use this term to refer to teacher candidates who are participating in a culminating clinical experience. The older term, "student teacher," no longer fits well with the intentionality of the clinical experiences that many contemporary teacher preparation programs now seek to provide their candidates.
4. We also used principal components analysis with the subset of interaction-style items and obtained results supporting the same interpretation.

REFERENCES

Armstrong, S. J., Allinson, C. W., & Hayes, J. (2002). Formal mentoring systems: An examination of the effects of mentor/protégé cognitive styles on the mentoring process. *Journal of Management Studies, 39*(8), 1111–1137.

Arnold, P. (2002). Cooperating teachers' professional growth through supervision of student teachers and participation in a collegial study group. *Teacher Education Quarterly, 29*(2), 123–132.

Atkins, P. W., & Wood, R. E. (2002). Self- versus others' ratings as predictors of assessment center ratings: Validation evidence for 360-degree feedback programs. *Personnel Psychology, 55,* 871–904.

Basadur, M., Graen, G., & Wakabayashi, M. (1990). Identifying individual differences in creative problem solving style. *Journal of Creative Behavior, 24*(2), 111–131.

Buros Center for Testing. (2012). *Mental measurements yearbook and tests in print* [online]. Lincoln, NE: University of Nebraska, Buros Institute. Retrieved from http://buros.org/

Clarke, A., Collins, J., Triggs, V., Nielsen, W., Augustine, A., Coulter, D., & ... White, J. (2012). The Mentoring Profile Inventory: An online professional development resource for cooperating teachers. *Teaching Education, 23*(2), 167–194.

Glenn, W. J. (2006). Model versus mentor: Defining the necessary qualities of the effective cooperating teacher. *Teacher Education Quarterly, 33*(1), 85–95.

Glickman, C. D. (1981). *Developmental supervision: Alternative practices for helping teachers improve instruction.* Alexandria, VA: Association for Supervision and Curriculum Development.

Greyling, W. J., & du Toit, P. H. (2008). Pursuing a constructivist approach to mentoring in the higher education sector. *South African Journal of Higher Education, 22*(5), 957–980.

Grisham, D. L., Ferguson, J. L., & Brink, B. (2004). Mentoring the mentors: Student teachers' contributions to the middle school classroom. *Mentoring & Tutoring: Partnership in Learning, 12*(3), 307–319.

Harrison, J., Lawson, T., & Wortley, A. (2005). Facilitating the professional learning of new teachers through critical reflection on practice during mentoring meetings. *European Journal of Teacher Education, 28*, 267–292. doi: 10.1080/02619760500269392

Heppner, P. P., & Petersen, C. H. (1982). The development and implications of a personal problem-solving inventory. *Journal of Counseling Psychology, 29*(1), 66–75.

Hudson, L. (1966). *Contrary imagination.* London, England: Penguin Books.

Iancu-Haddad D., & Oplatka, I. (2009). Mentoring novice teachers: Motives, process and outcomes from the mentor's point of view. *The New Educator, 5*, 45–65.

Kahan, D. (2002). Development and evaluation of a screening instrument for cooperating teachers. *Teacher Educator, 38*(1), 63–77.

Keirsey, D. (1998). *Please understand me II: Temperament, character, intelligence.* Del Mar, CA: Prometheus Nemesis Book Company.

Lesley, M. K., Hamman, D., Olivarez, A., Button, K., & Griffith, R. (2009). "I'm prepared for anything now": Student teacher and cooperating teacher interaction as a critical factor in determining the preparation of "quality" elementary reading teachers. *Teacher Educator, 44*(1), 40–55.

Lohman, M. C. (2004). The development of a multirater instrument for assessing employee problem-solving skill. *Human Resource Development Quarterly, 15*(3), 303–321.

Osunde, E. O. (1996). The effect on student teachers of the teaching behaviors of cooperating teachers. *Education,* 116612–11618.

Rhoads, K., Radu, I., & Weber, K. (2011). The teacher internship experiences of prospective high school mathematics teachers. *International Journal of Science & Mathematics Education, 9*(4), 999–1022.

Riding, R., & Cheema, I. (1991). Cognitive styles: An overview and integration. *Educational Psychology: An International Journal of Experimental Educational Psychology, 11*, 193–215. doi: 10.1080/0144341910110301

Russell, M. L., & Russell, J. A. (2011). Mentoring relationships: Cooperating teachers' perspectives on mentoring student interns. *Professional Educator, 35*(1), 16–35.

Stahlhut, R. G., & Hawkes, R. R. (1987, February). *Mentoring relationships during student teaching.* Paper presented at the National Conference of the Association of Teacher Educators, Houston, TX.

Stevens, J. (2002). *Applied multivariate statistics for the social sciences* (4th ed.). Mahwah, NJ: Erlbaum.

St-Jean, E., & Audet, J. (2011). The effect of mentor intervention style in novice entrepre- neur mentoring relationships. *Academy of Management Annual Meeting Proceed- ings, 2011-1,* 1–6. doi:10.5465/AMBPP.2011.65869654

Tripp, L., & Eick, C. (2008). Match-making to enhance the mentoring relationship in stu- dent teaching: Learning from a simple personality instrument. *Electronic Journal of Science Education, 12*(2), 41–65.

Vonk, J. H. C. (1996, April). *Conceptualizing the mentoring of beginning teachers.* Paper presented at the Annual Conference of the American Educational Research Associa- tion, New York, NY.

APPENDIX A: MENTORING STYLE INVENTORY

In typical cases, when are the following practices appropriate for student teach- ers? [Convergence Scale]

	From the beginning of student teaching onward (1)	Towards the middle of student teaching (2)	Near the end of student teaching (3)	After the stu- dent teacher's graduation (4)
Implementing their own lesson plans independently (1)	☐	☐	☐	☐
Developing new assessments on their own (2)	☐	☐	☐	☐
Transfer of responsibility for recording daily grades (3)	☐	☐	☐	☐
Transfer of responsibility for managing the grade book (4)	☐	☐	☐	☐
Assuming responsibility for all classroom instruction (5)	☐	☐	☐	☐
Grading tests (6)	☐	☐	☐	☐
Grading all tests, homework, and other assignments (7)	☐	☐	☐	☐

How comfortable are you with the following practices? [Collaborativeness Scale]

	Very un- comfortable (1)	Somewhat uncomfort- able (2)	Somewhat comfortable (3)	Very com- fortable (4)
Joint lesson planning with your student teacher (1)	☐	☐	☐	☐

	Very un-comfortable (1)	Somewhat uncomfort-able (2)	Somewhat comfortable (3)	Very com-fortable (4)
Encouraging your student teacher to use your assessments as a foundation for the creation of new assessments (2)	☐	☐	☐	☐
Co-creating assessments with your student teacher (3)	☐	☐	☐	☐
Encouraging your student teacher to use your lesson plans as a foundation for the creation of new lesson plans (4)	☐	☐	☐	☐
Co-teaching (5)				

In typical cases, when are the following practices appropriate for student teachers? [Convergence Scale]

	Always (1)	From the begin-ning of student teaching onward (2)	Towards the mid-dle of student teaching (3)	Near the end of student teaching (4)	Never (5)
Development of formative assessments (1)	☐	☐	☐	☐	
Using data from your formative assessments to inform and change instruction (2)					
Developing alternative remediation methods for use with students (3)					
Trying out new supplementary materials (4)					
Planning and implementing interdisciplinary lessons with more experienced teachers (5)					
Engaging in project-based instruction (6)					

Please put a check mark next to any practices you would ALWAYS allow a student teacher to use. (Leave blank any practices you would sometimes or never allow.) [Openness Scale]

- ☐ Use alternative teaching materials such as animals for dissection (1)
- ☐ Use alternative teaching methods such as role-playing (2)
- ☐ Use alternative teaching methods such as physically active games (3)
- ☐ Develop formative assessments based on curriculum guides (4)
- ☐ Engage in project-based instruction (5)
- ☐ Share students' work with a wider audience (6)
- ☐ Bring live animals to class to enrich instruction (7)
- ☐ Use cooperative learning (8)
- ☐ Divide the class into skill-based groups (9)
- ☐ Engage parents or community members in instruction (10)

APPENDIX B: NORMS BASED ON SAMPLE OF 793 TEACHERS

Scale	Continuum	Mean	SD
Directiveness	High scores = more directive Low scores = less directive	13.45	3.35
Collaborativeness	High scores = more collaborative Low scores = less collaborative	17.64	3.59
Convergence	High scores = more convergent Low scores = more divergent	14.41	4.25
Openness	High scores = more openness Low scores = less openness	6.0	2.43

PART II

MENTORING IN PROFESSIONAL FIELDS & THROUGH PROFESSIONAL ORGANIZATIONS

CHAPTER 5

PEER COACHING IN A CO-TEACHING MENTORING MODEL

Dianne M. Gut and Pamela C. Beam

ABSTRACT

Modeling a co-teaching relationship in a teacher education master's level STEM program and engaging in co-mentoring/peer coaching, two faculty members (general and special education) co-taught two semester courses to a cohort of teacher candidates in a one-year, field-intensive teacher preparation program. Pre-, post-, and delayed-post surveys tracked the development of candidates' understandings of co-teaching and the developmental relationships central to co-teaching. Candidates were required to co-teach two lessons with their cooperating teachers using a co-teaching model (one teach, one assist was not an option) and reflect on the experience. Finally, candidates completed weekly online reflections based on observations of co-teaching in the university classroom and co-teaching experiences in their seventh- through twelfth-grade classrooms. Using co-mentoring/peer coaching and collaboration lenses for analysis, perceptions of co-teaching reveal challenges and progress made in navigating and establishing developmental relationships within dyads in the areas of co-planning, co-assessing, classroom management, contrasting teaching styles, and expectations.

Mentoring for the Professions: Orienting Toward the Future, pages 87–109.

INTRODUCTION

Co-teaching offers a unique opportunity to utilize the strengths of individual teachers to enhance the learning environment, but it required communication and effort to make sure that both teachers are focused on the same goals and working in tandem. The extra effort is definitely worth the payoff in the end.

—Teacher Candidate

Collaboration and co-teaching are growing in popularity and use in the field of education. The benefits of having multiple professionals working collaboratively to increase outcomes for P–12 students have been documented in the literature, specifically for students across the full spectrum of grades, content areas, and abilities (Bacharach, Heck, & Dahlberg, 2010; Friend, 2007, 2008; Friend, Cook, Hurley-Chamberlin, & Shamberger, 2010; Johnson & Brumback, 2013). The traditional practice of mentoring (i.e., an experienced individual assisting a novice to develop knowledge and/or skills within a given context) has a long history and broad reach across education and other professions (Cain, 2009). A newer concept is the practice of co-mentoring or peer coaching, in which "two or more individuals voluntarily work together to help each other solve problems and grow professionally" (Savage, Savage, & Armstrong, 2012, p. 348). This chapter describes the use of co-teaching as a modeling tool and teaching approach from multiple perspectives: those of two university faculty who co-taught courses that included instruction on co-teaching and engaged in co-mentoring; as well as those of preservice teachers who experienced co-teaching in their university courses and employed it in their own clinical experiences with their mentor teachers.

Problem Statement

The purpose of this study was to examine changes in graduate teacher candidates' perceptions of co-teaching in response to (1) modeling by two university faculty members in co-taught classes, and (2) their direct personal experience with co-teaching in a K–12 classroom in which a cooperating teacher served as their co-teaching partner.

Definition of Terms

- *Alternative teaching.* This term refers to a co-teaching strategy that divides the class into groups. One teacher is responsible for the large group, and one is responsible for small-group instruction (Friend & Cook, 2003).
- *Co-mentoring.* Co-mentoring has been defined as "supportive assistance provided by several connected individuals...who share an association and common activity" characterized by reciprocal and mutual mentoring rather than traditional mentoring, which is hierarchical in nature (Bona, Rinehart, & Volbrecht, 1995, p. 119).

- *Co-teaching.* This term refers to the pairing of two teachers, typically one special education and one general education teacher, working together in a classroom to deliver instruction (Scruggs, Mastropieri, & McDuffie, 2007).
- *Cooperating teacher.* In this study, the cooperating teacher is the P–12 classroom teacher who serves as a mentor and co-teaches with the teacher candidate. "Cooperating teacher" is used synonymously with the term "mentor teacher."
- *Differentiated instruction.* Instruction that is responsive to variations in learners in a classroom is referred to as "differentiated instruction." Differentiation can occur in four areas: (1) content, (2) process, (3) products, and (4) learning environment (Tomlinson, 2000).
- *Dyad.* In this study, the term "dyad" refers to a pair of teachers who engage in co-teaching in the classroom. Such pairs typically consist of a general education and special education teacher, but can be two general education or two special education teachers.
- *One teach, one assist.* In this co-teaching strategy, one teacher has primary responsibility for teaching and the other circulates around the room, assisting students as needed (Friend & Cook, 2003).
- *One teach, one observe.* In this co-teaching strategy, one teacher is responsible for delivery of content, and the other observes for purposes of data collection or providing feedback (Friend & Cook, 2003).
- *Parallel teaching.* This term refers to a co-teaching strategy in which teachers divide the class in half, both teaching the same content (Friend & Cook, 2003).
- *Peer coaching.* In peer coaching, two colleagues engage in a mutually supportive relationship, working together in an effort to improve their teaching through the use of constructive feedback (Neubert & McAllister, 1993).
- *Station teaching.* In this co-teaching strategy, teachers divide both the content and the class, and each teaches different content (Friend & Cook, 2003).
- *STEM.* This acronym refers to the related fields of science, technology, engineering, and mathematics.
- *Teacher candidate.* In this study, "teacher candidates" refers to students enrolled in graduate level education courses and teaching part-time in the P–12 classroom.
- *Team teaching.* In this co-teaching strategy, both teachers deliver the same content at the same time to the whole class (Friend & Cook, 2003).
- *Year-long clinical placement.* Candidates are placed in a P–12 classroom for an entire school year. The first semester, they are required to spend three full days in the classroom, and the second semester, they are in the classroom full-time, completing a traditional student teaching experience.

Teacher Preparation Program

In this study, two university faculty members co-taught two classes to 12 teacher candidates enrolled in a teacher education master's level STEM program for career changers. The teacher candidates were enrolled in a one-year, field-intensive teacher preparation program. The field-intensive program began with the summer semester, and the co-taught university classes took place during fall semester, each taught by a general and a special education faculty member.

University-Level Co-Teaching

In the fall semester, teacher candidates were enrolled in *Managing and Monitoring Student Learning* and *Differentiated Instructional Adaptations*. The two classes met once a week and were scheduled back-to-back for a six-hour block of time. However, most weeks, the co-taught classes met for approximately three hours each week, with the remaining time reserved for additional time in the P–12 classroom and collaboration time for assignments. Both university instructors were present and co-facilitated instruction during the class time. Most often, a team-teaching form of co-teaching was used for instruction. In this co-teaching form, both instructors shared delivery of the content to the whole class, providing teacher candidates with both the general and special education perspective on the content. For example, when discussing classroom assessments, candidates received instruction on the aspects of quality assessments, as well as how they could be differentiated for learners at all levels. A discussion of the different types of assessments was enhanced with an analysis to determine which assessments would be most appropriate for specific learners, followed by an activity requiring candidates to adapt an assessment for all learners.

Managing and Monitoring Student Learning is a course designed to help general education teacher candidates (grades 7–12) become more proficient at managing classroom procedures and student behavior. This class provides teacher candidates with the skills needed to use classroom assessment data more efficiently and effectively through analysis and application, promoting data-driven decision making and problem solving. *Differentiated Instructional Adaptations* is a course designed to provide general education teachers with the skills needed to work with learners with diverse academic, social, and behavioral needs in inclusive classrooms. Course content focuses on collaboration strategies, curriculum accommodations, instruction and classroom management adaptations, and principles and skills for differentiating instruction in an inclusive classroom.

P–12 Classroom Co-Teaching

As part of their coursework, teacher candidates were required to co-teach a minimum of two lessons, based on Friend and Cook's (2003) models of co-teaching, with their cooperating/mentor teacher during the fall semester. Following their co-teaching experiences, teacher candidates were to record their personal reflections of the two separate events and share their reflections regarding the positives and negatives of the experience with all co-teaching teams during a facilitated meeting. The one-teach, one-observe, and one-teach, one-assist models were not allowable options, given that these models are the lowest levels of co-teaching and do not require equal engagement of both co-teachers. Rather, candidates were required to utilize parallel teaching, station teaching, alternative teaching, and/or team teaching.

LITERATURE REVIEW

Co-teaching is not new to the field of education and has been a focus of study for more than a decade. Its benefits for student learning as well as for co-teaching participants have been established in the literature. More recent focus has been on the benefits of the practice of co-teaching on the participants themselves (Barnes, 1999; Chapple, 2009; Goodnough, Osmond, Dibbon, Glassman, & Stevens, 2009; Scruggs, Mastropieri, & McDuffie, 2007). The focus of this more recent research has often been on a more experienced individual serving in a mentoring capacity for a novice or beginning teacher. A newer perspective is to examine the practice of co-teaching as a co-mentoring or peer-coaching opportunity. In this scenario, working collaboratively, peers serve as mentors to each other, thereby enhancing the growth and development of both individuals.

Co-Teaching

As the classrooms in the United States become increasingly more diverse, school systems must be ready to support students' diverse needs with strategies that enhance the educational experience for all children, while supporting those who struggle (Friend, 2007, 2008; Graziano & Navarrete, 2012; Jones & Morin, 2000; Walther-Thomas, Bryant, & Land, 1996). Co-teaching is one such strategy that helps address this need. Co-teaching is not a new concept and has in fact been in the literature since at least the mid-1990s (Jones & Morin, 2000; Walther-Thomas et al., 1996). However, the increase in both diversity and children with special needs in all classrooms, combined with federal mandates, has brought about a push to implement co-teaching in today's classrooms (Brinkmann & Twiford, 2012; Murawski & Dieker, 2004; Walther-Thomas et al., 1996).

In today's educational landscape, with federal legislation such as No Child Left Behind, along with greater reliance on high-stakes testing and academic standards, more and more school districts are counting on the concept of a co-teaching model to significantly improve the overall performance of all students, most specifically students with special needs (Brinkmann & Twiford, 2012; Graziano & Navarrete, 2012). In addition, the latest iteration of the Individuals with Disabilities Education Improvement Act (IDEIA), which mandated school systems' inclusion of students with exceptionalities into the general education classroom to the fullest extent possible, added more pressure for districts to find ways to support struggling students in all subject areas at all levels (Brinkman & Twiford, 2012).

Walther-Thomas et al. (1996) studied 23 schools over a three-year period as new co-teaching models were implemented in eight school districts. Teachers and administrators reported many student benefits. Students with disabilities developed more positive attitudes about school and working in an integrated classroom. Student motivation increased while overall dissatisfaction decreased, and students were able to celebrate their own academic and social strengths.

Often, a co-teaching dyad is made up of a general educator and an intervention specialist or special educator. Because of this, institutions of higher education have an opportunity in their programming to contribute significantly to the development of new teachers, both in working with other adults in the classroom and in building strategies new teachers can bring to their classrooms in order to serve all children's needs (Friend, 2007, 2008; Friend et al., 2010; Johnson & Brumback, 2013). Teacher educators also have some responsibility for the success of all children (Badiali & Titus, 2010), and with this type of approach, teacher educators may more fully meet their responsibility for contributing to the success of all children.

Co-teaching as a Mentoring Strategy

Teacher education has begun to shift its focus from predominately university-classroom-based instruction to clinically field-based instruction. A Blue Ribbon Panel commissioned by the National Council for Accreditation of Teacher Education (NCATE, 2010) recently set a national goal to reframe and reform teacher education by "turning teacher education upside down." In this new vision, clinical experiences form the basis for the application of theoretical concepts. In clinically based programs, partnerships and collaboration between P–12 schools and institutions of higher education are critical. Placing teacher candidates into classrooms earlier in their training as opposed to near the end, as was the case in traditional student teaching scenarios, means candidates have less experience and training during the earliest field experiences. These early field placements often occur in the first or second year of a candidate's teacher preparation. One strategy to address this lack of experience and knowledge and to support teacher candidates' early experiences is to employ co-teaching strategies. Using this instructional strategy, experienced teachers can model good teaching practices and gradually increase teaching opportunities for the novice teacher candidates. The use of co-teaching as a mentoring tool also has strong support in the literature.

Pugach and Wesson (1995) examined student and teachers' perceptions of co-teaching and found that teaming led to coordinated instruction, discussions about what and how content should be taught, and a more complete understanding of individual students' strengths and needs. Jimenez-Sanchez and Antia (1999) examined team-teaching pairs of deaf and hearing teachers and found that a team member with the most experience at the school took on the role of mentor for the team, assisting others with developing an understanding of classroom procedures. In a review of research on co-teaching and teaming, Pugach and Winn (2011) examined research findings with the purpose of determining how these practices support novice teachers. The researchers reached the following conclusion:

> On the whole, co-teaching and teaming continue to be viewed as beneficial by teachers, especially in terms of personal and professional support.... Also, it seems important for special education teachers to participate closely with their general education colleagues, both to widen the base of support they can tap into beyond special educators alone and to appreciate what they can learn from their general education colleagues. This can contribute to their socialization, not just as members of the professional special education community but also as members of the entire school community as a whole. (p. 43)

Co-Mentoring

A focus on co-teaching or collaboration as a form of co-mentoring is gaining popularity and subsequent focus in the literature. Savage and associates (2012) indicate that hallmarks of peer coaching are that "no person is regarded as superior to another" and that peer coaching is not focused on "quality assurance but [rather on] professional growth and change" (p. 348). They emphasize that a peer coaching or peer mentoring relationship must have a strong foundation based on mutual respect and trust designed to "build confidence and enhance a sense of professional self-worth" (p. 348).

In a non-teaching context, Creamer (2004) examined 24 pairs of disciplinary and interdisciplinary research/writing partners in higher education focused on how differences of opinion were handled between collaborative partners. The author proposed that "a shared worldview and familiarity with each other's expertise developed over time mitigate disciplinary differences among long-term collaborators" (p. 566). Participants viewed "differences of opinion as a valuable source of insight to complex problems" (p. 565). Nissilä (2005) concurred with the importance of a shared vision and suggested that "appreciating views other than one's own is the most important key success factor of a team," and that "the ability to genuinely learn and work together is a challenge. Collective reflection and regarding other people as esteemed colleagues...gives time and space to other people and will lead to a deeper understanding than one person alone can attain" (p. 209).

More specific to the education field, Goodnough and associates (2009) examined outcomes of co-teaching for members of teams they termed "co-learners," using a triad model comprised of two teacher candidates paired with one cooperating teacher. They described one outcome in the following way:

> The pairs naturally engaged in peer coaching.... [T]hey would plan a lesson together, and one pre-service teacher would implement the lesson while the other observed.

After completion of the lesson, the peer coach would offer critical feedback on the lesson. (p. 289)

Additionally, the teacher candidates reported that "working collaboratively with a fellow preservice teacher provided them with the opportunity to learn from each other and to enhance the quality of their teaching" (Goodnough et al., 2009, p. 290). One candidate indicated an appreciation of peer feedback, especially early on when relationships with cooperating teachers were still developing, and indicated that peer feedback was "more candid and straightforward" (p. 291) than feedback from cooperating teachers. Cooperating teachers in the triads also believed teacher candidates learned a great deal from each other after co-planning, co-teaching, and observing each other. Finally, cooperating teachers reported benefits from the collaboration, as all four commented on the extent of their own learning that resulted from exposure to varying perspectives and new ideas.

Barnes (1999) described a team-teaching approach used by two general education teachers (one teaching in the morning and one in the afternoon) and a special education teacher, along with a speech-language pathologist, and reported, "We all contribute insights that, when shared, can open up entirely new possibilities for seemingly intractable problems or difficulties" (p. 236). The author credited the trust developed among the professionals as providing a "basis for self-reflection and development" (p. 234).

In a survey of 92 general and special education teachers from across a range of grade levels and subject areas, Austin (2001) found that the teachers typically worked well with each other. They "solicited each other's feedback, and benefited from working together. Further, both groups generally agreed that co-teaching was a worthwhile experience that contributed to the improvement of their teaching" (p. 248). Austin reported that 91.4% of the special education co-teachers ranked the placement of student teachers in a collaborative teaching assignment as useful or very useful, as compared to 70.5% of the general education co-teachers; this was determined to be a statistically significant difference, and Austin speculated that this difference reflected their different roles in the classroom.

Peer Coaching

Unlike a typical mentoring situation involving a master paired with a novice teacher, peer coaching focuses on a pair of teachers with comparable status who teach the same content or grade levels, with the intent of producing increased levels of collegiality (Colucci, 2014; Conley, Bas-Isaac, & Scull, 1995; Jewett & MacPhee, 2012). Peer coaching can include both in-class and out-of-class activities. Out-of-class activities include, but are not limited to, co-planning, problem solving, reflective study groups, and curriculum development, while in-class activities include peer observations and note taking (Swafford, 1998).

Frequently, peer coaching is adopted as a building-wide initiative with multiple dyads, designed to foster a climate of teamwork. Collucci (2014) posits that a team atmosphere is especially important for new teachers and teachers struggling with particular issues, as it builds comfort, encouraging individuals to seek help and experiment with new ideas and instructional approaches. In a typical co-teaching arrangement, however, participants must be willing to observe as well as be observed. Peer coaching is reciprocal in nature, in that it uses frequent observations of one another by the two members of the dyad as a way to strengthen the reflective aspect of teacher growth and development (Trautwein & Ammerman, 2010). In addition, unlike a co-teaching dyad, peer coaching can be done in small groups (Shams & Law, 2012).

The literature is clear in its support of the peer-coaching strategy. Hyman (1990) perceived peer coaching to be a way for teachers to "professionalize" teaching by helping them conduct their own professional development, not unlike in other professions, thereby elevating the teaching profession. Additionally, teachers express an openness and willingness to try new instructional approaches when supported by peer coaching (Kohler, McCullough Crilley, Shearer, & Good, 1997). In many instances, teachers participating in a peer-coaching dyad reported improved outcomes related to the formulation of new ideas, confirmed belief in a strategy or strength, a changed sense of self, and adoption of new behavioral practices (Bruce & Ross, 2008; Swafford, 1998; Zwart, Wubbels, Bolhuis, & Bergen, 2008). Finally, peer coaching has been demonstrated to be a more effective and longer-lasting form of professional development, as compared to traditional inservice training or workshops, which typically last only one or two days (Stichter, Lewis, Richter, Johnson, & Bradley, 2006).

The benefits of co-teaching, co-mentoring, and peer coaching, from the inservice teacher perspective, are fairly well established in the literature. The purpose of this study was to examine changes in graduate teacher candidates' perceptions of co-teaching in response to modeling by two university faculty members in co-taught classes, and candidates' experiences in co-teaching with their cooperating teachers in the P–12 classroom. In the current study, co-teaching was used as a mentoring and co-mentoring/peer-coaching tool and was examined from the perspective of the teacher candidates enrolled in two co-taught university classes and placed in a year-long clinical field placement where their co-teaching was a course and program requirement.

METHODS

Context

This field-intensive, clinical STEM master's program required teacher candidates to be in a classroom three full days per week for the fall semester as well as take a full load of classes. Candidates began their work in the school when the local districts began classes, which included teacher inservice days before the middle and high school students began classes. Candidates followed the school calendar, so they took breaks with their school, rather than with the university.

Therefore, the first semester of fieldwork lasted approximately 18 weeks. The clinical model allowed candidates to implement co-teaching principles that were being discussed and modeled in the two co-taught university classes. As part of a class assignment during the fall semester, candidates were required to co-teach and co-plan on two separate occasions with their cooperating teacher, to operationalize how they would utilize co-teaching. During the second semester, candidates had full teaching responsibilities for their professional internship (student teaching), which occurred five days a week for the full school day. Therefore, the second semester lasted approximately 19 weeks.

Participants

- *Candidates*: Eleven co-teaching teams were dyads composed of a general education teacher candidate and a general education teacher assigned to the same classroom. One co-teaching team was a triad comprised of a general education teacher candidate placed with both an intervention specialist and a general education teacher. Nine of the candidates were placed in high school
- *Faculty*: The two college faculty members (one with secondary and extensive administrative experience and the other with preK through middle school special and general education experience) had a great deal of P–12 experience that was utilized and shared in class and through onllne discussion board responses. They also collectively had over 25 years of experience teaching at the university level.

Instruments/Procedure

Surveys

A 35-item online survey was created, following a review of relevant co-teaching literature (see Appendix for a copy of the complete survey). The survey was administered using Qualtrics, an online survey tool, three times over the course of the academic year (first week of the fall semester, last week of the fall semester, and last week of the spring semester). The first survey question asked the candidate for his/her birth date so responses could be matched for each participant across the three administrations. The remainder of the survey was made up of 14 open-ended questions (definition of co-teaching; philosophy of co-teaching; expected responsibilities in a co-teaching situation; expectations regarding discipline, classwork, shared materials, and homework) and 20 statements requiring a rating of "rarely," "sometimes," or "usually" (e.g., "I can easily read the nonverbal cues of others"; "I feel comfortable moving freely about the space in a co-teaching classroom regardless of whose room it is"; "I believe both teachers in a co-taught classroom need to agree on the goals of the classroom").

Discussion Board Posts

As a class assignment, candidates were required to make a weekly post to the class discussion board. Candidates were instructed to reflect on the co-teaching strategies observed in the co-taught classes, as well as any co-teaching experiences in their K–12 classrooms.

Data Analysis

Descriptive statistics were calculated for the forced-choice items from the survey. A phenomenological approach was used to analyze the open-ended responses from the pre-, post-, and delayed post-surveys, as well as the discussion board posts created by the teacher candidates as part of their weekly assignment. As defined by Lichtman (2010), phenomenology is used to describe and understand "the essence of lived experiences of individuals who have experienced a particular phenomenon" (p. 75).

RESULTS

Surveys: Forced-Choice Responses

Over time, teacher candidates' responses to the forced-choice questions indicate a more clearly defined understanding of the roles, responsibilities, and expectations related to co-teaching, reflecting development in their understanding of co-teaching processes. Table 5.1 summarizes findings from the questions most relevant to the focus of this chapter and provides a comparison of the means and standard deviations of responses from pre- (prior to classroom experience), post- (one semester of experience at midpoint of school year), and delayed post-surveys (at the end of a full academic year). Responses were rated on a 3-point scale with 1 = rarely, 2 = sometimes, and 3 = usually.

Surveys: Open-Ended Responses

With respect to the phenomenon being explored, candidates clearly developed a more in-depth understanding of co-teaching through their exposure in the university classroom and personal experiences in the P–12 classroom. Themes emerging from the data across all survey administrations included increased depth of understanding, increased specificity, and desire for more control, indicative of growing confidence in their skills, clear expectations, and a future orientation— specifically, how they intended to do things in the future.

Depth of Understanding

An analysis of the open-ended responses demonstrated a deepening understanding of co-teaching over time. Candidate responses to the pre-survey were superficial in nature, and they primarily defined co-teaching as "working together."

TABLE 5.1. Means and Standard Deviation by Question (1 = rarely; 2 = sometimes; 3 = usually)

Survey Item	Pre (n = 11) M (SD)	Post (n = 12) M (SD)	Delayed Post (n = 4) M (SD)
I can read the nonverbal cues of others	2.36 (.50)	2.67 (.49)	3.00 (.00)
I feel comfortable moving about the co-taught classroom	2.64 (.50)	2.67 (.49)	3.00 (.00)
I believe both teachers need to agree on the goals of the classroom	3.00 (.00)	2.92 (.29)	3.00 (.00)
I have presented lessons in a co-taught class	1.55 (.69)	2.33 (.49)	2.25 (.50)
I believe classroom rules and routines must be jointly developed	2.64 (.50)	3.00 (.00)	3.00 (.00)
I believe all materials should be shared	2.82 (.40)	2.75 (.45)	2.75 (.50)
I believe modifications of goals for students with special needs are the responsibility of both teachers	3.00 (.00)	3.00 (.00)	3.00 (.00)
I believe planning for classes is the shared responsibility of both teachers	2.55 (.69)	3.00 (.00)	3.00 (.00)
I believe the "chalk" should pass freely	2.55 (.52)	2.75 (.45)	2.75 (.50)
I believe common planning is important	2.40 (.48)	2.83 (.39)	3.00 (.00)
I believe that behavior management is a shared responsibility	2.91 (.30)	2.92 (.29)	3.00 (.00)

Note. Although the n is small across administrations, making it unreasonable to calculate mean differences, means and standard deviations were presented for ease of comparison.

In response to a question about expectations related to giving/receiving feedback, one candidate reported,

> If they [students] are not behaving in a manner that is respectful towards me or the other students, I tell them so. I would be open to my students informing me of faults in my teaching, as long as it was done in a respectful manner.

Increased Specificity

Post-responses were clearly based on actual experience, both in referencing strategies that were modeled and their own one-on-one teaching experiences. Their responses were more detailed and thoughtful, with explicit examples. Responses reflected deeper understanding of the co-teaching concepts, and definitions included specific examples of sharing duties and responsibilities, collaborating, and increasing student learning. For example, one candidate remarked, "Co-taught classrooms give students the opportunity to learn in a creative way from multiple skilled teachers and when done correctly have proven to be effective."

Desire for Control

Most commonly, when discussing the responsibilities they would like to have in the co-taught classroom, most candidates initially proposed a 50-50 split or shared responsibilities. Over time, however, some indicated they would prefer to have more control in the classroom, suggesting they "would probably prefer to be in charge," "take the leadership position," and "be given full authority for handling discipline issues." A desire for more control indicated confidence in their developing skills.

Clear Expectations

Over time, teacher candidates became clearer in their expectations and more directive in discussing how they would handle specific situations. Candidates addressed academic expectations for themselves and the students, as well as behavioral expectations, as reflected in the following responses: "Students should put forth their best effort and try all assignments. The students should feel comfortable to ask questions and know that I will assist them in understanding, but will not give answers." "Students will be assigned classwork based on their ability... gifted students might have five higher-level problems and other students might have 10 conceptual problems; this would depend and vary on the lesson." "Students should participate fully in classwork. Teacher should go over and scaffold students while completing work. Work done together in class should comprise the majority of the practice that students participate in."

Future Orientation

Finally, responses to the delayed post-survey at the end of the academic year, although limited in number, can be described as very specific, grounded in personal experience, and having a future orientation. Specifically, comments were stated in terms of what the teacher candidates intended to do in their own classrooms and expectations they would hold for students as well as co-teachers. In formulating their responses, candidates reflected on their successes and used them to determine a future plan of action.

Discussion Board Posts

An analysis of the weekly discussion board posts resulted in four major themes related to the co-teaching experience: defining roles, planning, classroom management, and setting and holding students accountable in regard to expectations. In general, candidates viewed classroom management and establishing behavioral expectations as separate from academic expectations. Finally, examples of specific co-mentoring among candidates are presented.

Defining Roles

Early posts demonstrate candidates' search for their roles as co-teachers in a classroom with experienced teachers, as in the following example:

I still haven't really had any teaching experiences yet, aside from going over the previous night's homework and walking around helping students with their work. It was a lot better than the past, but still trying to figure out my full current role as the second teacher in the room. My role has only solidified as a helper, but it feels more natural now, as it is known I will be taking over the classes during the second semester.

Planning

Issues with planning included how to plan for lessons and time management, as well as specifically planning for a co-taught lesson:

I am painfully aware that my time management skills need work. I never seem to be able to keep myself on schedule. I blame most of it on the fact that when I can get the kids involved in a topic, I want to see where they will go with it, so I keep feeding the conversation. This causes two problems. First, it usually throws my schedule off completely; also I tend to get into these conversations with the more advanced students, and the lower academic achievers don't bother to join, so they aren't getting anything out of it. I am aware of this issue and I have been working on it the last few weeks.

Classroom Management

One candidate was challenged early on, when attempting to discipline a student prior to having truly established the co-teaching roles of both teachers in the classroom:

On Friday another student was disciplined by my mentor teacher and sent to the hall, "to consider her choices." This was an implied purpose, not specified. After the specified time had passed, I went out into the hall to discuss the issues with this student. She came back into the classroom and rejoined the class. This same student again found herself unable to abide by the rules while getting ready for lunch, so once again she and I had a discussion about her behavior. I made certain to use "we" statements, to make sure that the student knew that the concerns I was discussing with her were shared by my mentor teacher as well. Upon returning to the classroom, my mentor teacher was clearly concerned about my discussion with the student. I explained the discussion, but I could see that it was still concerning her. We arranged a meeting for before school on Tuesday and discussed our issues. We had made a lot of assumptions about each other and had failed to actually set the boundaries. I was clearly overstepping my role as an "observer" by unintentionally derailing her discipline plan. We agreed to start over from square one, with our roles better defined and probably less confusing to the students.

Expectations

Candidates also reflected on how well they communicated their expectations to students and on challenges when things were not as clear as they should be:

I have also seen that the students are picking up on my expectations. When I teach the science lesson for the day, I always wrap up class by posing the "Question of the Day." It is a preview of the coming lesson, something that they can think about, but does not require any research. It usually takes the form of a yes-or-no question. I have made it clear to them that they should not only have their opinion, but my follow-up will always be for them to explain why. They have embraced this concept and are eager to share their answers the following day, and without prompting will explain their rationale for their answer.

Co-mentoring

Over time, the weekly online reflections emerged as a mechanism for co-mentoring among members of the cohort. Faculty instructors were able to gradually fade their comments on candidates' posts as candidates began to provide feedback to each other. Similar to their responses to the open-ended questions, confidence in their abilities once again manifested itself in the sharing of specific approaches to content delivery, strategies, lesson ideas, and general support. One such example follows:

> I designed the "Celebration of Knowledge" [assessment] for Friday and [cooperating teacher] gave it to them to take. About three quarters of the class was able to finish it in one period, but the other quarter has to finish on Monday. Already looking at the test, I see that I made one small error that messed up an entire question. As I am grading this weekend, I am trying to decide how I want to score this question, or even if I should count it at all.

In response, a peer suggested, "If the question was REALLY messed up, then I would either (a) throw it out, or (b) tell them that they don't get off that easily and have to complete the correct question for homework."

To which the original author replied,

> Some of the kids still have to finish the test today, so I just had them all do the correct question. Unfortunately, it was an easy typo to make.... It was supposed to be $y - 2x = x$ and I accidentally wrote $2x - y = x$.

In another instance, a teacher candidate was struggling with a less than ideal co-teaching situation to which a peer responded with a comment that provides evidence of peer-support and co-mentoring: "Hang in there. Having you there only improves the classroom environment, and I think the kids will appreciate your efforts, I'm sure."

Results of this study suggest that support for co-teaching on multiple levels (direct instruction, modeling, classroom practice, faculty mentoring, and peer coaching) helped candidates feel more comfortable and confident in utilizing co-teaching in their P–12 classrooms. In addition, explicitly mentoring cooperating teachers on the use of co-teaching strategies and requiring them to implement co-teaching with candidates benefitted not only the candidates but also helped cooperating teachers feel more comfortable about using co-teaching strategies more regularly.

As candidates moved into the second semester of their clinical experience (the traditional student teaching period), they were able to take the lead more frequently in co-teaching situations, and 75% came to believe "the chalk should pass freely between both teachers," indicating a clear growth in confidence and a changing perception of themselves as peers in the co-teaching relationship.

Discussion board posts indicated that co-teaching provided opportunities for cooperating teachers to serve as mentors for the teacher candidates. Additionally, candidates began to support each other via the discussion board posts and provide suggestions for each other, clearly engaging in peer coaching and co-mentoring.

Also evident from the data was the importance of developing a relationship between co-teachers who share the common goal of P–12 student learning. Open and clear communication about expectations for each other and for their students is critical in a co-teaching situation, as was demonstrated in survey results and discussion board posts.

DISCUSSION

Results of the surveys indicated that, with the exception of three questions, teacher candidates rated themselves as more frequently engaging in, or more strongly believing in, the importance of co-teaching-related behaviors as the year progressed. They perceived themselves as being more able to read the nonverbal cues of others, feeling more comfortable moving around in the co-teaching classroom, and, most notably, engaging in more co-taught lessons. Changes in candidates' attitudes towards co-teaching were reflected in responses to beliefs that classroom rules and routines should always be jointly developed, planning should be a shared responsibility, and common planning time should be allotted or created. These findings could be expected, given the additional co-teaching experiences teacher candidates were engaged in over the academic year, and the recognition that consistency and advanced planning are critical (Pugach & Wesson, 1995) for successful co-teaching.

Initially, candidates were unanimous in their belief that both teachers need to agree on the goals of the classroom, but, over time, the ratings were no longer unanimous. It is unclear what led to the change in ratings. One can speculate, however, that as teacher candidates amass experiences and develop confidence in their own abilities, they may establish different goals from those of their co-teacher. This could be the situation in instances where co-teachers have very different modes of instruction and content delivery, and it is a finding that will be tracked in future years to determine whether the results are consistent over cohorts. This finding can be related to Creamer's (2004) proposition that differences of opinion lead to unique insights and professional growth.

Candidates' ratings of their belief regarding the sharing of materials decreased over time, perhaps reflecting a desire to maintain ownership over the lessons and materials they developed. One candidate expressed a reluctance to turn over lessons for the co-teacher to teach, after working so hard to develop the lessons and associated activities. This individual wanted to be the one to lead the instruction, rather than sharing instruction with the co-teacher. Finally, candidates were consistent and unanimous across surveys in their belief that making accommodations for students with special needs was the responsibility of the co-teachers, echoing Pugach and Winn's (2011) sentiments regarding the benefits of teaming for providing services to P–12 students.

The discussion boards provided a venue for candidates to safely share their experiences and reflect on the co-teaching they were observing or engaging in. This venue, in effect, helped create the team atmosphere Colucci (2014) deemed important for new teachers, allowing them to share suggestions for content delivery, and for teachers who are struggling with particular issues such as dealing with differences in teaching styles within co-teaching teams.

Findings in this study support the traditional mentoring benefits derived from co-teaching situations. However, they also point to the reciprocal benefits between teacher candidates, as well as between candidates and their cooperating teachers. Future research will examine mentor teachers' perceptions of benefits of co-teaching, as well as co-mentoring between candidates and between university faculty members.

Limitations

Findings from this study are limited by several factors. The first limitation is the small sample size of participants in the study. Data from this study were derived from the first year of a three-year study. Participation in this grant-sponsored STEM master's program was highly selective and limited by available funds. Therefore, only 12 participants were admitted to the program for the first year. Subsequent years will provide additional data that can be analyzed in the aggregate across years. A second limitation was the unequal number of responses to the pre-, post-, and delayed post-surveys. The delayed post-survey was completed online at the end of the academic year when teacher candidates were working in the schools full-time and the researchers had limited contact with them—and, therefore, little control over the completion of the surveys. Based on the low response rate, changes have been made to the procedures to ensure increased participation in subsequent years.

CONCLUSIONS AND NEXT STEPS

With more than 25 years of combined experience at the university level, both faculty members were well-established in their content, practice, and expertise. Additionally, the two had a history of collaborating on many research projects, conference presentations, and curricular endeavors, establishing a bond of trust and shared confidence. Over the course of the semester, and more intentionally at the completion of the course, the dyad evaluated the courses and co-teaching experience. It was determined that the time allotted to the two classes (a co-taught three-hour block of time) was not sufficient to cover all necessary activities and learning expectations. Therefore, changes for the following year included having the classes meet for a five-hour block of time, with the entire time being co-taught, most often using a team-teaching approach. Further adjustments included adding activities that led to integrated discussions of accommodations that could be made on a daily basis, as well as providing additional practice in writing goals and objectives focusing on individual as well as whole-group/classroom needs. Finally, it was determined that candidates would be required to make a minimum of two discussion board posts each week—one they initiated and at least one in response to a peer's posting—a change designed to encourage additional dialogue among candidates.

These changes and next steps reflect outcomes of the co-mentoring between the two instructors that led to growth and development in shared understanding between the two faculty members regarding connections between their content areas of expertise, ways to better model co-teaching in the university classroom, and content delivery designed to enhance learning outcomes for teacher candidates.

It is strongly recommended that this new paradigm of co-teaching as a form of co-mentoring continue to be utilized and rigorously examined as a viable tool for teacher candidate development, as well as professional development for inservice teachers at the P–12 and university levels.

REFERENCES

Austin, V. L. (2001). Teachers' beliefs about co-teaching. *Remedial and Special Education, 22,* 245–255. doi: 10.1177/074193250102200408.

Bacharach, N., Heck T. W., & Dahlberg, K. (2010). Changing the face of student teaching through coteaching. *Action in Teacher Education, 32*(1), 3–14. doi: 10.1080/01626620.2010.10463538

Badiali, B., & Titus, N. E. (2010). Co-teaching: Enhancing student learning through mentor intern partnerships. *School-University Partnerships, 4*(2), 74–80.

Barnes, M. K. (1999). Strategies for collaboration: A collaborative teaching partnership for an inclusion classroom. *Reading & Writing Quarterly: Overcoming Learning Difficulties 15*(3), 233–238.

Bona, M. J., Rinehart, J., & Volbrecht, R. M. (1995). Show me how to do like you: Co-mentoring as a feminist pedagogy. *Feminist Teacher, 9*(3), 116–124. Retrieved from http://www.jstor.org/stable/40545722

Brinkmann, J., & Twiford, T. (2012). Voices from the field: Skill sets needed for effective collaboration and co-teaching. *International Journal of Educational Leadership Preparation, 7*(3), 1–13.

Bruce, C. D., & Ross, J. A. (2008). A model for increasing reform implementation and teacher efficacy: Teacher peer coaching in grades 3 and 6 mathematics. *Canadian Journal of Education, 31*(2), 346–370.

Cain, T. (2009). Mentoring trainee teachers: How can mentors use research? *Mentoring & Tutoring: Partnership in Learning, 17*(1), 53–66.

Chapple, J. W. (2009). *Co-teaching: From obstacles to opportunities* (Doctoral dissertation, Ashand University). Retrieved from https://etd.ohiolink.edu/

Colucci, A. (2014). The power of peer coaching. *Educational Horizons, 92,* 6–8.

Conley, S., Bas-Isaac, E., & Scull, R. (1995). Teacher mentoring and peer coaching: A micropolitical interpretation. *Journal of Personal Evaluation in Education, 9,* 7–19.

Creamer, E. G. (2004). Collaborators' attitudes about differences of opinion. *Journal of Higher Education, 75*(5), 556–571.

Friend, M. (2007). The coteaching partnership. *Educational Leadership, 64*(5), 48–52.

Friend, M. (2008). Co-teaching: A simple solution that isn't simple after all. *Journal of Curriculum and Instruction, 2*(2), 9–19.

Friend, M., & Cook, L. (2003). *Interactions: Collaboration skills for school professionals* (4th ed.). Upper Saddle River, NJ: Pearson Education.

Friend, M., Cook, L., Hurley-Chamberlain, D., & Shamberger, C. (2010). Co-teaching: An illustration of the complexity of collaboration in special education. *Journal of Educational & Psychological Consultation, 20*(1), 9–27.

Goodnough, K., Osmond, P., Dibbon, D., Glassman, M., & Stevens, K. (2009). Exploring a triad model of student teaching: Pre-service teacher and cooperating teacher perceptions. *Teaching and Teacher Education, 25,* 285–296.

Graziano, K. J., & Navarrete, L. A. (2012). Co-teaching in a teacher education classroom: Collaboration, compromise, and creativity. *Issues in Teacher Education, 21*(1), 109–126.

Hyman, R. T. (1990). Peer coaching: Premises, problems, potential. *Education Digest, 56*(1), 52–56.

Jewett, P., & MacPhee, D. (2012). Adding collaborative peer coaching to our teacher identities. *The Reading Teacher, 66*(2), 105–110.

Jimenez-Sanchez, C., & Antia, S. (1999). Team-teaching in an integrated classroom: Perceptions of deaf and hearing teachers. *Journal of Deaf Studies and Deaf Education, 4,* 215–224.

Johnson, N. H., & Brumback, L. (2013). Co-teaching in the science classroom. The one teach/one assist model. *Science Scope, 36*(6), 6–9.

Jones, S. L., & Morin, V. (2000). Training teachers to work as partners: Modeling the way in teacher preparation programs. *Delta Kappa Gamma Bulletin, 67*(1), 51–55.

Kohler, F. W., McCullough Crilley, K., Shearer, D. D., & Good, G. (1997). Effects of peer coaching on teacher and student outcomes. *Journal of Educational Research, 99*(4), 240–250.

Lichtman, M. (2010). *Qualitative research in education: A user's guide* (2nd ed.). Thousand Oaks, CA: Sage.

Murawski, W. W., & Dieker, L. A. (2004). Tips and strategies for co-teaching at the secondary level. *Teaching Exceptional Children, 36*(5), 52–58.

National Council for Accreditation of Teacher Education. (2010). *Transforming teacher education through clinical practice: A national strategy to prepare effective teachers. Report of the Blue Ribbon Panel on Clinical Preparation and Partnerships for Improved Student Learning.* Washington, DC: Author.

Neubert, C. A., & McAllister, E. (1993). Peer coaching in preservice education. *Teacher Education Quarterly, 20*(4), 77–84.

Nissilä, S. (2005). Individual and collective reflection: How to meet the needs of development in teaching. *European Journal of Teacher Education, 28*(2), 209–219.

Pugach, M. C., & Wesson, C. L. (1995). Teachers' and students' views of team teaching of general education and learning-disabled students in two fifth-grade classes. *Elementary School Journal, 95*(3), 279–295.

Pugach, M. C., & Winn, J. A. (2011). Research on co-teaching and teaming: An untapped resource for induction. *Journal of Special Education Leadership, 24*(1), 36–46.

Savage, T. V., Savage, M. K., & Armstrong, D. G. (2012). *Teaching in the secondary* school (7th ed.). Boston, MA: Pearson.

Scruggs, T. E., Mastropieri, M. A., & McDuffie, K. A. (2007). Co-teaching in inclusive classrooms: A metasynthesis of qualitative research. *Exceptional Children, 73*(4), 392–416.

Shams, M., & Law, H. (2012). Peer coaching framework: An exploratory technique. *The Coaching Psychologist, 8*(1), 46–49.

Stichter, J. P., Lewis, T. J., Richter, M., Johnson, N. W., & Bradley, L. (2006). Assessing antecedent variables: The effects of instructional variables on student outcomes through in-service and peer coaching professional development models. *Education and Treatment of Children, 29*(4), 665–692.

Swafford, J. (1998). Teachers supporting teachers through peer coaching. *Support for Learning, 13*(2), 54–58.

Tomlinson, C. A. (2000). *Differentiation of instruction in the elementary grades.* Retrieved from ERIC database. (ED443572)

Trautwein, B., & Ammerman, S. (2010). From pedagogy to practice: Mentoring and reciprocal peer coaching for preservice teachers. *Volta Review, 110*(2), 191–206.

Walther-Thomas, C. S., Bryant, M., & Land, S. (1996). Planning for effective co-teaching: The key to successful inclusion. *Remedial & Special Education, 17*, 255–265.

Zwart, R. C., Wubbels, T., Bolhuis, S., & Bergen, C. M. (2008). Teacher learning through reciprocal peer coaching: An analysis of activity sequences. *Teaching and Teacher Education 24*, 982–1002.

APPENDIX

Co-Teaching Survey

1.   Your birth date:

2.   My definition of co-teaching is:

3.   My attitude or philosophy regarding teaching all children in a co-taught classroom is:

4.   I would like to have the following responsibilities in a co-taught classroom:

5.   I would like my co-teacher to have the following responsibilities:

6.   I have the following expectations in a classroom regarding discipline:

7.   I have the following expectations in a classroom regarding class work:

8. I have the following expectations in a classroom regarding materials:

9. I have the following expectations in a classroom regarding homework:

10. I have the following expectations in a classroom regarding planning:

11. I have the following expectations in a classroom regarding adaptations for individual students:

12. I have the following expectations in a classroom regarding grading:

13. I have the following expectations in a classroom regarding noise level:

14. I have the following expectations in a classroom regarding cooperative learning:

15. I have the following expectations in a classroom regarding giving/receiving feedback:

16. I believe I can easily read the nonverbal cues of others.
    □ Rarely
    □ Sometimes
    □ Usually

17. I believe that I will feel comfortable moving freely about the space in the co-taught classroom, regardless of whose room it is.
    □ Rarely
    □ Sometimes
    □ Usually

18. I understand the content area curriculum standards specific to the potential co-taught classroom.
    □ Rarely
    □ Sometimes
    □ Usually

19. I believe both teachers in a co-taught classroom need to agree on the goals of the classroom.
    □ Rarely
    □ Sometimes
    □ Usually

20. I believe planning can be spontaneous, with changes occurring during the instructional lesson.
    □ Rarely
    □ Sometimes
    □ Usually

21. I have presented lessons in a co-taught class.
    - ☐ Rarely
    - ☐ Sometimes
    - ☐ Usually
22. I believe classroom rules and routines must be jointly developed.
    - ☐ Rarely
    - ☐ Sometimes
    - ☐ Usually
23. I believe there should be many measures used for grading students.
    - ☐ Rarely
    - ☐ Sometimes
    - ☐ Usually
24. I believe humor should be used in the co-taught classroom.
    - ☐ Rarely
    - ☐ Sometimes
    - ☐ Usually
25. I believe all materials should be shared in the co-taught classroom.
    - ☐ Rarely
    - ☐ Sometimes
    - ☐ Usually
26. I understand the methods and materials used in this content area.
    - ☐ Rarely
    - ☐ Sometimes
    - ☐ Usually
27. I believe modifications of goals for students with special needs are the responsibility of both teachers in a co-taught classroom.
    - ☐ Rarely
    - ☐ Sometimes
    - ☐ Usually
28. I believe planning for classes is the shared responsibility of both teachers.
    - ☐ Rarely
    - ☐ Sometimes
    - ☐ Usually
29. I believe the "chalk" should pass freely between both teachers.
    - ☐ Rarely
    - ☐ Sometimes
    - ☐ Usually
30. I believe a variety of classroom management techniques should be used to enhance learning of all students in a co-taught classroom.
    - ☐ Rarely
    - ☐ Sometimes
    - ☐ Usually

31. I believe that communication must be open and honest between the co-teaching partners.
    □ Rarely
    □ Sometimes
    □ Usually

32. I believe that fluid positioning of teachers in the classroom is unnecessary.
    □ Rarely
    □ Sometimes
    □ Usually

33. I believe it is important that time is allotted (or found) for common planning.
    □ Rarely
    □ Sometimes
    □ Usually

34. I believe that students should accept both teachers as equal partners in the learning process.
    □ Rarely
    □ Sometimes
    □ Usually

35. I believe that behavior management is the shared responsibility of both teachers.
    □ Rarely
    □ Sometimes
    □ Usually

CHAPTER 6

MENTORING FOR SUCCESS IN A TWO-YEAR DEGREE PROGRAM

Peer Mentors as Expert Helpers

Barbara A. Mahaffey and Alvin S. Mares

ABSTRACT

"New traditional students" enter college older than "traditional students" of the past and, often, with many adult responsibilities: employed full- or part-time, parenting a child or children, and paying for their own education. These students hope to gain knowledge and skills needed to obtain better careers, but many drop out before graduation. Research on college mentorship programs suggests their efficacy in improving retention, and some evidence suggests that peer mentoring may improve student persistence, not only for the mentee, but for the mentor as well. This chapter describes a peer mentoring program that supported students enrolled in an associate degree program in southwestern Ohio. The 52 mentors and mentees in the program were adults who returned to college to acquire new career skills in one of the helping professions. The authors discuss the need for the program, describe its structure and results, identify possible benefits of the program, and provide sample materials as takeaways.

Mentoring for the Professions: Orienting Toward the Future, pages 111–125.

INTRODUCTION

There is considerable enthusiasm and comparatively little research-based knowledge informing mentoring programs for college students. In the past decade, mentoring programs have proliferated and their benefits been extolled in spite of the lack of a consistent definition of mentoring or a generally accepted theoretical framework, problems that were identified more than twenty years ago by Jacobi (1991). Recently, however, researchers have addressed this issue and made progress toward validating a construct of mentoring (Crisp, 2009; Crisp & Cruz, 2009). In their critical review of the literature, Crisp and Cruz (2009) identified three commonalities among virtually all of the studies they examined: mentorships focus on the growth and accomplishments of the mentee and they include assistance of several kinds; mentoring may offer broad forms of assistance, such as assistance with career development; and relationships within the mentoring framework are personal and reciprocal. Crisp and Cruz noted four forms of support variables found in most college student mentoring programs:

- Psychological and emotional support
- Degree and career support
- Academic subject knowledge support
- Existence of a role model

Much of the research on mentoring for college students has focused on exploring student characteristics and barriers to staying in college, and Barefoot (2004) has recommended a change in focus from researching student traits to examining institutional and academic programs in order to explore the possibility of changing pedagogical aspects of classroom environments to enhance college student persistence. Though it is indeed time to go beyond simply considering student variables, this theme—the importance of preventing students' leaving college prior to earning a degree—is of vital importance. According to Hawley and Harris (2005–2006), student characteristics impacting persistence can be classified as focused on student achievement, motivation, aspirations, and expectations. Among the strongest predictors of attrition in the Hawley and Harris study (2005–2006) were the number of developmental classes required, the intention to transfer to a four-year institution, and English as a second language. Developers of mentorship programs often address one or more of these predictors in seeking to retain students through mentorships. Berkner, He, Cataldi, and Knepper (2002), for example, reported higher retention rates and student persistence being improved by the use of a mentoring program. The ongoing interest and growing emphasis, reflected in college funding sources, on the topic of persistence toward a degree is such that a scholarly journal, the *Journal of College Student Retention: Research, Theory & Practice*, is dedicated to theory, research, and practice related to the issue. Barefoot (2004) indicated that most of the literature has cited persistence as the major aim of mentoring. The work of Tinto (1993, cited in

Barefoot, 2004) and other scholars has led to an understanding of the need for integration of college students into both social and academic systems in improving their persistence toward a degree. College mentoring programs often seek to foster integration into both systems.

In addition to retention of students, some of the goals of college student mentoring programs, according to Howard and Smith-Goodwin (2010), are freshman acclimation, college and major program integration, peer support, and socialization. Putsche, Storrs, Lewis, and Haylett (2008) reported that a dedicated mentoring program coordinator, training of mentors, and appropriate matching of mentors and mentees were indicators of successful college student mentoring in a study of female undergraduates.

Because of a relative lack of research conducted with special populations, little is known about the nuances of college mentoring relationships and their possible benefits to some groups of students (Crisp, 2009; Hu & Ma, 2010). Brittian, Sy, and Stokes (2009) found that most African American students who did not participate in mentorship programs cited a lack of time as the major reason, though not being aware of mentoring programs was also reported as a reason by many African American students. The researchers also found that students who felt confident about their grades were less likely to participate as mentees; this factor may explain the slightly lower GPA they found for students who participated in mentoring programs in college. Another study found that Hispanic mentees, compared to Caucasian mentees, turned to their mentors for encouragement and support more frequently and regarded the mentorship experience as more important (Hu & Ma, 2010). Though academic support programs for at-risk college youth date back to the mid-1960s, when the Student Support Services Program was established by the United States Department of Education (Chaney, 2010), there is a need for more research on the effects of mentoring programs with new traditional students who belong to minority groups.

Some of the recent research on college student mentoring has examined the practice of having upper-level students mentor incoming freshmen in the same major programs. Howard and Smith-Goodwin (2010), for example, established a mentee and mentor cohort group in an athletic training program to increase retention by integrating freshmen students into the program. Rather than individually assigning new students to more experienced student mentors, new students were assigned to a mentoring cohort consisting of a group of 8–12 students in the program, including two seniors, two juniors, two to four sophomores, and four to six freshmen. The juniors and seniors in the cohort were designated as group leaders and were given guidelines for leading freshmen and sophomore members of their cohort. A survey administered to 69 cohort members of all four years in school found that 90% of the participants reported that the program was helpful to them in adjusting to the overall college environment.

Crisp and Cruz (2009), following Jacobi (1991), reported flaws in the definition of mentoring, methodological research design issues, and the theories used in some of the quantitative and qualitative studies they reviewed. They noted that prior college peer mentoring program research involved junior and senior students mentoring freshmen and was mostly conducted at institutions granting four-year degrees (Crisp, 2009). Only recently have researchers begun exploring community college mentoring programs (e.g., Crisp, 2009; Crisp & Cruz, 2009; Jaswal & Jaswal, 2008).

PEER MENTORING IN AN ASSOCIATE DEGREE PROGRAMS

College technology programs in community colleges have several primary goals, one of which is to train students to be workforce-prepared. Social service workplaces have changed job requirements, agency funding formulas, and legal and ethical standards. There has been an increase in the difficulty level of the basic knowledge, skills, and awareness needed for successful employment in the human services professions. A challenge for faculty who work with diverse students is how to retain the more capable and more experienced students, while training and addressing the needs of beginning freshmen who struggle to "get up to speed" quickly with workforce demands and pressures. A related challenge is that some college students require more assistance with preparing for a career, especially in jobs requiring multifaceted and ever-changing approaches to technology and human interaction—essential skills needed to work with clients. These challenges are important in providing effective career-focused technology programs to new traditional college students.

A promising means of meeting these challenges comes from the knowledge that new traditional college students who have succeeded to the point of being upperclassmen have much to offer in a mentoring program. Experienced adult college student mentors bring the following traits to bear in mentoring incoming students:

- Knowledge of workplace nuances and policies
- Savvy with navigating community resources or career contacts
- Experience with knowing "what works" to ensure success with assignments
- Survival tips after observing failures in college and the workforce

This section of the chapter describes a peer mentoring program offered in an associate degree-level human services technology (HST) program in southwestern Ohio. In 2012, 128 freshmen and sophomore students were enrolled in this two-year associate's degree program that prepares students to work in the field of human services. The program is housed at a branch campus of a public, four-year university. The mean age among those enrolled from 2005 until 2009 was 34, with ages ranging from 17 to 69 years. Although this program has been in existence since 1975, enrollments had doubled in 2005. This jump in enrollments came in conjunction with an economic downturn that resulted in a substantial interest in training or retraining for many individuals, especially in a field well known for helping clients to connect with resources. There is a wide variety of clients, social service agencies, and job titles in the human services profession (see Bureau of Labor Statistics, U.S. Department of Labor, 2013). Students in the HST program need to quickly assimilate the technological and human relations skills, such as helping clients become more self-sufficient, that comprise the major mission of careers in this field. Assisting clients to become more self-sufficient entails being aware of human services resources that might help them, as well as being able to assess clients' needs, determine resources to address their needs, access resources, help clients use resources effectively, and help assess the outcomes of the matches between clients and resources.

Because of the wide range of circumstances, maturity, and skill sets of people entering such a program and a campus retention rate of 72% between fall 2011 and fall 2012 among first-time full-time students pursuing a bachelor's degree (National Center for Education Statistics, 2014a), there was a need to provide an additional support system, such as a mentoring program. According to the National Center for Educational Statistics (2014b), nearly half (49%) of full-time students at Ohio University–Chillicothe (OU–C), where the HST program is located, drop out during their first year of school, and 25% graduate within six years of beginning their studies. The HST students were dropping out of college at a much higher rate starting about 2010; at times, between 50% and 67% of freshman students were not completing their first term of courses. Due in part to the recommendation offered by Crisp and Cruz (2009) to examine mentoring programs serving nontraditional student populations attending various types of institutions, the HST staff and an outside researcher designed an ongoing study. The college where the program is located is primarily an associate degree institution in which about 85% of HST students are first-generation college attendees.

Although the exact numbers have varied over the years, the typical student in the HST program is female and a college student mother. Female new traditional college student mothers from the mostly rural and small communities throughout southwestern Ohio were surveyed in 2008 about their needs and challenges. According to Hungerford (2006) and Morales (2008), student mothers and minority females are especially at risk for dropping out of college. Gonchar (1995) noted a critical need for child care in order to retain female students. Hungerford, Mahaffey, and Sill (2009) noted, in a presentation about their research, that mentors could assist with at-risk students' needs in regard to community resource education such as childcare, transportation, income and financial aid connections, social support, and emotional encouragement.

The HST program has always included field practice experience mentorship, provided by worksite supervisors, typically during the students' second year in the program. In light of overall campus and HST program retention rates of 50% and 33%, respectively, it was decided to try a novel approach to address the psychosocial and academic needs of the incoming college freshmen by supplementing formal academic advising and clinical field supervision with informal peer mentoring.

In the HST mentoring program designed to retain new traditional college students through the use of mentors and a mentoring course, second-year students become peer mentors and assist freshmen mentees who are anticipated to benefit from a variety of activities. This peer mentoring program does not replace the already existing support given to students through the various college offices, and the students are told to turn to faculty for basic career exploration and advice, help with making decisions about worksite choices and placements, and help with other issues and questions related to their studies. Rather, this program was designed to offer an additional support system that does not typically come from the faculty.

Freshmen college students entering the HST program in the fall term of 2012 were the first cohort eligible to be mentees, and upper-class undergraduate students were recruited to serve as their mentors. Freshmen student mentees were enrolled in a class entitled "Mentoring," and sophomore student mentors were enrolled in a class entitled "Applied Mentoring." After obtaining demographic data from all students who enrolled in the courses, the HST coordinator and faculty matched students at the beginning of each semester, and then maintained contact with mentors and mentees throughout the year to share information and to provide encouragement and support. Each student attended seminars and was given handouts, a Powerpoint presentation, and demonstrations/role plays using solution-focused brief therapy (SFBT), a model structure for short-term decision making and problem/conflict resolution (de Shazer, Berg, Lipchik, Nunnally, Molnar, Gingerich, & Weiner-Davis, 1986). On the first day of class, the syllabus was reviewed, including the schedule of topics to be discussed throughout the semester (see Figures 6.1 and 6.2).

The initial cohort of 25 students was recruited during the first year of the study, with an expected annual recruitment of 40 students during years two to five, for a total of 120 students, to replace participants who leave their programs or the university. The mentors and mentees attended class together. Data on the mentoring relationship (independent variable) and academic performance (dependent variable) were collected for all participants. Academic performance measures included grade point average (GPA), retention, and graduation rates. The retention rate was measured by determining whether the students were re-enrolled in their second year of the program. If a student graduated from the two-year degree HST program, then this was considered one of the successful outcomes of the mentoring study. Data gathering on each participant will continue semiannually, at the end of fall and spring semesters, for up to five years or until a participant graduates, transfers to another institution, drops out, or is dismissed from school, whichever occurs first. An important goal for this mentoring program is providing a smooth progression from the two-year HST pre-social work program to the four-year bachelor of social work program and graduation within five years of starting college. Success on this important goal will be assessed by comparing the six-year graduation rate with a bachelor's degree between mentoring program participants and other four-year public college branch campuses in Ohio, using

Date	Weekly Assignments
Week 1	Topic for the Week: Outline of the Course, Mentoring Ethics and Activities discussion. Review of Prof. Mahaffey's teaching philosophy. The syllabus will be reviewed and students will be shown how to join in Blackboard Discussion.
Week 2	Assignments: Work in small groups to discuss possible activities, barriers, and the project(s). Choose one topic from the Blackboard posting to discuss in class. Dr. Mares will present Solution Focused Brief Therapy for problem solving with mentees.
Week 3	Review of mentor relationship boundaries discussion. Students will turn in the first reflection card in class. Questions for reflection card: Tell what activities explored by the match. List areas of help needed by mentee. Create a possible problem list.
Week 4	Trip to the Library (there may be a Majors Fair or other event). Find an activity time with your mentee.
Week 5	Turn in the second reflection card. Help with possible Human Services Association or another student club event.
Week 6	Second meeting with Dr. Mares to discuss Solution Focused Brief Therapy and problem solving techniques. Discussion of a group activity.
Week 7	Turn in the third reflection card. Discuss additional needs for mentoring.
Week 8	Career exploration activity. Plan on visiting the Majors Fair with your mentee.
Week 9	Discuss another mentoring article or activity. Third meeting with Dr. Mares. Turn in the fourth reflection card.
Week 10	Turn in the fifth reflection card.
Week 11	Fourth meeting with Dr. Mares to learn Solution Focused Brief Therapy.
Week 12	Turn in the sixth reflection card. Reflect about time spent on the Trick or Treat Extravaganza with your mentee.
Week 13	Reminder: Turn in the mentoring folder next week with all paperwork. This week's topic: How to succeed throughout final exams.
Week 14	Final deadline for entering Blackboard submissions and all documentation. No final exam. Students will complete the two surveys about the mentoring experience.

FIGURE 6.1. Schedule of Activities

data published by the National Center for Education Statistics. Accomplishment of the following outcomes will be considered in judging the overall success of this peer mentoring program.

Process/Product Outcomes:

- Development of a customized peer mentoring program for Ohio University–Chillicothe (OU–C) human services technology (HST) students utilizing key elements of solution-focused brief theory (SFBT).
- Design of a peer mentoring program application form (see Figure 6.3)
- Adaptation of the College Student Mentoring Scale (CSMS, Crisp & Cruz, 2009). (This form was amended for the mentees to add the words "my

---

Topics for Blackboard Posting List for Mentoring

How does mentoring differ from my other learning experiences? Here are some common questions that you may write about in a reflective Blackboard Discussion journal.

1. How did I participate in class? What could I contribute to what was said?
2. What are my reflective thoughts about what was discussed in class - my thoughts, feelings, and behaviors about what was talked about in class?
3. Did I read any articles on mentoring this week before class? Did that help me?
4. Did I have any negative or positive reactions about what was discussed in class?
5. Do I agree or disagree with this week's class topic or any comment made by a class member?
6. Have I made any observations about world events that may relate to something that was discussed in class?
7. Have I noticed any of what I am learning that challenge my thoughts on diversity?
8. What have I noticed about my own anger/fears/emotions since beginning this class?
9. Have I changed any of my behaviors?
10. Have any of my beliefs/attitudes/opinions/morals changed while being in Human Services Technology classes (due to what I learned)?
11. Do I feel better qualified to mentor others as a result of what I learned in classes?
12. What was the most valuable experience or topic I learned in this class?
13. What can I teach someone so that she or he does not make a mistake?
14. What activities helped me to succeed?
15. Was the last activity I did with my mentor/mentee fun or interesting? How?
16. What was the most important lesson I learned?

FIGURE 6.2. Discussion Topics

mentor.") This is a survey with 25 statements that respondents score on a 5-point Likert scale (see Figure 6.4).

- Design of the Mentoring Relationship Scale (MRS)—a form on which the students rate the match relationships and contacts (see Figure 6.5).

Student/Program Outcomes

- 50% retention rate for first year of study
- 33% associate degree completion rate within four years of entering college
- 25% bachelor degree graduation rate within five years of entering college

Peer Mentoring Program Application

Student's Name: (please print)_____Today's Date: _____

Home Address: _____
                        (Street)   (City, State, Zip)
Home Phone: (_____)_____ Cell Phone: (_____)_____

Email (OU): _____

Email (Other): _____

Age: _____

Gender (circle): Male Female

Marital status (circle): Single Married Widowed/divorced

Race/ethnicity (circle all that apply): Caucasian African-American Hispanic Other_____

Educational goal (circle all that apply):

Associate Bachelor Grad/professional

Challenging life experiences (circle all that apply):

Homelessness   Foster care   Single parent   Delinquency   Alcohol/drug problems

LGBTQ   Physical health problems   Emotional problems   Domestic violence   Veteran

Do you have a natural or adoptive parent who has a four-year college degree? _____Yes_____No

FIGURE 6.3. Mentoring Application

The CSMS and MRS instruments will not be administered until the end of the current academic year, and thus data are not available to be summarized at this time.

It was anticipated that some students might experience a slight risk of embarrassment due to being considered a mentee. Students were told that they had the option of not participating in the study and could still be enrolled in the HST program and in the course entitled "Mentoring," taught by the HST coordinator. Students were also assured in a handout and orally that they could contact the HST coordinator with any question or concern about the mentorship. All participants signed an assent form agreeing to participate in a peer mentor relationship. Students were assured that their information would be confidential and that they not only had the right, but were welcome to contact the coordinator at any time by email or phone. The assent form also invited students to discuss any uncomfortable thoughts or feelings with the coordinator anonymously by note or by other methods if they preferred. After written consent and verbal assent were obtained,

College Student Mentoring Scale (CSMS)

While in college, I have had someone in my life who. . . .

(strongly agree = 5, agree = 4, neutral = 3, disagree = 2, strongly disagree = 1)

1. I look up to regarding college-related issues
2. helps me work toward achieving my academic aspirations
3. helps me realistically examine my degree or certificate options
4. I can talk with openly about social issues related to being in college
5. I admire
6. helps me perform to the best of my abilities in my classes
7. encourages me to consider educational opportunities beyond my current plans
8. I want to copy their behaviors as they relate to college-going
9. provides ongoing support about the work I do in my classes
10. gives me emotional support
11. encourages me to talk about problems I am having in my social life
12. sets a good example about how to relate to other people
13. helps me to consider the sacrifices associated with my chosen degree
14. expresses confidence in my ability to succeed academically
15. serves as a model for how to be successful in college
16. discusses the implications of my degree choice
17. makes me feel that I belong in college
18. encourages me to use him or her as a sounding board to explore what I want
19. shares personal examples of difficulties they have had to overcome to accomplish academic goals
20. helps me carefully examine my degree or certificate options
21. I can talk with openly about personal issues related to being in college
22. encourages me to discuss problems I am having with my coursework
23. questions my assumptions by guiding me through a realistic appraisal of my skills
24. recognizes my academic accomplishments
25. provides practical suggestions for improving my academic performance

FIGURE 6.4. College Mentoring Scale

students were given the name, phone number, and email address of a matched mentor.

In its initial and following years, the peer mentoring program's mentor–mentee relationships were same-sex relationships. Mentors were given mentee names, phone numbers, and email/text addresses during class times. In class, mentors

SW-HST Peer Mentoring Program **MENTORING RELATIONSHIP SURVEY** Rev. 6/10/12

Your name: _____ Today's date: ___/___/___

Name of mentor(ee): _____

Mentoring period (circle semester & complete year): Fall Spring Summer Year: 20___

Frequency of contact during period (circle): None Quarterly Monthly Biweekly Weekly Daily

Primary method of contact during period (circle one):

  In-person Phone Text Email Facebook Other: _____

Topics discussed (circle all that apply):

  Financial aid What to expect with classes What teachers are good Practicum/field issues

  Dealing with difficult professors Satisfactory Academic Progress Education/career options

  Other: _____

SFBT practice elements used (mentors only; circle all that apply):

  Problem Miracle Exception Scaling Compliment Homework What's better Coping

Mentoring relationship characteristics (*adapted from BBBS Strength of Relationship Survey*)
The following are some things people say about mentoring relationships. Please tell me how true it is
for you and how you feel about your mentor(ee). After each sentence, tell me if the statement is not
true at all, if it's not very true, if it's sort of true, or if it's very true. For example, if your mentor(ee)
always remembers your name, you would say "very true".

		Not true	Not very true	Sort of true	Very true
A	My mentor(ee) knows my name.	1	2	3	4
B	My mentor(ee) makes fun of me in ways I don't like.	1	2	3	4
C	My mentor(ee) almost always asks me what I want to do.	1	2	3	4
D	When I'm with my mentor(ee), I feel special.	1	2	3	4
E	Sometimes my mentor(ee) promises we will do something; then we don't do it.	1	2	3	4
F	My mentor(ee) is always interested in what I want to do.	1	2	3	4
G	When I'm with my mentor(ee), I feel excited.	1	2	3	4
H	When my mentor(ee) gives me advice, it makes me feel stupid.	1	2	3	4
I	My mentor(ee) and I like to do a lot of the same things.	1	2	3	4
J	When I'm with my mentor(ee), I feel sad.	4	3	2	1
K	I feel I can't trust my mentor(ee) with secrets—my mentor(ee) would tell my academic advisor.	1	2	3	4
L	My mentor(ee) thinks of fun and interesting things to do.	1	2	3	4
M	When I'm with my mentor(ee), I feel important.	1	2	3	4
N	When I'm with my mentor(ee), I feel bored.	4	3	2	1
O	I wish my mentor(ee) asked me more about what I think.	1	2	3	4
P	My mentor(ee) and I do things I really want to do.	1	2	3	4
Q	When I'm with my mentor(ee), I feel mad.	4	3	2	1
R	I wish my mentor(ee) knew me better.	1	2	3	4
S	When I'm with my mentor(ee), I feel disappointed.	4	3	2	1
T	When I'm with my mentor(ee), I feel happy.	1	2	3	4

FIGURE 6.5. Mentoring Relationship Scale

TABLE 7.1. Preliminary Results

	Total (n=52)		Mentor (n=11)		Mentee (n=41)		T-Test or Chi-Square		
	Mean/%	SD/N	Mean/%	SD/N	Mean/%	SD/N	t/X^2	df	p
Demographic characteristics									
Age (years)	33	11	31	12	33	11	-0.46	55	0.649
Female	77%	44	91%	10	74%	34	1.46	1	0.227
Race									
Caucasian	88%	50	100%	11	85%	39			
Black	5%	3	0%	0	7%	3			
Black/Caucasian	2%	1	0%	0	2%	1			
Other	4%	2	0%	0	4%	2			
Missing	2%	1	0%	0	2%	1	1.91	4	0.753
Marital status									
Single	60%	34	64%	7	59%	27			
Married	21%	12	36%	4	17%	8			
Divorced	18%	10	0%	0	22%	10			
Missing	2%	1	0%	0	2%	1	4.19	3	0.242
Enrollment characteristics (as of fall 2013)									
Major									
Human Services Technology	42%	24	18%	2	48%	22			
Social Work	25%	14	73%	8	13%	6			
Other									
Business	2%	1	0%	0	2%	1			
Communication	2%	1	0%	0	2%	1			
Early Childhood Education	2%	1	0%	0	2%	1			
Nursing	4%	2	0%	0	4%	2			
Undecided	12%	7	9%	1	13%	6			
Academic Probation	4%	2	0%	0	4%	2			
Missing	9%	5	0%	0	11%	5	17.71	8	0.024
Progress									
Number of units earned to-date	51	43	108	38	36	29	6.81	50	0.000
Number of terms enrolled	8	5	13	3	6	4	4.41	50	0.000
Number of years enrolled	3	2	4	1	2	1	4.40	50	0.000
Estimated no. classes taken per year	5	4	7	2	5	4	1.31	49	0.198
Estimated no. classes taken since enrolling	13	11	27	10	9	7	6.76	50	0.000
Commute home to campus (miles)	11	10	15	13	10	9	1.44	55	0.156
Educational goal									
Associate	18%	10	0%	0	22%	10	11.10	5	0.049
Associate or Bachelor	7%	4	0%	0	9%	4			
Bachelor	37%	21	27%	3	39%	18			
Bachelor or Graduate	2%	1	9%	1	0%	0			
Graduate	23%	13	46%	5	17%	8			
Undecided	14%	8	18%	2	13%	6			
Risk factors									
First generation	86%	49	91%	10	85%	39	0.28	1	0.599
Single parent	39%	22	18%	2	44%	20	2.40	1	0.122
Emotional condition	28%	16	18%	2	30%	14	0.66	1	0.417
Alcohol or drug	23%	13	27%	3	22%	10	0.15	1	0.694
Domestic violence	14%	8	9%	1	15%	7	0.28	1	0.599
Homeless	9%	5	9%	1	9%	4	0.00	1	0.967
Physical condition	7%	4	9%	1	7%	3	0.09	1	0.764
Academic achievement									
Retention (1-year: fall 2012-fall 2013)	65%	34	100%	11	56%	23	7.39	1	0.007
Cumulative grade point average	2.46	1.18	3.03	0.46	2.30	1.26	1.86	50	0.069

were trained in brief contact etiquette, given guidelines on appropriate relationship ethical standards, and topics for discussion with mentees, and were asked to engage in discussion about needed mentoring activities. To provide structure to the peer mentoring program, mentors were asked to contact the mentees at least once monthly and fill out time sheets with data about the topic(s), activity(ies), and time spent with the mentee.

Due to the historically high drop-out rate during students' first year on campus, a few other caveats were added to the design of this new peer mentoring program intervention. If the mentoring relationships established during the first year of the project/study continues, the mentor or mentee will check in with the coordinator yearly until either the mentor or mentee leaves school (e.g., graduates, transfers to another institution, drops out, is dismissed). When mentors leave, their mentees will be reassigned to other mentors. When mentees leave, new mentees will be recruited and assigned to their mentors. During the first year of the program, students made a list of possible mentor/mentee activities:

- Visits to college advising, financial aid, disability services, and other offices for student support
- Visits to the library, college tutoring center, and help desk advising
- Trips to social events in the community and college
- Attending research and health fairs
- Social meetings to discuss life events and problem exploration
- Weekly check-ins about college attendance issues via cell phone/text or Blackboard

Preliminary Results

Data collected so far indicated that the HST adult student peer mentoring program appears to have been largely successful. Students in the first mentoring cohort (i.e., those enrolled between July and September 2012) experienced a 65% retention rate, compared to the historically lower rate of 35% in past years, prior to the implementation of the peer mentoring program. See Table 6.1 for data based on the 2012–2013 mentoring program. In addition, all of the mentors remained enrolled in college a year later, in the fall term of 2013. As Corso and Devine (2013) found, mentoring programs for college students may be of great benefit to the college student mentors.

DISCUSSION

Students appear to have benefitted from the initiation of the peer mentoring program, with some of the mentors noting an increase in their motivation, commitment to college, and sense of pride because of their contribution to the success of at-risk students. Most of the students were engaged in the training sessions and reported using the SFBT to help others address issues and overcome problems experienced throughout the year. The same-sex relationships may have been an important element of the program, at least for the women who had children. The mentors in the new cohort class talked, for example, about ways to find childcare. This kind of advice was cited by the new mentees as one of the factors that kept them coming to classes during the first year of the mentoring program. One surprise is that the peer student mentors reported as much benefit from the course and peer relationships as the mentees. Additionally, the HST coordinator experienced a relief from answering repeated questions from the incoming students. There were no reported incidents of inappropriate relationships.

Future research is needed to ascertain the adult college mentoring program benefits, constraints, retention, persistence, and other factors associated with student success. It is recommended that other technology and career training programs attempt mentoring programs, perhaps using some of the resources offered in this chapter. The possible benefits are vast, especially when considering that mentoring programs with proficient students as mentors offer few risks and have many possible benefits. One of those benefits is the enhancement of student survival, acclimation, and decision-making skill sets. Those experiential skills, once learned by the mentees, can translate into skills and tools they then can use in their fieldwork with clients.

Although it is difficult to measure relationship dynamics fully, possible development of working alliances, networking, and role-modeled successes throughout the career for mentees and mentors are a few of the possibilities offered by college mentoring programs such as this one.

REFERENCES

Barefoot, B. O. (2004). Higher education's revolving door: Confronting the problem of student dropout in US colleges and universities. *Open Learning, 19*(1), 9–18.

Berkner, L., He, S., Cataldi, E. F., & Knepper, P. (2002). *Descriptive summary of 1995–96 beginning postsecondary students: Six years later: Statistical analysis report.* Washington, DC: National Center for Education Statistics, U.S. Dept. of Education, Institute of Education Sciences.

Brittian, A. S., Sy, S. R., & Stokes, J. E. (2009). Mentoring: Implications for African American college students. *Western Journal of Black Studies, 33*(2), 87–97.

Bureau of Labor Statistics, United States Department of Labor. (2013). Social and human service assistants. *Occupational outlook handbook, 2012–13 Edition.* Retrieved from http://www.bls.gov/ooh/community-and-social-service/social-and-human-service-assistants.htm

Chaney, B. W. (2010). *National evaluation of Student Support Services: Examination of student outcomes after six years. Final report.* Rockville, MD: Westat.

Corso, J., & Devine, J. (2013). Student technology mentors: A community college success story. *Community College Enterprise, 19*(2), 9–21.

Crisp, G. (2009). Conceptualization and initial validation of the College Student Mentoring Scale (CSMS). *Journal of College Student Development, 50*(2), 177–194.

Crisp, G., & Cruz, I. (2009). Mentoring college students: A critical review of the literature between 1990 and 2007. *Research in Higher Education, 50*(6), 525–545.

de Shazer, S., Berg, I. K., Lipchik, E., Nunnally, E., Molnar, A., Gingerich, W., & Weiner-Davis, M. (1986). Brief therapy: Focused solution development. *Family Process, 25*(2), 207–222.

Gonchar, N. (1995). College student mothers and on-site child care: Luxury or necessity? *Social Work in Education, 17*(4), 226–234.

Hawley, T. H., & Harris, T. A. (2005-2006). Student characteristics related to persistence for first-year community college students. *Journal of College Student Retention: Research, Theory & Practice, 7*(1/2), 117–142.

Howard, L. A., & Smith-Goodwin, E. A. (2010). Student-to-student mentoring for retention: Both groups benefit. *Athletic Therapy Today, 15*(3), 14–17.

Hu, S., & Ma, Y. (2010). Mentoring and student persistence in college: A study of the Washington state achievers program. *Innovations in Higher Education, 35*, 329–341.

Hungerford, G. (2006, May). The plight of student mothers on campus. Paper presented at the 2nd Annual National Symposium of Parents in Higher Education, Columbus, Ohio.

Hungerford, G., Mahaffey, B. A., & Sill, S. (2009, December 9). *Student mothers at Ohio University: Is anyone listening?* Powerpoint presentation, Ohio University.

Jacobi, M. (1991). Mentoring and undergraduate academic success: A literature review. *Review of Educational Research, 61*(4), 505–532.

Jaswal, F., & Jaswal, T. M. (2008). Tiered mentoring to leverage student body expertise. *New Directions for Community Colleges, 144*, 55–61.

Morales, E. E. (2008). Exceptional female students of color: Academic resilience and gender in higher education. *Innovative Higher Education, 33*(3), 197–213.

National Center for Education Statistics. (2014a). *Digest of Education Statistics. Table 326.30. Retention of first-time degree-seeking undergraduates at degree-granting postsecondary institutions, by attendance status, level and control of institution, and percentage of applications accepted: 2006–2012.* Retrieved 9/8/2014 from http://nces.ed.gov/collegenavigator/?s=all&zc=45601&zd=O&of=3&id=204820#retgrad.

National Center for Education Statistics. (2014b). *College navigator Ohio University-Chillicothe Campus. Retention and graduation rates.* Retrieved on 9/8/2014 from http://nces.ed.gov/collegenavigator/?s=all&zc=45601&zd=O&of=3&id=204820#retgrad

Putsche, L., Storrs, D., Lewis, A. E., & Haylett, J. (2008). The development of a mentoring program for university undergraduate women. *Cambridge Journal of Education, 38*(4), 513–528.

Tinto, V. (1993). *Leaving college: Rethinking the causes and cures of student attrition* (2nd ed.). Chicago, IL: University of Chicago Press.

CHAPTER 7

MENTORING AND OTHER PROFESSIONAL SUPPORT FOR FACULTY IN INSTITUTIONS OF HIGHER LEARNING

A Study Report

Justina Osa, Andrean Oliver, and Tracy Walker

ABSTRACT

Several factors contribute to the rationale for mentoring for early-career faculty members as they face the challenges of a new position. The research literature identifies benefits to faculty members and to the university as outcomes of mentoring. This study surveyed full-time, tenure-track faculty members at a higher education institution to solicit their perceptions on mentoring—whether it is beneficial, what kinds of support they received as new faculty members, what mentors do to support and develop mentees' professional growth, and what they regard as potential problems in, or barriers to, mentorships for faculty in higher learning. Though only a small proportion (18%) of the survey recipients responded to the survey, thus limiting the generalizability of the results, these faculty perceptions of mentoring programs for new faculty members indicate favorable attitudes toward such mentorships, and the recognition that among the potential problems are lack of administrative support and possible mismatches between mentors and mentees. A needs assessment to determine faculty mentoring needs is provided as a takeaway.

Mentoring for the Professions: Orienting Toward the Future, pages 127–143.
Copyright © 2015 by Information Age Publishing

INTRODUCTION

The easiest and sometimes most effective way for a new employee to learn his or her way around a job is to be paired with a veteran who can show him or her the ropes. This type of informal, unstructured mentorship, once a common practice, may not be adequate in today's more complex, cross-functional workplace. Some organizations have taken mentoring to the next level by formalizing their programs, an approach in which the mentor helps the protégé achieve clearly defined goals (Bowers, 2002). Organizations have long used mentoring to complement training and professional development in their efforts to increase employee productivity and retention (Welp, 2002).

Higher education institutions may now be facing conditions that make mentoring programs even more important to early-career faculty than they have been in the past. Currently, in many higher education institutions, a climate characterized by decreased funding, downsizing of faculty, increased workloads, and reduced availability of funding for academic development and research prevails (Adams, 2002). These conditions impact all faculty, as scholars endeavor to remain viable in the academy. Moreover, research shows that the early-career phase of a faculty position in an institution of higher learning is very challenging and stressful, conditions that suggest the need for a systematic and sustained support system (Rice, Sorcinelli, & Austin, 2000). Although mentoring has a strong track record, it is challenging to design an effective mentoring program in an institution of higher learning because there is no "plug and play" formula that applies to all mentoring situations. Each institution would therefore need to develop its own mentoring program, one that fits its particular circumstances and is adequate for its needs.

What is Mentoring?

Numerous theories and myths attempt to trace the origin of the term "mentor." While none of them definitely explains the origins of the word "mentor" as we know it today, almost all point to the image of a trusted adviser, counselor, or teacher who uses his or her knowledge to guide and support others (Sorcinelli, 2010). Traditionally, the literature about mentoring stereotypes mentors as older, wiser, more experienced persons and mentees as younger, less experienced protégés.

The more contemporary view expands the idea of who can be the mentor and who can be the mentee. According to Smith (2007), a mentor nowadays can be a coworker or a peer, someone who is equal in status and in age to the mentee. A peer who is a mentor can be more experienced than the mentee or at the same developmental level. The current view of mentoring is that it is less about seniority and teaching and more about sharing and development. In its purest sense, mentoring is about supporting and developing the all-around growth of protégés, not just making them better at their jobs (Bowers, 2002). Smith (2007) viewed mentoring as "a particular mode of learning wherein the mentor not only supports the mentee, but also challenges them productively so that progress is made" (p. 277).

In the current discourse on mentoring, the term has come to be used for a variety of relationships. Some of its synonyms include *role model, coach, guide, sponsor, friend,* and *adviser* (Penner, 2001). In the contemporary world, more-over, organizations derive benefits by viewing mentoring broadly, as Ferman defines it. According to Ferman (2002), mentoring is

> a process whereby one is assisted, guided and advocated for by another...[usually]
> more experienced...person.... It can lead to and overlap with networking and other
> collaborative endeavours and can occur in many and varied modes, ranging from
> frameworks characterized by hierarchy and formality to those marked by informal-
> ity and a peer relationship. (p. 47)

BACKGROUND

In institutions of higher learning, tenure and promotion requirements have often been sources of stress, pain, frustration, insecurity, and failure among faculty. Considering this source of tension, faculty perceptions regarding the lack of col-legial relationships, supportive environments, and mentoring have been given as reasons for leaving institutions of higher learning (Barnes, Agago, & Coombs, 1998; Cropsey, Barrett, Klein, & Hampton, 2004).

With tenure and promotion requirements as an ever-present source of stress, and with an increasing number of challenges, such as increasing student diversity, larger class sizes, greater expectations of accountability, and more complex tech-nology, early-career faculty in institutions of higher education often find them-selves in a difficult and vulnerable position. Ewing and associates (2008) propose that interventions such as mentoring may contribute to the reduction of stress, thus enhancing productivity and job satisfaction.

In a study of 430 faculty members and administrators with academic rank, Queralt (1982) found that faculty who had mentors displayed a significantly high-er level of career development than those who did not. Using the criteria of pub-lication status, grant acquisition, appointment to leadership roles, academic rank, yearly gross income, job satisfaction, and career satisfaction, Queralt determined that faculty members with mentors achieved more success than their counterparts without mentors.

Other scholars have also claimed that junior faculty benefit from participating in a mentoring program (e.g., Boyle & Boice, 1998; Deneef, 2002; Draine, Hyde, & Buehlman, 1999). According to Leslie, Lingard, and Whyte (2005), mentoring is necessary for a successful academic career. Driscoll (2004) provided an anal-ogy for mentoring that helps to make its value clear:

> When trees start growing again in a forest where there were trees before, the roots
> of the trees that went before help to strengthen the roots of the trees now growing.
> The trees now growing end up having stronger and deeper roots, and consequently,

these trees are more able to help younger trees growing nearby because their strong, extensive root system helps the root system of these younger trees to grow strong. Similarly, faculty, who were once rookies, are well equipped to mentor the current rookies who are trying to grow strong, deep roots in their respective fields. (p. 6)

For an early-career scholar, accepting a tenure-track position at an institution of higher education can be a mystifying experience and lead to feelings of helplessness. For example, new faculty may not fully understand the performance expectations the university has for them, and they may not be fully certain of their role on the university campus and in the community. In addition, work settings can have "hidden norms, values, and rules" that "could be crucial elements for newcomers to negotiate in terms of their fuller participation and navigation in the discourse [of the university] community" (Gravett & Petersen, 2007, p. 194).

Although the challenges associated with being an early-career academic may be long past for some readers, most people who have had that experience will recall stumbling through the maze of unfamiliar rules and regulations, finding a way around a new discipline, and eventually getting their bearings within the department, school, and university (Bell & Treleaven as cited in Devlin, Nagy, & Lichtenberg, 2010). Junior or new faculty begin their careers with idealistic expectations (Rice et al., 2000) and high levels of enthusiasm (Sorcinelli, 1994), often to become dissatisfied, stressed, and even physically ill (Hill, 2004; Olsen & Sorcinelli, 1992).

Rice and associates (2000) conducted a longitudinal study to examine the experiences and needs of junior faculty in higher education. The study participants expressed confusion about the tenure system and how it worked, and they described limited engagement with a community and the experience of living an unbalanced lifestyle. Participants also reported about loneliness, isolation, competition, and even incivility. Almost all these faculty members reported feeling overworked, with a loss of personal, family, and leisure time.

As the discussion has thus far shown, several circumstances contribute to the need for faculty to be mentored. For newly employed faculty, problems result from feelings of isolation, insecurity, and uncertainty. They need to develop a sense of belonging, to cultivate trusted friends and colleagues, to function effectively in an unfamiliar academic environment, to interact well with faculty who come from diverse backgrounds and have diverse experiences, to understand and navigate the unique features in the new institution, and to distinguish between the truth and the various myths and stories heard via the grapevine. Furthermore, in an era of career switching, when individuals begin second, third, and even fourth careers over the course of their lifetimes, it is probable that many new faculty members will experience confusion regarding role expectations; acceptable workplace behaviors; organizational culture; and the knowledge, skills, and dispositions that are needed for survival in the university community. Mentoring performs a psychosocial function by providing friendship, confirmation, and role modeling—supports that are reported to increase a mentee's sense of competence and feelings of self-worth and thus improve his or her effectiveness in the workplace (Donnelly & McSweeney, 2011).

PURPOSE

Some academics have been fortunate to have colleagues who make time to assist them, or to have an informal mentor with whom they can share ideas or labor over a research grant or from whom they can seek "just-in-time" guidance. For others, a formal mentoring program provides opportunities for support as they are getting started, as well as for ongoing career development. But, as Bell and Treleaven (as cited in Devlin et al., 2010) ask, how can an academic who faces any of the many possible challenges, especially early in his or her career, be paired with the right mentor, and what can early-career faculty members' experiences of receiving and giving career support tell us about the nature and benefits of mentoring, as well as conditions that constrain its effective use in institutions of higher education?

The purpose of this study was to investigate mentoring experiences and other forms of career support of faculty members in an institution of higher learning. Of particular interest were support mechanisms relating to faculty work in the areas of teaching, research and publication, and service. The study gathered information from faculty members employed at one institution of higher education on the nature and extent of mentoring and other forms of career support.

Research Questions

The four specific research questions that guided the study were:

1. What do faculty members think of mentoring?
2. What are the areas in which faculty members receive professional support?
3. What did mentors do to support and develop the all-around growth of mentees?
4. What are the hindrances to mentoring in an institution of higher learning?

METHODOLOGY

This study used a survey to collect information regarding faculty members' perceptions of the need for a mentoring program on the campus of one institution of higher education. The institution is located 20 miles south of Richmond, Virginia, and serves a majority African American student population of approximately 5,500. The researchers sent the survey to the entire faculty at the institution. Among the faculty, 55% are male and 45% female. Fifty-five percent are African American, 32% are European American, 12% are Asian, and 1% are Hispanic.

In addition to obtaining information on faculty perceptions about the mentoring they had received, the researchers also sought information about what the faculty thought a mentoring program ought to be like. The proposal to conduct the research using human subjects was submitted to the institutional review board (IRB), which approved the study. Consent was provided by all participants before completing the electronic survey.

Participants

Participants included in this study were both tenured and untenured faculty members at one institution. The 262 faculty members who were eligible to participate held the ranks of instructor, assistant professor, associate professor, or full professor during the 2010–2011 academic year. Faculty administrators in the position of dean or above were not included in the study sample, nor were adjunct faculty.

Instrumentation

The researchers developed survey items to document the types of mentoring that faculty members had received, as well as their views about the types of mentoring that faculty members ought to receive. They included items representing best practices for mentors and mentees found through a thorough review of the literature. Using an expert panel of professionals familiar with mentoring, the researchers sought information needed in order to determine if the individual items related to the overall functioning of the survey (DeVellis, 2012). The panel examined the items for clarity and sources of bias as well as for their relevance to the domain of mentoring—a process that established the face validity of the final instrument, which included 13 items.

Procedures

Using Qualtrics, an online survey tool, the researchers posted the 13 final items, thereby making them accessible to eligible faculty participants. The survey link was sent via email to all eligible faculty members. Information typically included on informed consent forms was included on the first page of the online survey. Necessary information, including the purpose of the study, was also included on the first page. Survey respondents were also assured that their confidentiality would be protected. Respondents were informed that by clicking to proceed to the next page to begin the survey, they were giving their tacit consent to participate in the study. In order to ensure as large a return rate as possible, the researchers sent follow up email messages periodically to prospective study participants.

RESULTS

Included in the items on the survey were several eliciting information about the participating faculty members themselves. In this section of the chapter, we present this demographic information first; then we turn to a consideration of responses to the survey questions related to mentoring.

In total, 45 of 262 eligible faculty members completed the entire survey, providing a response rate of approximately 18%. Among the respondents, length of employment in an institution of higher education varied. Fourteen percent (14%) had worked in higher education for only one to three years. Twenty-four percent (24%) had worked in higher education for four to six years. Only 12% indicated employment for seven to nine years and 10% for 10 to 12 years. The largest proportion of the survey's respondents had worked in higher education for over 12 years (40%). Respondents were also asked to indicate their current rank. The rank of respondents also varied. The lowest responding group were faculty members holding the rank of instructor (12%) followed closely by those holding the rank of professor (17%). Twenty-four percent (24%) held the rank of assistant professor while the largest proportion of respondents held the rank of associate professor (46%). Fifty-two percent (52%) stated they were tenured faculty, while 48% stated they were non-tenured faculty.

The first survey item asked respondents if they had ever had a formal mentor as part of their participation in a mentoring program. The number indicating participation in a mentoring program was split equally, with 50% responding "yes" and 50% responding "no." Sixty-four percent (64%) of those faculty members who responded that they had received assistance from a mentor indicated that the experience was "very beneficial." Fourteen percent (14%) felt the experience was "beneficial," while 18% stated it was "somewhat beneficial." Only 5% indicated that the mentoring experience was "not beneficial." Faculty members then responded to a question asking them to indicate all areas in which they had received assistance from a mentor during the mentoring experience. They were allowed to select multiple categories. Figure 7.1 below displays their responses.

As Figure 7.1 indicates, the most frequently marked domains of faculty work for which faculty members received mentoring assistance were "understanding the culture of the institution" and "resource awareness" (64% in each domain). Responses showed that faculty members had also received considerable assistance with several other domains, with 59% marking these domains as indicative of the types of support that their mentoring experience had provided: "possible solutions to problems," "professional development," and "attending conferences." Fifty-five percent (55%) reported that they had received assistance with "professional presentations" and "teaching strategies," whereas 50% indicated receiving mentoring assistance with "teaching content." For all other domains, fewer than 50% of respondents indicated receiving assistance from mentors.

The survey also sought to determine the strategies mentors used to provide support to faculty members. These data are displayed in Figure 7.2. A very large proportion of respondents (86%) indicated that their mentors helped them by modeling professionalism, and a large proportion (71%) indicated that their men-

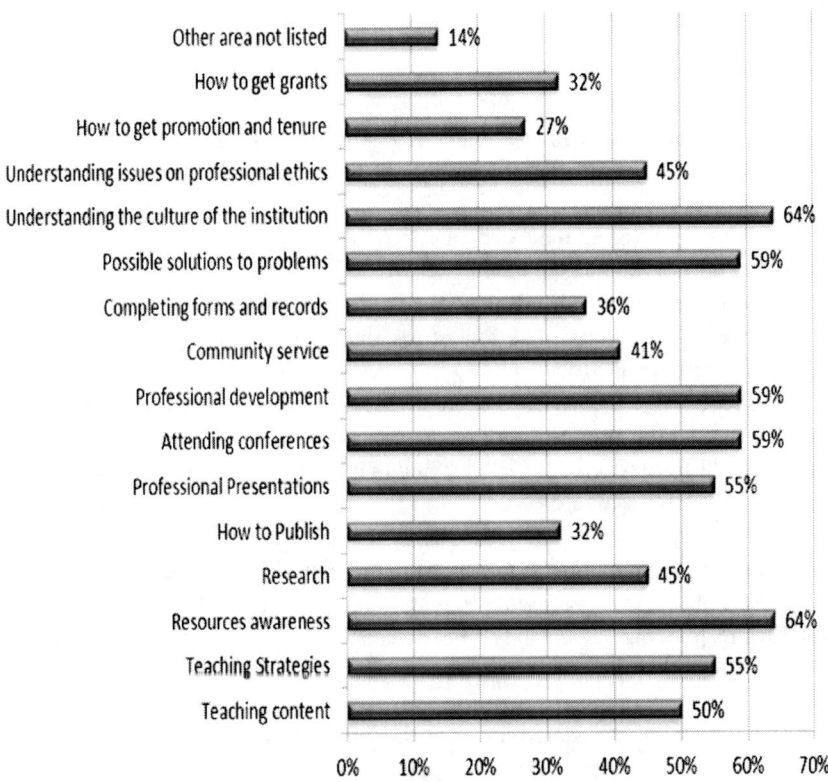

FIGURE 7.1.   Domains of mentoring support

tors assisted them by valuing their knowledge and experience as well as by shar-ing in their personal success and failures.

Respondents were asked if they thought having a mentor is important for new-ly employed faculty. Almost all indicated that they did in fact believe that a men-tor is important (95%). Faculty members were also asked to further explain their reasons for believing that having a mentor is important to new faculty. Content analysis showed that 54.1% of the participants' comments belonged in a category that the research team labeled, "having someone to count on/having someone to answer questions." A total of 10.7% responses fit into a category that the research team labeled "increase in new faculty retention and tenure." Another group of responses totaling 10.7% fit into a category that the research team called, "better understanding of culture and politics in higher education." Several other unique comments were received, and these comments are also important to consider. These responses included the following:

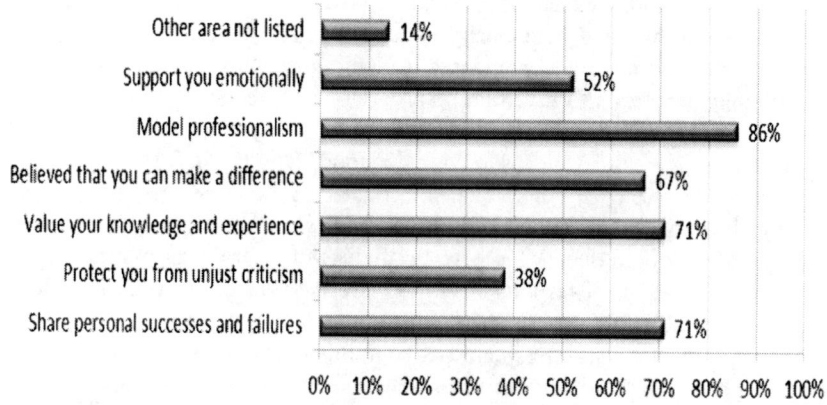

FIGURE 7.2. Mentoring strategies

- Model appropriate faculty expectations
- Having mentors can upgrade morale
- Getting published
- Mentors are better than learning the ropes alone
- Assistance with advising and teaching

The researchers asked faculty members if they would advise their institution to establish a formal mentoring program. Eighty-eight percent (88%) said there should be a formal program. Respondents were asked to explain why they thought their university should consider such a program. The open-ended responses were recorded and categorized. Forty percent (40%) of those who supported a formal mentoring program expressed the view that all new faculty should be required to participate in such a program. Ten percent (10%) noted that a formal mentoring program would require "carefully chosen mentors," and 10% thought it would be a good idea for mentors to receive some form of compensation. Furthermore, 10% also offered comments supporting the practice of locating the mentoring program at the departmental level, and 10% suggested that new faculty should be allowed to select their own mentors. Unique responses (that is, responses that did not fit into any of the categories mentioned above) indicated that a mentoring program would be useful because: (1) it would provide "assistance with publications and grants" and (2) it would be helpful "for strategic planning purposes." One faculty member suggested that, for the purpose of sharing information, a faculty orientation would be better than a mentoring program.

In response to a question about the training of mentors, 85% of respondents indicated that there should be formal training. As to what the training should entail, various responses were received. Half of the respondents agreed that a formal training program did not need to be extensive. Twenty percent (20%) thought that a training program could help clarify expectations and time commitments. Ten percent (10%) offered unique responses. Among those who responded positively regarding the need for a formal training program, all agreed with three additional suggestions: (1) "both parties should be trained," (2) "there is a science and art to the mentoring process that needs to be understood," and (3) "a formal mentoring program would allow for consistencies in managing how mentees are guided." Additionally, those who responded positively indicated that the success of a mentoring program would depend, in part, on the use of a screening process for selecting mentors. Several respondents who were in favor of a formal mentoring program reported being unsure about what strategies to recommend for making such a program successful. Respondents who did not support the use of a formal mentoring program provided comments indicating that informal mentoring is better than formal mentoring, and that it may be difficult to train faculty in ways that would enable them to become effective mentors.

In response to a question about how mentors should be assigned, various responses were prevalent (see Figure 7.3). A large number of respondents (69%) agreed that mentors should be assigned by discipline. Fifty-two percent (52%) thought that mentors should be assigned based on the specific needs of the mentee. Only 2% thought the selection process should be random. Six percent offered additional comments. One suggested that the mentoring program should "have mentor profiles available to new faculty" so that the new faculty members could find faculty mentors whose interests and experience would fit their needs. Another suggested that the mentoring program should hold an event where mentees could mingle with potential mentors and determine with whom they might have the best rapport.

The survey also asked faculty to identify possible impediments to the success of a mentoring program (see Figure 7.4). Several possible impediments were included on a list, and respondents could select all those that they thought were salient. Eighty percent (80%) thought that a lack of time was an impediment for

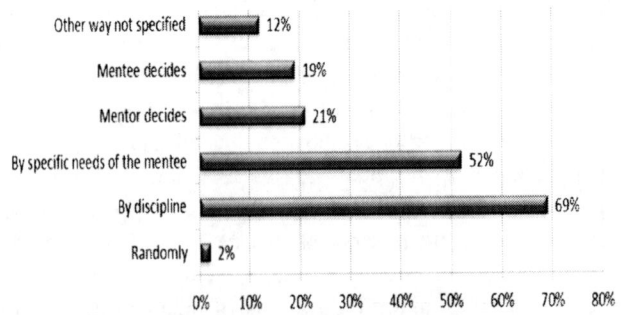

FIGURE 7.3.   How mentors should be assigned to new faculty members

successful implementation of a mentoring program. Seventy-three percent (73%) thought that limited support from the institution would be an impediment. Sixty-three percent (63%) thought that a possible impediment would be incompatibility between the mentor and mentee. Several respondents offered unique responses, suggesting that "cultural differences," "lack of desire for mentoring," and "professional jealousy" might be impediments to the success of a mentoring program.

Finally, faculty members were asked to provide any additional feedback for consideration in the development of a formal mentoring program at their institution. Responses varied considerably; we list several of the most provocative comments below:

- "A mentoring program is a must for all institutions of higher learning."
- "I was in a mentoring program at another institution, and it was incredibly helpful."
- "A mentoring program needs to be practical and useful. Assessment of the program HAS to include significant qualitative components or it will be just another program that makes the university look good while making little difference to the issues it would be designed to address."
- "I wish I had a mentor when I was a new faculty member. It would have made my professional life much easier."
- "Given the pressure to teach a lot of sessions to unprepared students and the large amount of administrative work, to get participation, there should be a financial incentive."
- "There should be institutional support and structure to support mentoring; however, it must be a natural mentor-mentee fit for it to be successful."
- "I think that this is *extremely* important and I plan to develop this in our department."

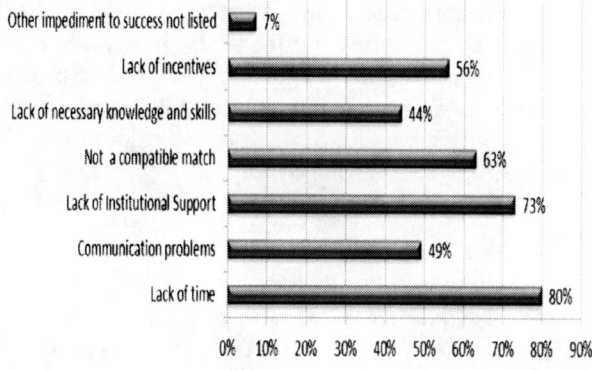

FIGURE 7.4. Possible impediments to the successful implementation of a mentoring program

DISCUSSION

Mentoring has long been viewed as a powerful means of enhancing the professional success and personal well-being of faculty members, especially new and early-career faculty members (Sorcinelli, 2010). Having a good mentor early in a scholarly career can mean the difference between success and failure (Wilson-Ahlstrom, Ravindranath, Yohalem, & Tseng, 2010). This study addressed research questions about the mentoring and other professional support provided to faculty members at a public institution of higher learning in the Eastern part of the United States. Study participants represented tenured and tenure-track faculty at the instructor, assistant, associate, and full professor ranks during the 2010–2011 academic year. The four research questions that guided the study were: (1) What do faculty members think of mentoring? (2) What are the areas in which faculty members receive professional support? (3) What did mentors do to support and develop the all-around growth of mentees? and (4) What are the hindrances to mentoring in an institution of higher learning? In this discussion section, the researchers examine the extent to which the data collected and analyzed answered the research questions.

Research Question 1

What do faculty members think of mentoring? Responses to the survey showed that 64% of responding faculty agreed that mentoring is "very beneficial." This view was further supported by the fact that an overwhelming number of participants agreed with the statement that there should be a formal mentoring program in their institution. This positive view of mentoring is in line with the existing literature on mentoring as far back as 1991. Sands, Parson, and Duane (1991), for example, stated that "mentoring" had become a "buzzword" in higher education. In fact, what has been written since that time about mentoring suggests that whether one is a student, a beginning faculty member, or an administrator, one would benefit from interacting with a mentor. In recent years, the practice of mentoring has become pervasive, and the study of mentoring programs has proliferated. We believe that increased attention to mentoring programs reflects the fact that the benefits of mentoring programs are substantial, not only for individual protégés and mentors, but also for their organizations (Noe, Greenberger, & Wang, 2002; Wanberg, Welsh, & Hezlett, 2003).

Research Question 2

What are the areas in which faculty members receive professional support? Fifteen domains of faculty practice were identified as possible areas in which faculty members might receive professional support. These areas include: teaching content, teaching strategies, resources awareness, research, how to publish, professional presentations, attending conferences, professional development, community service, completing forms and records, possible solutions to problems, understanding the culture of the institution, understanding issues on professional ethics, how to get promotion and tenure, and how to get grants. In addition to rating the importance of the domains in this list, participants were given the opportunity to identify additional areas in which faculty members receive professional support. Areas that participants identified included university politics, how to mentor graduate students, and how to establish a productive research lab. It is not surprising that the top five domains identified by respondents as those in which faculty members actually do receive professional support are: (1) understanding the culture of the institution, (2) resource awareness, (3) possible solutions to problems, (4) professional development, and (5) attending conferences. These findings are consistent with literature in the field. As this literature suggests, mentors can provide support in a variety of domains of faculty work. Especially helpful are "near peers," who are just two to three years ahead of a first-year faculty member. These colleagues may offer the best advice for handling difficult situations because they have the most recent experience of how institutional culture, practices, and policies affect junior faculty members' lives (Reimers, 2010).

Research Question 3

What did mentors do to support and develop the all-around growth of mentees? Participants were given the option to indicate their agreement with one or more of the following options: share personal successes and failures, protect you from unjust criticism, value your knowledge and experience, believed that you can make a difference, model professionalism, and support you emotionally. Most respondents agreed that modeling professionalism and sharing personal successes and failures are the most important practices that mentors use in providing support to and developing the all-around growth of mentees. According to Truman (2009), among many others, behavior modeling has been associated with higher learning outcomes compared to other training approaches. Shared accountability for accomplishments also has received support in recent research. The practices that participants selected seemed, based on our reading of the relevant literature, to fit with prevailing wisdom about adult learning.

Research Question 4

What are the hindrances to mentoring in an institution of higher learning? Respondents indicated agreement by selecting possible impediments from the following list: lack of time, communication problems, lack of institutional support, not a compatible match, lack of necessary knowledge and skills, and lack of incentive. Study participants indicated that one of the relatively serious hindrances to mentoring is "not a compatible match" (63%), suggesting the need for further scrutiny of the methods universities use for pairing mentors with mentees. This finding seems to indicate that the strategy for pairing mentors with mentees is crucial. Participants indicated that mentors and mentees should be assigned "by discipline" (62%) and "by specific needs of the mentee" (55%).

Limitations of the Study

Certain limitations of the study suggest that its findings should be viewed with some caution. First, the study reported on faculty perspectives from only one institution of higher learning. Its findings, therefore, do not necessarily generalize to faculty at other institutions. Second, the response rate at the one institution was relatively low (18%) despite the fact that the researchers sent several electronic requests to all faculty. Finally, some issues relating to faculty mentoring may be controversial, so faculty respondents may not have been comfortable sharing less popular views about the practice.

CONCLUSION

Research has consistently found mentored individuals to be more satisfied and committed to their professions than non-mentored individuals (Wanberg et al., 2003). Mentored individuals often earn higher performance evaluations, receive higher salaries, and make faster career progress than their non-mentored counterparts (American Psychological Association, 2006). Furthermore, when professionals experience success and operate in an anxiety- and stress-free workplace, they are less likely to fail or leave their jobs. The results of this study support the findings from existing studies on the positive impact of mentoring on the experiences and performance of early-career faculty members (Agunloye, 2013; Boyd, 2002).

Mentoring has been recognized as an effective strategy for reducing the stress, pain, frustration, insecurity, and failure that many new faculty members experience in institutions of higher learning. Nevertheless, a mentoring program or other program of professional support for faculty should not be yet another top-down requirement imposed on faculty. Rather, it should be a way of thinking and behaving that recognizes the responsibility that faculty members have for setting their own career goals, determining the processes for attaining their goals, and providing collegial support to one another.

Based on literature on mentoring and the results of this study, institutions of higher learning are encouraged to give new or junior faculty members the professional gift of a mentor. This practice benefits the mentor, the mentee, and the institution as a whole. Conducting a needs assessment is the first step in designing a mentoring program. A needs assessment can provide information about the professional supports that might be useful for early-career faculty members and that are also feasible for the institution of higher education. In general, a needs assessment offers a systematic process for looking at a situation—a process that enables decision makers to understand the situation fully and, through such understanding, find clues to help them determine what to do to improve the situation.

Below is a practical "takeaway"—a step-by-step guide for conducting a needs assessment—that can be followed by any institution of higher learning that is considering providing mentoring and/or other professional support to its faculty.

Conducting a Needs Assessment Relating to Mentoring or Other Professional Support for Faculty

There are a few steps to conducting a good needs assessment. They include:

1. Set the goal or goals for conducting the needs assessment.
2. Identify individuals and focus groups to participate in the needs assessment.
3. Form a task force to be charged with the responsibilities associated with conducting the needs assessment.
4. Select survey items and develop the survey.
5. Distribute the survey online.
6. Collect and analyze the data collected.
7. Design structured questions to guide the focus group sessions. Findings from the online survey could inform the questions for the focus group sessions.
8. Select facilitators and provide standard instructions for holding the focus group sessions.
9. Hold the focus group sessions.
10. Analyze the information gathered.
11. Compile the needs assessment report.
12. Share the report with campus administrators and faculty.

REFERENCES

Adams, K. (2002). *What colleges and universities want in new faculty.* Washington, DC: Association of American Colleges and Universities.

Agunloye, O. O. (2013) *Impact of mentoring program on faculty performance in institutions of higher education: A developing country study.* Retrieved from http://www.toknowpress.net/ISBN/978-961-6914-02-4/papers/ML13-343.pdf

American Psychological Association. (2006). *Introduction to mentoring: A guide for mentors and mentees.* Retrieved from http://www.apa.org/education/grad/intro-mentoring.pdf

Barnes, L. L. B., Agago, M. O., & Coombs, W. T. (1998). Effects of job-related stress on faculty intention to leave academia. *Research in higher education, 39*(4), 457–469.

Bowers, T. (2002). *TechRepublic community.* Retrieved from http://www.techrepublic.com/article/download-this-powerpoint-to-make-a-case-for mentoring/1051314

Boyd, D. (2002). *The impact of mentoring on adjunct faculty performance: Eastern University.* Retrieved from http://ahea.org/files/pro2004boyd.pdf

Boyle, P., & Boice, B. (1998). Systemic mentoring for new faculty teachers and graduate teaching assistants. *Innovative Higher Education. 22.* 157–179.

Cropsey, K. L., Barrett, K. A., Klein, W. S., & Hampton, C. L. (2004). *Reasons for faculty attrition among respondents to a faculty exit survey.* Richmond, VA: Virginia Commonwealth University, School of Medicine, MCV Campus.

Deneef, A. L. (2002). *The preparing future faculty program: What difference does it make?* Washington, DC: Association of American Colleges and University.

Devlin, M., Nagy, J., & Lichtenberg, A. (2010, July). *Research and development in higher education: Reshaping higher education. Paper presented at the meeting of the 33rd HERDSA Annual International Conference, Melbourne, Australia.* Retrieved from http://www.herdsa.org.au/wp-content/uploads/conference/2010/papers/HERDSA2010_Bell_A.pdf

DeVellis, R. F. (2012). *Scale development: Theory and applications.* Thousand Oaks, CA: Sage.

Donnelly, R., & McSweeney, F. (2011). From humble beginnings: Evolving mentoring within professional development for academic staff. *Professional Development in Education, 37*(2), 259–274.

Draine, B., Hyde, J., & Buehlman, J. (1999). Mentoring for faculty and academic staff: Three programs at the University of Wisconsin Madison. In J. Z. Daniels (Ed.), *WISE best practices guidebook: Mentoring programs* (pp. 23–28) Champaign, IL: Committee on Institutional Cooperation.

Driscoll, D. M. (2004). *Mentoring and diversity: A handbook for faculty mentoring LSAMP Indiana students in science, technology, engineering, and mathematics fields.* Retrieved from http://www.purdue.edu/ethics/contribute_pdf_docs/DiversityResourceGuide_04r.pdf

Ewing, R., Freeman, M., Barrie, S., Bell, A., O'Connor, D., Waugh, F., & Sykes, C. (2008). Building community in academic settings: the importance of flexibility in a structured mentoring program. *Mentoring and tutoring: Partnership in learning, 16*(3), 294–310.

Ferman, T. (2002). Academic professional development practice: What lecturers find valuable. *The International Journal for Academic Development, 7*(2), 146–158.

Gravett, S., & Petersen, N. (2007). You just try to find your own way: The experience of newcomers to academia. *International journal of lifelong education, 26*(2), 193–207.

Hill, N. R. (2004). The challenges experienced by untenured faculty members in counselor education: A wellness perspective. *Counselor Education and Supervision, 44,* 135–146.

Leslie, K., Lingard, L. & Whyte, S. (2005). Junior faculty experiences with informal mentoring. *Medical Teacher, 27*(8), 693–698.

Noe, R. A., Greenberger, D. B., & Wang, S. (2002). Mentoring: What we know and where we might go. *Research in Personnel and Human Resources Management Book, 21,* 129–173

Olsen, D., & Sorcinelli, M. D. (1992). The pre-tenure years: A longitudinal perspective. In M. D. Sorcinelli & A. E. Austin (Eds.), *Developing new and junior faculty: New directions for teaching and learning* (pp. 15–26). San Francisco, CA: Jossey-Bass.

Penner, R. (2001). Mentoring in higher education. *Direction, 30*(1), 45–52. Retrieved from: http://www.directionjournal.org/issues/gen/art_1162_.html

Queralt, M. (1982, April). *The role of the mentor in the career development of university faculty members and academic administrators.* Paper presented at the annual meeting of the National Association of Women Deans, Administrators, and Counselors, Indianapolis, IN. (ERIC Document Reproduction Service No. ED 216 614)

Reimers, T. (2010). *Mentoring best practices: A handbook.* Albany, NY: University at Albany, State University of New York. Retrieved from http://www.albany.edu/academics/mentoring.best.practices.toc.shtml.

Rice, R., Sorcinelli, M., & Austin, A. (2000). *Heeding new voices: Academic careers for a new generation.* Washington, DC: American Association for Higher Education.

Sands, R. G., Parson L. A., & Duane, J. (1991). Faculty mentoring faculty in a public university. *The Journal of Higher Education, 62*(2), 174–193. Retrieved from http://www.jstor.org/stable/1982144. doi: 10.2307/1982144

Smith, A. (2007). Mentoring for experienced school principals: Professional learning in a safe place. *Mentoring and Tutoring, 15*(3), 277–291. doi:10.1080/13611260701202032.

Sorcinelli, M. D. (1994). Effective approaches to new faculty development. *Journal of Counseling & Development, 72,* 474–479. Retrieved from http://works.bepress.com/marydeane_sorcinelli/12

Sorcinelli, M. D. (2010). *Building a network of mentors: A guide for engineering educators.* Retrieved from: http://cleerhub.org/resources/2

Truman, G. E. (2009): Behaviour modeling, instruction and exploration training approaches in group and individual contexts. *Behaviour & Information Technology, 28*(6), 493–524. doi:10.1080/01449290601177037.

Wanberg, C. R., Welsh, E. T., & Hezlett, S. A. (2003). Mentoring research: A review and dynamic process model. *Research in Personnel and Human Resources Management, 22,* 39–124. doi: 10.1016/S0742-7301(03)22002-8.

Welp, J. (2002). *How to set up a formal mentoring program.* Retrieved from http://www.techrepublic.com/article/how-to-set-up-a-formal-mentoring-program/1051313

Wilson-Ahlstrom, A., Ravindranath, R., Yohalem, N., & Tseng, V. (2010). *Pay it forward: Guidance for mentoring junior scholars.* Washington, DC: The Forum for Youth Investment.

CHAPTER 8

FIRST BOSSES AS EARLY CAREER MENTORS FOR WOMEN IN RETAIL MERCHANDISING

Allison Thornburgh and V. Ann Paulins

ABSTRACT

In an effort to gain insight into the supports that facilitated their careers, this investigative pilot study explored the lived experiences of early career mentoring among seven women who have achieved mid-level career success in the retail industry. Specifically, the study considers the ways these women's first bosses served (or not) as mentors and conduits to career development networks. Although preliminary and ungeneralizable, the outcomes of this research offer ideas for consideration in appointing mentors to women in early stages of retail careers and for women who are themselves seeking mentors.

INTRODUCTION

Women hold the majority of positions in the retail industry; however, they hold disproportionately few top leadership positions. According to the National Association of Female Executives (NAFE), only four retailers in the United States

Mentoring for the Professions: Orienting Toward the Future, pages 145–171.

145

qualified in 2013 to be one of the Top Companies for Executive Women, a designation based on the "percentage of females who work in a retail company, as well as the percentage of females who are senior managers, corporate executives, P&L [profit and loss] executives, CEO [chief executive officer] direct reports, among other executive markers" (Farfan, 2013, p. 2). Farfan reports that, among these four top companies, although the percentage of female employees ranges from 33 to 57%, only 20 to 43% of senior managers are women, and the highest percentage for corporate executives is 36%. In 2011, only two CEOs out of the top 100 retail companies listed in Stores.org were women; by 2013 the number of women CEOs had grown, but only to seven. This trend is similar among the Fortune 500 companies, which showed 22 women (approximately 4%) in CEO roles in 2013 ("Women CEOs in the Fortune 500," 2013). In the 21st century, gender equity is clearly not yet the norm and cannot be recognized as evident until there are proportional numbers of women and men in top leadership positions, reflecting the population of employees in given fields.

Mentoring opportunities early in women's careers may be influential in their pursuit of, preparation for, and interest in career leadership. In fact, Broadbridge (1999) found that mentoring is an important element in the career development of retail professionals; additionally, lack of mentoring was identified as one of the top three problems encountered by managers in retail settings (Broadbridge, 1998). It is not known how, or whether, current mentoring practices within the retail industry are adequately preparing women to move through the ranks to assume advanced leadership positions. Hale (1995) explored the mentoring of women in organizations and concluded that mentoring specific to women is needed in order to position them—in numbers exceeding the current status quo—as legitimate high-level leadership candidates. Interestingly, Eddleston, Baldridge, and Veiga (2004) observed differing effects of mentoring for men and women, with women receiving fewer benefits in terms of promotions than men received.

Fran Yoshioka, independent trend consultant and visiting professional-in-residence at Ohio University, sharing her views and concerns about mentors for today's young professionals during a lecture she delivered in April, 2013, reported that her early mentors were her bosses. She attributed much of her success over a three-decade career to her first boss, who was her mentor. Yoshioka noted that she felt that her first boss invested in teaching her new employee, thus making the protégé more valuable to her. In return, Yoshioka, the protégé, looked up to the mentor, emulated her, and set career goals as encouraged by her mentor. Yoshioka indicated concern that (1) first bosses may not readily take on nurturing, teaching mentor roles today, and (2) young women may not readily seek mentors.

In light of Yoshioka's observations and the need for more proportionate representation of women in business's top ranks, it seems important to understand the infrastructure supporting women's leadership advancement in the retail industry—particularly through mentoring in the first job. The role of the first boss in the lived experiences of female leaders needs to be explored, as an initial step, to gain insight into the dynamic relationships of mentors and protégés early in careers. Better understanding of the ways first bosses have influenced women who have accomplished success in retail careers may reveal appropriate mentoring strategies for future female leaders. Our exploratory study addresses whether or not first bosses are positioned to serve as mentors, and, if so, how they mentor and what factors empower them to be effective mentors.

RELATED LITERATURE

Mentors, according to Kram (1983), perform "a variety of functions that support, guide, and counsel the young adult" (p. 608). Effective mentors understand that they must be dependable, engaged, authentic, and aware of the needs of the protégé (Kram, 1983) through acting as role models (Cordova, Shaughnessy, & Neely, 1990; Noe, 1988) and instructors for networking and career strategies (Cullen & Luna, 1990). Mentors help novices, or protégés, understand and absorb organizations' cultural and social norms and assist new employees to learn what they need to know to succeed in their jobs (Kram, 1983). Career mentors do so by playing many roles—teacher and supporter, organization counselor, professional career guide, financial sponsor, and supportive boss (Phillips-Jones, 1982). Levesque, O'Neill, Nelson, and Dumas (2005) identified five career mentoring behaviors most often acknowledged in the literature: "championing, exposure and visibility, coaching, informational support, and political assistance" (p. 438). Mentors can present challenging work assignments and introduce protégés to influential industry contacts (Noe, 1988).

Successful leaders are likely to benefit from a variety of people providing mentoring throughout their lives (Baugh & Sullivan, 2005; Higgins & Kram, 2001). Referred to as developmental networks (Higgins & Kram, 2001; Molloy, 2005) or developer relationships (Cotton & Shen, 2013), a "portfolio" of influential people contributes to personal and professional development. In addition to bosses, Baugh and Sullivan (2005) identified work colleagues, both in- and outside one's organization, and subordinates as potential developmental mentors. Cotton and Shen (2013) observed that family members, work peers, CEOs, and even idols one has never met offer important developmental guidance and support. Molloy (2005) suggested that the range of supports people need is individual and may differ depending on personality and career goals.

Career Mentors

Of the five types of mentors that Mentros and Yang (2006) identified (career mentors, research mentors, project mentors, co-mentors, and lead mentors), this project focuses on the role of career mentors. According to Mentros and Yang, career mentors provide support for protégés because of shared work environments where mentors work closely with protégés and are in positions to share knowledge and experience. Mentoring during career planning and developmental life stages has been explored and deemed valuable toward student success (Kane, Healy, & Henson, 1992) and in the workplace (Chandler, Kram, & Yip, 2011; Fagenson-Eland, Baugh, & Lankau, 2005). Kane and associates found that providing students with mentoring experiences further strengthens their skills, solidifies their sense of work ethic, and enhances their confidence in job performance. After interviewing 505 students, they discovered that, through mentoring, students improved time management skills, gained corporate-specific communication skills, enhanced self-discipline, and developed abilities to initiate business-related activities.

Mentoring can be beneficial for both organizations and individuals. Retention of high-quality employees and strategic planning for future workplace leadership are two important organizational benefits of mentoring (Broadbridge, 1998, 1999). Allen, Eby, Poteet, Lentz, and Lima (2004) performed a meta-analysis to explore career-oriented benefits of mentoring. Interestingly, their accumulated evidence indicated that mentoring more positively affects subjective measures of career success (e.g., satisfaction) than objective career success measures (e.g., salary and promotions). They suggested further research to understand the conditions that contribute to protégés' most beneficial outcomes of mentoring.

Mentor–Protégé Relationships

The mentor–protégé relationship is a critical aspect in mentoring success. As scholars have noted, mentoring relationships can emerge in a variety of ways, and—often related to the way the relationship emerges—the fit between the parties in this developmental relationship contributes to the level of success of the mentoring experience (Fagenson-Eland et al., 2005; Kram, 1983; Parise & Forret, 2007; Phillips-Jones, 1982; Ragins, 1989).

Kram (1983) described three ways that mentoring relationships develop. Mentors may be assigned when people join organizations; such assignment creates formal mentoring relationships. Formal mentors could be peers, knowledgeable and experienced coworkers, or supervisors or team leaders. Alternatively, mentoring relationships can arise with time, when working relationships solidify with one member emerging as a guide to the other, less experienced colleague. Finally, mentors can be sought by novice employees wanting guidance and enhanced experiences for career growth.

Parise and Forret (2007) investigated the benefits of formal mentoring programs. They considered voluntary versus required participation, mentor's roles in being paired with their protégés, mentor training, and institutional support for the mentoring program, and found that "mentors whose participation in the program was more of a voluntary nature (non-formal) were more likely to perceive it to be a rewarding experience" (p. 236). They found that institutional or management support for mentoring programs was also positively related to successful mentor experiences. Further, Parise and Forret (2007) observed that mentors' involvement in being matched to protégés reduced their perceptions of bias in mentoring programs. Similarly, informal mentoring relationships were associated with successful outcomes when compared to formal mentoring programs in a study conducted by Nicholson (1996), who noted that, for women, lack of long-term networks (and thus access) to informal networking presents a barrier that can further disadvantage them in comparison to men. In fact, Powell (1999) observed that informal mentoring has emerged as an especially effective networking vehicle—for men. She explored ways in which traditional mentor roles navigate power (over protégés) and maintain the status quo by supporting "good old boy" pathways to career advancement.

Phillips-Jones (1982) explored the relationships that mentors and protégés develop, providing insight into potential problems of the relationships. Challenges such as the time it takes to mentor (and be mentored), poorly matched mentor and protégé assignments or choices, lack of mutually shared expectations for protégé success, inappropriate use of power by the mentor, jealousy of the protégé by the mentor, and potential sexual attraction and tension between the partners were presented as important issues to consider and negotiate when entering into mentoring relationships (Phillips-Jones, 1982). Fagenson-Eland and associates (2005) investigated the extent to which 27 mentor–protégé pairs agreed about their developmental mentoring relationships and communication practices. Significant congruency was found between the pairs, except when large differences in age or work tenure between the mentor and protégé occurred. Burke and McKeen (1997) found that better mentor outcomes arise when mentors have direct supervisory roles and when organizations are supportive of the mentoring relationships. Despite the positive prospects of mentoring, Eby, Allen, Evans, Ng, and DuBois (2008) suggest caution with respect to overestimating the effects of mentoring, noting that in their meta-analysis of research, limited mentoring-related outcomes, particularly in career areas such as promotions and salary, emerged. According to Eby and associates, "in terms of workplace mentoring...larger gains may be likely in terms of enhancing helping behavior, situational satisfaction and attachment, and interpersonal relationships, whereas smaller gains may be likely in terms of enhancing job performance" (2008, p. 265). Clearly, more insight into workplace mentoring experiences leading to career success and leadership attainment is needed.

Trait and Behavioral Theories of Leadership

Bass (1990) defines leadership as

> the focus of group processes as a matter of personality, as the exercise of influence, as particular behaviors, as a matter of inducing compliance, as a form of persuasion, as a power relation, as an effect of interaction, as a differentiated role, as an instrument to achieve goals, and as initiation of structure. (p. 38)

Thus, leadership involves both personality traits and behavioral actions. Through an extensive review of leadership literature, Derue, Nahrgang, Wellman, and Humphrey (2011) summarized documented leadership behaviors as either (1) task-oriented, (2) relationship-oriented, (3) change-oriented, or (4) passive, and noted that leaders are generally evaluated on their abilities to complete tasks (or lead others to complete tasks), their relational dynamics, and their ability to effect change.

Thomas Carlyle, author of the "great man" leadership theory prevalent in the 1840s, stated that "the history of the world is but the biography of great men" (1841/1888, p. 32). Carlyle believed that effective leaders are gifted; they have divine inspiration and are born with the "right" characteristics. According to this precursor of the trait theory of leadership, people are either born to lead or not. This idea, predominant throughout the 19th century, resulted from and led to research studying the styles and accomplishments of famous, if highly disparate, men, such as Abraham Lincoln and Alexander the Great (Cherry, 2012).

Expanding this personological view of leadership, Allport and Odbert's (1936) work drew from two of the most comprehensive dictionaries of the English language to extract 17,953 personality-describing words. The list was reduced to 4,504 adjectives that Allport and Odbert believed were descriptive of observable and relatively permanent traits. In the 1940s, Raymond Cattell (1946) acquired the Allport–Odbert list of adjectives and decreased the list to 171 by disregarding synonyms. Through further research, Cattell developed the 16 Personality Factor Model. This model measures personality based upon 16 traits: abstractedness, apprehension, dominance, emotional stability, liveliness, openness to change, perfectionism, privateness, reasoning, rule-consciousness, self-reliance, sensitivity, social boldness, tension, vigilance, and warmth (Eysenck, 1967). Using Cattell's 16 Personality Factor Model (1946), Tupes and Cristal (1967) discovered five recurrent aspects of personality: agreeableness, culture, dependability, emotional stability, and surgency. These evolved into what is now described as the "Big Five personality traits" (Costa & McCrae, 1992): openness, conscientiousness, extraversion, agreeableness, and neuroticism (listed in that order and commonly referred to as OCEAN).

Recent investigations of leadership styles have focused on tasks, relationships, and change agency, categorizing leader behaviors into styles described as either transactional (task-oriented, contingent reward) or transformational (relationship-oriented, nurturing, and empowering), with passive leadership categorized as laissez-faire, or leadership by exception (Bass, 1990; Derue et al., 2011; Jogulu & Wood, 2006; Judge & Piccolo, 2004). According to Bass (1997), "the transactional–transformational paradigm views leadership as either a matter of contingent reinforcement of followers by a transactional leader or the moving of followers beyond their self-interests for the good of the group, organization, or society by a transformational leader" (p. 130). Transformational leadership, viewed as a nurturing, supportive (mentor-oriented) approach, was defined by Steven Covey (1989) as representing the "ability to 'transform' people and organizations...to change them in mind and heart; enlarge vision, insight, and understanding; clarify purposes; make behavior congruent with beliefs, principles, and values; and bring about changes that are permanent, self-perpetuating, and momentum- building" (p. 287). Interestingly, according to Judge and Piccolo (2004), transformational and transactional leadership are not mutually exclusive, and each style can be deemed advantageous over the other, depending on the circumstances and environment.

Jogulu and Wood (2006) performed a meta-analysis of literature about early leadership theories specifically to learn how such theories might enhance the profiles of women as leaders. They observed that women were noticeably absent from any consideration of leadership traits in early work, and they found that as behavioral leadership theories emerged in the 1930s, women continued to be excluded primarily because women leaders did not comprise a critical mass from which behaviors could be observed and assessed. Stanford, Oates, and Flores (1995), along with Helgesen (1990), suggested that certain feminine characteristics (traits *and* behaviors) advantage women in leadership capacities. These characteristics typically reflect good communication skills, such as attentive listening and empathy.

Theorists have sought to determine whether innate personality traits contribute to and can be used to predict leadership ability. The validity of trait theory has met with scrutiny (Pervin, 1994), with scholars appropriately concerned that measuring leadership capacity based on supposed innate qualities does not take into account the ability of people to learn and develop skills. Derue and associates (2011) called for efforts to integrate trait and behavioral theories of leadership, remarking that trait theories have critical limitations for understanding leadership, but also noting that personality traits contribute to leadership effectiveness through behaviors and relationships. They determined, through extensively reviewing literature and integrating trait and behavioral theories in their meta-analysis, that behaviors, rather than traits, are more valuable predictors of leadership effectiveness. It is noteworthy, however, that Derue and associates observed an interaction between traits and behaviors and suggested that behaviors can mediate traits (e.g., proactive behaviors may temper neuroticism; unpopular behavior may negate agreeableness). In their analysis, three traits—conscientiousness, extraversion, and agreeableness—were identified as the most important of the Big Five in predicting leadership success. Further, Derue and associates (2011) observed that conscientiousness and agreeableness were most highly associated with improving the performance of those being led and that conscientiousness and extraversion were most highly associated with positive evaluations of leadership effectiveness. Derue and associates (2011) suggest that assessment of personality traits can be helpful in predicting leadership effectiveness, and they encourage organizations to emphasize agreeableness, conscientiousness, and extraversion when selecting leaders.

METHODS

The literature supports the notion that mentoring is an important element of leadership, often exhibited by supervisors. For employees in early career positions, first bosses must offer guidance and direction. The extent to which business professionals emerge as mentors may be related to their personality traits and leadership styles. Because women need opportunities to develop leadership skills to advance into top leadership positions in the retail industry, knowledge about key characteristics of effective early career mentors could be an important first step. Insights based on this knowledge should prove valuable to organizations seeking ways to improve their workplace diversity, responsiveness to employee needs, infrastructures that support positive teamwork, strategies for employee transitions, including upward mobility, and continuity of workplace knowledge and culture. Using the qualitative methods described below, we explored career women's perceptions of whether and how their first bosses mentored them, as well as how their first bosses' personality traits and leadership behaviors contributed to the developmental relationship.

Participants

Our eligibility criteria required that participants be women who had achieved mid-level career leadership positions[1] in the retail industry. Participants for this study were recruited using a convenience sampling method. Emails were sent to potential participants through a university-sponsored list-serve for retail merchandising students and graduates. Additionally, personal emails were sent to prospective participants who were recommended by faculty, personal acquaintances, and industry professionals known to the researchers; word-of-mouth, personal networking processes, and the snowball effect were all employed. As a result, seven eligible women were identified who agreed to participate.

Interview Protocol

In this exploration, we probed into the professional experiences of the women to learn about the ways their first bosses influenced their careers and whether and how these first bosses remained mentors throughout these women's careers. Each woman had a different experience and perspective; therefore, a conversational interview-based protocol was used to create a comfortable environment allowing for in-depth conversation, as suggested by Berg (2009). The interviews were conducted individually to build trust and rapport between the primary investigator and participants and to focus on the lived experiences of each participant. A semi-structured interview protocol was employed, with 11 consistent questions investigating participants' current positions, supervisory roles and experiences, first career positions, work histories, first bosses' roles and influences in their careers, developmental and mentoring networks, and views of the role and importance of mentoring in general. Probing questions were posed as the interview responses were generated.

Questions were presented in a manner that required description by the participants (e.g., "Tell me about your current position," "Describe your work history," and "Tell me about the boss at your first career position"). To address leadership styles of first bosses, participants were informed of the following:

There are three recognized management styles: transactional, transformational, and laissez-faire. Transactional leaders establish a give-and-take relationship, clarify responsibilities, and reward or correct followers for the outcome. Transformational leaders are ones who establish themselves as a role model; they mentor and empower followers, encouraging them to develop to their full potential. Laissez-faire leaders fail to take responsibility for managing and have a lack of involvement.

Participants were then asked, "Which category would you say your first boss would fit into? Explain and give examples."

To investigate the relationships between personality traits and mentoring, participants were instructed as follows:

> I am going to ask you to rank and explain your first boss in the five personality traits that are used to describe human personality: openness, conscientiousness, extraversion, agreeableness, and neuroticism. Please rate them on the scale one being poor and 10 being excellent and give examples that demonstrate.

Each of the five traits questions was presented in a defining manner, such as, "How would you rate your first boss in openness, which is described as exhibiting creativity, nonconformity, autonomy, and unconventional qualities?"[2] After selecting the rating, the participants were asked to provide examples that demonstrated how their bosses exhibited the traits.

After reporting personality trait ratings and selecting leadership style categories, the women provided illustrative examples to justify their choices. These descriptions enabled the researchers to understand more fully the thought processes and experiences of the interview participants, and the descriptions served to provide surface validity to the data.

The interviews were audio recorded and then transcribed in their entirety for analysis. For ease of reporting and to protect identity, each participant was assigned a pseudonym: Amanda, Brittany, Cassie, Danielle, Emily, Faith, and Gabrielle. Table 8.1 presents profiles of our seven participants.

Data Analysis

The data collection and analysis were undertaken not to create broad generalizations, but to document collective voices of these seven women and their experiences with first bosses as mentors for the purpose of preliminary (or pilot) work toward developing a grounded theory. Once the qualitative data were transcribed and analyzed, observations of similarities and differences among the woman's experiences were noted, through a constant comparative method, to generate emergent themes. The data analysis and development of overarching themes were initially conducted independently by each investigator, and then the investigators compared their observations and analyses, refining categories and ensuring documented evidence of the final themes presented here.

TABLE 8.1.   Participant Career Experiences

Pseudonym	Current Position	Scope of Employee Supervision Current Number Supervised	First Career Position
Amanda	Retired from Direct Marketing Position	50 (In last position)	Fashion Board Committee
Brittany	Vice President of Planning	7 Directly 14 Total in Team	Merchandise Training Program
Cassie	Project Manager	1 Directly 20–30 Depending on project	Executive Training Program
Danielle	Merchant	1 Currently Has Supervised More	Assistant Buyer
Emily	Director for Private Brand	5	Cosmetic Division
Faith	Merchandise Manager	3	Internship in Corporate Merchandising Office: Led to Merchant Training Program
Gabrielle	Recruiting Coordinator	1 Directly 100 Indirectly	Sales Associate

Limitations

While the small number of interview participants prevents generalization of results, the knowledge gained provides guidance for further investigation about first
bosses' mentoring roles. The variety of mid-level leadership positions represented
here offers opportunities to consider different experiences, but also contributes to
limited ability to draw comparisons between women with similar positions or career paths. All of the first bosses in this study were female, thus disallowing comparison between male and female first bosses. The geography of the participants,
which was primarily, but not exclusively, Midwestern and Southeastern United
States, may affect interpersonal relationships and work cultures, and thus affect
relationships between mentors and protégés. For example, when Cassie, who is
from the Midwest but moved to New York, was asked how she would rate her
first boss on agreeableness, she said, "I don't know if it's New York, but I haven't
really seen a lot of agreeableness; as a result I don't know if it's everywhere but
definitely at my company, and to be a project manager you have to have kind of
an edge about you."

Furthermore, our study considered the experiences of women who reached
mid-level career success; through this analysis we cannot know whether the experiences of women who have been unable to progress successfully to mid-level
leadership are different from the experiences of the women in our study. Neither
are the voices of the few women who have reached high-level leadership positions

included here, thus limiting the contributions of our data to a certain segment of career women.

Despite these limitations, this exploratory research provides a basis for new insights. Perhaps most importantly, the research provides a means of identifying mentorship issues worthy of further research.

RESULTS

All seven first bosses emerged as influential reference people or members of the women's developmental networks, though only six of the seven participants identified their first bosses as mentors. Our data generated, through the voices of our participants, action-based descriptions of first bosses as mentors because they showed the following behaviors:

- Guiding the women through professional development aspects of the industry, such as relationship building
- Inspiring and motivating their new-to-career employees
- Teaching technical and task-oriented industry practices
- Demonstrating leadership, whether positive or negative

Specifically, Faith's first boss "acclimated me to the retail industry." Similarly, Amanda reflected, "I learned a lot about the retailing business from her." Gabrielle revealed that her first boss "has always given me a lot of guidance and...helped me to see another career path that I didn't even know was out there." This guidance aspect was perhaps most evident in Emily's summary: "My first boss set the tone for what your work ethics are or what your habits are and how you treat people, so I think your first boss is critical in what you develop [into] for the rest of your life." Emily elaborated further, saying that her first boss guided her through "the correct etiquette when calling on a customer, and how to handle 'no.'"

The first bosses motivated and inspired by empowering the new employees to make decisions (Amanda, Cassie, Gabrielle), trusting in and believing in the protégé's abilities (Gabrielle), having high performance expectations (Danielle), and instilling confidence in them (Cassie). Gabrielle considers her first boss's "faith and belief" in her as the reason for her own career success. Cassie revealed that her first boss "definitely gave me a lot of direction and a lot of opportunity to show her what I could do, and she kept giving me more and more as I asked for it."

Brittany's first boss taught her about the aspects of the retail industry by "being a good teacher and explaining why business processes work the way they do." Amanda shared that she learned how to analyze figures from her first boss, a skill that she used throughout her career and has emphasized with her own employees over the years. Cassie said that her first boss "took me under her wing, developed me into a strong assistant in tandem with my boss, and kind of got me on the right direction to become an associate...and then a product manager." Emily observed that her first boss "is one of those people who explained to you and helped you with everything."

Danielle reported that her first boss had, in fact, been instrumental in her career development, though she did not see their relationship as one of mentor–protégé. The complexity of the first boss relationship with a career novice is illustrated in Danielle's insightful statement:

[A]s the first person I worked under...I think at first I didn't know how to take it. Then I actually realized much later that she was the kind of person who would give you a hard time along the way but really it was for your own good because I found out that she actually really always pushed for the people on her team. I found out much later...she always pushed for an opportunity for me and she always kind of went to bat for me and she got me promoted and things like that.

As a role model, Brittany noted that she "recognized early on that I don't want to be a boss like that person," whereas Cassie reflected that she leads with a different personality style than her first boss, but nevertheless "[took] a lot of how she managed and [is] using that today." Specifically, Cassie observed her first boss's effective open-door policy and noted, "I learned that she allowed me to [come in and talk about things] and I saw in other instances where bosses didn't and what happened to the people underneath them, so I think that was probably the biggest impact that she has had on my career." Danielle shared that her first boss's "assertiveness and expectations, for basically perfection is something that I have been very tuned into and is something that I definitely expect [as a supervisor], and I think part of that is because I was managed that way [by my first boss]."

Analysis of Personality Traits of First Bosses

The rankings that each of the seven women designated for her first boss on the Big Five personality traits (Eagly & Carli, 2007) are shown in Table 8.2. There were no observed differences between transactional and transformational first bosses in reference to these personality traits. Interestingly, it was noted that conscientiousness and extraversion were positive for all first bosses, and strongly positive for the four bosses who were long-term mentors.

Brittany described her first boss as conscientious because she was dependable and did not change her expectations of employees; Cassie explained her first boss's conscientiousness by reflecting, "She was very conscientious of everything that happen[ed] on a day-to-day basis; whether she was involved in it or not, she knew what was going on." With a clear illustration, Emily described her first boss as being "just very conscientious in how she dealt with people, whether it was just returning a phone call immediately or sending somebody a note, meeting every deadline; she was very conscientious in that way." Similarly, Gabrielle said that her boss "was very aware of what you've achieved and thank[ed] you for your efforts, and then you could always depend on her." Danielle's lower score for conscientiousness was explained through Danielle's' perception of the inconsistency

TABLE 8.2.   Participants' Ratings of the Big Five Personality Traits of their First Bosses

| Personality Traits[1] of First Boss | First Boss was Categorized: | | | | | | | |
| | Transactional Leader | | | Transformational Leader | | | | |
	Amanda	Brittany	Faith	Cassie	Danielle	Emily	Gabrielle	Mean
Openness: Exhibiting creativity, nonconformity, autonomy, and unconventional qualities	9	4	7	5	7	8	8	6.9
Conscientiousness: Exhibiting achievement orientation and dependability	10	9	5	9	5	10	8	8.0
Extraversion: Exhibiting sociability, assertiveness, activity, and positive emotions	10	N/A[2]	5	8	9	9	10	8.5
Agreeableness: Exhibiting caring, trusting, compliant, and gentle qualities	8	2	9	6	6	6	10	6.7
Neuroticism[3] Exhibiting poor emotional adjustment and negative emotions	1	7	5	2	7	2	1	N/A

Notes: 1 = Poor execution; 10 = excellent execution
[1]Definitions from Eagly and Carli (2007), p. 40.
[2]Missed question
[3]Upon analysis and reflection it was apparent that participants rated neuroticism differently; some participants associated a low number with positive (lack of) neurotic traits while others associated a high number with positive (lack of) neurotic traits.

of her boss's actions and expectations. Similarly, Faith cited indecisiveness as the reason for her boss's low ranking. With respect to extraversion, Gabrielle stated, "In the retail industry, you have to be very extraverted and very positive." Danielle described how extraversion presented itself in her first boss by stating, "Especially when she presented in front of a room, you could tell she was extraverted. She was engaging; and I think she took time around the office to be social with people." In support of the first boss's ability to network and connect her protégé to other influential people, Cassie recalled, "[S]he was somebody who was in meetings. She was a friend with a lot of people in the company." Furthermore, Faith described her first boss as someone who "was always positive; she never looked at the negative, [but rather] turned the negative into a positive."

Agreeableness reflected a wider range of ratings than any of the others, with 2 (Brittany) as the low score and 10 (Gabrielle) as the high score. Several of the respondents qualified their ratings, describing their boss's quality of agreeableness with comments such as, "[she was] not a softie" (Cassie) and "[she was] assertive and business-like" (Danielle), demonstrating that lower ratings on the agreeableness trait are not in contradiction with positive leadership.

The personality trait, neuroticism, presented challenges for analysis in this study. Upon reflection about the data, it was apparent that some participants interpreted first bosses who possessed neurotic qualities as exhibiting "poor execution," while others with first bosses who did not possess neurotic qualities rated those bosses with "poor execution." Thus no meaningful rating data were generated for analysis purposes. Nevertheless, the qualitative comments (which were limited because the participants offered little explanation) were reviewed and were included in the qualitative data analysis and presentation.

Analysis of First Bosses' Leadership Styles

Table 8.3 presents summary information about the mentor roles and leadership styles of first bosses and project participants. Commensurate with literature supporting leadership effectiveness and interrelatedness of both transformational and transactional leadership behaviors, three bosses designated by the participants as transformational leaders and three designated as transactional leaders were labeled as mentors by the participants. Interestingly, Danielle categorized her first boss as a transformational leader, but she was the only woman who did not identify her first boss as a mentor. Although six of the seven women identified their first bosses as mentors, the types of mentorship that they described varied. Three participants, (Amanda, Brittany, and Faith) categorized their first bosses as transactional leaders. The other four (Cassie, Danielle, Emily, and Gabrielle) categorized their first bosses as transformational leaders. These seven women's designations of leadership styles were substantiated through their explanations of first bosses' behaviors. Amanda, for example, noted that her first boss was "all business, always." Brittany stated that her boss offered "rewards for results." She further elaborated, "Responsibility was given as it was proven." Faith reflected that her boss's learning status limited her ability to be fully transformational, though this status enhanced the boss's ability to be empathic toward someone learning a new position.

Emily's transformational boss explained the mistakes and successes she had made with her employees to show them how to handle a given specific issue in anticipation of their future encounters with similar situations. Cassie and Gabrielle categorized their first bosses as transformational because they were empowered and had the trust of their bosses to make decisions. Danielle observed that her first boss set very high expectations and was often difficult to please; however, she also provided opportunities and advocated for Danielle's career success.

When these seven women were asked whether they saw themselves emulating their first bosses, the women with transformational bosses all said "yes," and women with transactional bosses reported either limited emulation or said "no."

Interestingly though, of the four women with transformational first bosses, only one (Gabrielle) cited relationship-oriented transformational qualities, such as mentoring characteristics and positivity, that she seeks to emulate. As noted in the previous section, Cassie, Danielle, and Emily referenced management styles rather than personality traits as qualities they seek to emulate.

Among the women who reported having transactional first bosses, only Amanda acknowledged a degree of emulation. She reflected that her own educational preparation, which was limited in analytical foundation, supported her need to emulate her first boss's strong analytical skills. Brittany replied with an emphatic "no" when asked whether she emulates her first boss. She explained that she recognized early on that she did not "want to be a boss like that," and she noted, "I have modeled behavior to pretty much 100% opposite." Faith also replied "no" to the question about emulating her first boss.

Whether or not the women said they see themselves as emulating their first bosses, all of the women described their first bosses as having influenced their careers. The nature of the first bosses' influence varied from positive to negative, depending on the individual situations. Notably, the three transactional bosses had influences on their protégés that were task-oriented and based upon industry knowledge. The task-oriented learning outcomes reflect transactional leadership and communication in which performance is rewarded based on proper execution of the job. Among the women who reported having transformational first bosses, the influences on their careers went beyond task-oriented items to include more holistic career-shaping outcomes, reflective of transformational leadership. Cassie revealed that her boss emphasized and modeled the importance of forming relationships with her assistants and associates and of having an open-door policy; and she also reported that her boss gave her confidence. Danielle said, "My first boss had a great impact on my career because I think she set the bar so high that I could never reach it; as she did that, she kind of pulled me along with her; and I think her expectations always set me up to have high expectations. So I think even as I progress even more, the sky is always the limit." Gabrielle described her first boss's strong influence as the reason she established her career. Cassie, Danielle, Emily, and Gabrielle all described their first bosses as having transformational leadership behaviors; their descriptions show that these bosses exhibited mentoring roles (or in the case of Danielle, influences) through their supportive transformational leadership.

Brittany and Faith reported that their first bosses were short-term mentors, offering support for the protégés within a discrete timeframe. Brittany stated that her first boss was a mentor "in short term, at the beginning stages," but Brittany quickly outgrew the relationship. She observed, "it was proprietary for her to mentor [me]...we were kind of connected at the hip. Her success depended on mine." When Brittany got promoted, she recalled, she was no longer a resource for her first boss, and, subsequently, the first boss discontinued her role as Brittany's mentor. Similarly, Faith and her first boss were learning their positional

TABLE 8.3. Project Participants' Perceptions of Leadership Styles and Mentor Relationships

	Amanda	Brittany	Cassie	Danielle	Emily	Faith	Gabrielle
First boss's leadership style	Transactional	Transactional	Transformational	Transformational	Transformational	Transactional	Transformational
Reported leadership style of bosses substantiated in interview statements?	Yes	Yes	Yes	Yes	Yes	Yes	Yes
Did mid-level leader emulate first boss? How?	Limited Analytical work	No	Yes Managerial style	Yes Assertiveness & high expectations	Yes Models work ethic &work habits	No	Yes Positive & open-minded style
Was the first boss influential? How?	Yes Modeling tasks	Yes Instructional	Yes Empowering, instilling confidence	Yes Set high bar	Yes Role model & consultant	Yes Acclimation to industry; learning initial tasks	Yes Empowering, exhibited belief in women; Inspirational role model

Was the first boss a mentor?	Yes	Yes	Yes	No	Yes	Yes	Yes
Duration of mentoring relationship	Career-long	Short-term	Career-long	NA	Career-long	Short-term	Long-term
Does the mid-level leader consider herself a mentor? How?	Yes; Provides encouragement	Yes; Provides feedback in safe zone	Yes; Offers career advice & advocacy	Yes; Role model; open door	Yes; Share information; discuss strategies	Yes; Consultant outside of supervisor role	Yes; Offers career guidance to employee(s)
What is the importance of mentoring?	Encouragement; role modeling	Feedback and guidance outside of supervisory roles	Acclimation to company culture and specific job tasks	Guidance outside of supervisor relationship; encouragement for career reflection & development	Learning & sharing information through informal supportive relationships	Teaching skills & company culture	Guidance through self-discovery & career development
Other influential mentors?	Professional contact	More senior colleagues	Boss's boss	Formal workplace mentor	Another boss	Bosses who later became professional colleagues	Parent who is also employed in the industry

responsibilities together, with Faith occupying the position that her boss had just been promoted from. When Faith was asked whether she considered her first boss to be a mentor, she responded, "At the time I thought she was a mentor to me." Faith considered her first boss a mentor at the time but, upon reflection about what a mentor should be, would not consider her a mentor now, meaning her first boss was not a long-term mentor. Faith recalled, "She was learning to be a merchant at the same time I was learning to be an assistant...so she was very understanding of what I was going through and the training and making sure I had everything I need[ed]." When Faith's boss left the company, the mentoring relationship ceased.

Amanda, Cassie, Emily, and Gabrielle noted that their relationships with first bosses emerged into long-term mentoring relationships—with the first bosses providing guidance throughout the majority of the protégés' careers. Amanda noted that her first boss was a mentor, and they are still very good friends. Similarly, Emily indicated that today, several decades after working for her, the mentor "is still a very good friend." She illustrated their relationship by saying, "I still talk to her; I still run things by her. She continues to be an influence in my life."

Five of the women said that their first bosses were formal mentors. Amanda was the only interviewee who described her first boss-mentor relationship as informal. The structured nature of boss/subordinate seemed to define the formal mentoring relationship. Amanda explained that she and her first boss worked in tandem and that theirs was not a firmly established, traditional boss/employee relationship. Despite the reported formal nature of these mentoring relationships, Emily and Faith advocated for informal mentoring as more effective. Emily elaborated, saying that, having experienced both formal and informal relationships as the mentor, the "formal mentorship program that our company has...always felt forced; it always felt like we have to do this; we need to meet once a week, or whatever it is." She continued by describing her preference for more fluid relationships, in which employees or other protégés approach her about specific current situations and seek advice. Faith stated that "mentorship isn't something you can force, it kind of happens organically." Brittany did not commit to a preference for informal versus formal mentoring, but suggested that effective mentors need not be direct supervisors, but workplace relationships between more senior employees and less experienced protégés should provide the support of regular interaction and a shared understanding of company mission and tasks.

How First Bosses Mentor

All of the first bosses were described as being mentors, with the exception of Danielle's transformational first boss. This mentor role shows the importance first career bosses have on new employee career paths. Interestingly, in this population, the positions that these first bosses held were fairly entry level. While their positions as supervisors placed them in leadership roles, their relative lack of leadership and career experiences might have affected their ability to be highly effective transformational leaders, perhaps due to being inexperienced as bosses.

One of Emily's reflections, about being more impressionable during that time in her career, supports this possibility. Faith also stated, "At that time in my career, yes, she was a mentor to me. As I furthered my career I do have mentors in my life, and when I look back, she wasn't the mentor that I would have needed to take me to the next level."

In examining the first boss, it became evident that the women were probably more impressionable at that early point in their careers because it was their first career position and they were learning about the industry. Faith described her relationship with her first boss as a mentor relationship at the time because she was more impressionable in her first career position. She did not have another boss to compare with that first boss, and she did not yet possess the experience to fully understand good leadership versus bad leadership practices. The experiences of the first boss and that boss's preparation to be a supervisor, teacher, and a mentor—as well as the boss's leadership ability—clearly affect the success of the relationship for the early career employee.

Beyond First Bosses—Developmental Networks and Transitions to Mentorship

All of the women noted other influential mentor(s) in their careers (see Table 8.3), and all agreed that mentorship leads to leadership success in the retail industry. Faith stated that she thinks it is "extremely key to have a strong mentor to survive and thrive in the retail industry." Cassie noted that it is important to have a mentor just to ask questions. She emphasized the point that, whether a novice is fresh out of college or switching into a new company, she needs someone to go to for help. Danielle said, "I think the importance of mentoring is guidance outside of your day-to-day experiences and what your supervisor is expecting of you, and I think it should be positive encouragement with the ability to be realistic about the subject at hand." Gabrielle described the importance of mentoring related to helping protégés find new opportunities or new insights about themselves; she identified guiding and coaching people through their professional and personal lives as contributions that have positive effects.

Each of the women stated that she considers herself a mentor to others. Brief summaries are presented in Table 8.3 indicating how the women mentor others. Gabrielle described a protégé whom she encouraged and facilitated in the transformation from her part-time job into a full-time career, just as Gabrielle's first boss had done for her. She attributed the guidance and mentoring of her first boss to her success in helping her own employees. Faith explained that the two women whom she currently mentors are in different companies, which she prefers, as she believes that the mentor relationship is better when she is not the direct boss. Emily said that she has mentored formally and informally and that the formal mentorship program that her company offered always felt forced. Danielle explained, "I think it's very important to set an example and act as some type of role model for especially people who are younger in their careers, and I always try to make myself an open door so that no one would ever be afraid to approach me." Interestingly, Brittany has been a role model many times in her career, and she said that informal mentoring has always turned out to be the best.

Emergent Themes Leading to Suggestions for Future Research

Insights were gained regarding the role that first bosses play as primary early career mentors in the development of female leaders in the retail industry. In summary, drawing from the content analysis, the collective voices of the women interviewed for this study revealed nine emergent themes: (1) first bosses are influential, and generally seen as mentors, though the role of mentor is not consistent nor fully defined across participants; (2) first bosses seem to be, by virtue of their supervisory positions, in roles as formal mentors; (3) in response to prompting through the interview questions, both personality traits and leadership styles are reflected upon as descriptions of how first bosses mentor; (4) mentoring effectiveness is not necessarily associated with transactional or transformational leadership; (5) transformational first bosses, but not transactional first bosses, are emulated; (6) with respect to emulating first bosses, participants tend to note task-oriented rather than relationship-oriented criteria; (7) long-term mentoring is reflected in relationship-based descriptions, such as being approachable, empowering, and inspiring; (8) mentorship is seen as supporting leadership success in the retail industry, and (9) the participants, who have reached mid-level career success, see themselves as mentors and seek to mentor others.

Commensurate with the nature of exploratory qualitative research, the emergent themes identify topics that invite further inquiry. Therefore, areas that our study suggests warrant future research include (1) analysis of the relationship between first boss supervision and mentoring; (2) identification of the mentor qualities and environmental conditions that lead to long-term versus short-term mentoring relationships; (3) continued development of an integrative theory, including both personality traits and behavioral leadership styles of first bosses that shape their relationships with, and abilities to mentor, new employees; (4) the relative value of formal versus informal mentoring programs, especially for employees in first career positions; (5) the ways that companies and industry can build a sustainable infrastructure that empowers women to be mentored and then become mentors; and (6) the dynamics that the sex of the first boss may introduce into the supervising and mentoring relationship.

Relationship between First Boss's Supervision and Mentoring

Bosses influence and have power over employees. Because all first bosses were influential in the careers of the interviewees, and most were expected, by virtue of their supervisory positions, to teach and guide their new-to-career employees, support for further investigation of the relationship between first bosses and new employees is evident. Future research should include inquiry regarding personality traits (specifically whether high levels of openness, conscientiousness, extraversion, and agreeableness enhance a mentor's effectiveness) and leadership behaviors. While this study supports the notion that transactional and transformational leadership qualities are not exclusive, further investigation of the way they are exhibited by first bosses will enhance our understanding of the relationship between leadership style and effective mentoring. There is clear evidence that first bosses can mentor but some question about the efficacy of first bosses to serve as mentors, particularly in the long term.

Long-Term versus Short-Term Mentor Relationships

Expectations for first bosses to serve as short- versus long-term mentors should be considered and included in future analyses, particularly in light of our observation that transformational leaders emerged as career-long mentors more often than transactional leaders. In terms of company and industry goals for sustainability through leadership transition planning, it could make a difference whether the first boss is a transformational or transactional leader, because transformational first bosses are perhaps more likely to be emulated than are transactional first bosses. Additionally, support for the understanding of transactional and transformational leadership styles was evidenced in the interviews; the women in our study reported more relationship-oriented influences when describing transformational bosses, and more task-oriented items when describing transactional bosses. No evident differences emerged with respect to exhibition of Big Five personality traits (openness, conscientiousness, extraversion, agreeableness, and neuroticism) for transformational as compared to transactional first bosses.

Integrative Theory—First Bosses' Personality Traits and Behavioral Leadership Styles

Content analysis revealed that first bosses were influential because they provided instruction, acclimated new employees to the industry, set high expectations for performance, served as role models, inspired their employees to be confident and seek career challenges, and empowered their new-to-career subordinates through delegation of work. These behaviors, which reflect both transformational and transactional leadership styles, are measurable in ways different from personality traits. Nevertheless, first-boss personality traits (commensurate with Barrick & Mount, 1991) of conscientiousness and extraversion seem positively related to bosses' likelihood to serve as long-term mentors and to former employees' seeking to emulate first-boss leadership qualities (e.g., style of management, modeling work ethic and work habits, exhibiting positive attitudes) that are often described as mentoring behaviors (see Tables 8.2 and 8.3). We conclude that, as Derue and associates (2011) suggest, a more fully integrated theory of mentoring that includes both personality and behavioral dimensions needs to be developed, and we advocate for inclusion of both personality traits and behaviors in further (more comprehensive and generalizable) research about first bosses as mentors.

Formal versus Informal Mentor Programs in the Retail Industry

The roles of first bosses to teach job tasks, acclimate new employees to the company culture, guide protégés through relationship building and professional networks, and provide novices feedback about work habits and expectations seemingly lend themselves to formal mentoring programs. In contrast, informal relationships seem to lend better support for career-long professional development. Future research that focuses on formal versus informal mentors, and which are more effective, would contribute positively to the body of research. It would be helpful to understand the value of having a network of mentors who are called on in certain situations versus having one mentor who is called upon in every situation.

Sustainable Infrastructure to Support Cyclical Mentoring

Women need to continue to seek and secure mentors who can assist them with career development. Strong mentors at the first-boss level will set the standard for mentoring practices that may support women's advancement into top leadership positions. Ways to develop and sustain cyclical mentoring could enhance the transition of women into top leadership ranks.

First Bosses' Gender and Early Career Mentoring

All first bosses in this study were women, and therefore we did not glean any insight into similarities or differences in mentoring relationships based on gender. Because previous research has indicated that few differences exist between women and men in terms of their expectations from mentors (Levesque et al., 2005), the mentoring relationships between men and women, particularly in the retail industry, where women are disproportionately absent from leadership roles, need further exploration. We emphasize that, because a desired outcome of this inquiry was to build knowledge leading to infrastructures for empowerment of female leaders in the retail industry, the topic of gender roles and mentoring remains a necessary area of inquiry.

CONCLUSIONS

First bosses emerge as important contributors to women's career development networks; therefore, people who are first bosses need to realize the importance of their roles. Likewise, new-to-career protégés benefit from understanding ways that their first bosses can be mentors and recognizing how mentors play key roles in their career development. Retail companies seeking to recruit new employees who transition into organizational leaders should take note that the personality traits of conscientiousness and extraversion seem to enhance first bosses' abilities to emerge as effective mentors. Additionally, the personality traits of conscientiousness and extraversion may contribute to long-term mentoring relationships.

Both transactional and transformational leadership styles are effective in the role of first boss, each supporting effective motivational qualities through behaviors such as teaching workplace culture and skills, setting high expectations for novice employees, and demonstrating (ideally positive) professional interactions. Regardless of the leadership style of the first boss, the first-boss position has an important influence on the new employee.

There is evidence that the behaviors and personality traits of the first boss temper the mentor–protégé relationship. Therefore, careful selection of the management team seems prudent. Retailers' strategies to identify and place employees in first-boss roles should consider that appropriate combinations of personality traits and leadership behaviors are likely to contribute to the long-term career opportunities of new female recruits, and perhaps also to the stability of the retailers' own workforce.

Given that opportunities for quality mentoring may be limited to early career women in retail merchandising positions and that the role first bosses play in advanced career development is limited, companies are encouraged to implement mentoring infrastructures beyond first bosses. Preliminary evidence from this research indicates that additional mentoring networks may be particularly likely to enhance long-term mentoring opportunities that guide women into leadership roles. Retail companies are encouraged to experiment with formal mentor structures, building development networks for emerging leaders, and providing ways for employees to participate in informal mentoring programs. With documentation and analysis, innovative mentoring systems can provide data further contributing to development of grounded theory.

NOTES

1.   *Mid-level leadership* was defined by Clark and associates (1999) as "having authority over a significant part of the institution or company, while still being accountable to higher authorities" (p. 66).
2.   Definitions for personality traits were derived from Eagly and Carli (2007, p. 40).

APPENDIX A: SUGGESTED GUIDELINES
FOR WOMEN SEEKING MENTORS

Based on this research, the following practical guidelines are presented for women who are new to careers and seeking mentors as pathways to career development:

•   Observe your work environment and your professional industry environment to identify potential career mentors.

- Seek prospective mentors who are well connected and therefore are in a position to enhance your developmental network.
- Seek to build relationships with industry leaders; consider leaders close to your own career position as well those in highly aspirational positions.
- Ask leaders directly regarding their willingness to provide you guidance commensurate with the role of a mentor.
- Ask your company to support your efforts to seek mentoring.

APPENDIX B: SUGGESTED GUIDELINES FOR PROSPECTIVE MENTORS TO NEW-TO-CAREER WOMEN

Career professionals who seek to become mentors to new-to-career women can use these guidelines as they embark on mentoring activities:

- Inventory your personality traits (OCEAN); consider ways that your strengths and areas of challenge fit with the needs of new-to-career women.
- Consider your leadership style; regardless of transactional or transformational behaviors, seek to motivate, teach, and enhance career networks for the protégé.
- Be aware of your position as a role model and the responsibilities that carries.
- Seek to build relationships that will be sustainable over time with new-to-career women.
- Seek to empower the protégé with responsibilities on the job and within the profession.

REFERENCES

Allen, T. D., Eby, L. T., Poteet, M. L., Lentz, E., & Lima, L. (2004). Career benefits associated with mentoring for protégés: A meta-analysis. *Journal of Applied Psychology, 89*(1), 127–136.

Allport, G. W., & Odbert, H. S. (1936). *Trait-names: A psycho-lexical study.* Princeton, NJ: Psychological Review Company.

Barrick, M. R., & Mount, M. K. (1991). The big five personality dimensions and job performance: A meta-analysis. *Personnel Psychology, 44*(1), 1–26.

Bass, B. M. (1990). *Bass & Stogdill's handbook of leadership: Theory, research, and managerial applications* (3rd ed.). New York, NY: Free Press, Collier Macmillan.

Bass, B. M. (1997). Does the transactional-transformational leadership paradigm transcend organizational and national borders? *American Psychologist, 52*(2), 130–139.

Baugh, S. G., & Sullivan, S. E. (2005). Mentoring and career development. *Career Development International, 10,* 425–428.

Berg, B. E. (2009). *Qualitative research methods for the social sciences* (7th ed.). Boston, MA: Allyn & Bacon.

Broadbridge, A. (1998). Barriers in the career progression of retail managers. *The International Review of Retail, Distribution and Consumer Research, 8*(1), 53–78.

Broadbridge, A. (1999). Mentoring in retailing: A tool for success? *Personnel Review, 28*(4), 336–355.

Burke, R. J., & McKeen, C. A. (1997). Benefits of mentoring relationships among managerial and professional women: A cautionary tale. *Journal of Vocational Behavior, 51*, 43–57.

Carlyle, T. (1888). *On heroes, hero-worship and the heroic in history*. New York, NY: Frederick A. Stokes & Brother. Retrieved from http://www.questia.com/read/1444983/on-heroes-hero-worship-and-the-heroic-in-history (Original work published 1841)

Cattell, R. B. (1946). *Description and measurement of personality*. Yonkers-on-Hudson, NY: World Book Company.

Chandler, D. E., Kram, K. E., & Yip, J. (2011). Mentoring at work: New questions, methodologies, and theoretical perspectives. *Academy of Management Annals, 5*(1), 519–570.

Cherry, K. (2012). The great man theory of leadership. Retrieved from http://psychology.about.com/od/leadership/a/great-man-theory-of-leadership.htm

Clark, M. C., Caffarella, R. S., & Ingram, P. B. (1999). Women in leadership: Living with the constraints of the glass ceiling. *Initiatives, 59*(1), 65–76.

Cordova, F., Shaughnessy, M., & Neely, R. (1990). Mentoring women and minorities in higher education. In A. D. Johnson & P. Mroczek (Eds.), *Mentoring minorities and women: A challenge for higher education* (pp. 13–17). DeKalb, IL: Northern Illinois University Press.

Costa, P. T., & McCrae, R .R. (1992). *Revised NEO personality inventory (NEO PI-R) and NEO five-factor inventory (NEO-FFI)*. Odessa, FL: Psychological Assessment Resources.

Cotton, R. D., & Shen, Y. (2013). The company you keep: The relational models and support expectations of key developer relationships, *Career Development International, 18*(4), 328–356

Covey, S. R. (1989). *The seven habits of highly effective people: Restoring the character ethic*. Melbourne, Australia: Business Library.

Cullen, D. L., & Luna, G. (1990). A comparative study of female mentors in academe and for higher education In A. D. Johnson & P. Mroczek (Eds.), *Mentoring minorities and women: A challenge for higher education* (pp. 18–23). DeKalb, IL: Northern Illinois University Press.

Derue, D. S., Nahrgang, J. D., Wellman, N., & Humphrey, S. E. (2011). Trait and behavioral theories of leadership: A meta-analytic test of their relative validity. *Personnel Psychology, 64*(1), 7–52.

Eagly, A. H., & Carli, L. L. (2007). *Through the labyrinth: The truth about how women become leaders*. Boston, MA: Harvard Business School Press.

Eby, L. T., Allen, T. D., Evans, S. C., Ng, T., & DuBois, D. L. (2008). Does mentoring matter? A multidisciplinary meta-analysis comparing mentored and non-mentored individuals. *Journal of Vocational Behavior, 72*(2), 254–254.

Eddleston, K. A., Baldridge, D. C., & Veiga, J. F. (2004). Toward modeling the predictors of managerial career success: Does gender matter? *Journal of Managerial Psychology, 19*, 360–385.

Eysenck, H. J. (1967). *The biological basis of personality*, Springfield, IL: Thomas.

Fagenson-Eland, E. A., Baugh, S. G., & Lankau, M. J. (2005). Seeing eye to eye: A dyadic investigation of the effect of relational demography on perceptions of mentoring activities. *Career Development Journal, 10*(6/7), 460–477.

Farfan, B. (2013, February 14). 2013 best U.S. retail industry companies for women in leadership positions—NAFE. Retrieved from http://retailindustry.about.com/od/best-retail-jobs-employers/a/Nafe-Ranks-Best-Retail-Chains-For-Women-To-Work-Manage-And-Get-Promoted.htm

Hale, M. M. (1995). Mentoring women in organizations: Practice in search of theory. *American Review of Public Administration, 25*(4), 327–339.

Helgesen, S. (1990). *The female advantage: Women's ways of leadership*. New York, NY: Doubleday Currency.

Higgins, M., & Kram, K. E. (2001). Reconceptualizing mentoring at work: A developmental network perspective. *Academy of Management Review, 26*, 264–288.

Jogulu, U. D., & Wood, G. J. (2006). The role of leadership theory in raising the profile of women in management. *Equal Opportunities Journal, 25*(4), 236–250.

Judge, T. A., & Piccolo, R. F. (2004). Transformational and transactional leadership: A meta-analytic test of their relative validity. *Journal of Applied Psychology, 89*(5), 755–768.

Kane, S. T., Healy, C. C., & Henson, J. (1992). College students and their part-time jobs: Job congruency, satisfaction, and quality. *Journal of Employment Counseling, 29*, 138–144.

Kram, K. E. (1983). Phases of the mentor relationship. *Academy Of Management Journal, 26*(4), 608–625. doi:10.2307/255910

Levesque, L. L., O'Neill, R. M., Nelson, T., & Dumas, C. (2005). Sex differences in the perceived importance of mentoring functions. *Career Development International, 10* (6/7), 429–433.

Mentros, S. E., & Yang, C. (2006). *The importance of mentors. Cultivating careers.* Retrieved from http://www.educause.edu/research-publications/books/cultivating-careers-professional-development-campus-it/chapter-5-importance-mentors

Molloy, J. C. (2005). Development networks: Literature review and future research. *Career Development International, 10*(6/7), 536–547

Nicholson, P. (1996). *Gender, power and organisation*. London: Routledge.

Noe, R. A. (1988). An investigation of the determinants of successful assigned mentoring relationships. *Personnel Psychology, 41*, 457–479.

Parise, M .R., & Forret, M. L. (2007). Formal mentoring programs: The relationship of program design and support to mentors' perceptions of benefits and costs. *Journal of Vocational Behavior, 72*, 225–240. doi:10.1016/j.jvb.2007.10.011

Pervin, L. A. (1994). A critical analysis of current trait theory. *Psychological Inquiry, 5*(2), 103–113.

Phillips-Jones, L. (1982). *Mentors & protégés*. New York, NY: Arbor House.

Powell, B. J. (1999). Mentoring: One of the master's tools. *Initiatives, 59*(1), 19–31.

Ragins, B. R. (1989). Barriers to mentoring: The female manager's dilemma. *Human Relations, 42*, 1–22.

Stanford, J. H., Oates, B. R., & Flores, D. (1995). Women's leadership styles: A heuristic analysis. *Women in Management Review, 10*(2), 9–16.

Tupes, E. C., & Cristal, R. E. (1967). *Recurrent personality factors based on trait ratings.*

Technical Report ASD-TR-61-97. Lackland Air Force Base, TX: Personnel Laboratory, Air Force Systems Command.

Women CEOs in the *Fortune* 500. (2013, May). *CNN Money.* Retrieved from http://management.fortune.cnn.com/2013/05/09/women-ceos-fortune-500/?iid=F500_sp_river

Yoshioka, F. (2013, April). *Career advice for merchandising students.* Department of Human and Consumer Sciences Visiting Lecturer Series, Lecture conducted from Ohio University, Athens, OH.

CHAPTER 9

THE STANFORD WAY

A Case for Mentoring Female Coaches in Women's Basketball

Tara VanDerveer, Vikki Howard, and Beth VanDerveer

ABSTRACT

Opportunities for women in coaching NCAA basketball continue to dwindle. Providing women with support and guidance through mentoring is a necessary mechanism through which coaching skills and opportunities are cultivated. The Stanford Way offers one model of leadership-mentoring that has successfully created coaching opportunities for many women who played and coached for the Stanford women's basketball team.

INTRODUCTION

Collegiate women's basketball in the United States has undergone significant changes over the past 40 years as a result of legal and cultural changes. Coaching opportunities for women have gone from almost none, to very many, to gradually fewer and fewer. The purpose of this chapter is to describe the history of women's involvement in coaching basketball, the trajectory of which explains the need for

Mentoring for the Professions: Orienting Toward the Future, pages 173–186.
Copyright © 2015 by Information Age Publishing
173

effective mentoring practices. While research on mentoring of collegiate basketball coaches is limited, it is widely acknowledged that a form of apprenticeship or mentoring is a necessary element of coaching development (Nash, 2003). For the purpose of this analysis, a definition of mentoring is taken from Jones, Harris, and Miles (2009), who describe sports coaching mentoring as "learning from more senior others." Although mentoring research suggests that a range of tactics is effective, it is generally acknowledged that each mentor–mentee relationship is unique and therefore defies standardization (Jones, et al., 2009). At Stanford University, Hall of Fame coach Tara VanDerveer purposefully mentors coaches at many levels, from camp counselors to "top 20" coaches. The Stanford Way, the apprenticeship model used by VanDerveer and other coaches at Stanford, is described in this chapter and analyzed according to mentoring leadership practices considered important to effective development of protégés.

HISTORY OF WOMEN IN COLLEGIATE BASKETBALL COACHING

In the 1970s, a wave of young women entered the coaching profession to take over fledgling women's basketball programs and replace the corps of physical education professors who were also part-time coaches. They formed a generation of coaches who would become the royalty of women's basketball ranks, and included Pat Head-Summit, Jody Conradt, Vivien Stringer, Sylvia Hatchell, Muffet McGraw, Teresa Grentz, MaryAnn Stanley, Joan Bonvicini, Kay Yow, Barbara Stevens, and Tara VanDerveer. These women took advantage of a unique moment in history when opportunities for women were legally mandated, and each is among the top 30 "winningest" coaches of all time. Title IX of the Education Amendments of 1972 provided protection against sexual discrimination of girls and women and had an immediate and powerful impact on the engagement of females in sports. According to this law, "No person in the United States shall, on the basis of sex, be excluded from participation in, be denied the benefits of, or be subjected to discrimination under any education program or activity receiving Federal financial assistance" (as cited in United States, Department of Education, Office for Civil Rights, 1998, para. 1).

Prior to the passage of Title IX, boys and men participated in sports in staggering disproportion. For example, in 1970–1971, only 7% of all athletes participating in high school sports were girls. In 2012, girls made up nearly half of all athletes, or about 42% (Anderson, 2013). In collegiate athletics, the increase was more than 100% (Hattery, 2012).

Ironically, at the same time that girls and women have been given better chances to play, women's opportunities to coach at the college level have actually declined. The decline began in 1979, when 58% of coaches of female sports were women, compared to 42.9% in 2012 (Anderson, 2013). Cooky and Lavoi (2012) reported, moreover, that just 15% of head coaching, administrative, and media positions in athletics go to women, and that women are expected to perform better, are paid less, and have more limited promotional opportunities than males in athletics.

Significantly, prior to 1982, all women's collegiate athletics were administered by the Association of Intercollegiate Athletics for Women (AIAW). For logistical, financial, and strategic reasons, the AIAW and the National Collegiate Athletic Association (NCAA) merged, and women's athletics came under the umbrella of the formerly men's-only organization. Hailed as the gateway to greater visibility, financial support, and talent development, this merger was embraced by women coaches and athletic directors (O'Reilly & Cahn, 2012). While the expected benefits did accrue, female sports now became an attractive opportunity to men as well as women. Unlike the invisible barrier keeping women out of the coaching ranks of male sports, no such barrier kept men from competing with women for jobs coaching women. According to Hattery (2012), as money and prestige increased, men began to flock to intercollegiate women's coaching, thereby limiting opportunities for women. NCAA women's basketball, the sport with the greatest prestige and resources, has seen the greatest influx of male coaches, with possibilities of employment for women getting smaller each year (Hattery, 2012).

The increasing dominance of men in coaching NCAA women's basketball is a concern for two important reasons. First, women are increasingly deprived of opportunities, in spite of a legal mandate that NCAA programs provide women with equal opportunities to participate as players, coaches, and administrators. This is a fairness issue as well as a legal one. Several discriminatory factors contribute to these lost opportunities for women: athletic directors' (mostly male, as indicated earlier) likelihood to hire coaches of the same gender (Acosta & Carpenter, 2008) and reliance on their friends for recommendations when hiring (Gogol, 2002); inequalities in compensation; incompatibility of women's values and level of comfort within a predominantly masculine environment in sports (Kilty, 2006); homophobia (Krane & Barber, 2005); a widely held perception that men are inherently better at coaching than women (Norman, 2010); and lack of female mentors (Kilty, 2006). Second, women's interest in advancement is inhibited by these and other factors. Female assistant coaches express less interest and initiative in advancement to head coaching positions than do male assistant coaches (Cunningham & Sagas, 2002). The factors that contribute to this lack of self-determination align with factors that contribute to the demise of females heading sports teams.

MENTORSHIPS AS A MEANS TO INCREASE WOMEN'S OPPORTUNITIES IN COACHING

In one response to declining numbers of women in coaching, the United States Olympic Committee (USOC) and NCAA sponsor an annual coaching conference for women to promote retention of female coaches, attract minority women to coaching, and provide training to improve coaching performance (Kilty, 2006). An important thread of this conference is mentorship. Mentoring female coaches is a potentially powerful strategy to overcome barriers to women's entry into coaching NCAA basketball and to stem the loss of female talent. Dr. Judith Sweet, Co-Director of The Alliance of Women Coaches, identifies mentorship as a key to finally achieving equal opportunities. According to Sweet, "the [female athletes] I admire the most are those who embrace their responsibilities to be role models and advocate for gender equity...all of whom have been leaders in the Women's Sports Foundation and have mentored future leaders" (United States Sports Academy, 2012, para. 10).

Bloom, Durand-Bush, Schinke, and Salmela (1998) studied coach–mentor relationships and found that elite coaches had been mentored during their early and mid-careers, though these mentor relationships tended to evolve serendipitously or were specifically sought out by the developing coach. These coaches believed that such mentorship was both the most powerful, authentic means of learning skills and values and was essential to maximizing their coaching potential. This finding was corroborated by Sagas, Paetzold, and Ashley (2005), who concluded that the support (mentorship) of a head coach for an assistant was essential to the success of an assistant coach.

Mentoring is a special form of leadership. Collins (2001) and a research team from Stanford University found that the most effective, or "Level 5," leaders behave in the following ways:

- Model a paradoxical mix of personal humility and professionalism
- Display a compelling modesty, are self-effacing and understated
- Attribute success to factors other than themselves
- Display a workmanlike diligence—more plow horse than show horse
- Set up their successors for even greater success

What distinguishes these leaders is that they typify what Tony Dungy, former Super Bowl winning coach of the Indianapolis Colts, considers a mentoring leader (Dungy & Whitaker, 2010). For our purposes, there are three major elements that differentiate this type of mentor leader from others:

- It is really not about them. They lead to add value to the lives of those they lead. They are humble people and lead by example.
- They take a long-term perspective. They know a team must get results to survive, but they also know that building and developing people for the long run means tolerating some mistakes.
- Mentor leaders are focused on mentoring leaders who develop other mentor leaders. It is the ongoing legacy they are concerned about. (Dungy & Whitaker, 2010, p. 19)

The Stanford coaching–mentoring model discussed below aligns with the elements of Collins's leader–mentor framework. The Stanford Way is an unambiguous set of expectations that form the behaviors and attitudes for senior mentors to model as they provide explicit leadership in the art of coaching and personal development.

COACH–MENTOR: THE STANFORD WAY

Mentoring women in coaching may take many forms. For the purposes of this discussion, mentoring takes three forms of support for emerging female coaches. Formal mentoring is a quasi-contractual relationship whereby an expert coach plans and executes advisement of philosophy, skills, and connections. By contrast, an expert coach may be an informal mentor in an unstructured and more spontaneous relationship that is intentional but not necessarily systematic or obligatory. Finally, mentoring may be indirect when an expert coach, whose values are appreciated and skills communicated without the expert coach's explicitly teaching those skills, is viewed as a role model by emerging coaches. All three forms of mentoring are important to the advancement of emerging coaching talent, though not well researched in NCAA women's basketball. Mentoring in all three forms is explored in the following description of the Stanford Way, a model for the philosophy and execution of mentorship.

Philosophy

Posted in the hallways and locker room is the Stanford Way motto that articulates team expectations: "Accountability, Toughness, and Giver" (See Figure 9.1). From the beginning, new team members are advised of and held to the values identified in this motto. Central to the initial indoctrination of team members is an emphasis on "representing." Protégés are reminded that they should always act to embody the reputation of the name on their shirts. They're asked to keep track of their adherence to the philosophy implied by the motto. They're told, "Here is your notebook—and everything goes in the notebook, including daily accounting of basketball activities that you do (notes from meetings with staff, notes from practice, scouting, recruiting)." The notebook is a continual reference and

The Stanford Way		
Accountability	Toughness	Giver
Dependability	Physical Strength	Enthusiasm
Consistency	Confident	Unity
Discipline	Aggressive	Energy
Competitiveness	Resilient	Unselfishness
Take Ownership	Whatever it takes	Leadership
Work Ethic	Have a motor	Commitment
		Investment

FIGURE 9.1. The Stanford Way motto, posted in the player locker room

reflection. It becomes, in effect, the protégés' basketball roadmap. The Stanford system, one that has led to perennial success, is revealed in this notebook. Much of the Stanford system is about routines that have proven successful. For example, because of the system, players would easily be able to run their practice without coaches on the court, moving seamlessly from drill to drill, transitioning quickly and maximizing efficiency. In this way, players become part of the corps of coaches and, in fact, often actual future coaches through this implicit mentorship.

Perhaps the most important tenet of the Stanford Way is *accountability*. Standards are high, and protégés understand that their performance is important and that failure to perform is unacceptable. While perfection is not expected, effort is. The Stanford Way is a "no excuses" culture. However, in order for this philosophy to be fair and engender mutual trust, objectives are transparent, with clarity about respective responsibilities and criteria by which performance will be evaluated. If a game tape is needed by the next day, it is expected that whoever receives the assignment will find a way to get it done; if practice is rescheduled at the last minute, everyone on the team is expected to adapt and be ready without fail. When protégés are unable to perform a duty reliably after having received specific instructions and feedback, that responsibility is taken away. While rare, this happens on occasion. For example, a protégé was relieved of the privilege of writing to prospects and their parents when feedback and edits did not improve the student's writing ability. In other words, the student's letters did not represent the Stanford Way; for the sake of the team and program, the privilege needed to be withdrawn.

Framework

Today, developing the talent and passion of women who will become coaches is accomplished in much the same way that trade guilds transferred knowledge for centuries. That is, protégés become understudies or apprentices as they gradually learn the trade. At Stanford, the trade is learned through careful scaffolding and a multilayered process. Using a low frustration/high success approach, protégés are initially taught easy tasks at which they can be successful, where they can build confidence and learn to become part of the culture. Gradually, tasks become more varied and more challenging as protégés master each skill and establish their commitment to the Stanford Way.

Coaching basketball in the NCAA has eight primary performance categories: coaching players' basic and advanced basketball skills, personal and academic advisement of student-athletes, conditioning, scouting competing teams, scheduling of games and related events, recruiting a continuous flow of talent, fundraising, and marketing/promotions of team. Each of these areas may be further broken down. Coaching and teaching basketball skills, for example, includes planning practices, coaching during practice, goal setting, in-game management, individual workouts, and video feedback sessions with individual players and the team. Obviously, each of these categories can be further articulated: planning practice

Recruiting Tasks and Subtasks
Communication with Recruits
- Respond to general correspondence from HS/club basketball coaches, recruits, and family as allowed by NCAA (1)
- Targeted letters to juniors/seniors (3)
- Letters to family (3)
- Letters to recruits' coaches (1)
- Social media: Facebook/blogs, Twitter, Instagram (1)
- Phone calls and texts making direct contact with recruits (1/2)
- Emails to recruits (1)

Evaluate Talent
- Assess Stanford's talent needs (2)
- Access recruiting services (1)
- Watch and evaluate unsolicited tapes of players (1)
- Plan recruiting trips, including personnel assignments to watch/evaluate talent based upon research of games, tournaments, clinics, etc. (3)
- Evaluate talent based upon Stanford assessment tool(s) (3)
- Rank recruits according to talent and need (3)

Assess Academic Potential
- Gather potential recruits' data on GPA, standardized test scores (2)
- Make preliminary assessment as to likelihood of being admitted by Stanford (2/3)
- Assist high probability recruits in completing application for admission (3)
- Communicating with admissions on progress of application for admission (3)
- Communicating admission/non-admission to applicants (no person except the head coach ever makes this call—yet VanDerveer will explain to protégés how she communicates this sensitive information)

Special Projects Conducted to Separate Stanford from Other Top Basketball Programs
- Creative mailings: quotes, puzzles, wanted posters, did you know, etc. (1)
- Involving team in recruiting process (2/3)

Campus Visitations
- Schedule travel logistics (2)
- Plan and execute activities (2)
- Campus tours (1/2)
- Formally meet with parents and recruits (2/3)

Home Visitations
- Schedule home visits and travel logistics (2)
- Travel to and visit with recruits, their families, and coaches (2/3)

Post-Signing Contact with Recruits
- Logistical contacts (e.g., housing, academic advising) (1/2)
- Social contacts (following HS academic and basketball progress, etc.) (1)
- Basketball logistics (e.g., conditioning, skill development) (1)

FIGURE 9.2. Ranking of difficulty and order of protégé assignments for subtasks for recruiting: Rank of "1" is entry level assignment; rank of "2" represents modestly complex skill; rank of "3" is advanced skill/responsibility

involves team collaboration of dissecting film, identifying individual and team strengths, determining priorities for skills training, integrating scouting priorities into practice plans, identifying key plays and defenses to be taught and relative drills, and allocation of teaching roles. Each task can be ranked according to relative complexity/difficulty, and assigned to new coaching members by likelihood of success (see example, Figure 9.2). Actual assignments are adjusted based upon assessment of the talents new coaches possess when joining the team. Further, all coaching assignments are subject to the permissive or restrictive NCAA guidelines.

Mentees may progress through stage assignments as they master skills, though not necessarily in a linear or non-overlapping fashion. Importantly, tasks are not simply assigned, but scaffolded. For example, letter writing is not just a means of communicating content, but a means of communicating the Stanford Way itself. That is, a letter represents the Stanford culture in terms of linguistic precision and conveys the program philosophy. Initially, new letter writers will be given examples of letters to recruits and their families. In fact, a letter-writing series has already been developed, and protégés may adapt these letters rather than "reinventing the wheel." Subsequent drafts are reviewed and edited by a veteran member of the coaching staff prior to a letter's being mailed. This oversight continues until a protégé demonstrates sufficient mastery. At the same time this skill is being mastered, new tasks are assigned and similarly scaffolded.

The Stanford head coach is not the only mentor, and coaches are not the only protégés. Every member of the Stanford program plays a part in the teaching and learning process. For example, although Head Coach VanDerveer sees herself as ultimately responsible for development of the entire community, relationships are not hierarchical, but interdependent. Associate Head Coach Amy Tucker provides guidance and support to those subordinate to her. At the same time, her advisement of Coach VanDerveer is both expected and valued. In fact, as the recruiting coordinator, Tucker is considered the team's expert, and is, therefore, a mentor to both VanDerveer and other members of the team. In this way, bidirectional mentoring weaves and binds all strands together, strengthening the organization.

In Practice

From the beginning, new members of the Stanford basketball team are invited into the culture. The most important and ongoing aspect of this invitation is the opportunity to sit in coaching planning meetings. Here, all the secrets of coaching are revealed—strategy, philosophy, psychology, and decision making. These meetings are daily and sometimes last two to three hours. The coaching team reviews film, plans practices, discusses talents, and provides each other with feedback on coaching behavior. All coaches have the duty and opportunity to take center stage in (among other things) diagramming plays, critiquing video, and evaluating player roles and contributions.

The Stanford Way of mentoring is an immersion model, whereby protégés are expected to be a part of "all things" according to their respective levels of knowledge and skill development. In other words, protégés learn the business through purposeful engagement in authentic and relevant tasks and persistent observation of veterans of the staff. Moreover, participation is highly collaborative, with all members of the Stanford team committed to each other. As an example, one new coach lacked the sophistication in technology needed to break down tapes, so the video technologist stepped up to provide both training and most of the actual work until the protégé became competent and confident at a task that a majority of coaches are proficient at upon hire. This interdependency is a part of a winning formula at Stanford—if everyone is helping everyone be their best, this will give Stanford the best chance of being successful on the court.

There are two caveats about the mentorship philosophy at Stanford that bear discussion. First, VanDerveer believes that one variable contributing to the demise of females in coaching is a relative intolerance of females who have encountered a rough period in coaching. Women who have been fired from a position as head basketball coach find that second chances are rare, as compared to those given men in coaching. Stanford feels it is important for the game to keep highly competent women in coaching and encourages their reentry into the game, either by directly hiring or by providing professional support of or networking for meaningful reentry into the profession. In one instance, the head coach of a top Division I program was released when her contract expired. VanDerveer invited her to Stanford and hired her as part of the staff for a year. The next year, with her feet on the ground and confidence regained, this woman was hired to coach another struggling program. She quickly rebuilt the program to contention, and subsequently challenged Stanford in the second round of the NCAA tournament (Stanford prevailed).

A second Stanford approach to basketball is an open-door advocacy for the game. That is, anyone who has a passion for basketball is a welcome beneficiary of formal or informal mentorship. Outside of a specific game plan, no play, no strategy, no philosophy of the game is so sacred that it will not be shared. High school, college, and professional coaches call VanDerveer for ideas and advisement. A young coaching staff at Penn State University, consistently a top-20 team, has been mentored annually by VanDerveer in the off-season.

Coaches and prospective coaches are invited to watch most practices and video sessions and meet directly with her and other members of the team. One season, the head coach at San Jose State attended every single practice. Even at her summer camps, Tara VanDerveer offers after-hours coaching clinics for camp counselors. There is no time that she won't take the time to grow the game. Furthermore, this professional generosity is not gender-specific. Men and women seek mentorship and are granted access to the full measure of knowledge and wisdom available—that is the Stanford Way.

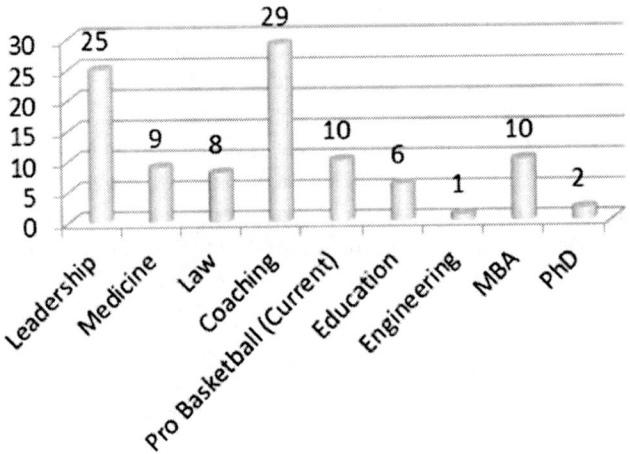

FIGURE 9.3. Current career positions and accomplishments of former Stanford women's basketball (107 total) who played for VanDerveer (1986-2013). Source: http://www.stanfordfbc.org/FBCFiles/alumni_alphabetical.htm

Outcomes

Proof of the mentoring efficacy of the Stanford Way is found in the accomplishments of those who have been a part of the system. While the primary focus

TABLE 9.1. Former Stanford Women's Basketball Players (out of 107 total former players) who have coached or are currently (2013) coaching basketball or working in other basketball-related professions such as broadcasting (1986–2013). Source: http://www.stanfordfbc.org/FBCFiles/alumni_alphabetical.htm

	Division I	Other College	K-12	Other Basketball Career	Total
Head Coach	4	1 + [1]	9		15
Other Coach	6 + [6]	[1]	1		14
Other Basketball				8	8
Retired Coach	6*	2*			
Assistant Stanford	5*				
Total	16	3	10	8	37

[] Past Coach
*Duplicate Entry

of this chapter is on the mentorship of women in coaching, the more important vision is in the mentorship of women in general. Evidence of the impact of the Stanford Way comes from the postgraduate accomplishments of her players as professionals and coaches (see Figure 9.3 and Table 9.1). Further evidence is provided in the career opportunities created for coaching protégés. Of the 14 former assistant coaches who were mentored under the Stanford Way, 10 became coaches elsewhere and two became executives in the Women's National Basketball Association (WNBA). Of the 10 who coached elsewhere, eight became head coaches of Division I women's basketball programs and/or the WNBA, including prestigious positions at the University of Washington, University of California–Berkley, and University of Wisconsin. Four of these coaches were invited to be part of the Stanford team after being fired elsewhere; three of these rescued coaches later became head coaches at Division I programs after leaving Stanford.

THEORETICAL ANALYSIS OF THE STANFORD WAY

It is possible to analyze the Stanford Way by using Kram's (1985) framework of functions of mentorship (Bower, 2010). Kram posited two aspects of mentoring—career-related and psychosocial:

Career-Related Functions

1.   *Sponsorship* is when a head coach helps promote the talent and potential of an emerging coach by highlighting her/his abilities. This happens at the end of the process, once Stanford protégés have demonstrated mastery and are prepared for other coaching opportunities where they might use their talents more independently.
2.   *Exposure/visibility* is a networking function whereby an emerging coach is introduced to important figures in coaching. This stage also occurs deep in the process. As a part of the Stanford experience, protégés meet other coaches at practices, conferences, and the NCAA tournament.
3.   *Protection* of emerging coaches keeps their workload reasonable. Clearly, the easy-to-challenging Stanford approach to task assignment is consistent with this principle.
4.   *Coaching* skills in basketball execution are developed with respect to scouting, recruiting, teaching, and so on. An immersion model of mentorship at Stanford exposes protégés to all essential aspects of coaching. Moreover, consistent high expectations ensure that these skills are mastered at a high level.
5.   *Challenging assignments* provide safe risk-taking so that emerging coaches develop self-confidence and competency. Stanford is one of a handful of elite programs in NCAA basketball. To remain in its lofty position is more challenging than one might imagine. Additionally, success leads to confidence, and success is in abundance.

Psychosocial Functions

1. *Role modeling* requires that the head coach be valued and respected by the emerging coach in terms of skills, values, and philosophy.
2. *Acceptance and confirmation* builds confidence and trust, and is based upon encouragement and support provided by the mentor.
3. *Counseling* helps the emerging coach work through personal problems that may interfere with success.
4. *Friendship* provides a context for shared experiences and builds a foundation for communication.

Three C's and the Stanford Way

Interdependence is fundamental to human relationships as "the 'interpersonal reality' within which specific motives are activated, toward which cognition is oriented, and around which interaction unfolds" (Rusbult, Kumashiro, Coolsen, & Kirchner, 2004, p. 138). Mentorship efficacy, then, relies on the degree of interdependence between mentor and protégé. The degree of interdependence between mentor and emerging coach is thought to increase when there is an increase in the 3Cs (Jowett & Nezlek, 2011): *closeness*—affective ties based upon trust, appreciation and respect; *commitment*—mutual motivation to maintain relationship over time; and *complementarity*—cooperation based upon responsiveness and willingness to interact.

It is clear from the description above that the Stanford Way is compatible with the 3Cs. As mentioned, from the beginning protégés begin building an interpersonal foundation as they are folded into the Stanford culture—the Stanford family.

CONCLUSIONS

The story of women's NCAA basketball is one of irony. A federal law that promised to open doors for women led to a pattern of hiring in coaching that has closed doors. Purposeful mentorship is a necessary solution to reopening those doors. This chapter provides a description of one mentoring model—the Stanford Way. Principles and practices of this model are compatible with theoretical frameworks that provide direction in mentoring. Still, much greater commitment to and understanding of best mentoring practices are needed if women are to fulfill the promise of Title IX.

REFERENCES

Acosta, R. V., & Carpenter, L. J. (2008). *Women in intercollegiate sport: A longitudinal study—A thirty-one year update 1977–2008*. West Brookfield, MA: National Association for Girls and Women.

Anderson, P. M. (2013). Gender equity forty years later: A look at Title IX's impact on American sport. *International Sports Law Journal, 13*(1–2), 1–6. doi: 10.1007/s40318-013-0001-9.

Bloom, G. A., Durand-Bush, N., Schinke, R. J., & Salmela, J.H. (1998). The importance of mentoring in the development of coaches and athletes. *International Journal of Sport Psychology, 29*, 267–281.

Bower, G. G. (2010). The examination of mentoring relationship between the head coach and assistant coaches of women's basketball teams. *Advancing Women in Leadership, 31*, 1–7.

Collins, J. (2001). *Good to great: Why some companies make the leap...and others don't.* New York, NY: Harper Collins Publishers Inc.

Cooky, C., & Lavoi, N. M. (2012). Playing but losing women's sports after Title IX. *Contexts, 11*(1), 42–46.

Cunningham, G. B., & Sagas, M. (2002). The different effects of human capital for male and female Division I basketball coaches. *Research Quarterly for Exercise and Sport, 73*, 489–495.

Dungy, T., & Whitaker, N. (2010). *The mentor leader: Secrets to building people and teams that win consistently.* Carol Stream, IL: Tyndale House Publishers.

Escobedo, D. (2012). *Trailblazer in women's athletics reflects on Title IX.* United States Sports Academy. Retrieved from http://ussa.edu/news/trailblazer-in-womens-athletics-reflects-on-title-ix/

Gogol, S. (2002). *Hard fought victories. Women coaches making a difference.* Terre Haute, IN: Wish.

Hattery, A. J. (2012). They play like girls: Gender and race (in)equity in NCAA sports. *Wake Forest Journal of Law & Policy, 2*, 247–533.

Jones, R. L., Harris, R., & Miles, A. (2009). Mentoring in sports coaching: A review of the literature. *Physical Education and Sport Pedagogy, 14*(3), 267–284.

Jowett, S., & Nezlek, J. (2011). Relationship interdependence and satisfaction with important outcomes in coach-athlete dyads. *Journal of Social and Personal Relationships, 29*(3), 287–301. doi: 10.1177/0265407511420980

Kilty, K. (2006). Women in coaching. *The Sport Psychologist, 20*(2), 222–234.

Kram, K. E. (1985). *Mentoring at work.* Glenview, IL: Scott Foresman.

Krane, V., & Barber, H. (2005). Identity tensions in lesbian intercollegiate coaches. *Research Quarterly for Exercise and Sport, 76*, 67–82.

Nash, C. (2003). Development of a mentoring system within coaching practice. *Journal of Hospitality, Leisure, Sport & Tourism Education, 2*(2), 39–48.

Norman, L. (2010) Feeling second best: Elite women coaches' experiences. *Society of Sport Journal, 27*(1), 89–104.

O'Reilly, J., & Cahn, S. K. (Eds.). (2012). *Women and sports in the United States: A documentary reader.* UPNE.

Rusbult, C. E., Kumashiro, M., Coolsen, M. K., & Kirchner, J. L. (2004). Interdependence, closeness, and relationships. In D. J. Mashek, & A. Aron (Eds.), *Handbook of closeness and intimacy* (pp. 137–162). Mahwah, NJ: Lawrence Erlbaum.

Sagas, M., Paetzold, R., & Ashley, F. (2005). Relational demography in coaching dyads. *Physical Educator, 62*(2), 103–112.

United States, Department of Education, Office for Civil Rights. (1998, August). *Title IX and Sex Discrimination. Title IX*. Retrieved from http://www2.ed.gov/about/offices/list/ocr/docs/tix_dis.html

United States Sports Academy. (2012, August 15). *Trailblazer in women's athletics reflects on Title IX*. Retrieved from https://ussa.edu/news/trailblazer-in-womens-athletics-reflects-on-title-ix/

CHAPTER 10

A LEARNING OUTCOMES MODEL FOR MENTORING ADJUNCT FACULTY

Richard G. Maybee

ABSTRACT

Largely in response to economic issues, universities of higher education have increased their hiring of part-time adjunct instructors. In 2011, adjunct faculty accounted for 50% of instructors in degree-granting institutions. Studies indicate that adjunct instructors have less access to faculty development resources, may not have office space to meet with students, and have less prestige than their full-time counterparts. These and other important characteristics of adjunct positions are typically not well addressed by institutional administrators. In response to unmet needs of adjuncts, a learning-outcomes model for adjunct mentoring is proposed as part of the solution. The model is based on a one-to-one, full-time faculty-to-adjunct relationship, although it could be adapted to a group environment. The model offers five representative communication tools as vehicles to achieve five representative learning outcomes. An important feature of the model is its flexibility to use revised and/or new communication tools and learning outcomes beyond those offered. Criteria for a good adjunct mentor program are given to assist departments, deans, and institutional faculty development efforts. The model holds heuristic value for helping to meet adjunct instructor needs.

Mentoring for the Professions: Orienting Toward the Future, pages 187–203.

187

INTRODUCTION

In an effort to cut costs, institutions of higher education today have increased their absolute and proportional use of part-time instructors (Perez & Litt, 2012). According to the National Center for Education Statistics' *Digest of Educational Statistics* (2012), part-time adjunct faculty in 2011 accounted for 50% of all faculty teaching in degree-granting institutions of higher education. A survey report by Hart Research Associates conducted for the American Federation of Teachers (2010) indicated that this percentage is higher in community colleges, with 70% or more of the instructional workforce in those institutions represented by adjuncts.

Contingent, part-time higher education faculty members will be referred to as *adjunct faculty* or *adjuncts* in this chapter's discussion. Common job titles include "lecturer," "instructor," or "adjunct professor." Although institutions of higher education use different terms to refer to adjuncts, and although their employment may be short-term or long-term, these faculty members receive part-time contracts that specify term-by-term or limited-time service for a particular rate of pay. Adjuncts are not eligible for tenure or long-term contracts and usually are not eligible for promotion. Job benefits, such as health insurance, are often not offered to adjunct faculty.

The use of adjuncts will probably continue to increase. According to Terry Hartle, senior vice president of the American Council on Education, the continuing increase is primarily in response to economic conditions (Raab, 2013). Cutbacks to higher education and rising benefit costs increase pressure for employing more adjuncts (Perez & Litt, 2012). In "The Adjunct Explosion," McArdle (2006) quotes Christian Gregory, a highly regarded adjunct English instructor at Auburn University, who offers his perspective on changes in institutional behavior toward adjunct instructors: "In the early 90's, universities began to adopt the management techniques of business: outsourcing to minimize labor costs. The easiest way to do that? Increase adjuncts" (p. 159).

Not only is their employment more precarious that that of other faculty members, but adjunct faculty often complain that they are marginalized by the institutions they serve. In addition to receiving no or few benefits, they often are hired just before the beginning of a term, get little support from their departments or full-time colleagues, and rarely receive faculty development opportunities (Kezar, 2012). Despite these and other less than desirable conditions, adjuncts continue to seek employment and do what they can to survive while meeting the teaching requirements of the institutions that employ them.

This chapter first examines adjunct faculty needs. Second, it proposes a model for mentoring adjuncts based on communication tools and learning outcomes derived from those adjunct needs. Third, it suggests a set of criteria for operating a successful adjunct mentoring program.

ADJUNCT FACULTY NEEDS

Are the complaints of adjunct instructors justified? Is there evidence supporting these concerns? Research suggests that there is a strong basis in reality for a broad spectrum of adjunct faculty needs.

Hutti, Rhodes, Allison, and Lauterbach (2007), in response to concerns for adjunct faculty retention and appreciation, conducted a survey sent to 278 part-time faculty members at the University of Louisville. The majority of the respondents had taught at the university for one to six years, and 66% had received prior training on teaching methodologies. Based on the survey responses, the top six learning needs were (1) "Facilitating student engagement in the classroom"; (2) "Instructional design"; (3) "Diversity in the classroom"; (4) "Teaching with technology;" (5) "Testing and evaluation"; and (6) "Online learning" (p. 33). In a second needs assessment of 67 part-time faculty members who participated in a part-time faculty institute, Hutti and associates (2007) found the top six learning needs to be (1) "Teaching to different learning styles"; (2) "Strategies for enhancing active learning"; (3) "Motivating students"; (4) "Teaching for deeper learning"; (5) "The art of leading an effective discussion"; and (6) "Engaging the quiet student" (p. 36). It should be noted that the above needs are strongly weighted toward pedagogical issues due to the identified purpose of both surveys, which focused on instructional needs.

Nolan, Siegrist, and Richard (2007) reported on the development of the five-year success plan for part-time faculty at Delgado Community College (March, 2005) at Delgado Community College in New Orleans. This plan utilized information from two focus groups—one for part-time faculty and another for supervisors of part-time faculty. The outline of the comprehensive college-wide plan was developed during a workshop led by an external consultant. The office of faculty and staff development and the faculty evaluation and improvement instruction committee produced the final plan, which identified eight goals based on the most common needs of adjunct faculty at the community college. It is clear that adjunct faculty needs were listened to and covered a range of important issues framed, in the plan, in terms of goals addressing adjunct faculty needs for the following:

- recognition and appreciation "of the impact part-time faculty have on student success, recruiting and retention"
- to "feel valued, supported and included...a sense of belonging"
- "a space of their own and access to the classrooms in which they teach"
- "orientation...that meets their needs"
- "training and [to] exhibit familiarity with administrative policy and procedure"
- "learning-centered, instructional enhancement activities"
- "opportunities to interact with other part- and full-time faculty"
- "recognition and/or events that demonstrate appreciation and recognition of the contributions of part-time faculty" (Nolan et al., 2007, pp. 90–91).

After a reorganization and an expansion of its mission in 2004, Shepherd University, Shepherdstown, West Virginia, found, in the fall of 2005, that its part-time faculty outnumbered full-time members by 50%. Part-time faculty taught nearly 50% of the university's 100-level courses and nearly 40% of its general education courses (Renninger, Holiday, & Carter, 2007). In response to this information, a training series and guidebook were proposed to increase Shepherd University's adjunct faculty members' awareness of campus resources available to assist students. In 2006, the proposal was adopted, and a committee composed of a cross-section of university staff and faculty was formed to assess adjunct faculty needs. A training session was scheduled, and a campus-wide survey of adjunct faculty and department chair needs was conducted. Information from the survey was used to develop the "Guide for New Faculty at Shepherd University" and to provide content for a training event. Numerous adjunct faculty needs emerged from the responses to the survey:

- information about media and library resources
- results of outcomes research on the effectiveness of various teaching practices and classroom management
- information about organizational structure, staff, key contacts and phone numbers, and resources locations
- information about basic procedures, pay periods, grading, and add/drop processes
- information about teaching, testing, lecturing strategies, and information about student motivation
- information about technology in the classroom
- more frequent communication among members of departments
- access to office space, computer, and printer
- to be provided with the school handbook and schedule

The response to the subsequent adjunct training event was "overwhelmingly positive" (Renninger et al., 2007, p. 205). Renninger and associates report that adjunct faculty "felt they were receiving information, recognition, and attention that had not previously been given to them," and they found the seminar "very informative," "inspirational," and "much needed" (p. 205). Attendees also reported that they were able to meet and collaborate with other adjunct faculty. Many in attendance indicated that they planned to use information from the training in their upcoming course preparation and syllabi.

Forbes, Hickey, and White (2010) report on a survey of adjunct nursing school faculty needs at Adelphi University with 65 respondents. At the time of the survey, adjunct faculty development consisted mainly of unstructured and informal oversight. The school offered a one-hour, non-mandatory orientation program. The survey included open-ended questions asking about suggestions for orientation and obstacles to teaching. The results were content-analyzed and revealed the following under the cluster of "orientation": the need for "written guidelines," "help with technology," and "a more available 'go-to' person" (p. 120). A question asking about "obstacles to teaching" yielded three clusters: "communication," "feeling isolated," and "lack of guidance" (p. 120). Under the cluster, "communication," the following problems were noted: "unclear communication," "inconsistent messages," and "inaccurate information" (p. 120). Under the cluster "feeling isolated," several needs were revealed: "limited contact with faculty," "not knowing 'who's who,'" and "no one around to help" (p. 120). Under the cluster of "lack of guidance," adjunct faculty needs included "student roster confusion" and "technology help" (p. 120). Forbes and associates (2010) concluded that "role ambiguity was identified by the responses of adjunct faculty relating to inconsistencies regarding guidelines, unclear expectations, inconsistent messages" (p. 121). Almost all adjuncts indicated that "orientation was inadequate" and that written guidelines would be useful (p. 121).

According to Forbes and associates (2010), as a result of the survey and input from key administrators, five major categories of adjunct-related initiatives were developed and implemented at Adelphi University over a two-year period: (1) "creating an overall infrastructure for adjunct faculty needs," (2) "formal orientation and staff support," (3) "faculty course coordinators," (4) "integrating adjunct faculty into the school's total faculty," and (5) "adjunct faculty and formal coursework for development" (p. 123).

These efforts show that careful research can result in the promotion of solutions directed at meeting the real needs of adjunct instructors. It should be noted that when there has been little response to adjunct needs, instances of adjunct faculty organizing have occurred. For example in 2011, the adjunct faculty at St. Joseph's University in Philadelphia, concerned about "low pay and a lack of job security and health benefits" formed an association to address these issues (June, 2012, p. 7). Leaders of the association met with university administrators and received raises and grant money for financial assistance to attend conferences when they present a paper.

From her position as professor and chair of history at North Seattle Community College, Nutting (2003) reflected on a number of obstacles negatively influencing effective teaching by adjunct instructors. Among these obstacles is lack of space for adjuncts, who often have no on-campus place where they can meet with students, work, or store materials. Another obstacle involves oversight: "Seldom do full-time faculty or administrators mentor part-timers, observe them regularly, or evaluate their work" (p. 36). Few adjuncts receive support for professional development, according to Nutting, or "get to vote on campus initiatives, new hires, policy changes or union contracts that affect them" (p. 36). She also noted that part-time faculty often are "excluded from committee and college meetings, institutional searches and even division and department meetings, mailing lists, and mailboxes" (pp. 36–37). Nutting observed that adjunct faculty members are seldom recognized for excellent teaching, for publishing, or for service. She noted that faculty adjuncts receive little collegial support from full-time faculty, some of whom regard part-time faculty as "substandard" (p. 37). Nutting also found that few part-timers "get to assess the institutions where they work or make suggestions on how to improve teaching and learning in their disciplines or to provide support services to students" (p. 37). Nutting (2003) suggests that remedies include being more collegial, improving communications, being more inclusive in institutional affairs, and improving mentoring.

Finally, in her 1998 doctoral dissertation, Merodie Anne Hancock (1998) reports on the results of the in-depth, three-round Delphi technique she used to survey adjunct professor needs at Old Dominion University in Norfolk, Virginia. Hancock's third-round survey of 57 respondents resulted in sixteen items with means ranging from 2.7–3.9 on a five-point scale. The top eight ranked adjuncts needs, with means from 3.7 to 3.9, are listed below:

- "Opportunities for peer support and knowledge exchange...and collegiality" (p. 56)
- "Training in academic use of computer technology to include hardware, presentation and discipline specific software, Internet, on-line library" (p. 56)
- "Professional development: opportunities to attend, with financial assistance and certificate training" (p. 58)
- "Ways to provide inputs on textbook selection course development, and faculty feedback to department chairs" (p. 57)
- "Informative sessions on methods of accessing support equipment, staff, supplies, etc., particularly during off-hours when adjuncts are on campus" (p. 56)
- "How to enhance learning for adult and traditional students with use of technology" (p. 56)
- "Ongoing faculty development program addressing topics such as syllabus development and course requirements and objectives" (p. 58)
- "Orientation meeting/literature for adjuncts to cover...university policies and procedures" (p. 56)

Hancock's (1998) results from Old Dominion University are highly consistent with other adjunct faculty needs assessments. Hopefully, institutions of higher education are responding to the plight of adjunct instructors with programs that ameliorate these discriminating practices.

The needs discussed in the research studies above can be summarized as eight themes of faculty development. Some of the needs were mentioned more frequently in the literature, yet upon reflection, all seem equally important:

1. Need for adjunct faculty orientations and written material covering, at a minimum, policies, procedures, key persons, resources, and expectations

2. Need for adjunct instructors to have access to basic resources, such as work space, office space to meet with students, supplies, copying, and assistance

3. Need for collegiality with full-time staff, fellow adjuncts, and a sense of belonging to the institution

4. Need for mentoring that allows the adjunct to observe good teaching and to be evaluated on his or her teaching

5. Need for research-based information on the teaching effectiveness of different teaching methodologies, classroom management, and student motivation

6. Need for assistance with understanding and operating classroom technology

7. Need for specific knowledge of student-centered, participative teaching techniques and guidance on designing better tests, evaluations, assessments, and rubrics

8. Need for respect, recognition, feeling valued, and appreciation for good teaching

MENTORING: ONE FACULTY DEVELOPMENT APPROACH TO MEETING ADJUNCT NEEDS

Calls for faculty development often fall on deaf ears due to low institutional priorities and budget constraints. Yet some perceive faculty development as a high priority. Altany (2011), for example, notes that faculty development is a key to faculty motivation and vitality. Altany concludes, "Professional development promotes faculty responsibility for continuous career-long growth based not only on the trial and error of experience, but also on theory, research, and professional collaboration with colleagues" (p. 6). Adjunct instructors, as well as other faculty members, are in need of faculty development opportunities through which they can learn about learning, about teaching, about students, and about themselves.

When institutions of higher education respond to adjunct faculty needs in development programs, they tend to do so in two ways and to varying degrees: adjunct orientations and handbooks and adjunct mentoring programs (Ziegler & Reiff, 2006). Most of the literature suggests that both orientations and handbooks are optimal for full adjunct and new faculty development (Howard & Hintz, 2002; West, Borden, Bermudez, Hanson-Zalot, Amorim, & Marmion, 2009). Adjunct faculty mentoring can be defined as occurring when "a mentor demonstrates behaviors of guiding, nurturing, and modeling for the continued advancement" of the mentee (Smith & Zsohar, 2007, p. 184). Typically, in mentoring programs, seasoned faculty member are mentors of adjunct faculty (Culleiton & Shellenbarger, 2007). Although mentoring is often seen as a continuous process of professional development, short-term mentoring time frames may better fit the often inconsistent scheduling of adjunct instructors. Action plans are essential for short-term mentorships, but they play an important part in any adjunct mentoring program. The value of the action plan is that it provides a framework for conduct and evaluation of the mentor–mentee relationship experience. Action plans set forth in writing what is to be accomplished during the mentoring time period (Cohen, 2000). Without an action plan, accountability for success is limited to subjective impressions. Action plans make use of objectives in the form of specific learning outcomes. In addition, these plans can establish a schedule for mentor–mentee meetings; set the length of the meetings; and clarify acceptable communication roles, methods, and procedures. This section of the chapter presents a learning outcome-based model of adjunct faculty mentoring that incorporates various communication tools to facilitate desired outcomes (see Figure 10.1). With the mentor–mentee relationship as the core of the model, five communication tools are viewed as essential in facilitating five representative learning outcomes.

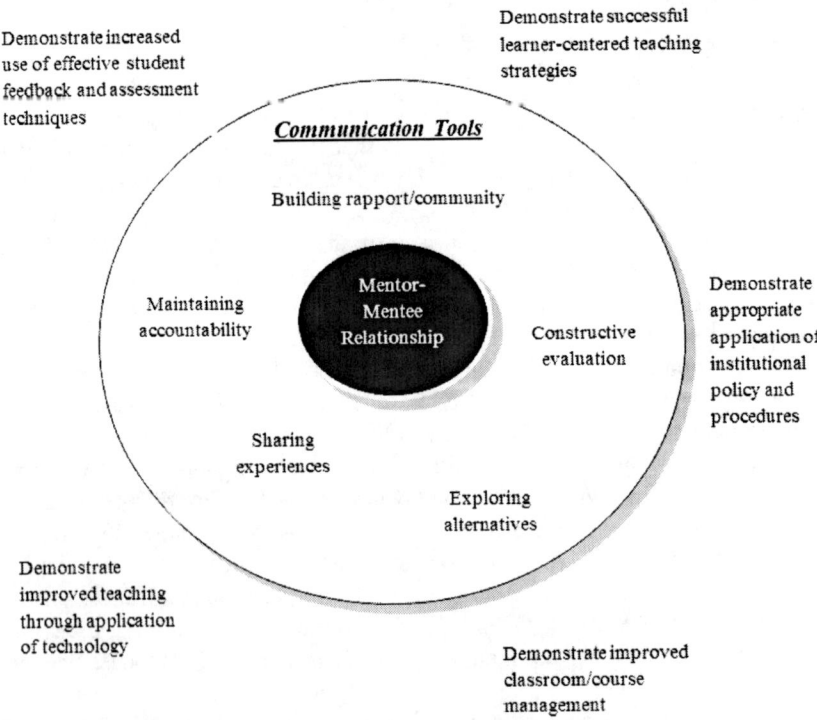

FIGURE 10.1. This figure represents a sample model reflecting the outcomes and communication tools used to process attaining the outcomes.

Communication Tools

Based on the adjunct needs previously discussed, the author developed the following five communication tools, which satisfy many of the functional and socioemotional needs of adjunct instructors. These tools serve to facilitate the process of attaining learning outcomes. These tools are common to healthy working relationships, a commonality that supports their importance in a mentor–mentee relationship.

Communication Tool One: Building rapport and community with full-time instructors and other adjuncts

Mentors and mentees can use empathic and active listening through which they seek to understand and accept the others' points of view, and show genuine interest in each other. Mentors can introduce adjuncts to full-time faculty and to other adjuncts to build rapport and a sense of community among faculty.

Communication Tool Two: Constructive evaluation of adjunct teaching and class management

Through observation and conversation, mentors can evaluate adjuncts' classroom questioning methods, attitudes, and behavior, critical thinking, ways of providing feedback to students, and teaching strategies. Mentors can also invite adjunct faculty to observe the mentor's classroom teaching and management style.

Communication Tool Three: Seeking alternative methods, attitudes, and techniques

Mentors can help adjuncts to understand proven methods and alternatives, set realistic expectations, and review contexts. They can help mentees to compare gains versus losses regarding classroom teaching and relational strategies.

Communication Tool Four: Sharing mutually relevant experiences between mentor and mentee

Mentors can share personal experiences and information relevant to the adjunct's needs, referring the adjunct to appropriate resources and making suggestions for alternative courses of action. Key to this communication tool is sensitivity to the mentees' needs and interests.

Communication Tool Five: Maintaining accountability for action plans, progress, introspection, and evaluation

Mentors should help adjuncts make action plans, record progress, and reflect upon and evaluate the mentoring relationship. Key to this communication tool is sensitivity to mentees' need for constructive feedback.

Learning Outcomes

Learning outcomes are critical to the success of the proposed model. They provide both a focus on the topics to be learned and the criteria for determining whether success in learning has been achieved. Learning outcomes provide the basis for evaluation of the mentor–mentee relationship, and accountability in the mentoring program. The learning outcomes in the proposed mentoring model were developed by the author and are based on common adjunct faculty needs as identified in the research. They are achieved through using the five communication tools listed above. The interaction process between a seasoned mentor and the adjunct mentee will utilize most, if not all, of the core communication tools. While other outcomes may occur, the dynamic interpersonal interaction in this model is directed toward achieving the following representative learning outcomes:

Learning Outcome One: Demonstrate successful learner-centered teaching strategies

Adjunct mentees can research and apply various teaching methodologies that are student-centered, active learning-based, and oriented toward student participation. Guidance for particular teaching strategies can be provided through the experiences of the mentors. The mentees can pilot a given teaching approach, and then the mentors, after observing the mentees in the classroom, can provide constructive feedback and coaching.

Learning Outcome Two: Demonstrate appropriate application of institutional policies and procedures

Certainly, this outcome is one of high priority among adjunct faculty. Knowing what to do and how to do it, according to established institutional policies and procedures, adds needed clarity to an often-overwhelming adjunct experience. This is especially true of the adjuncts' initial employment with the organization. Mentors can reinforce policies and procedures and can help adjunct faculty establish priorities. Mentors need to monitor the actions of the adjuncts in order to provide clarification when necessary. Mentors should make themselves available to adjuncts in order to facilitate the accomplishment of this outcome.

Learning Outcome Three: Demonstrate improved classroom/course management

Adjunct mentees can research best practices in classroom management, apply these to their teaching, and evaluate the effectiveness of the approaches in their classrooms. Mentors can coach adjunct mentees regarding those practices and give feedback after observing the mentees' teaching.

Learning Outcome Four: Demonstrate improved teaching by applying technology

This outcome, in part, depends on the specific kinds of technology and accessibility at the adjunct's college or university. In general, however, mentors can refer the adjuncts to the appropriate personnel who have responsibility for the technology. The institution needs to make the technology support staff available to the adjuncts during the times when the adjuncts are working. It is important that adjuncts assume responsibility for initiating requests for assistance well before the start of class. Mentors may have advice for adjunct mentees regarding technology based on successful applications from the mentors' own experience. This guidance may include presentation techniques or specific sites useful in teaching a particular class.

Learning Outcome Five: Demonstrate increased use of effective student feedback and assessment techniques

After consultation with their mentors, adjunct mentees can research best practices related to classroom feedback and student progress measurement as applied to a particular discipline. In addition, schools have different evaluation requirements, often at the departmental level. Adjunct mentees should query their mentors regarding appropriate evaluation methods for the course and department. For instance, the evaluation of student writing has seen a resurgence in the classroom and can be considered as a primary measure of academic progress. Mentors can view the results of student assessment and feedback strategies and give guidance to their mentees.

Alternative Model Configurations

The learning outcomes chosen for the representative model above were developed from the themes reflected in the literature on adjunct needs. Alternative configurations are possible in the model, such as reducing the overall number of learning outcomes and/or creating new learning outcomes not included in the representative model. Figure 10.2 provides a blank model, into which any number of communication tools and learning outcomes can be entered. The number and kind of learning outcomes can be fully customized to meet the needs of individual adjunct instructors or groups of adjuncts teaching in related disciplines. An alternative model could, for example, reduce the number of learning outcomes to just two, such as *demonstrate successful learner-centered teaching strategies* and *demonstrate improved classroom/course management*. This configuration would be especially appropriate when a short-term mentoring relationship is primarily focusing on classroom teaching and management.

Although the five communication tools are viewed as core processes for almost all mentor–mentee relationships, they too can be modified to meet particular department or institutional preferences. *Building rapport and community with full-time and other adjuncts*, for example, might be dropped as a communication tool when the primary focus in the mentoring relationship is on evaluating teaching and promoting good classroom management. Thus, the model is particularly useful in that it allows considerable flexibility, yet retains the essential idea that learning can occur best when specific learning outcomes are identified and a core of good communication skills is acknowledged as essential to facilitating the mentor–adjunct relationship.

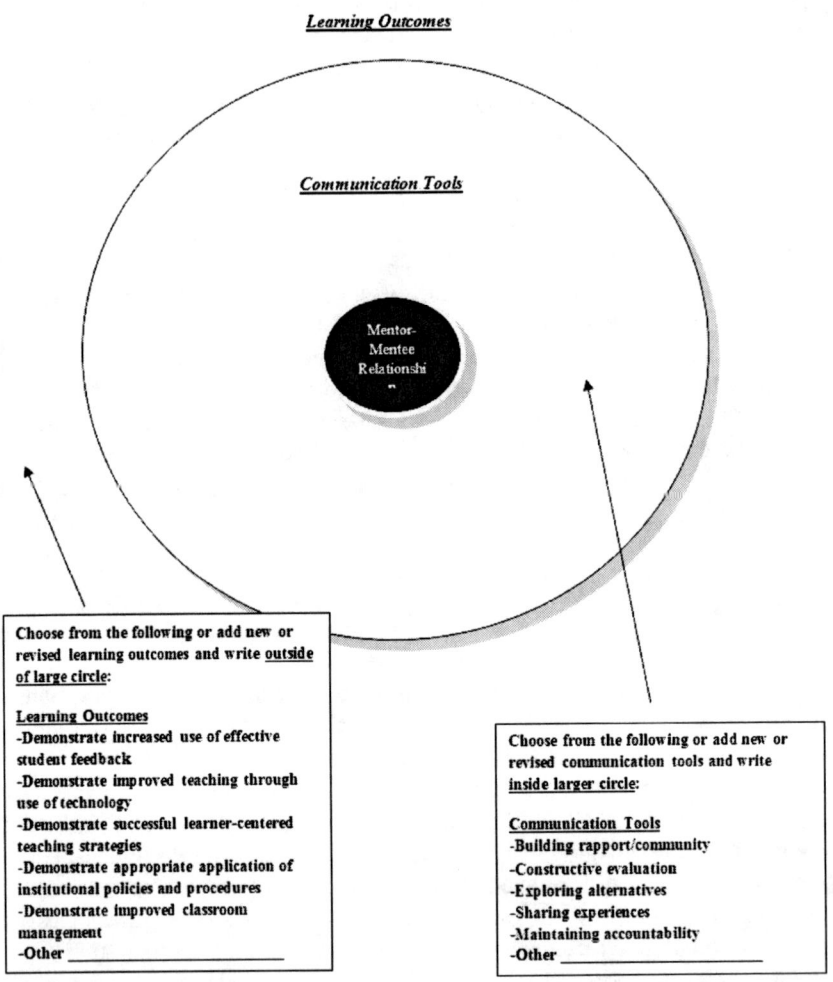

FIGURE 10.2.   Using this "build-your-own" model the desired learning outcomes are chosen from the box on the lower left and entered around the outside of the large circle. Communication tools are chosen from the box on the lower right and placed inside the large circle. The resultant model is then used to structure the focus of the mentor–mentee relationship relative to the desired outcomes and facilitative processes.

MENTOR–MENTEE COMMUNICATION CYCLES

It is important to understand that the learning outcomes mentoring model promotes a realistic view of the mentor–mentee relationship. The mentoring relationship is not a strictly task-oriented process. In the best relationships, there is considerable give-and-take, with participants often moving from task to socioemotional functions, as needed, to get the work accomplished and to maintain the relationship. This process, especially in the mentor–mentee relationship, can be viewed as involving different stages of communication. These stages, or cycles, often repeat over time during the relationship. Group dynamics literature provides a cyclic perspective on mentor–mentee relationships and is helpful to an understanding of the underlying process active in the learning outcomes model. Building on the successive stage development group dynamics theory of Tuckman (1965) and Tuckman and Jensen (1977), researchers believe that groups and relationships cycle through various stages, often reentering previous stages to meet an emerging need (Arrow, 1997; Wheelan & Hochberger, 1996). The following adaptation of the four basic stages in group development, identified by Wheelan and Hochberger (1996), can be applied to the faculty mentor–adjunct mentee relationship:

- The orientation stage usually occurs during the initial meeting, and the mentee typically agrees with the mentor's suggestions, demonstrating few conflicts.
- The conflict stage usually follows the orientation; the mentor and mentee begin expressing different views on issues until they reach agreement on how things should be done. This stage can be short or, depending on the nature of the relationship, can last for a number of meetings.
- The structure stage evidences cooperative attitudes and mutual input of mentor and mentee; they spend their meeting time planning how the tasks will be performed.
- The work stage constitutes the essential task work of the mentor–mentee relationship. The mentee reports on progress, and the mentor gives feedback with suggestions for corrections or new directions. Plans are revised and new plans created.

The length of each stage in the mentor–mentee relationship can vary in time— in minutes, hours, or days. There is often considerable cycling back and forth from one stage to another as the need for clarification occurs. In shorter-term relationships, there is a need to move to the work stage more quickly in order not to waste valuable time. Ideally, the majority of time is spent in the work stage, where productivity is at its highest. The concept of communication stages as operating in the learning outcomes model of the mentoring relationship is an important process dimension of the mentor–adjunct relationship.

Overview of Criteria for Effective Adjunct Mentoring Programs

Lastly, it seems relevant in the discussion of a mentoring model to include criteria for implementation of a workable adjunct mentoring program. Many readers may not understand the importance of a good working structure necessary to support a viable adjunct mentoring system. Research suggests that mentoring programs are best when they include the following elements (Johnson, 2007; Nolan et al., 2007; Zutter, 2007):

Administration and full-time faculty commitment

Without the commitment of school and department administration and full-time faculty, an adjunct mentoring program is hard to start and can quickly become ineffective.

An administrative coordinator with mentoring management software

A full- or part-time coordinator is essential to the successful operation of any adjunct mentoring system. Continuity and accessibility to management are important in coordinating mentor–mentee relationships. Establishing matching criteria, matching mentors and mentees, developing the structure for learning outcome plans, conducting evaluations, and relating to the administration are all essential responsibilities of a mentoring program coordinator. In addition, coordinating mentor–mentee pairs and plans is a primary function and may benefit from the use of appropriate software to help make efficient use of resources, for example, Chronus Mentor software at www.Chronus.com/software/chronus-mentor is designed to help manage mentoring programs.

A clearly defined matching process where similarity is a priority

Whenever possible, matching mentors and mentees along lines of similar interests can be beneficial to the mentoring experience (Russell & Adams, 1997).

Mentor and mentee orientations

Without orientations regarding roles and procedures, the program is likely to have difficulty getting off the ground and maintaining healthy progress.

Frequency and duration of contacts made clear

The heart of any mentor program is the contact between mentor and mentee, whether face-to-face, online, or by phone. These contacts should be structured with scheduled meetings and guidelines for contact that balance the needs of the mentee with the responsibilities of the mentor.

Established relationship boundaries and roles

Mentors and mentees, especially when they are of the opposite sex, need to establish clear role boundaries. Mentors should be assertive in clarifying boundaries at the beginning and during the relationship. Out-of-bounds behavior is not to be tolerated, as professional ethics and university policies apply to mentorships as fully as to other programs governed by the institution.

An updatable action plan/agreement with realistic priorities prepared at the beginning of the relationship

An essential part of a successful mentor program is to establish realistic learning outcomes according to mentee priorities. These outcomes should be measured and adjusted, if needed, as the relationship progresses.

Periodic evaluations and contact with mentor program coordinator

Accountability for progress is critical to any mentor program. In most cases, this involves providing periodic mentor and mentee reports to the mentor program coordinator. Problems can be resolved with the intervention of the program coordinator. It is important that both the mentor and mentee have access and trust in the mentoring program coordinator.

Summative program evaluation

At the end of each reporting period (e.g., term, semester, etc.) the program coordinator can report to his or her supervisor. The report should include the progress and results of the mentoring pairs working together during that term, as well as the overall results of the program during that period.

CONCLUSION

As expenses and enrollments continue to rise, institutions are hiring more adjunct instructors as a cost-saving measure. Adjunct faculty members have a variety of important needs that are identified in the research literature. As the number of adjunct faculty continues to increase, it is important for institutions of higher education to address these needs. Currently, most such efforts take the form of orientations/handbooks or mentoring programs. The learning outcomes mentoring model presented in this chapter can foster an effective, interactive, and dynamic mentor–mentee relationship. The core communication tools identified in the model can help adjuncts achieve the five learning outcomes and meet their relational, pedagogical, and technical needs—this is especially true for those new to an institution. Variations on the model allow for an alternative number and kind of learning outcomes, as well as alternatives for the communication tools to meet local needs. The primary value of the model, as discussed, is that it can serve as a heuristic for developing new approaches to mentoring programs. Overall, the learning outcomes mentoring model offers a flexible and useful approach to designing and implementing an adjunct faculty mentoring program.

TAKEAWAY: CUSTOM MODEL ORGANIZER

Figure 10.2 above demonstrates the possibilities for development of custom adjunct faculty learning-centered mentoring models to meet different adjunct faculty needs. When the mentor and adjunct develop an action plan, they can use this "build-your-own" organizer to create the learning outcomes that form the basis of the plan. They can also choose or create the specific communication tools they wish to use as the methods for reaching the learning outcomes. Each mentoring relationship is different, and thus, there is a need to customize the basic model of the action plan for each circumstance.

Using contents of the text boxes in the "build-your-own" model in Figure 10.2, desired learning outcomes can be chosen and entered around the outside of the larger circle. Revised or completely new learning outcomes can also be entered outside the larger circle. Communication tools can be selected and entered inside the larger circle. Revised or new communication tools can also be developed and added inside the larger circle as needed. Caution should be used in reducing the number of communication tools, as these are the primary means in academia for reaching the learning outcomes selected. The resulting model forms the basis for the action plan, objectives, and accountability process of the mentor–mentee relationship.

REFERENCES

Altany, A. (2011). Professional faculty development: The necessary fourth leg. *The Teaching Professor, 25*(6), 6.

American Federation of Teachers. (2010). A national survey of part-time/adjunct faculty. *American Academic, 2*, 3–15.

Arrow, H. (1997). Stability, bistability and instability in small group influence patterns. *Journal of Personality and Social Psychology, 72*, 75–85.

Cohen, N. (2000). *A step-by-step guide to starting an effective mentoring program.* Amherst, MA: HRD Press.

Culleiton, A., & Shellenbarger, T. (2007). Transition of a bedside clinician to a nurse educator. *MEDSURG Nursing, 16*(4), 253–257.

Forbes, M. O., Hickey, M., & White, J. (2010). Adjunct faculty development: Reported needs and innovative solutions. *Journal of Professional Nursing, 26*(2), 116–124.

Hancock, M. A. (1998). *Urban university adjunct faculty perceptions of professional development needs.* Norfolk, VA: Old Dominion University.

Howard, B. C., & Hintz, S. S. (2002, May). *Adjunct faculty orientation and mentoring: Developing and retaining the best!* Paper presented at the Annual Meeting of the national Institute for Staff & Organizational Development, Austin, TX.

Hutti, M. H., Rhodes, G. S., Allison, J., & Lauterbach, E. (2007). *Part-time faculty institute: Strategically designed and continually assessed.* In R. E. Lyons (Ed.), *Best practices for supporting adjunct faculty* (pp. 32–48). Bolton, MA: Anker Publishing Company.

Johnson, W. B. J. (2007). *On being a mentor: A guide for higher education faculty.* Mahwah, NJ: Lawrence Erlbaum.

June, A. W. (2012, November 5). Adjuncts build strength in numbers. *The Chronicle of Higher Education.* Retrieved from http://chronicle.com/article/Adjuncts-Build-Strength-in/135520/

Kezar, A. (2012). *Embracing non-tenure track faculty: Changing campuses for the new faculty majority.* New York, NY: Routledge.

McArdle, E. (2006). The adjunct explosion. *University Business.* Retrieved from http://universitybusiness.ccsct.com/page.cfm?p=159

National Center for Education Statistics. (2012). *Digest of education statistics,* Table 290. Retrieved from http://nces.ed.gov/programs/digest/d12/tables/dt12_290.asp

Nolan, G., Siegrist, C., & Richard, N. (2007). A mentoring network for adjunct faculty: From proposal to pilot to five-year plan. In R. E. Lyons (Ed.), *Best practices for supporting adjunct faculty* (pp. 81–106). Bolton, MA: Anker Publishing Company.

Nutting, M. M. (2003, Fall). Part-time faculty: Why should we care? *New Directions for Higher Education, 123,* 33–39.

Perez, S., & Litt, A. (2012, November). *The work of the university: The adjunct phenomenon.* Retrieved from http://www.academia.edu/2100902/The_Work_of_the_University:_The_Adjunct_Phenomenon

Raab, B. (2013, April 9). Meet your new professor: Transient, poorly paid. *In Plain Sight.* Retrieved from http://inplainsight.nbcnews.com/_news/2013/04/09/17658326-meet-your-new-professor-transient-poorly-paid?lite

Renninger, L., Holiday, S., & Carter, M. (2007). Initiating a support system for adjunct faculty: The first year. In R. E. Lyons (Ed.), *Best practices for supporting adjunct faculty* (pp. 199–216). Bolton, MA: Anker Publishing Company.

Russell, J. E. A., & Adams, D. M. (1997). The changing nature of mentoring in organizations: An introduction to the special issue on mentoring in organizations. *Journal of Vocational Behavior, 51,* 1–14.

Smith, J. A., & Zsohar, H. (2007). Essentials of neophyte mentorship in relation to faculty shortage. *Journal of Nursing Education, 48*(4), 184–186

Tuckman, B. W. (1965). Developmental sequences in small groups. *Psychological Bulletin, 63,* 384–399.

Tuckman, B. W., & Jensen, M. A. C. (1977). Stages of small group development revisited. *Group and Organizational Studies, 2,* 419–427.

West, M. M., Borden, C., Bermudez, M., Hanson-Zalot, M., Amorim, F., & Marmion, R. (2009). Enhancing the clinical adjunct role to benefit students. *Journal of Continuing Education in Nursing, 40*(7), 305–310.

Wheelan, S. A., & Hochberger, J. M. (1996). Validation studies of the group development questionnaire. *Small Group Research, 27,* 143–170.

Ziegler, C., & Reiff, M. (2006). Adjunct mentoring, a vital responsibility in a changing educational climate: the Lesley University adjunct mentoring program. *Mentoring and Tutoring, 14*(2), 247–269.

Zutter, C. (2007). Mentoring adjunct instructors: Fostering bonds that strengthen teaching and learning. In R. E. Lyons (Ed.), *Best practices for supporting adjunct faculty* (pp. 68–80). Bolton, MA: Anker Publishing Company.

CHAPTER 11

MENTORING DOCTORAL STUDENTS

Gregory D. Foley

ABSTRACT

This chapter addresses the formation of scholars via doctoral education. It considers the nature of doctoral education and the role of mentoring throughout the entire process—both the formal stages of the doctoral process and the many other occasions for mentoring in the formation process. The chapter interweaves theory and research with anecdotes and practical advice. It draws on the author's own mentoring of graduate students as well as recent perspectives on doctoral education in general and on doctoral study in mathematics education in particular. Although a main focus is on adviser as mentor—where "adviser" is taken to mean the major professor, supervisor, and committee chair of the emerging scholar who is pursuing a doctor of philosophy degree—other mentoring roles, such as class professor or committee member that are essential in graduate education are addressed. The chapter closes with a discussion of roles, goals, and benefits of mentoring doctoral students.

INTRODUCTION

Each individual begins doctoral study with a unique combination of prior knowledge, expertise, and experiences as well as tentative goals and aspirations. Thus,

Mentoring for the Professions: Orienting Toward the Future, pages 205–221.

the wise doctoral adviser will leverage the student's existing proficiencies; help the student develop new ones; induct the student into the academy and specialty; help the emerging scholar shape, clarify, and pursue a research agenda; and launch the newly fledged scholar on a productive career path. Despite such individualization based on a student's background and aims and despite the fact that one advising style does not fit all students or all situations, there is a clear goal in doctoral advising: the formation of a scholar who can advance the frontiers of knowledge.

Mentoring for the PhD begins during the process of responding to inquiries and reviewing applications, and it continues through graduation and beyond. The advice given while students are first beginning to consider doctoral studies is critical, as is the assistance when students seek employment once fully fledged. This essay considers the nature of doctoral education and the role of mentoring throughout the entire process. The chapter interweaves theory and research with anecdotes and practical advice.

- Readers will learn specific strategies for building a community of scholars among doctoral students.
- Readers will receive tips on how to help students learn the literature, learn the field of specialty, make professional presentations, and write for publication.
- Readers will receive advice on apprenticeships and other professional activities to complement course work, comprehensive exams, and the dissertation process.

A mentor is one who provides sage guidance to someone less experienced. According to the National Academy of Sciences (1997), a mentor is part adviser, part teacher, part role model, and even part friend. To provide a context for the role of mentor in doctoral education, the chapter begins with a discussion of the characteristics and aims of doctoral study. Next, mentoring students through their many stages in the process of earning a doctorate is considered; these include major rites of passage, such as taking comprehensive exams and writing the dissertation, as well as other important steps such as applying for the program and applying for employment upon completion of the degree. This is followed by a discussion of other occasions for mentoring that occur along the way. The chapter concludes with closing thoughts about roles, goals, and benefits of mentoring doctoral students.

THE NATURE AND PURPOSE OF DOCTORAL EDUCATION

A *doctor* is a deeply knowledgeable scholar who serves as a member of the community of creators and caretakers for a field of intellectual study. *Doctoral education* is the process of formation of such scholars and prepares them for the role of stewardship for the field (Golde, 2006; Walker, Golde, Jones, Bueschel, & Hutchings, 2008).

Thus, to understand doctoral education, it is essential to conceptualize the nature of an intellectual field. Many, perhaps most, modern fields of study are both disciplines and professions. Bass (2006) makes this case for the field of mathematics:

> Mathematics is a *discipline*—a domain of knowledge, an intellectual heritage with ancient roots, with language and methods for analysis and understanding of aspects of the worlds that we inhabit and experience. And mathematics is now a *profession* as well—an intellectual community dedicated to knowledge generation, application, conservation, and transmission, and interacting with other domains and institutions of learning and with the larger society. (p. 102)

My field—mathematics education—is the offspring of the ancient discipline of mathematics "(Reyes & Dossey, 2008; Reyes & Kilpatrick, 2001) and the ancient profession of teaching. This interdisciplinary area of study emerged as a field in its own right in the 1950s. To become a doctor of philosophy of mathematics education, an individual advances beyond being a master teacher of mathematics. A doctor is a scholar who creates new knowledge within a field of study and who serves as a steward of the discipline and a caretaker of the profession (Golde, 2006; Walker et al., 2008). This is true not just for mathematics or mathematics education, but in general. Nonetheless, in the spirit of Bass's (2006) list for mathematics, following is a list of what being a doctor comprises for mathematics education:

- Mastery of core knowledge in learning theory, curriculum and instruction, educational assessment, teacher education, and educational research methods
- Mastery of these same areas as they apply to teaching and learning mathematics, statistics, and mathematical modeling
- Working knowledge of mathematics, statistics, and mathematical modeling at the baccalaureate level in all three of these fields and at the master's level or beyond in at least one of these fields, plus an understanding of the history and philosophy of mathematics
- Pedagogical knowledge and technological pedagogical knowledge in mathematics, statistics, and mathematical modeling
- Working knowledge of the tools and methods of inquiry used in mathematics education
- Deep knowledge of the research literature in mathematics education as well as an understanding of the history and trends of school mathematics curriculum, instruction, assessment, and policy
- Judgment of the educational significance of emerging results in mathematics education

- The ability to ask and hone questions of educational significance in mathematics education and to design and conduct research to reduce the uncertainty of the answers to such questions
- Practical experience in designing and conducting small research projects or assisting with large research projects—before writing the dissertation proposal
- Practical experience in proposing and presenting talks and papers at conferences
- Practical experience in writing for publication in refereed professional journals
- Practical knowledge in developing curricula, teaching, supervising clinical experiences, conducting teacher professional development, and facilitating seminars
- Knowledge and disposition to mentor researchers in mathematics education and present the ideas of mathematics education to diverse audiences including school administrators, parents, and the general public

In addition, the doctoral student is well advised to establish a professional network of colleagues in mathematics education and to propose, conduct, and prepare a comprehensive written report of an individually designed research study addressing a significant educational issue that will advance the field of mathematics education and will prepare the scholar for future research.

To be sure, the list above sets an ideal standard—one that few doctoral students will have achieved by the time they graduate with the PhD, but this list serves several purposes. It clarifies the complexity and high expectations of doctoral education and provides a basis for developing similar lists for other fields of study. Each field would have similarly demanding desires for the knowledge, skills, and dispositions of its PhDs. The list suggests that the scope of doctoral study cannot be captured by a set of courses alone, nor by the dissertation alone, nor by apprenticeship alone, nor by any single activity, strategy, or method. These multifaceted goals demand a multitude of methods for their achievement. For purposes of this chapter, the list provides a framework for topics to be considered; that is, it serves as a list of areas for potential mentoring of doctoral students.

As Kwiram (2006) notes, mentoring is a natural fit for the formation of a scholar who is eager to learn:

> Education...works best when there is a strong motivation on the part of the student—a natural curiosity, an insatiable desire to understand, a question that just has to be answered. When this quest is coupled with an informed and inspiring mentor who can guide the intellectual exploration with the appropriate resources, one has an optimum learning environment: Aristotle at one end of the log and Alexander at the other! (p. 141)

It is difficult to imagine doctoral study without mentoring. The mentor–protégé relationship is at the heart of doctoral education.

The balance of the chapter examines the many forms that this relationship takes over the course of a student's journey through doctoral study. The next two sections of the chapter are organized according to the steps and components included in a doctoral program: first, mentoring during the progression of stages in the process, and second, other opportunities for mentoring along the way.

MENTORING ACROSS THE STAGES OF THE DOCTORAL PROCESS

Mentoring students through their many stages in the process of earning a doctorate calls for a variety of strategies. This part of the chapter begins with the earliest stage of students who are beginning to consider doctoral study; continues through the formal steps of obtaining approval for a program of study, completing written and oral comprehensive exams, and conducting and defending a dissertation; and concludes with post-degree considerations.

Mentoring Those Seeking Doctoral Study

Advising and mentoring persons who are contemplating doctoral study can take many forms. An undergraduate about to complete a program may ask about future study. Should the student jump immediately into graduate study or gain experience as a practitioner? As the National Academy of Sciences (1996) points out, there is no one-style-fits-all mentoring. The astute mentor is a good questioner and an excellent listener. There is no one best path for all students. The mentor observes, listens, probes, and helps the student understand his or her own motivations, interests, and desires as well as short-term and long-range objectives. The wise adviser gives advice that is in the student's best interest, in keeping with the student's strengths, weaknesses, personality, and situation.

Personal experience suggests that the optimal progression for a particular student might be to get a job and return for graduate study after seasoning and experience, or to pursue a master's degree in another department or at another university and then return for doctoral study. Mentoring options could include providing information about various programs, sending students to other professionals on campus, contacting a colleague at another institution, or writing letters of support or introduction.

An individual with a bachelor's degree and some years of experience still may benefit from a master's degree. This is certainly the case in mathematics education, though it is not true for every field of study (Golde & Walker, 2006). One of the very best doctoral students that I have ever encountered came to me in just such a situation. I advised that he seek and obtain a master's degree in mathematics before applying for doctoral study in mathematics education. This particular path has worked brilliantly for this individual, who has achieved virtually all of the proficiencies listed above.

Some students who possess a good deal of experience, a master's degree, and an overall strong background may have goals and interests that you and your institution cannot fulfill. The only fair thing to do is to direct the student elsewhere so that the student can be better served. A good mentor focuses on doing what is right for the student. Treat the student seeking your advice with care and compassion. And never let yourself get too busy to take time for your students and for persons making inquiries about your program.

Mentoring During the Application and Selection Process

Applications for doctoral programs typically are preceded by inquiries, sometimes a year or more in advance of the application. Taking time for inquiries is one of the best recruitment strategies in the long run. This advice from two of my own mentors—Alan Osborne and Richard J. Shumway—has helped me build the mathematics education PhD program at Ohio University.

Once a prospective student has made a formal application, give the application a careful reading and thoughtful consideration. Triangulate by getting the opinions of other colleagues even if this is not required at your institution. Conduct a face-to-face interview if possible; if not, use the Internet to simulate a face-to-face interview. Next to selecting new faculty colleagues, selecting doctoral students is the most important decision that a university department makes. This is a multi-year commitment of time and resources, both for the doctoral student and for the department. And like a faculty member, a doctoral student becomes an integral part of the department and someone with whom you will interact on a regular basis for many years. Ultimately, if successful, doctoral students will be formed into colleagues who will teach at sister institutions and who will be part of your profession and your professional network.

Mentoring as Doctoral Study Begins

As noted above, each person enters into doctoral study with a unique set of prior knowledge, expertise, and experiences. In order to form well-rounded scholars, the doctoral mentor builds on students' existing strengths and guides them through new challenges to help develop additional areas of capability. Pairing up a new student with a compatible mentor is key. Ideally, mentors adapt to meet the needs of the students in their charge. This does not mean mentors bow to the whims of students. On the contrary, for me, this has often meant "putting my foot down" or "digging in my heels," sometimes in new and creative ways.

I have adopted a policy of *absolute rigid flexibility*. That is, I stay firm on matters of principle, but am flexible in as many other ways as is reasonable. In mathematics education, for example, the standard writing style in most journals is that of the American Psychological Association (APA, 2010). To encourage students to learn APA style, to become comfortable with this style, and to develop as writers, I require them to write papers early and often, and I provide detailed feedback. The lack of flexibility in this regard pays dividends when students propose conference papers, write for publication, and work on their dissertations.

At Ohio University, we have new doctoral student orientations at the university, college, and department levels. And we invite new students to social events. Making expectations clear from the beginning, providing a sense of belonging, and offering opportunities to meet faculty and other students are first steps in the process of welcoming new students into the intellectual community—a community of which they will be a part for three or more years. As Walker and colleagues (2008) note, "Intellectual community is not simply a feel-good atmosphere.... Intellectual community serves multiple purposes, from improving knowledge production to reducing isolation and attrition" (p. 121).

Providing an appropriate first internship and the right mix of classes *ab initio* is important as well. Within the program of study, absolute rigid flexibility comes into play once again. Students are required to take some core classes (and eventually all of them), but not all students need to proceed through the program at the same pace. Students develop best when there is room for elective courses. The wise mentor gets to know new students as soon as possible and begins planning course-taking patterns and assistantship assignments during the interview process.

Many other aspects of helping students early in their program of study are addressed under the section, "Other Occasions for Mentoring." Next, several formal steps in the doctoral process are examined.

Program of Study Committee Meetings

At Ohio University, the first time a student forms and meets with a committee of faculty members occurs when the student seeks approval for his or her program of study. Thus, this is the first major step on the road to completing the dissertation. Students select the group of faculty members before whom they will defend the list of courses that they have selected to serve as the foundation of their dissertation. Often this same committee will continue with the student through comprehensive exams, the dissertation proposal, and the dissertation defense. In any case, the student's mentor helps the student think through who might be best suited to assist them with the tasks that lie ahead.

This is a major transition point for students. The mentor needs to help each student ask and answer some key questions. How will the professors whom the student knows as teachers interact as part of a committee? What roles are needed within the committee? For mathematics education students, often the committee members correspond to the four major areas of study: educational foundations, educational research, mathematical sciences, and mathematics education. These are the same areas on which they will be tested during the written and oral comprehensive examinations.

The program of study meeting is an opportunity for four (or more) members of the graduate faculty to learn in depth about the candidate's interests and, often, the candidate's intended dissertation topic. This allows the committee to determine readiness for the comprehensive exams and dissertation and to offer advice to the student. The student still has one primary mentor but now has three additional mentors, and the four together act as a mentoring team. This is a new dynamic in the mentoring process and is a powerful experience for the emerging scholars. They obtain a new sense of what it means to seek membership in the academy.

Mentoring During Comprehensive Exams

The committee mentors the student not only by examining the candidate on the program of study but also by posing the exam questions in a way to propel the student into work on the dissertation. Mentoring occurs by getting the student to grapple with important issues that are germane to the dissertation topic. Richardson (2006) emphasizes the importance of both formal knowledge and practical knowledge for a PhD program in education. Berliner (2006) focuses on psychological foundations and a deep understanding of research methodology. A student at the comprehensive exam stage needs all of these cognitive tools to be ready for the dissertation. If all goes well, the end of the oral exam becomes a discussion in preparation for the dissertation proposal.

Mentoring Throughout the Dissertation Process

The adviser typically develops a close mentoring relationship with the candidate during the (sometimes protracted) dissertation process. If mentoring has occurred according to plan up to this point, the dissertation process may not be so long and arduous. If the student already knows how to write well and in a manner appropriate to the discipline, if the student has a strong set of research tools, and if the student has completed earlier research studies from start to finish, then the dissertation is a natural next step. But even in the best of circumstances, the adviser will spend many hours guiding the student. The doctoral dissertation requires original and independent work, and the student may be surprised to find that the adviser will offer many more questions than answers and will place the onus of the work on the student in order to develop the individual's independence as a researcher and scholar.

If the adviser has inherited a student from another professor at the dissertation stage, a new and strong mentor–protégé relationship will need to be formed. Many of the processes discussed earlier in this essay will need to be addressed. My personal experience suggests that this situation will challenge the mentor, and extra time at the beginning of this new relationship will be required to nurture and develop the student and to establish clear expectations.

Kilbourn (2006, pp. 572–573) offers a set of 15 excellent questions from the perspective of the reader to direct a student through the process of developing a dissertation proposal. Six of the 15 questions are as follows:

- "How informative is the introduction? Is it easy to understand?"
- "How long before you understand what the proposal is about?"
- "Are the questions that the study will address clear? Do they seem reasonable, given the nature of the problem?"
- "Is the literature review adequate, and is it conceptually integrated with the problem and the questions posed?"
- "Are the methods of the study spelled out in concrete detail? Will they have a good chance of answering the questions the study poses?"
- "Is the researcher's role in the inquiry clear and acceptable, given the nature of the problem?"

Though intended for students writing a qualitative proposal, these questions have proven useful to my students and me for quantitative research proposals as well—and for research papers and full dissertations. The questions serve as a nice guide for mentors and student alike. Heid and Blume (2011) offer useful suggestions concerning the research question, literature review, and theoretical framework.

Mentoring Beyond the Dissertation

When a student earns the doctorate, the adviser's work is not complete. The mentor–protégé relationship is ongoing and permanent, much like the parent–child relationship. This view of mentoring is a tradition in the mathematical sciences, as evidenced by the Mathematics Genealogy Project (2013) web site, which maintains a record of persons who have earned doctorates in the mathematics sciences and their academic descendants in the form of a family tree. As of April 4, 2014, this site had records of 169,358 such individuals. The great mathematician Carl Friedrich Gauss, for example, had 10 students and 62,868 descendants, and Leonhard Euler, who was perhaps the most prolific writer among mathematicians, had six students and 82,817 descendants. These two mentors have had a powerful influence on the course of mathematics, both through their own work and through the work of their descendants.

Each doctoral adviser, usually in a much smaller way, influences his or her academic descendants. Helping them to find a suitable position after graduation is a crucial aspect of launching newly fledged doctors of philosophy on a successful career path. The adviser's goal is to help each doctoral student find an appointment that fits the student's expertise, interests, and aspirations. This goes beyond writing letters of support and begins long before graduation through assisting students in developing networks of colleagues at the state, national, and international levels. If the scholar is well formed, achieving such milestones as promotion and tenure will be natural consequences in the course of time.

OTHER OCCASIONS FOR MENTORING

In *The Formation of Scholars* (2008), Walker and colleagues emphasize the importance of a department's collective responsibility in creating an intellectual community to nurture the fledgling scholars and its responsibility to provide doctoral students with purposeful opportunities for apprenticeship. This part of the chapter considers these mechanisms as occasions for mentoring.

Mentoring via the Doctoral Seminar

Known to some as a professional seminar (or "pro sem"), the departmental doctoral seminar is an important vehicle for mentoring and filling the gaps in the development of scholars that cannot easily be done any other way. Such a seminar is especially helpful to students early in their doctoral studies. In some departments, the doctoral seminar might be considered a formal step in the doctoral process. Based on my own experience, however, such a seminar works best as a way of inviting students into a department's intellectual community.

In 2009, the graduate faculty in the department of teacher education at Ohio University, in an effort to reinvigorate our doctoral program, read and discussed *The Formation of Scholars* (Walker et al., 2008). As a result, we agreed that one key step in updating and improving our program would be to create a departmental doctoral seminar. Started by the faculty, it quickly became popular with students even though no course credit is awarded for participation.

John E. Henning, department chair at the time, and I agreed that we would lead the seminar. This seminar essentially is a biweekly group mentoring session that covers a wide range of ever-evolving topics on roughly a two-year cycle. Seminar sessions are informal, and the discussions are always rich. Formats vary. Sometimes professors present their research interests or discuss personal experiences in writing for publication, searching for employment, or other topics of current or periodic interest. On other occasions, doctoral students present their research results, whether from their dissertation or other projects, or they may describe the process involved in a recently published work. Topics have included developing a program of study, forming doctoral committees, completing comprehensive exams, and navigating the dissertation process. The time spent mentoring in the doctoral seminar can avoid having to explain the same thing repeatedly to individual students. The doctoral seminar has created a strong intellectual community within the department. Students develop an understanding of the work of being a professor and the variety of ways professors organize, conceptualize, and approach such work. Professors get to know the current concerns of students and are reminded that each year brings a new group of individuals eager to be initiated into the profession.

Teaching Classes as a Mentor to Develop Scholars

As the 1970 Graham Nash song says, "Teach your children well.... Feed them on your dreams." When teaching at the doctoral level, I have found it important to hold virtually nothing back. The students will benefit from hearing their professors' true thoughts, hopes, and aspirations. Putting students face-to-face with the ideas, issues, arguments, dilemmas, confusions, and contradictions within the discipline and at the interface between the profession and the world at large best serves their development. The professor as mentor guides doctoral students through cognitive dissonances of a higher degree than the students have faced in the past. To become full-fledged scholars, the individuals pursuing the doctorate must learn how to grapple with tough issues and how to take a position and defend it with appropriate evidence and arguments.

In order to develop these high-level skills, it is necessary for class assignments and class activities to be authentic. It is important to assign challenging readings that cause students to think, that familiarize them with the top minds in the field, and that lead to rich classroom discourse. Discourse should, of course, take both written and oral forms. In this manner, students will learn to read, write, speak, and listen within the discipline. They will learn to write papers of varying lengths on a wide array of topics that are sufficiently open-ended so that students can learn how to ask questions that are significant within the area of study. The professor as mentor can help the novice student negotiate the dissonance of such open-ended assignments. Students are best served if they write papers often, experience the review process, and revise their papers in keeping with what the review process teaches them.

A strategy that I use is to allow students two weeks to write a paper, then have pairs (or sometimes trios) of students exchange papers and give each other written and oral feedback according to a rubric. Lastly, I give students an additional week to revise the paper and turn in both the original and the revised versions. This produces better work, is more authentic, models peer review, familiarizes the students with standards for professional writing, leads to deep engagement in each other's ideas, and creates an intellectual community within the class. Furthermore, it gives me an opportunity not only to guide students in developing their ability to articulate their thoughts in written form but also to coach students on appropriate collegial interactions. And students get to take on roles that are important to the profession.

In order to develop these emerging scholars, tasks that are assigned in doctoral classes are not only authentic and genuine but also cognitively demanding. That is, the work requires a host of mental functions, such as memory, problem solving, communication, application, and analysis. In addition to assigning papers, I ask students or small groups of students in advance of a class session (and sometimes on the spot) to ask questions to stimulate a discussion on assigned readings. Formal presentations by individuals and small groups of students provide the professor the opportunity to create a conference environment within the classroom and to mentor students on how to behave in such a setting.

I always have required term papers in doctoral courses in education. Recently, I have used the final exam period as a time for students to present their results to each other. In this way, their work becomes more public. It alters the mindset of the students; they now prepare their thoughts for a relatively diverse audience, instead of for a single individual. Knowing that they will present their ideas to the entire class generally improves the quality of the term papers and makes the assignment more authentic—closer to the work they will do as a member of the profession.

Guest speakers can broaden and deepen the content of a course. Bringing in experts is a way to mentor students by preparing them for similar interactions at professional conferences. Interacting with outside speakers builds student confidence and introduces students to a wider intellectual community. Occasionally, students will follow up with such speakers and develop a protégé–mentor relationship with the speaker. The Internet makes virtual visits possible, thus greatly increasing the feasibility of such mentoring opportunities.

Online instruction is becoming popular. Many of the doctoral courses offered through the department of teacher education at Ohio University now have a hybrid format—with class sessions alternating between everyone participating in a face-to-face manner one week and a mixture of face-to-face and online participation the next. This has allowed the department to serve students in a much larger geographic region than in the past. This approach also models (hopefully effective) online instruction, makes hybrid and online formats feel like a natural way to teach, and mentors students in how to use and orchestrate such instructional technology.

Mentoring Through Meaningful Assistantships

Many doctoral students work as teaching assistants or research assistants. Actually, at the doctoral level, I prefer the terms *graduate teaching associate* (GTA) and *graduate research associate* (GRA). Such arrangements are "win-win." These are worthwhile, developmental experiences for the doctoral students, and they add capacity and value to departmental activities. In the case of the GTA, the instruction performed by the doctoral students benefits the undergraduate students being taught. Such values and benefits are most likely to occur when GTAs and GRAs serve as protégés under the guidance of a faculty mentor.

Using Practicum Courses as Mentoring Opportunities

A good practicum course combines theory and research results for some practical purpose. I will cite some examples from my own work in mentoring doctoral students enrolled in such courses.

In one case, a group of five doctoral students worked together under my guidance to complete a practicum. With my encouragement and mentoring, they decided to go individually into the field to do classroom observations, to meet weekly to discuss what they found, and all the while to use their collective experiences to develop an observation protocol that focused on teacher behaviors that were most likely to elicit and enhance student learning. The agreed-upon intended purpose of the protocol was *not* to evaluate the teachers being observed; instead, the goal was to develop a protocol for research purposes. The protocol would be designed to see whether a particular professional development program had an impact on the classroom behavior of the teachers who had participated in the program. Some issues that arose included, how do you measure a teacher's use of cognitively demanding tasks, of formative assessment, or of purposeful classroom discourse? The students employed the theories and research results that they had read about and discussed in prior on-campus classes, and they learned how difficult it is to put such ideas into practice in the form of an observational protocol. Students consequently gained an appreciation for existing observation protocols and developed acumen in selecting such protocols.

Other students have worked with faculty teams to develop mentor–protégé relationships between practicing teachers and teacher candidates in schools where undergraduates were gaining clinical experience. Some doctoral students who were classroom teachers have chosen their own classroom as a practicum laboratory. International students on scholarships, which free them from needing a GTA or GRA position to support their doctoral studies, sometimes have opted to engage in a research project of personal interest or to support an ongoing grant-sponsored project.

Mentoring While Conducting Research

Doctoral students who conduct their own research or who "piggyback" on existing projects are mentored through the institutional review board (IRB) process for conducting research that involves human subjects. For many students, the IRB process initially seems daunting or even scary. But they can be mentored to view the process as genuinely helpful. The IRB form essentially is a checklist for designing a research study. It asks questions that researchers should be asking themselves as they plan their studies.

The mentoring continues as the research phase begins. Even though the IRB process has caused the student to think through the research in advance, unexpected circumstances invariably arise. Guiding students over, around, or through these obstacles builds their self-confidence and prepares them to write strong dissertation proposals and to carry out the associated dissertation research.

Once a doctoral student completes a research investigation, it is a natural next step to make the results public. This can be done via a presentation at the departmental doctoral seminar (discussed earlier), a talk at a college-wide research forum, a poster at a university research day, a poster or paper at a professional meeting, or an article in a refereed journal. Most students need encouragement and advice as they make their way through these increasingly challenging modes of publication.

Mentoring via Professional Conferences

Mentors help doctoral students become familiar with various professional organizations and conferences. Mentors introduce students to colleagues at conferences, as well as allow students some space to select and attend presentations and other events on their own. Again, the same approach cannot be used for all students; emerging scholars differ in personality, self-confidence, maturity, and experience. The mentor assesses and guides students on an individual basis. A student's first conference often is in the role of an attendee, just to get the lay of the land and absorb the ambiance of the meeting. After that, students can make presentations and become actively engaged as full participants. Many conferences, even large national or international ones, are student-friendly. Mentors can encourage students to participate in such events.

An important mentoring strategy is to copresent with students. This allows students to serve in an apprentice role before presenting with other students or by themselves. Some conferences virtually require an individual to be a copresenter before being accepted as a lead presenter. In any case, the mentor can provide a measure of guidance that is customized to the individual student and the particular situation.

At Ohio University, both the university and the Patton College of Education offer support for student travel to attend professional meetings. This support is greater if the student will present a talk and greater still if the student will present a research paper. Such incentives are extremely important for doctoral students, who typically operate on a very limited budget.

Mentoring While Writing for Publication

At Ohio University in the department of teacher education, writing for publication in refereed journals is an expectation for doctoral students. It is also the topic of a required course in the doctoral program and the focus of a great deal of mentoring within the department. There are many parallels between presenting at conferences and writing for publication. As noted above, mentors help their protégés scrutinize and select appropriate conferences as outlets for their work. Such scrutiny is equally important when it comes to picking the right journal for a student's manuscript.

Several of my students have revised term papers into a form suitable for publication in a professional journal. Students are often surprised when I advise them to repurpose and publish their ideas. But this is the bonus that results from doing authentic and original work for class assignments.

Mentoring by Encouraging Initiative

As just noted, students do not always fully appreciate the value of their own ideas and creativity. Doctoral mentors challenge and cajole their charges. Often students have accomplished a great deal of initial thought and labor along a particular path, and they need to be coaxed to take the next step. At other times, students need to be persuaded to take the first step on what may turn into a valuable journey. One of my most treasured experiences as a doctoral mentor occurs when a student thanks me for encouraging words that I provided and that led them to substantial accomplishments.

Mentoring by Forwarding Information

Sometimes mentoring can be as simple as forwarding to students an email message that announces a scholarship opportunity, a special conference, or a call for papers. Forwarding an article from a listserv may be just what a particular student needs to fill a gap for a paper currently in progress. Sifting through the barrage of print and electronic mail and funneling relevant information to specific students shows that you are aware of their interests and, in some cases, may provide an opportunity for them to pursue their dreams and aspirations.

FINAL THOUGHTS

Mentoring Roles, Goals, and Benefits

Although this chapter has focused mostly on the role of doctoral adviser as mentor, it has also touched on the role of group mentoring through graduate classes, practica, and the doctoral seminar. To paraphrase a well-known maxim, it takes a college to mentor a doctoral student. Teaching and committee service offer important mentoring roles for faculty and are a good training ground for the ultimate doctoral mentoring role of faculty adviser.

Mentoring doctoral students involves forming scholars, preparing stewards, and launching careers. Mentoring includes developing students' ability to engage in inquiry, to become a part of an intellectual community, and to form networks with fellow scholars at various levels. Mentoring is not a one-way street. Mentoring does not just benefit the protégé; mentors gain a great deal by interacting with emerging scholars because each step in the mentoring process provides the mentor an opportunity to revisit important aspects of becoming a scholar and reminds the mentor of what is needed to be a steward of the discipline. Mentoring not only helps form the protégé as a scholar but also advances the scholarship of the mentor.

What Then Is Doctoral Mentoring?

Mentoring is an integral part of doctoral education and can take place every day. Mentoring is not something doctoral faculty do on a part-time basis. It is not reserved for office hours or for chance meetings in the hallways or around campus.

Mentoring is a mindset. Every encounter, whether face-to-face, by telephone, or via the Internet, is an opportunity to mentor the student, to shape the scholar, and to develop capacity and independence. A successful doctoral program is infused with mentoring—by design. The faculty and other doctoral students need to see themselves as a mutually supportive intellectual community that is intertwined with larger such communities at the state, national, and international levels.

Mentoring is essential in the formation of scholars. The words "discipline" and "disciple" have the same root. With the proper guidance, the doctoral scholar will make the transition from disciple, or follower, to leader and professor. After all, a doctoral scholar is in training to become a professor—one who professes and is a member of a profession. To profess is to declare, to acknowledge, to vow, or to promise. Our students of today are the promise for tomorrow. Mentoring is the mechanism to fulfill this promise.

TAKEAWAY

In the spirit of Wiggins and McTighe (2006), first create a list of what you expect your doctoral students to know and be able to do. Next, make these expectations clear to your students. Finally, work with your department colleagues to create an intellectual community within your department that embraces your doctoral students and provides them with daily opportunities to develop the expected knowledge and capacities.

ACKNOWLEDGMENTS

I thank my many mentors, especially L. Ray Carry and Alan Osborne, as well as my graduate faculty colleagues in the Department of Teacher Education, the Patton College, and Ohio University, especially John E. Henning and George A. Johanson—all of whom have influenced my views on mentoring doctoral students. Moreover, I acknowledge and thank the doctoral students I have had the pleasure to work with over the years, many of whom are now my colleagues.

REFERENCES

American Psychological Association. (2010). *Publication manual of the American Psychological Association* (6th ed.). Washington, DC: Author.

Bass, H. (2006). Developing scholars and professionals: The case of mathematics. In C. M. Golde & G. E. Walker (Eds.), *Envisioning the future of doctoral education: Preparing stewards of the discipline. Carnegie essays on the doctorate* (pp. 101–119). San Francisco, CA: Jossey-Bass.

Berliner, D. C. (2006). Toward a future as rich as our past. In C. M. Golde & G. E. Walker (Eds.), *Envisioning the future of doctoral education: Preparing stewards of the discipline. Carnegie essays on the doctorate* (pp. 268–289). San Francisco, CA: Jossey-Bass.

Golde, C. M. (2006). Preparing stewards of the discipline. In C. M. Golde & G. E. Walker (Eds.), *Envisioning the future of doctoral education: Preparing stewards of the discipline. Carnegie essays on the doctorate* (pp. 3–20). San Francisco, CA: Jossey-Bass.

Golde, C. M., & Walker, G. E. (Eds.). (2006). *Envisioning the future of doctoral education: Preparing stewards of the discipline. Carnegie essays on the doctorate.* San Francisco, CA: Jossey-Bass.

Heid, M. K., & Blume, G. W. (2011). Strengthening manuscript submissions. *Journal for Research in Mathematics Education, 42,* 106–108.

Kilbourn, B. (2006). The qualitative doctoral dissertation proposal. *Teachers College Record, 108,* 529–576.

Kwiram, A. L. (2006). Time for reform? In C. M. Golde & G. E. Walker (Eds.), *Envisioning the future of doctoral education: Preparing stewards of the discipline. Carnegie essays on the doctorate* (pp. 141–166). San Francisco, CA: Jossey-Bass.

Mathematics Genealogy Project (2013), Department of Mathematics, North Dakota State University Fargo. Retrieved from http://genealogy.math.ndsu.nodak.edu/

Nash, G. (1970). *Teach your children.* On D. Crosby, S. Stills, G. Nash, & N. Young, *Déjà vu* [audio record album] (side 1, track 2). New York, NY: Atlantic Recording

National Academy of Sciences. (1997). *Adviser, teacher, role model, friend: On being a mentor to students in science and engineering.* Washington, DC: National Academy Press.

Reys, R. E., & Dossey, J. A. (Eds.). (2008). *U.S. doctorates in mathematics education: Developing stewards of the discipline.* Conference Board of the Mathematics Sciences Issues in Mathematics Education, Vol. 15. Providence, RI: American Mathematical Society, in cooperation with Washington, DC: Mathematical Association of America.

Reys, R. E., & Kilpatrick, J. (Eds.). (2001). *One field, many paths: U.S. doctoral programs in mathematics education.* Conference Board of the Mathematics Sciences Issues in Mathematics Education, Vol. 9. Providence, RI: American Mathematical Society, in cooperation with Washington, DC: Mathematical Association of America.

Richardson, V. (2006). Stewards of a field, stewards of an enterprise. In C. M. Golde & G. E. Walker (Eds.), *Envisioning the future of doctoral education: Preparing stewards of the discipline. Carnegie essays on the doctorate* (pp. 251–267). San Francisco, CA: Jossey-Bass.

Walker, G. E., Golde, C. M., Jones, L., Bueschel, A. C. & Hutchings, P. (2008). *The formation of scholars: Rethinking doctoral education for the twenty-first century.* San Francisco, CA: Jossey-Bass.

Wiggins, G., & McTighe, J. (2006). *Understanding by design* (2nd ed.). Upper Saddle River, NJ: Pearson Merrill Prentice Hall.

PART III

MENTORING WITH DIFFERENT POPULATIONS

CHAPTER 12

MENTORING DIVERSE DOCTORAL STUDENTS

Lessons from the Field

Martha N. Ovando

ABSTRACT

This chapter aims at contributing to an enhanced understanding of what is needed to promote and enact mentoring. As universities and graduate schools increase in student diversity, there is a need to provide ongoing support to a more culturally diverse graduate student body, taking into account students' distinct backgrounds that influence their doctoral studies. Based on the author's experience of mentoring doctoral students from diverse backgrounds for several years, former protégés' perspectives, and a review of the pertinent literature, four essential components that facilitate a productive relationship between a mentor and a protégé through mentoring are examined: an operational definition of mentoring, attributes needed in mentoring doctoral students, diverse doctoral students' needs and contributions, and faculty contributions to the mentoring process. How universities and graduate schools foster successful mentoring experiences is analyzed in light of its importance for

Mentoring for the Professions: Orienting Toward the Future, pages 225–241.
Copyright © 2015 by Information Age Publishing
All rights of reproduction in any form reserved.

students from diverse backgrounds, and a list of conversation starters that faculty may use as they contemplate the idea of engaging in mentoring of diverse doctoral students is provided as a takeaway.

INTRODUCTION

Mentoring has been a focal point in many different fields, including business and education. According to Reddick, Griffin, and Chertwitz (2011), the declaration of a National Mentoring Month in January of 2010 reinforced "the power of mentoring and its impact on youth" (p. 59). The prominence and contributions of mentoring in higher education have been noted, particularly as they relate to mentoring diverse doctoral students who come from various cultural backgrounds. Studies have addressed a number of areas related to mentoring, including mentoring of single groups, such as African American graduate students (Reddick & Young, 2012), the mentoring experience as a way to nurture aspiring researchers of color (Davidson & Foster-Johnson, 2001), alternative perspectives and models of mentoring (Darwin & Palmer, 2009), and mentoring doctoral students in single education fields such as educational leadership programs and in adult literacy and numeracy (Tracey, 2012; Young & Harris, 2012).

As graduate school efforts to diversify the doctoral student body are underway, there is a need to provide ongoing mentoring support to more culturally diverse candidates, taking into account students' multicultural backgrounds, as those backgrounds may affect their doctoral journey in different fields. It is not only the mentees who will benefit: "Mentoring functions related to cultural and ethnic diversity deal with improving the mentor's understanding of the different graduate school and workplace experiences that are faced by the culturally distinct protégé" (Davidson & Foster-Johnson, 2001, p. 562). Similarly, according to Reddick and Young (2012), "Working with students of color is having respect and understanding for the influence that issues of race and ethnicity have on their lives" (p. 420). Graduate schools are in search of ways to ensure that diverse doctoral students not only enroll in graduate school but also complete their degrees in a timely fashion, and mentoring has been recognized as a promising avenue to this end. As Young and Harris (2012) affirm, mentoring "can be seen as an investment for reducing program attrition and increasing satisfaction" (p. 340).

This chapter proposes to contribute to an enhanced understanding of what it actually takes to promote a positive and productive mentoring relationship between a professor and a doctoral student. A discussion of information gained while mentoring diverse doctoral students may offer valuable information for those interested in mentoring endeavors intended to meet the needs of doctoral students from various cultural backgrounds during their educational journey, and to increase graduation rates. Based on the author's extensive experience and lessons learned from interacting with and mentoring diverse doctoral students, including Mexican American, African American, and Asian American male and female students, as well as the perspectives from former protégés (through nomination letters); and a review of the pertinent literature, this chapter specifically centers attention on four essential elements, consideration of which may facilitate a mutually rewarding relationship between a professor and a protégé through mentoring. These are (1) definition of mentoring, (2) specific attributes of mentoring discovered in practice, (3) diverse doctoral students' needs and contributions, and (4) what faculty may bring to the mentoring process. In view of its importance to the success of mentorships for diverse doctoral students, how institutions of higher education offering graduate programs may continue to support and sustain successful mentoring experiences for all students is also a focus of attention.

MENTORING DEFINED

Mentoring has a long history and has advanced into various fields, including higher education. As mentoring has evolved, various definitions have attempted to capture its true spirit. For instance, as a component of induction programs for beginning teachers, mentoring has been highlighted as making a positive difference in the professional growth of both new teachers and experienced teachers (Bowden, 2004). Others affirm that mentoring is a "challenging and mutually enriching relationship" (Trubowitz, 2004, p. 59). At the higher education level, mentoring has been identified as an avenue to support and guide graduate students to navigate the doctoral journey successfully. According to Davidson and Foster-Johnson's (2001) research on mentoring graduate researchers of color, "Mentoring is a dynamic process between two individuals. It consists of activities and interactions that may be related to work, skill acquisition, and social and emotional aspects of the mentor or the protégé" (p. 549). It should also be noted that successful mentoring of doctoral students addresses personal, professional, and/or academic development. Mullen (2012) sees mentoring as having key core characteristics and suggests that "cornerstone tenets of mentoring are lifelong, humanistic learning, and reflection upon learning as well as social self-reflection by the engaged mentoring parties" (p. 9).

Conceptions of mentoring tend to vary according to the specific context in which mentorship is implemented, and these conceptions usually include a description of the relationship between the mentor and the protégé (Davidson & Foster-Johnson, 2001), an explanation of purposes for specific student groups (Reddick et al., 2011), contributions to the successful navigation of doctoral studies (Ovando, Ramirez, & Shefelbine, 2008), recognition of mentoring's effectiveness for students and its rewarding nature for faculty (Berret, 2011), and details of its merit in facilitating the development of graduate students of color (Young & Brooks, 2008). For purposes of this chapter, mentoring can be viewed as "a journey of mutual discovery in which a faculty member makes a commitment to foster the personal and professional development of a doctoral student" (Ovando, 2012, p. 2). A special emphasis is placed on mentoring as a professional relationship, one that is not short-lived but that might extend beyond the doctoral journey and become "a lifetime professional relationship" (Ovando, 2010, p. 1). Furthermore, in my experience working with diverse doctoral students, including students from various cultural backgrounds, I have discovered that a mentoring relationship, as a professional relationship, has specific attributes that combine to result in a powerful strategy that leads mentees to successful completion of doctoral studies.

ATTRIBUTES OF MENTORING

While mentoring has been used and valued in business and higher education, and information regarding various models of mentoring has advanced in recent years, it is relevant to distinguish clearly its inherent characteristics as a promising strategy to support diverse graduate students who aspire to navigate the doctoral journey successfully. Mentoring may be formal or informal, transformative, reciprocal, focused on activities of the doctoral pathway, inspirational, stimulating, and promotional.

Mentoring may take two basic forms, *formal* and *informal*. On the one hand, formal mentoring tends to "direct attention to the factors that create mentor–mentee relationships that provide growth and satisfaction for both participants" (Trubowitz, 2004, p. 59). A formal mentoring relationship is usually designed to achieve specific organizational goals by providing general guidelines related to the mentoring process/steps, knowledge and qualifications of mentors, stages of the development of mentoring relationships, selection and appointment of mentors, and timelines and duration of the process, as well as specific outcomes. In formal mentoring programs, mentors and their protégés are typically matched by a third party (Davidson & Foster-Johnson, 2001). Further, formal mentoring programs usually last from six months to a year, with limited communication between the mentor and protégé, usually based on organizational purposes (Kram, 1988).

During my practice as a mentor, I have come to realize that, while formal mentoring has the potential to assist doctoral students, it might not be as satisfying or impactful as informal mentoring. In most cases, including the diverse doctoral students with whom I worked, informal mentoring relationships tend to be self-initiated by the mentee and evolving in nature, usually going from an initial professor–doctoral student interaction to a true professional partnership. From the perspective of one of my former protégés, "True mentoring evolves in just this way. While I will always consider her [the mentor] a role model, I am honored that she considers me a colleague." It was also noted by a protégé that, to engage in an informal mentoring relationship, "you really don't need a formal appointment... mentoring is a personal and professional commitment for reciprocal growth and learning, and...through an honest mentoring relationship, one can make an important emotional and intellectual difference in the individual development of others" (Ovando, 2010, p. 2). Informal mentoring relationships tend to build on commonly shared interests and professional growth needs and aspirations of both the mentor and the protégé. They require a mutual commitment to agreed-upon goals and expectations that will lead to a productive relationship that may expand beyond the initial stages to become ongoing and long-term and to yield mutual satisfaction. In this context, mentoring outcomes, specific activities, and timelines are jointly selected and not necessarily prescribed by institutional guidelines. Furthermore, as Davidson and Foster-Johnson (2001) explain, "Whereas individuals in formal mentoring relationships may receive explicit organizational recognition for their participation, they are less likely to receive the intrinsic rewards that individuals in informal mentoring relationships often report" (p. 551).

In my experience, it is apparent that mentoring diverse doctoral students can be *transformative*, positively influencing a protégé in a way that results in his or her considering new pathways and aspirations. As a former Mexican American protégé explained, "My [mentor] sent me on a journey from which I will never return. This has been a journey that has not only touched and changed my life but also all those around me." A true and meaningful mentoring relationship illuminates alternative avenues for the development of a protégé, with the potential to change the protégé's course of action. "A mentor encourages you to stretch beyond your own reach and find new frontiers," stated a female former protégé. Another observed, "Her experience and expertise placed her unmistakably at a level that I thought I could not achieve. Yet her guidance, advice, and modeling allowed me to dream that I could get there. [She] has not only extremely high standards for herself and her students, [but] she also motivates individuals to raise their own aspirations."

In addition, it is apparent that mentoring is often *reciprocal* in nature, benefitting both the protégé and the mentor. While the protégés were able to gain considerable knowledge and professional wisdom from our close and honest association, I, as a mentor, was also able to gain new information and insight related to their field of specialization and their own background and culture, which enabled me to enhance my own expertise and capacity to better serve as a mentor of diverse doctoral students. Further, this experience illustrated that, at times, both I as a mentor and doctoral students as protégés can face frustration and disappointment and yet celebrate happy occasions as well. Further, through the mentoring relationship, it was possible for both to learn lessons related to the persistence, motivation, and commitment needed to pursue a professional goal.

Such reciprocity has recently been highlighted by President Obama, who said, "The mentor usually gets as much or more out of [mentorship] than the mentee" (Obama, Saldana, & Obama, 2010, p. 32). Others agree that effective mentoring affords specific benefits to those who commit to mentoring. For example, Reddick et al. (2011) suggest that mentors develop "a deeper perspective on self and discipline, needed advising skills essential for future careers, an opportunity to contribute to diversity in academia, and an awareness of the reciprocal nature of mentoring relationships" (p. 64).

During my work with diverse doctoral students, I also discovered that mentoring is mainly *focused on activities related to the doctoral journey.* This was particularly the case with students who were not familiar with the expectations of graduate school. Thus, *first*, it was necessary to socialize graduate students to the academic environment by introducing them to graduate school expectations and norms, as well as to other faculty and university staff. Supporting this concept of socialization of graduate students through mentoring, researchers who addressed support for graduate students of color confirm that mentoring relationships "provide opportunities for access to different kinds of experiences and information about academic and social expectations of the institution and the profession" (Young & Brooks, 2008, p. 399). Socialization through mentoring becomes essential, particularly for students who come from diverse backgrounds, including women, as these students face additional academic challenges that require bold and innovative approaches to assist them during and even after their doctoral studies.

Second, the mentoring experience turned to aspects of scholarly work, making sure that protégés became familiar with the expectations and requirements of doctoral assignments and projects. As Reddick et al. (2011) describe the mentoring relationship, mentors "are responsible for developing a strategy for exposing students to relevant activities and experiences," and protégés "learn about the unique aspects of graduate study and engage in a wide range of activities, including the completion of scholarly research, writing for scholarly audiences and participating in seminars" (p. 60).

Third, the mentoring relationship expanded to aspects related to the development of aspiring researchers. Mentoring activities related to research were also progressive in nature, going from initial basic advising related to scholarly endeavors to sharing and, ultimately, letting the protégé lead. As a former protégé explained in a letter describing our relationship,

> [She] expressed her excitement about advising and working with me as a graduate student when I first started my doctoral program at a [major university].... When I first started my tenure track position five years ago, she readily offered her assistance. Since then she has provided invaluable guidance about the tenure process, building a research agenda, suggestions for submission of manuscripts, writing with clear purpose, and collaborating on several research projects. In fact, we have published articles together and [she] allowed me to be the first author.

Fourth, during the mentoring experience and through purposeful activities, my protégées were able to expand professional *networking* opportunities. Doctoral students were introduced to other professionals in the field and were encouraged to become members of key professional associations and learned societies. As stated by a colleague, through a letter, on behalf of the author, "While serving as a mentor and guide through the proposal process, she also helps students and junior colleagues develop networks through introductions to key researchers in the field at state and national conferences" (Bumphus, 2009, p. 1). As Young and Brooks (2008) report, "effective support for graduate students of color includes opportunities for career advancement such as attendance to national conferences, publication opportunities, internship experiences, and chances to network with practitioners, scholars, and other graduate students of color within the university and nationally" (p. 401).

From my experience working with diverse doctoral students, it became apparent that mentoring may be *inspirational in character.* Through inspirational mentoring, it is possible to plant a seed of interest in higher goals and to offer reasons for doing, visualizing, or engaging in activities that have the potential to lead the protégé to a course of action that will then lead them to the successful achievement of a professional purpose, thus contributing to an enhanced self-confidence. Through motivational conversations with protégés, we, as faculty, may help them visualize future professional roles and alternative career paths. A former protégé explained the effects of this strategy:

> [Faculty] encouraged me to pursue doctoral studies. Prior to considering this degree, I assumed that PhDs were for highly intellectual people who were so brilliant that I would have never considered myself in that league. These faculty members encouraged me to consider myself "in that league" and they also demystified the doctoral experience for me, and portrayed it as something attainable.

Mentoring that is inspirational in nature is intentional and long-term; therefore, it does not end when a protégé successfully navigates a doctoral program. It extends beyond graduate school, encouraging protégés' aspirations to higher levels of achievement. As a former protégé observed, the mentor's "outstanding professional example continues to inspire me in the areas of scholarship, service and teaching." As a transformative experience, Mentoring of doctoral students may offer the support needed "to transition them from coursework to completion of the dissertation to ongoing growth as lifelong learners" (Young & Harris, 2012, p. 351).

As inspirational mentoring may make an important emotional and intellectual difference in the personal and professional development of the protégé, it was apparent from my work with doctoral students that mentorships can also be *stimulative,* as they may enliven hope. Engaging in mentoring of diverse doctoral students allowed me the opportunity to help protégés shape a positive anticipation of what they could realize by going even beyond what they anticipated. This, in turn, fostered faith and energy in them to see the possibilities that they might not have visualized as attainable. I learned that, as mentors, we can instill in doctoral students a strong belief and feeling that they are capable of pursuing their dreams, and that with dedication and self-discipline these dreams may, in time, become a reality in their professional and personal future. In a former Asian American protégé's words, "In a mere three years, [the mentor] not only planted the notion of hope in me, but she taught me how to sustain it, and how to give back to others. [She] is an architect of hope."

In addition, it was apparent to me that mentoring might be *promotional* of an ethical commitment from both mentor and protégé. While working with various groups of doctoral students, I came to realize that it was necessary to be honest and to devote time, knowledge, and energy, and that doctoral students were genuinely committed to investing in the mentor–protégé relationship by being respectful, meeting deadlines, agreeing to fulfill mutually agreed duties, asking relevant questions to clarify expectations, and exchanging personal and professional information, as well as clearly communicating any concerns. Along with others, I suggest that by "openly and honestly communicating with faculty, diverse doctoral students may be able to overcome certain obstructing factors" (Ovando et al., 2008, p. 51). Given that certain factors might block diverse doctoral students' progress—factors such as fear of scholarly writing, time constraints, separation from families, negative stereotypes, job-related demands, and unfamiliarity with higher education academic demands—researchers suggest that doctoral students of color must also demonstrate "responsibility, capability, and timeliness; diligently approaching studies and classroom performance; and, as noted, expressing interest in opportunities for growth and learning beyond the classroom" (Reddick & Young, 2012, p. 415).

While the above suggests that mentorships with diverse doctoral students may reflect specific characteristics, I have also come to realize that understanding of individual protégés' needs is essential. This understanding of individual students includes recognizing that their cultural background, experiences, and knowledge contribute to a productive mentoring relationship.

PROTÉGÉS' NEEDS AND CONTRIBUTIONS

During my experience working with doctoral students, it was apparent that they were in search of avenues to satisfy certain personal, academic, and professional needs. However, the depth and scope of such needs seemed to depend on their diverse cultural backgrounds. For instance, some needed ongoing support to navigate the institutional environment, information about institutional expectations, clarification of institutional culture and norms, as well as academic protocols and etiquette. As Young and Brooks (2008) report, "although it can be argued that all graduate students, regardless of race, must overcome issues of socialization on entering graduate school, interviewees explained that people of color are more likely to begin their programs lacking the social, political and cultural capital necessary for success" (p. 407).

Diverse doctoral students also need role models from similar cultural backgrounds, particularly due to the lack of diversity among faculty in most universities. The protégés I worked with were interested in learning how to have access to faculty who represented minority populations so they could not only candidly express academic concerns but also share personal struggles without fear of being criticized. In my experience as a mentor from a different cultural background, I realized that it was essential not only to listen but also to share personal and professional challenges faced during my own doctoral journey. This candid exchange served to validate the protégés' concerns and fears as legitimate. In my opinion, for diverse doctoral students, "getting to know faculty, particularly minority professors is essential to their success" (Ovando et al., 2008, p. 51).

Other doctoral students expressed a need to learn how to approach and communicate with faculty who did not share the same cultural background. This appeared to be particularly challenging for female Mexican American students who were first-generation doctoral students. As Davidson and Foster-Johnson (2001) assert, "everyone has different ways of communicating, regardless of race, gender, or ethnic background. Added to these differences, however, are unique variations in communication methods that are inherent to particular cultures and countries" (p. 563).

Further, others affirm that diverse graduate students need continuous support throughout their doctoral studies, addressing the various stages of their program. For instance, Young and Brooks (2008) note, "effective support for graduate students of color includes opportunities for career advancement such as attendance at national conferences, publications opportunities, internship experiences, and chances to network with practitioners, and other graduate students of color within the university and nationally" (p. 401). Diverse graduate students may also need to develop the ability to question the canons, to reduce isolation, to learn to speak up in class, and to avoid suffering from stereotypes (Regents of the University of Michigan, 2012). In my practice as a mentor, I came to realize that diverse doctoral students' needs varied depending on their cultural background, level of experience, and professional aspirations, as well as on the specific stages of their doctoral programs. Thus, meeting the unique diverse needs of these students required individually tailored attention and support so they could be able to experience success.

Whereas the above account is not inclusive of all diverse doctoral students' needs, it was apparent from my mentoring experience that it was essential to acknowledge that their needs might be compounded by their expectations as adult learners who bring considerable professional and personal experiences to their doctoral studies. Therefore, their learning needed to be guided by the tenets of andragogy (English, 1999; Zachary, 2000), a primary tenet being that education should be "driven by the heart and soul of the learner's personal/professional goals" (Harris, 2005, p. 160) and transformational in nature. According to Mezirow (2000), a transformative learning process evolves through certain clarifying stages, including "a disorienting dilemma," of which there may be many for any doctoral student and particularly for a doctoral student from a culturally different background and calling for both a "critical assessment of assumptions" and the "recognition that one's discontent and the process of transformation are shared," and, especially for the "provisional trying of new roles" and "building competence and self-confidence in new roles and relationships" (p. 22).

On the other hand, I also became aware of how important it was to recognize that protégés may significantly add to the mentoring process and outcomes. Protégés' contributions included sharing information about their cultural backgrounds, traditions and norms; bringing additional resources to my attention; providing insight to generate plans of action; and providing a different lens to address academic issues and solve problems. As a result, the role of the protégés changed from a passive and receptive one to an active one. As Fischler and Zachary (2009) noted, both the mentor and the mentee "work to achieve goals that they mutually define to develop skills, abilities, knowledge and/or thinking" (p. 6). Similarly, recent researchers affirm that "mentors empower their protégés through sharing knowledge, advice, and insights, and evaluations of their protégés' work, while allowing for discourse and reflection. However, protégés may also contribute to the relationship, sharing their own insight and reflections with their mentors" (Hansman, 2012, p. 373).

In my experience, protégés engaged in the mentoring relationship brought to the process a high level of personal motivation to pursue a doctoral degree and to be successful. Protégés also demonstrated a high level of willingness to invest their energy and time to achieve a goal, thus becoming highly self-disciplined, fulfilling graduate school duties and job responsibilities as well as family obligations. Doctoral students' "inner desire is a key factor to endure the demands and challenges associated with the requirements of a doctoral degree" (Ovando et al., 2008, p. 48).

It can also be asserted that diverse doctoral students may bring nontraditional experiences and perspectives that can be eye-opening for those of us unfamiliar with other cultures. We can benefit most from such learning if it is built on our understanding that to engage in mentoring diverse graduate students we need to become familiar with different cultures and expand our own knowledge base. Such knowledge facilitates our endeavors to tailor mentoring activities to students' distinct needs and to enhance the mentoring relationship.

Protégés' knowledge, insights, and experiences indeed add to the richness and outcomes of the mentoring relationship. However, it is essential to also acknowledge that faculty contributions are vital, given their positions, experiences, and familiarity with the rigor and expectation of academia and doctoral studies.

FACULTY CONTRIBUTIONS TO MENTORING

Faculty members are in a position to play a key role and make important contributions to the development of diverse doctoral students through mentoring. However, during my experience in working with doctoral students, it became clear that there was a need to reflect on my own personal beliefs, understanding of other cultures, personal professional path, and knowledge. Such reflection was instrumental in understanding the students' diverse needs and aspirations, and led to my offering individualized personal support and showing genuine concern as well as honoring protégés' experiences and contributions to the mentoring process. This experience echoes Davidson and Foster-Johnson's advice that "mentors acquire knowledge based on introspective evaluation of their own personal attitudes and prejudices, conversations and shared learning experiences with their protégées, and assessment of their organization" (2001, p. 564). Further, faculty contributions to mentoring have been recognized as incalculable by researchers who focused on diverse students' success in navigating the doctoral journey. Clearly, students value and respect mentors who take the time to share their own experiences and suggest ideas to become successful (Ovando et al., 2008).

Research indicates that faculty members who work with graduate students of color are not only knowledgeable about institutional cultural diversity issues but are also willing to engage in specific actions that may foster a positive academic experience for the protégé. For instance, Davidson and Foster-Johnson (2001) report that faculty who engage in mentoring of graduate students of color tend to act in the following ways:

- Adopt and articulate a personal policy toward diversity
- Ensure that diversity objectives are embedded in the curriculum, where appropriate
- Promote the formal examination of race, ethnicity, and cultural issues in research by having faculty–student discussions of proposed research and published scholarly works
- Have protégés maintain diaries or logs of their graduate school experience (an approach often used in the disciplines of organizational behaviors, anthropology, and women's studies)
- Assign issues or questions for protégés to write about. Provide supportive feedback through confirmatory comments and suggestions
- Employ a variety of teaching approaches to address diversity issues in class content (e.g., guest speakers or videotapes)
- Use reflective teaching strategies and group dialogue to encourage communication between students about issues related to race and culture
- Collaborate with protégés on research projects that incorporate issues of culture and race
- Work with protégés in identifying appropriate professional organizations, conferences, and scholarly outlets for future work related to their areas of research interest (p. 567)

In my work, I have highlighted the fact that faculty members who perform the role of mentor of diverse doctoral students bring the following to the mentoring process (Ovando, 2012):

- An understanding of mentoring and a willingness to become mentors
- The knowledge of institutional culture, expectations, traditions, and spoken or unspoken protocols
- An awareness of the diverse cultural backgrounds, needs, aspirations, and limitations of the protégé
- Expertise in research and various methodological paradigms
- The wisdom and experience associated with scholarly work

- Personal and professional life experiences
- The willingness to initiate, develop, and sustain a professional relationship with the protégé
- The motivation to return benefits experienced during their own development
- The capacity to practice responsive and sensitive listening
- A genuine desire to connect with doctoral students (p. 3)

Further, Reddick and Young (2012), who examined mentoring practices to support doctoral students of color, remind us that faculty contributions may be more effective when faculty strive toward the following strategies and commitments:

- Being a race-conscious mentor; having concern for student mentees beyond the instrumental aspects of the relationship
- Unpacking the hidden curriculum and making transparent the implicit rules of the department and/or institution
- Developing and sustaining both formal and informal structures
- Opening doors and helping to foster networks
- Having knowledge and respect for newer conceptualizations of mentoring (incorporating technology and new media)
- Staying current with critical epistemological and research methodologies that may be of interest to students of color (pp 419–420)

While knowledge of different cultures, expertise in research, and understanding of cultural diversity in specific institutions and departments are relevant components of the work of faculty as mentors, bringing to the attention of doctoral students information about external forms of support and professional networks may also enhance their success. For instance, faculty may encourage their protégés to actively seek participation in organizations such as the Barbara Jackson Scholars Program, Mexican American Legal Defense and Education Fund, National Association for the Advancement of Colored People, National Indian Education Association, or National Association of Asian American Professionals.

The effectiveness of mentoring diverse doctoral students depends to a great extent on the contributions of both the protégé and the faculty members who perform the role of mentor. Mentoring of these students, however, may only render the desired outcomes as institutions of higher education and specifically graduate schools embrace mentoring as a serious organizational commitment.

HIGHER EDUCATION CONTEXT

Higher education institutions, particularly graduate schools, are concerned with graduation rates of doctoral students. The attrition rate for diverse doctoral students, including women and minorities, appears to be higher than for their counterparts (Young & Harris, 2012), and some graduate programs aim to promote higher completion rates for students from different backgrounds through mentoring. However, there is a need to ensure that the institutional culture and norms reflect a welcoming and nurturing environment. As Brown, Davis, and McClendon (1999) remind us, "We must begin to pay attention to the institutional processes that affect students of color as they matriculate through graduate programs nationwide. The structures, the norms, practices and personnel will ultimately govern whether the career trajectories of these students will be positive or negative" (p. 117).

It is imperative that institutions of higher education search for, or create, the kind of support structures that may enhance diverse doctoral students' success. Based on a study of avenues and practices to support students of color in educational administration, Young and Brooks (2008) identified the following support strategies:

- Substantive and race-sensitive orientation programs
- Faculty–student study and reading groups centered on issues of diversity (including cohorts)
- Introduction to a diverse curriculum
- Systematic introduction to faculty and graduate students of color in other fields of inquiry at the university
- Race-sensitive multidisciplinary research colloquia
- Financial support to attend national-level conferences (p. 413)

It has also been noted that universities have began to establish institution-wide policies and procedures with the potential to promote mentoring and to enhance graduation rates. Such policies may accomplish the following (Ovando, 2012):

- Reflect a welcoming culture and environment conducive to diverse doctoral student success and ongoing support at all levels
- Demonstrate a commitment to promote positive academic experiences for all doctoral students
- Value and respect doctoral students' multicultural backgrounds and diversity
- Foster, support, and reward faculty who serve as mentors of doctoral students
- Provide clear and accessible information about expectations and requirements
- Facilitate access to additional learning opportunities beyond the established curriculum
- Promote hiring, supporting, and retaining faculty and administrative staff committed to serving doctoral students from diverse backgrounds (p. 3)

Institution-wide policies and procedures may serve to guide the design, practice, and evaluation of mentoring endeavors that hold promise. On the other hand, some researchers advance the notion that, at the department level, certain actions and initiatives may directly influence the willingness of faculty to serve as mentors for diverse doctoral students. For example, Davidson and Foster-Johnson (2001) propose that departments create specific guidelines to address the various design aspects of a mentoring program, including training in issues of cultural diversity for faculty so that they may be better prepared to be mentors and do so effectively.

By creating policies and practices to support all doctoral students, including those from different cultural backgrounds, institutions of higher education are in a better position to consider the importance of and need for program support, selection of participants and ongoing evaluations:

> If the resources (both human and financial) are to be invested in mentoring programs, those responsible for planning and implementing programs must be willing to commit time, resources, and energy to such programs. Indeed, all parties have a responsibility to make mentoring work so that it can be a positive force for individuals and their organizations. (Hansford, Ehrich, & Tennent, 2004, p. 536)

While higher education institutions have begun to make concerted and intentional efforts to foster mentoring of diverse doctoral students, it is relevant to acknowledge that certain external factors, emerging expectations, and demands make the task of mentoring a challenging one. Thus, universities and researchers may engage in inquiry that illuminates innovative ways of mentoring, as well as other avenues that could contribute to enhancing diverse doctoral students' success. As Rath (2012) states, "research mentoring is a welcome step away from the 'training' model of development and toward a more flexible, immediate and community-building understanding of on-going, situated learning" (p. 516).

CONCLUDING THOUGHTS

Mentoring has gained high prominence in higher education, particularly in graduate schools interested in fostering higher completion rates and reducing attrition as well as enhancing diversity. Therefore, researchers and practitioners are interested in gaining additional insight relative to mentoring as a strategy to create a positive institutional environment conducive to a successful culmination of doctoral studies. In an attempt to highlight insights acquired from a personal experience in working with diverse doctoral students and to provide a practical point of view, this chapter has focused on a definition of mentoring, attributes of mentoring, doctoral students' (protégés') needs and contributions, faculty contributions, and how institutions of higher education may enhance the promise of mentoring as an avenue to offer valuable support to doctoral students from different backgrounds.

Providing positive experiences to diverse doctoral students can no longer be left to chance or to a few servant-oriented, unselfish faculty who are willing to invest time and energy in mentoring of doctoral students at a professional cost and risk. It is of utmost importance that universities in general, and graduate schools in particular, embrace an ethical commitment not only to recruit, select, and admit aspiring students from different cultural backgrounds but also to create the conditions that positively influence their academic progress and success in their own specializations. At the same time, it is essential that higher education institutions "contemplate the need to recruit, hire, support and retain faculty who come from diverse backgrounds, have a true understanding of the challenges associated with doctoral work, and can relate to the unique needs of diverse minority aspirants" (Ovando et al., 2008, p. 53). Additionally, a more inclusive reward system than is currently in existence must be put in place so that faculty are not only encouraged, but inspired to engage in mentoring with a true spirit of service and to "move thoughtfully and boldly from awareness and advocacy, and finally into action" (Young & Brooks, 2008, p. 417). Faculty who understand the need for mentoring for diverse students have an important responsibility:

> Faculty committed to facilitating and enacting such change must increase awareness and concern among colleagues, graduate students of color, and White graduate students regarding issues of race and focus on understanding how best to support the success of future leaders of color. (Young & Brooks, 2008, p. 417)

Finally, as we continue to engage in mentoring endeavors, it is incumbent upon us as faculty to reflect on our own positionality, feelings, beliefs, and values as well as our collective perceptions related to working with different groups of doctoral students. For instance, it would be enlightening to have conversations with other faculty about mentoring experiences: how does one start mentoring; what is effective, what is not as effective; what challenges are faced and how are these overcome; what institutional arrangements and resources are most helpful; what institutional barriers can be detrimental to the protégés; what, if any, discrimination issues emerge, and how can these be addressed; what are the most common concerns of protégés; what are the most pressing needs of doctoral students from various cultural backgrounds; what can be learned from interacting with diverse doctoral students; what external resources are available; and the like. By discussing these and other related aspects of mentoring, we will enhance our collective capacity, and, in turn, we will be able to ensure that mentoring diverse doctoral students yields positive outcomes for all, including the protégé, the mentor, and the institution at large.

REFERENCES

Berret, D. (2011, January 10). Mentoring 101. *Higher Ed*. Retrieved from www.insidehighered.com/news/2011/01/10mentoring_is_good_teaching_in_college

Bowden, S. H. (2004). Top ten list for choosing to become a mentor. *Young Children, 59*(4), 78–79.

Brown, M. C, Davis G. L., & McClendon, S. A. (1999). Mentoring graduate students of color: Myths, models and modes. *Peabody Journal of Education, 74*(2), 105–118.

Bumphus, W. G. (2009). Mentoring award nomination letter. The University of Texas at Austin.

Darwin, A., & Palmer, E. (2009). Mentoring circles in higher education. *Higher Education Research and Development, 28*(2), 125–136.

Davidson, M. N., & Foster-Johnson, L. (2001). Mentoring in the preparation of graduate researchers of color. *Review of Educational Research, 71*(4), 549–574.

English, L. M. (1999). An adult learning approach to preparing mentors and mentees. *Mentoring and Tutoring: Partnership in Learning, 7*(3), 195–202.

Fischler, L. A., & Zachary, L. J. (2009). Shifting gears: The mentee in the driver's seat. *Adult Learning, 20*(1&2), 5–9.

Hansford, B. C., Ehrich, L. C., & Tennent, L. (2004). Formal mentoring in education and other professions: A review of the literature. *Educational Administration Quarterly, 40*(4), 518–540.

Hansman, C. A. (2012). Empowerment in the faculty-student mentoring relationship. In S. Fletcher & C. Mullen (Eds.), *The Sage handbook of mentoring and coaching for education* (pp. 368–382). Thousand Oaks, CA: Sage.

Harris, S. (2005). *Changing mindsets of educational leaders to improve schools: Voices of doctoral students.* Lanham, MD: Rowman & Littlefield Foundation.

Kram, K. E. (1988). *Mentoring at work: Developmental relationships in organizational life.* Lanham MD: University Press of America.

Mezirow, J. (2000). Learning to think like an adult: Transformation theory: Core concepts. In J. Mezirow & Associates (Eds.), *Learning as transformation: Critical perspectives on a theory in progress* (pp. 3–33). San Francisco: Jossey-Bass.

Mullen, C. A. (2012). Mentoring: An overview. In S. Fletcher & C. Mullen (Eds.), *The Sage handbook of mentoring and coaching for education* (pp. 7–23). Thousand Oaks, CA: Sage.

Obama, B., Saldana, A., & Obama, M. (2010, January 20). Remarks by the President and First Lady in honor of National Mentoring Month [News release]. Retrieved from www.Whitehouse.gov/the-press-office/remarks-president-and-first-lady-honor-national-mentoring-month

Ovando, M. N. (2010, October 28). Appreciation remarks. J. Scribner Mentoring Award Presentation, University Council of Educational Administration Annual Convention, New Orleans, LA.

Ovando, M. N. (2012, February). *Mentoring diverse doctoral students: Lessons learned.* Paper presented at the Excellence in Mentoring Lecture Series, The University of Texas, El Paso.

Ovando, M. N., Ramirez, A. Jr., & Shefelbine, J. (2008). Successfully navigating doctoral studies in school leadership: Diverse minority voices. *Journal of Border Educational Research* [Special Issue], *7*, 41–56.

Rath, J. (2012). Research mentoring in higher education. In S. Fletcher & C. Mullen (Eds.), *The Sage handbook of mentoring and coaching for education* (pp. 506–519). Thousand Oaks, CA: Sage.

Reddick, R. J., Griffin, K. A., & Cherwitz, R. A. (2011). ViewPoint: Answering President Obama's call for mentoring: It's not just for mentees anymore. *Planning for Higher Education, 39*(4), 59–65.

Reddick, R. J., & Young, M. D. (2012). Mentoring graduate students of color. In S. Fletcher & C. Mullen (Eds.), *The Sage handbook of mentoring and coaching for education* (pp. 412–429). Thousand Oaks, CA: Sage.

The Regents of the University of Michigan. (2012). *How to mentor graduate students: A guide for faculty*. Retrieved from www.rackham.umich.edu/publications/

Tracey, S. (2012). The role of mentoring in adult literacy and numeracy in Northern Ireland. In S. Fletcher & C. Mullen (Eds.), *The Sage handbook of mentoring and coaching for education* (pp. 430–440). Thousand Oaks, CA: Sage.

Trubowitz, S. (2004). The why, how, and what of mentoring. *Phi Delta Kappa, 86*(1), 59–62.

Young K., & Harris, S. (2012). Mentoring doctoral students in educational leadership programs. In S. Fletcher & C. Mullen (Eds.), *The Sage handbook of mentoring and coaching for education* (pp. 339–353). Thousand Oaks, CA: Sage.

Young, M. D., & Brooks, J. (2008). Supporting graduate students of color in educational administration preparation programs: Faculty perspectives on best practices, possibilities and problems. *Educational Administration Quarterly, 44*(3), 391–423.

Zachary, L. (2000). *The mentor's guide: Facilitating effective learning relationships*. San Francisco, CA: Jossey-Bass.

CHAPTER 13

WOMEN FACULTY IN STEM AND THE VALUE OF MENTORING IN ADVANCING THE FIELD

Maureen Doyle-Scharff and Valerie Martin Conley

ABSTRACT

A gender gap with respect to employment and status of women in the STEM fields is prevalent in institutions of higher education in the United States, especially with respect to the attainment of leadership positions. Institutions of higher education, therefore, and the government agencies providing them with support hope to increase women's participation, status, and opportunities for career advancement in these fields. When surveyed, female faculty members indicate that they are interested in receiving various sorts of support for career development. The related literature, moreover, suggests that mentoring programs are among the successful strategies for providing such support. The literature also acknowledges that mentoring of female faculty, especially in the STEM fields, must address their unique needs, cultural barriers in general, and specific institutional barriers. Both traditional and nontraditional approaches offer promise. The National Science Foundation's ADVANCE program supports a variety of programs, many using mentoring models, to expand career opportunities for female faculty members in STEM fields. This chapter describes several mentoring programs for women STEM faculty, including those at Brown University, the University of Rhode Island, and the University of Miami. It also describes more extensive efforts to address the career advancement interests of female faculty, particularly those who aspire to leadership positions.

Mentoring for the Professions: Orienting Toward the Future, pages 243–258.

INTRODUCTION

A gender gap in faculty membership and status is prevalent in the STEM fields, academic medicine, and the business arena, especially with respect to senior leadership roles (Chesler & Chesler, 2002; Jolliff, Leadley, Coakley, & Slone, 2012; Nonnemaker, 2000). A considerable amount of energy and resources has been deployed over the past two decades to assess the root causes of this disparity, especially in academia, in the hope that solutions can be identified and implemented. The disparity is manifested in a number of ways: fewer women hold senior faculty and administrative positions; fewer opportunities exist for junior faculty to advance in their careers; fewer mentors and considerably smaller networks are available to women, which leaves them feeling isolated, unappreciated, and more apt to leave their employer or academia altogether; and an unsupportive environment exists for women, which creates dissatisfaction in their work and job (Wasburn, 2007). In a study that looked at attitudes, performance and treatment of women and minority faculty in STEM fields, women reported perceiving the environment as unsupportive, and experienced more discrimination than STEM men (Blackwell, Snyder, & Mavriplis, 2009).

Several reasons can be cited to explain such disparity. The most obvious is that if there are fewer women students in the STEM fields, presumably there will be a smaller pool of qualified women to choose a career in academia. This shortage of female faculty is often explained in social science research by a *deficit model* blaming socialization factors, both formal and informal, for women's lower rate of entry into the sciences than the rate of entry for men. This theory suggests that structural obstacles lead to the exclusion of women scientists by providing fewer chances and opportunities over the course of a career, inevitably leading to worse career outcomes as a group (Sonnert & Holton, 1996). Yet another explanation is the *difference model*, which references gender differences between women and men in psychosocial constructs like behavior, attitudes, goals, and ambitions. The difference model suggests that social norms and cultural patterns shape the behavior of individuals and the characteristics of social institutions, which can negatively impact a woman's drive to be successful on a professional level, leading to avoidance of those activities (including employment) that are more "male oriented." Finally, according to this model, epistemological differences between men and women make the construct of science incompatible with "women's ways of knowing" (Sonnert & Holton, 1996).

These theories notwithstanding, many believe that the culture and politics of higher education specifically are at the heart of the problem (Gibson, 2006). One cannot just hire more women—they'll still leave if the environment is not supportive. Kulis, Sicotte, and Collins (2002) studied the problem of women's underrepresentation in the sciences, noting that the pipeline metaphor often used to explain this deficit is as much about increasing the number of women entering the field as it is about preventing leakage down the line. Deploying strategies like faculty development and mentoring programs to transform the culture of higher education and to support women faculty in their career development, advancement, and desire to stay in academia is a key to movement in a positive direction.

When surveyed, women faculty at all levels list numerous desires when it comes to career development support. Mentoring is often included on the list (Nemiro, Hacker, Ferrel, & Guthrie, 2009). Countless studies have shown the value of mentoring, both formal and informal, on the careers of both men and women (Wasburn, 2007). A particular emphasis on providing mentoring opportunities for women faculty in STEM could prove to be a significant factor in shifting the academic culture and environment, particularly in the STEM fields, enabling women faculty to thrive and advance. This chapter will discuss the challenges faced by women faculty in STEM and the role mentoring can play in overcoming these challenges, and will also provide examples of actual mentoring programs and initiatives, many supported by the National Science Foundation (NSF) and developed specifically to advance the careers of women faculty in STEM.

WOMEN FACULTY IN STEM: THE GENDER GAP

Although academic institutions have worked tirelessly over the past decade to improve academic culture and climate for women, many still observe the marginalization of women faculty (Gibson, 2006) and an unsupportive or "chilly climate" (Hall & Sandler, 1984). Some scholars argue that the competitive nature of STEM fields and academic medicine is in direct contrast or conflict with the female preference for cooperative and interactive learning and exchange (Ginorio, 1995). Indeed, there exist many cultural barriers that prevent women from advancing in their careers in the STEM fields. These barriers not only limit opportunities for women leaders and role models, but they can also have a serious impact on the recruitment of young women into STEM programs.

Although progress can be reported on the increased numbers of women entering faculty positions in academia, the data representing women in higher ranks are not as positive. For example, in recent years, medical schools have seen more women pursue an academic career than men. However, the number of women who advance to full professor or administrative leadership positions is significantly less than the number of men who achieve these positions (Nonnemaker, 2000, p. 401).

Stereotypes, based both on myth and reality, can be used to explain this trend: the "good ol' boys club" that represents men in leadership positions both in academia and business and the complacency on the part of current leadership that does not see this disparity as an issue, or the overall chilly climate that awaits newly hired women in academic departments where few women leaders and role models exist to help guide them (Hall & Sandler, 1984). Implications of this invisible discriminating environment are far-reaching for both women faculty and students (Wasburn, 2007).

Communication differences between men and women could be partially to blame for the lack of support, career development, and advancement of women in academia. Men tend to express themselves through assertive speech, with a style that is impersonal and abstract. They come across as competitive and often control the conversation (Hall & Sandler, 1984). Women, on the other hand, tend to be less assertive, more inclusive, have a personal style, be polite, be viewed as hesitating, and, more often than not, use "we" versus "I" (Hall & Sandler, 1984, p. 5). With these differences in mind, it is not hard to understand why, when women are mentored by men, the mentee often expresses less satisfaction with respect to the mentoring experience that do mentees in other combinations. In contrast, the dynamic when a woman mentors another woman is viewed more favorably, including in terms of more social engagement (Ragins & Cotton, 1999).

The lack of senior female faculty role models/mentors can have a negative impact on junior female faculty and female student recruitment/retention (Johnsrud, 1991). Turnover in STEM women faculty is tied closely to dissatisfaction with research support, advancement opportunities, and freedom to express ideas (Xu, 2008). Traditional norms of autonomy, individualism, and competition in higher education, especially in the STEM fields, are contrary to the potential that higher education offers as a collegial community that, by its nature, exists to grow and develop all of its citizens. It is this cooperative type of environment that is more aligned with the preferences of women (Johnsrud, 1991).

MENTORING OF WOMEN FACULTY: A LIMITED RESOURCE

Since 2001, the National Science Foundation (NSF) has invested over $100 million in support of the ADVANCE program (Increasing the Participation and Advancement of Women in Academic Science and Engineering Careers). The goal of this transformative program is to identify opportunities to "increase the representation and advancement of women in academic science, technology, engineering and mathematics (STEM) careers, thereby contributing to the development of a more diverse science and engineering workforce" (NSF, 2013, p. 1).

Research from various ADVANCE grants has shown that women faculty members take longer to reach tenure and are promoted far less than their male counterparts (University of Michigan NSF, 2008). Participating in a mentoring relationship or program can lead to improved job satisfaction, promotion, and retention for women faculty (Ragins & Cotton, 1999). In STEM programs particularly, mentoring programs contribute to a supportive environment necessary for both recruitment and retention of women faculty (Nemiro et al., 2009). Workload issues have been cited as the primary reason for female faculty's not having enough time to participate in faculty development initiatives (which rarely include formal mentoring programs) (Nemiro et al., 2009).

At research institutions, mentoring is often associated with clinical research (a mentor is a National Institutes of Health requirement for all "K" Career Development Awards; NIH, 2013). However, formal mentoring programs (outside of a research track) are a common request when junior and tenure-track faculty members are asked to identify strategies that would help in their professional development (Nemiro et al., 2009). Unfortunately, few women faculty have access to this type of program, and as noted above, even when professional development programs are offered, rarely have the time to engage in additional activities beyond those defined by their job (Nemiro et al., 2009).

There are many similarities between the STEM fields and medicine, especially when it comes to academic environment and faculty demographics, so some of the research focused on female faculty in academic medicine may prove to be relevant in studying disparities in STEM. Bickel et al. (2002) evaluated data from a benchmark survey conducted by the American Association of Medical Colleges (AAMC) and in-depth interviews of 34 department chairs and two division chiefs to better understand barriers and opportunities for advancement of women faculty in the medical school environment. The findings confirmed the existence of barriers that included traditional gender roles, sexism that is still pervasive in the arena, and the "lack of effective mentors" (p. 1047). The authors' recommendations specific to mentoring included holding all senior faculty (both men and women) accountable for the successful advancement of junior faculty, with a focus on helping men become better mentors to women (Bickel et al., 2002). This suggests that in order to leverage the value and advantage of formal mentoring, especially for STEM women faculty, leadership must make intentional changes and adjustments to the culture of their institutions, imbedding faculty development and mentoring into the roles and responsibilities of all faculty members. These same leaders must, however, be mindful of the differences between men and women in terms of wants, needs, and communication styles in order to maximize the effects of these resources.

UNIQUE NEEDS OF WOMEN FACULTY IN STEM AND THEIR IMPLICATIONS FOR MENTORING: OPPORTUNITIES AND PITFALLS

Successful mentoring of female faculty, especially in the STEM fields, must recognize the unique needs, cultural issues, and barriers that exist for this faculty type (Hall & Sandler, 1984; Pololi, 2010). In fact, different mentoring models can have a different impact on female faculty (Chesler & Chesler, 2002). In this section we'll explore different types of mentoring models and their potential fit for women faculty in STEM.

Traditional Mentoring Models

The traditional model of mentoring can be divided into two categories: informal and formal. Both types can be defined as a relationship between two people: a mentor (the person with more experience) and the protégé or mentee (the person more junior, with less experience). The goal of this relationship is for the mentor to advise, coach, and guide the mentee in training, development, and decision making related to job and career strategies. Informal mentoring usually happens spontaneously. More often than not, it is the responsibility of the mentee to find a mentor, establish the context of the relationship, and drive any discussions between the two parties. Informal mentor relationships do not have a finite time-frame and can often span the length of the mentee's career. Evidence suggests informal mentoring relationships are more effective than formal mentoring programs (Chao, Walz, & Gardner, 1992).).

Formal mentoring programs are an intentional part of faculty development initiatives that have a specific form and structure, and often include tools, resources, time commitments, schedules, and other collateral factors that help to enable and develop a strong mentor/mentee relationship. The duration of a formal mentoring program is typically finite, with the mentoring relationship concluding at the end of the program. However many relationships endure beyond the confines of the program itself. Although when compared to informal mentoring in any employment setting, regardless of gender, formal mentoring is not considered as impactful on career advancement as its informal counterpart, it is believed that due to cultural norms and the barriers that exist for junior and women faculty in academia, formal mentoring may be more effective (Boice, 1993). Cross-gender versus same-gender mentorship pairs, discussed above, can pose challenges for men in effectively mentoring women since the style, approach, and experience of the male as a mentor may not be appropriate for the female mentee (Bickel et al., 2002). Traditional mentoring models may suffice when it comes to meeting the needs of women faculty, especially if the alternative is no mentoring relationship at all. Nonetheless, the cultural norms and obstacles discussed earlier may prove to be barriers to a woman's full engagement in a mentoring program, especially if few options exist to engage with other women as role models or mentors.

Nontraditional Models

Recently, different types of mentoring models have begun to appear in the literature and in practice, both in the business world and in academia. Peer mentoring is one such model. Peer mentoring can be formal or informal, but often requires participants to take the initiative in creating a community (Driscoll, Parkes, Tilley-Lubbs, Brill, & Pitts Bannister, 2009). The peer mentoring community has more than two members, is non-hierarchical, flexible, and focuses on the empowerment of its participants (Wasburn, 2007). Another example of a nontraditional mentoring program is collaborative or group mentoring. In this case, several senior faculty members will mentor a group of junior faculty. The construct of this program is that of strategic collaboration, including networking activities and peer-to-peer partnerships. Collaborative group mentoring helps to develop a collegial environment and atmosphere for the mentors and the mentees, a development that is particularly beneficial to women (Pololi, Knight, Dennis, & Frankel, 2002; Wasburn, 2007). Of course, the support structure required to implement such a program is imperative and must include senior administrative support both functionally and financially—in the scheduling of regular meetings and design of contracts, for example—and could include interpersonal skills training and other professional development tools. Peer and group mentoring models may be more aligned with the needs of women faculty, and therefore viewed more favorably by women, offering not only the value of a mentoring relationship or relationships, but an opportunity to interact and interface with peers (especially other women) in a safe, collegial, inclusive setting.

Mentoring Webs: A Case Study

A program that may be of particular interest to institutions seeking to transform their culture in support of women faculty in STEM is the story of Stevenson University's School of the Sciences (SOS). At its core, Stevenson's SOS mentoring program looks like facilitated group mentoring. It is this, but much more. The mentoring web, as it is called, is an intentional, socially constructed, comprehensive faculty development program that includes regular meetings, shared leadership, and book clubs.

This formal, structured mentoring program, designed to promote faculty growth and development, includes two key components:

- Faculty Mentoring and Evaluation Committee—all promotion-eligible faculty are required to have one
- New Faculty Orientation Program—"Faculty 101" includes a professional development plan (Gorman, Durmowicz, Roskes, & Slattery, 2010)

When female faculty members with an interest in leadership are asked what they need to succeed, they often mention self-reflection opportunities, business acumen/skills, and mentoring (O'Bannon, Garavalia, Renz, & McCarther, 2010, p. 172). Importantly, faculty development programs that acknowledge female leadership style attributes like consensus building, empowerment, compassion, and challenging the status quo can more appropriately meet the unique needs of women faculty in their quest for leadership positions (O'Bannon et al., 2010). Ultimately, trust is the cornerstone of any effective mentoring program (Wasburn, 2007).

The ADVANCE Program and Its Commitment to Mentoring

Nearly every ADVANCE grant recipient has a program that focuses on mentoring. The NSF ADVANCE website (2013) boasts a dedicated section that highlights these mentoring programs and resources. In an effort to provide real-world solutions to the disparities found in STEM, we offer the following examples of innovative mentoring programs and resources that have been funded through the ADVANCE program and could serve as potential opportunities for other academic institutions interested in implementing a mentoring strategy for women faculty in STEM.

Administrator Shadowing Program—Brown University

The Administrator Shadowing Program at Brown University targets women faculty interested in advancing in their career in pursuit of a position in administration. The program gives these faculty members the opportunity to experience firsthand the work, processes, and leadership aspects of administrative positions. The pairing of faculty with administrators is based on mutual interests, availability, and project timing, and the relationship typically lasts for a semester. In addition to providing women faculty with a better understanding of what it takes to move into an administrative position, the mentoring relationship seeks to build leadership skills required of administrators in academe.

ADVANCE Faculty Mentoring Handbook—University of Rhode Island

A valuable resource for any formal mentoring program, either new or existing, is the *ADVANCE Faculty Mentoring Handbook* developed by the University of Rhode Island. This comprehensive guide was developed for mentors and mentees alike and begins with an overview of the concept of mentoring. Included in the handbook is a realistic look at mentoring—that it can be a fair amount of work, and that you can expect to get out of the relationship what you put into it. The more participants are committed to its success, the more likely it is that the relationship will achieve that success. Offering guidelines for mentors, mentees, and department chairs, the handbook also identifies characteristics of a successful mentoring relationship, specifically for women mentees. Lastly, it describes the role of the ADVANCE program office and the role it can play in assisting mentors and mentees, providing resources, advice, and guidance to ensure a positive outcome for all parties involved in the mentoring program.

The Mentoring Relationship—Cornell University

Cornell University has published a document that outlines relevant information on mentoring and the mentoring relationship for mentors of new or junior faculty. Beginning with an overview of the academic institution, it discusses resources available and the value of developing a network of peers and senior faculty. In addition, questions on career direction and development are addressed, as well as recommendations on aspects of professional development that might be of value to a mentee. Importantly, *The Mentoring Relationship* covers the pitfalls of a mentoring relationship that can be avoided, or at least managed for success. These include understanding the time commitment required for a successful relationship, setting appropriate expectations for both parties, knowing what to do with a relationship mismatch, and recognizing that as a mentee develops and grows in her or his career, so will the mentee's needs and expectations of a mentoring relationship.

Speed Mentoring—University of Miami

The Miller School of Medicine at the University of Miami runs a program called Speed Mentoring, which serves as a precursor to a formal mentoring relationship between a mentor and mentee. Similar to the concept of speed dating, the goal of the program is to introduce junior faculty and postdoctoral students to senior faculty. Typically scheduled for an hour in length total, the session is divided into five- or eight-minute intervals, for which mentees come prepared with their CV or a topic for discussion and move from one senior faculty to another. Mentees have two minutes to record or organize their notes between each round. Each session is followed by an opportunity to socialize, reflect, and assess the various conversations. It is through this effort that mentees can identify potential mentors, with whom they may ultimately be matched via a formal mentoring program.

Advancing the Field of Women Faculty in STEM: Future Opportunities

As important and valuable as mentoring is in advancing the careers of women faculty (Wasburn, 2007), mentoring alone may not be enough. Many of the previous examples suggest that mentoring is most impactful when it is part of a comprehensive faculty development strategy. Academic institutions willing to invest time and resources in faculty development programs, especially those that take into account the unique needs of women, will reap the benefits and rewards of a satisfied, engaged, and motivated professorate. All of the following leadership programs focusing on women faculty include a mentoring component utilizing one or more of the different mentoring models discussed earlier. These are but a few examples of intentional initiatives with the specific purpose of advancing women faculty in their chosen field.

The Leadership Institute, University of Missouri-Kansas City

Funded through an NSF ADVANCE award, this program was developed and delivered by the faculty and staff at the Midwest Center for Nonprofit Leadership at the University of Missouri–Kansas City. The goal of the program is to increase the number of women leaders in the STEM fields by assisting them to prepare for leadership roles (O'Bannon et al., 2010). Consisting of two sessions, each lasting two days, the program includes prework and homework and is interactive by design in the hope of bridging the gap between faculty and leadership responsibilities. Topics covered include leadership dynamics in a higher education setting, personal leadership inventory, communication skills, self-awareness, strategic financial management, and the value of participating in a mentor relationship while building internal and external stakeholder networks. The program culminates in the development of a personal action plan (O'Bannon et al., 2010).

Summer Institute for Women in Higher Education

The Higher Education Resource Services (HERS) hosts three annual leadership institutes: one at Bryn Mawr College, one at University of Denver, and another at Wellesley College. Whether participating in the two-week residential program at Bryn Mawr or Colorado, or the four-part weekend program at Wellesley, participants are offered an intensive immersion into leadership and management challenges. Topics of interest include leading and managing change, financial environment, mock interviews with C-Suite leadership, leadership mapping exercises (making use of instruments such as the Myers-Briggs personality inventory, for example), and the utilization of a coaching and mentoring tool (HERS, 2013).

Women Faculty Mentoring Program, University of Wisconsin–Madison

The university-wide Women Faculty Mentoring Program at the University of Wisconsin–Madison was implemented to support, develop, and retain junior women faculty throughout the tenure process. Junior faculty members who apply to the program are matched with a tenured woman with similar interests but who works outside her department. It is a multiyear program, and mentoring pairs last for a year with the intent to complement/supplement the mentoring efforts of individual departments (University of Wisconsin–Madison, 2013).

The program includes evaluation and assessment throughout the duration of the mentoring relationship, from both the mentor's and mentee's perspective. In addition to the mentoring pairs, participants are encouraged to engage in peer mentoring groups that help mentees to develop a network and a sense of inclusion across the university. Sponsored events are the cornerstone of the program and include a mentoring luncheon, an annual reception, and a conversation series featuring guest speakers on topics of interest to women faculty (University of Wisconsin–Madison, 2013).

ELAM—Executive Leadership in Academic Medicine, Drexel University

A one-year part-time fellowship program, ELAM exists to enable senior women faculty to "effect sustained positive change as institutional leaders" (Drexel University, 2013). Targeting women faculty at schools of medicine, dentistry, and public health, the ELAM program includes education, a personal leadership assessment, coaching, networking, and mentoring. Of particular note is a key requirement of a fellow's participation: Her dean must nominate and mentor the faculty member throughout the duration of the program, culminating with joint attendance at the program's closing forum. The success of the ELAM program cannot be overestimated. When entering the program in 1995, 38% of ELAM's first class held significant leadership positions within higher education. Five years later, 80% of that same first class held similar positions (Richman, Morahan, Cohen, & McDade, 2001).

These programs and many others around the country have begun to make an impact in advancing the careers of women faculty. Future opportunities for women faculty in STEM specifically are virtually endless, and institutions seeking to enhance their faculty development programs need only to look to their neighbors for inspiration and ideas. These opportunities will not, however, come easily without the commitment of academic leaders and the very women who choose this path.

CONCLUSIONS

Implementation of programs similar to those described above, yet on a smaller scale, at individual institutions or among a consortium of regional colleges and universities, may help STEM administrators in their efforts to improve the recruitment, advancement, and retention of women faculty. Likewise, grassroots efforts by female faculty themselves could prove to be a successful strategy in expanding and enhancing networks and career development opportunities for female STEM faculty. The challenges most academic institutions face in dealing with disparities between men and women faculty in the STEM fields continue to persist. Progress has been made, however, in large part due to the ADVANCE program and the grants it disperses throughout academia. Research supported through the ADVANCE program confirms the important role mentoring plays in career development and advancement of women faculty. This evidence suggests that academic institutions interested in advancing women faculty in the STEM fields would benefit from the implementation of a formal mentoring program. Recently, a variety of mentoring techniques has begun to emerge. These techniques are seemingly better tailored to the needs of women faculty's leadership style and learning preferences. A number of mentoring programs and resources now exist that leverage these women-centric concepts, many of which are available as open source materials on institutions websites.

Ultimately, the future of women faculty in STEM, and whether or not parity can be reached with their male counterparts, is dependent upon the commitment of academic leadership and its desire to purposefully engineer a more welcoming, inviting, supportive, and stimulating work environment for female faculty. Of course, the responsibility also lies on the shoulders of current and future women faculty at all levels of leadership and responsibility.

Margaret Mead is credited with saying, "Never underestimate the power of a few committed people to change the world. Indeed it is the only thing that ever has." The leadership programs highlighted in this chapter, developed and often facilitated by women, serve as a testimony to this quote. A good place to begin a change strategy for any STEM program would be the implementation of a mentoring program. Cited as a key resource to help in their professional development (Nemiro et al., 2009), women faculty would benefit from this type of support from their leaders and peers. Indeed, the power of mentoring and its impact on female faculty career development and job satisfaction could serve as a catalyst for the change so desperately needed in the STEM fields.

TAKEAWAY EXAMPLES

The Mentor/Mentee Checklist that follows is only one of many resources available on the Internet, as indicated by the resource list that follows the checklist.

STEM Women Faculty

Mentee Checklist

Before the meeting with your mentor…

.... Remember, you are responsible for facilitating this relationship. Don't expect your mentor to drive it forward.

.... Ask yourself – What are my goals and expectations? Why do I want a mentor? How can a mentor assist me in meeting these goals? What are my competency levels as a teacher, researcher, administrator, and in the community? Where do I want them to be?

.... Take the initiative. Introduce yourself by phone, letter or email. Invite your mentor to meet; suggest potential topics. Agree on confidentiality and no-fault termination.

.... Avail yourself of any tools or resources your institution provides faculty involved in a mentor/mentee relationship.

.... Ask your mentor for her CV. Identify key steps in her career path that seem valuable and prepare questions for your first meeting.

.... Make a list of some of the challenges you've faced as a STEM faculty member. Be prepared to discuss with your mentor, and ask if she faced similar challenges during her career.

.... Update your CV and send it to your mentor.

.... Ask yourself: What skills do I need to learn or improve? What do I want to change about my work style? What professional networks do I seek? What do I want out of this relationship?

During the meeting…

.... Discuss your short- and long-term professional goals (e.g., grants, manuscripts, courses, networking) and work together to develop steps to reach these goals; make them time-bound.

.... Determine frequency of meetings. This will vary based on individual needs, but often occurs once a month, and at least quarterly. The extent of interaction can range from a brief email or phone "check-ins" to lengthy follow-up meetings.

.... Suggest potential topics for future meetings. (Examples: setting and achieving goals, managing time effectively in an academic environment, balancing personal and professional life, negotiating for what you want/need, completing manuscripts, etc.)

After the meeting and throughout the relationship…

.... Establish your own checklist for follow up. Keep an ongoing portfolio of activities & works in progress. Check your timeline.

.... Re-evaluate the mentoring agreement annually.

STEM Women Faculty

Mentor Checklist

.... Be sure that your mentee knows how to contact you (e.g., email, telephone, fax, etc.). Request contact information from your mentee.

.... Familiarize yourself with your institution's promotion/tenure policies and avail yourself of any tools or resources your institution provides faculty involved in a mentor/mentee relationship.

.... Introduce yourself by phone, brief letter or email. Invite your mentee to a meeting; suggest potential topics. Agree on confidentiality and no-fault termination.

.... Obtain your mentee's CV prior to the first meeting so that you already know important professional information.

.... Set aside about an hour for the first meeting with your mentee. You may want to conduct the first meeting away from the office, or go to your mentee's office. Use this hour to learn about other aspects of your mentee. What are her interests and hobbies? Share similar information about yourself.

.... Discuss your expectations and your needs with your mentee. Work with your mentee on yearly goals for the mentoring relationship (meeting time, etc.). Plan to meet at least quarterly with your mentee.

.... To chart her success, help your mentee develop a checklist that you both can follow.

Adapted from Georgetown University Office of Faculty and Academic Affairs
http://www1.georgetown.edu/gumc/evp/facultyaffairs/about/

RESOURCE LIST

For additional details and information on the programs and initiatives highlighted in this chapter, please visit the websites provided below:

Administrator Shadowing Program—Brown University http://www.brown.edu/Administration/Provost/Advance/shadowing.html

ADVANCE Faculty Mentoring Handbook—University of Rhode Island http://oied.ncsu.edu/faculty/wp-content/uploads/2013/04/Faculty_Mentoring_Handbook_pdf-1.pdf

ELAM—Drexel University https://www.drexelmed.edu/Home/OtherPrograms/Executive-LeadershipinAcademicMedicine.aspx

The Leadership Institute—University of Missouri-Kansas City http://bloch.umkc.edu/mw-cnl/

The Mentoring Relationship—Cornell University http://www.advance.cornell.edu/documents/The-Mentoring-Relationship.pdf

Mentoring Webs—Stevenson University http://stematsu.org/

Speed Mentoring—University of Miami http://www.as.miami.edu/seeds/speedmentoring

Summer Institute for Women in Higher Education—HERS http://www.hersnet.org/her-shighereducationresourceservices.htmsisihtm.asp

Women Faculty Mentoring Program—University of Wisconsin-Madison http://www.provost.wisc.edu/mentor.htm

REFERENCES

Bickel, J., Wara, D., Atkinson, B., Cohen, L., Dunn, M., Hostler, S., ... Stokes, E. (2002). Increasing women's leadership in academic medicine: Report of the AAMC Project Implementation Committee. *Academic Medicine, 77*(10), 1043–1061.

Blackwell, L. V., Snyder, L. A., & Mavriplis, C. (2009). Diverse faculty in STEM fields: Attitudes, performance, and fair treatment. *Journal of Diversity in Higher Education, 2*(4), 195–205. doi:10.1037/a0016974

Boice, R. (1993). New faculty involvement for woman and minorities. *Research in Higher Education, 34*(3), 291–341.

Chao, G. T., Walz, P., & Gardner, P. D. (1992). Formal and informal mentorships: A comparison on mentoring functions and contrast with nonmentored counterparts. *Personnel Psychology, 45,* 619–636. doi: 10.1111/j.1744-6570.1992.tb00863.

Chesler, N. C., & Chesler, M. A . (2002). Gender-informed mentoring strategies for women engineering scholars: On establishing a caring community. *Journal of Engineering Education, 9*(1), 49–55.

Drexel University College of Medicine. (2013). ELAM® Fast Facts. Retrieved from www.drexelmed.edu/elam.

Driscoll, L., Parkes, K., Tilley-Lubbs, G., Brill, J., & Pitts Bannister, V. (2009). Navigating the lonely sea: Peer mentoring and collaboration among aspiring women scholars. *Mentoring & Tutoring: Partnership in Learning, 17*(1), 5–21. doi:10.1080/13611260802699532

Gibson, S. K. (2006). Mentoring of women faculty: The role of organizational politics and culture. *Innovative Higher Education, 31*(1), 63–79. doi:10.1007/s10755-006-9007-7

Ginorio, A. B. (1995). *Warming the climate for women in academic science.* Washington, DC: Association of American Colleges and Universities, Program on the Status and Education of Women.

Gorman, S. T., Durmowicz, M. C., Roskes, E. M., & Slattery, S .P. (2010). Women in the academy: Female leadership in STEM education and the evolution of a mentoring web. *Forum on Public Policy: Journal of the Oxford Roundtable, 2,* 1–21. Retrieved from http://files.eric.ed.gov/fulltext/EJ903573.pdf

Hall, R. M., & Sandler, B. R. (1984). *Out of the classroom: A chilly climate for women?* Washington, DC: Association for American Colleges.

HERS/Higher Education Resource Services. (2011). About HERS (Higher Education Resource Services). Retrieved from http://www.hersnet.org/abouthers.asp?menu=About%20HERS

Johnsrud, L. K. (1991). Mentoring between academic women: The capacity for interdependence. *Initiatives, 54*(3), 7–17.

Jolliff, L., Leadley, J., Coakley, E., & Slone, R. A. (2012). Women in academic medicine statistics and medical school benchmarking, 2011–2012. Retrieved from https://www.aamc.org/members/gwims/statistics/

Kulis, S., Sicotte, D., & Collins, S. (2002). More than a pipeline problem: Labor supply constraints and gender stratification across academic science disciplines. *Research in Higher Education, 43*(6), 657–691.

National Science Foundation (NSF). (2013). ADVANCE program description. Retrieved from http://www.nsf.gov/funding/pgm_summ.jsp?pims_id=5383

National Institutes of Health (NIH), Office of Extramural Research. (2013). Research career development "K" awards. Retrieved from http://grants.nih.gov/grants/policy/nihgps_2012/nihgps_ch12.htm

Nemiro, J. E., Hacker, B., Ferrel, M. L., & Guthrie, R. (2009). Using appreciative inquiry as a tool to instigate transformational change in recruiting and developing women faculty in STEM disciplines. *International Journal of Gender, Science and Technology, 1,* 5–35. Retrieved from http://genderandset.open.ac.uk

Nonnemaker, L., (2000). Women physicians in academic medicine: New insights from cohort studies. *New England Journal of Medicine, 342,* 399–405.

O'Bannon, D. J., Garavalia, L., Renz, D. O., & McCarther, S. M. (2010). Successful leadership development for women STEM faculty. *Leadership and Management in Engineering, 10,* 167–174.

Pololi, L.H. (2010). *Changing the culture of academic medicine: Perspectives of women faculty.* Hanover, NH: Dartmouth College Press.

Pololi, L. H., Knight, S. M., Dennis, K., & Frankel, R. M. (2002). Helping medical school faculty realize their dreams: An innovative, collaborative mentoring program. *Academic Medicine: Journal of the Association of American Medical Colleges, 77*(5), 377–384. Retrieved from http://www.ncbi.nlm.nih.gov/pubmed/12010691

Ragins, B. R., & Cotton, J. L. (1999). Mentor functions and outcomes: a comparison of men and women in formal and informal mentoring relationships. *Journal of Applied Psychology, 84*(4), 529–50. Retrieved from http://www.ncbi.nlm.nih.gov/pubmed/10504893

Richman, R. C., Morahan, P. S., Cohen, D. W., & McDade, S. A. (2001). Advancing women and closing the leadership gap: The Executive Leadership in Academic Medicine

(ELAM) program experience: *Journal of Women's Health & Gender-based Medicine, 10*(3), 271–277.

Sonnert, G., & Holton, G. (1996). Career patterns of women and men in the sciences. *American Scientist, 84*(1), 63–71.

University of Michigan NSF. (2008). *Assessing the academic work environment for science and engineering and social science faculty at the University of Michigan in 2006: Gender, race, and discipline in department- and university-related climate factors.* ADVANCE REPORT. Ann Arbor, MI: Author. Retrieved from http://www.advance.rackham.umich.edu/ADV-FacultyClimate-Rpt2-final.pdf

University of Wisconsin–Madison. (2013). Office of the Provost women faculty mentoring program. Retrieved from http://www.provost.wisc.edu/mentor.htm

Wasburn, M. (2007). Mentoring women faculty: An instrumental case study of strategic collaboration. *Mentoring and Tutoring, 15*(1), 57–72. doi:10.1080/13611260601037389

Xu, Y. J. (2008). Gender disparity in STEM disciplines: A study of faculty attrition and turnover intentions. *Research in Higher Education, 49*(7), 607–624. doi:10.1007/s11162-008-9097-4

CHAPTER 14

ADVENTURES IN COLLABORATION

Mentoring, Instructional Rounds, and Shared Leadership in Improving Teaching and Learning in a Rural School District

James A. Salzman and Karen Boch

ABSTRACT

The chapter describes the application of principles of mentoring within the context of the development of a rural district leadership team (DLT). The two authors, a university-based professional development consultant and the school district's superintendent, discuss the use of a university faculty member in a group-mentoring role as the DLT members learn about and implement instructional rounds in their school district. The authors describe the gradual release of responsibility as DLT members develop formal protocols and procedures while concurrently building capacity to mentor new members as district staff integrates instructional rounds into their school improvement process. Finally, they discuss the ways in which the district intends to sustain the practices after the formal university–school collaboration is completed.

Mentoring for the Professions: Orienting Toward the Future, pages 259–275.

It's 7:30 a.m. on a Wednesday in November. It's still dark outside as members of Wellston City School District's Leadership Team (DLT) settle themselves into their seats before the start of a day of instructional rounds in the middle school. This is the third year that the district has engaged in the process, and the protocols are well known. But today there's a bit of a twist. Instead of being led by the university consultant, DLT members, most of them classroom teachers, will be leading and facilitating the activities. Each day devoted to instructional rounds (IR) begins with an opportunity for the DLT members to hone their skills. Dave and Belinda get the attention of their peers and use one of the reading protocols to facilitate the processing of the article they chose on the problem of practice. Following them, Tammy and Bronwyn show a teaching video they found that highlights a teacher's use of formative instructional strategies. They remind their colleagues to describe, not evaluate, what they see and hear in the video. Both of these activities are designed to orient team members to the problem of practice for which they will be observing in classrooms.

After processing the video, DLT members form predetermined teams of four or five to go into classrooms to observe. Each team will observe four classrooms for approximately 20 minutes apiece; generally teams are able to observe 16 to 20 classrooms on any IR day. This year, the DLT members want to focus on specific grade bands, so this day's observations are done in sixth- through eighth-grade classrooms. While in the classrooms, each member takes notes individually on what he or she sees and hears as it relates to the problem of practice. Observers pay close attention to the three elements—students, teachers, and content—of the instructional core, holding onto the mantra of instructional rounds: "If you can't see [the problem of practice] in the core, it's not there" (City, Elmore, Fiarman, & Teitel, 2009, p. 27). What they are especially attentive to is in what ways the tasks that are being assigned to students allow for the problem of practice to reveal itself.

When they return to the presentation room, each team member silently identifies representative, sometimes unique, pieces of evidence of the problem of practice in action from their notes and places each one on individual post-it notes. The members of the teams then take turns placing different post-it notes on a large poster while they debrief on what they saw. In this case, the groups decide that they will all process the notes using the same structure that related to district professional development on formative instructional practice in which teachers had engaged. Post-it notes start to populate the categories of "Learning Targets" (both clear and unclear), "Feedback" (examples of student-to-teacher and teacher-to-student), and "Ownership" (with examples of how students show ownership of the goals of the lesson and how teachers do so).

When all groups have processed their team observations, each team reports its findings. This day, the facilitators choose to process by doing a gallery walk, with one team member staying with the poster and group members traveling to each poster to compare and contrast what they saw in different classrooms. Since no classroom identifiers are on the post-it notes, DLT members are looking for the patterns that arise as teachers in these grade bands implement formative instructional practices in their classrooms. When the gallery walk is done, group members propose differ-

ent recommendations for what the principals and their building leadership teams (BLT) can do to improve teaching and learning in their schools. These recommendations are made in three layers: (1) what can be done by the next BLT meeting, (2) what can be done by the next month, and (3) what can be done by the end of the year. The BLT members will then get the recommendations and create an action plan for moving the middle-school building forward. As the day comes to a close, DLT members do a plus/delta evaluation of what worked and what could be improved for the next meeting. Immediately following this evaluation, Jim, the university consultant who has been observing and taking notes on the group interactions throughout the day, provides the group with feedback on his perceptions of the successes of the day and recommendations for consideration as the DLT members continue to hone their group learning. Finally, DLT members volunteer to lead various aspects of the next IR meeting, and the day ends.

INTRODUCTION

Just as professional staff in a hospital use rounds to determine the health of their patient load and how best to use their resources on any given day, DLT members are able to take the pulse of the school, as it reveals itself in the instructional core, so that teachers and administrators can monitor efforts at improving teaching and learning and make adjustments efficiently. The scene described above is an example of a day of instructional rounds within the Wellston City School District in Wellston, Ohio. We should note that the day described is one that took place in the third year of an ongoing project and the processes and leadership described may be different from more traditional school improvement models. What is unique to our experiences in schools is the distributed leadership within the DLT and the intentional building of capacity, especially of classroom teachers, to lead the school change efforts from within the district. And the question that drives this chapter is: How did Wellston City Schools get to this place?

The chapter describes the application of principles of mentoring within the context of the development of a rural district leadership team (DLT). Recognizing that definitions of mentoring abound, Eby, Rhodes, and Allen (2010) generalize that mentoring "(1) reflects a unique relationship between individuals...; (2) is a learning partnership...; (3) is a process defined by the types of support provided...; (4) is reciprocal, yet asymmetrical...; and (5) is dynamic [i.e., changing over time]" (p. 10). In this chapter, the two authors, a university-based professional development consultant and the school district's superintendent, discuss the use of a university faculty member in a group-mentoring role as the DLT members learn about and implement instructional rounds in their school district. They also describe the gradual release of responsibility as DLT members develop formal protocols and procedures while they build capacity to mentor new members as district staff integrates instructional rounds into their school improvement process. Finally, they discuss the ways in which the district intends to sustain the practices after the formal university–school collaboration is completed.

MENTORING AND INSTRUCTIONAL ROUNDS

Mentoring in education has been the subject of a good deal of interest since the 1980s. In its seminal days, lacking a literature base, education scholars looked to business literature for their models, which tended to focus on a traditional pairing of a single mentor with a mentee. This was often not a comfortable fit because schools form quite different organizations and cultures than business. For instance, in business, the early literature often touted the successes of mentoring relationships in which the mentors were same-sex and eight to 25 years older than their protégés (Kram, 1983, 1985; Levinson, Darrow, Klein, Levinson, & McKee, 1978). The rationale behind this was clear. In the business world, the mentor is a role model for the protégé and is able to provide a concrete picture of where the protégé can be in time with hard work, dedication, and documented accomplishments. That type of hierarchy, however, doesn't always exist in K–12 education. In states like Ohio, with formal mentoring programs, a career-changing new teacher may be older than the accomplished mentor assigned to work with him or her. And whether in business or education, formalized mentoring relationships do put strains on resources, both fiscal and human. In recent years, however, *group mentoring* has become a topic of interest for business as a cost-efficient way of changing learning structures, enculturating individuals into the operations of the business and accelerating individuals into leadership roles (Emelo, 2011; Jones, 2006). In this case, a university based professional developer, with experience in facilitating instructional rounds, used a group mentoring structure to assist the district leadership team as they worked to change their culture and move more staff into leadership roles.

Instructional rounds (IR) in educational settings, founded upon and modified from the medical rounds model, provide a structure for engaging in this type of group mentoring (City et al., 2009). In this case, it also rested upon some assumptions about the relationship between the mentor and the staff. Rather than positioning the relationship as one of expert to novice, the IR mentor acted as more of a consultant, engaging staff in dialogue about the state of current practices and the ideal outcomes teachers could attain in schools as they revolved around the instructional core—teachers, students, and content—and as they were most clearly reflected in the tasks that teachers require of students. This type of professional development is often associated with communities of practice (Wenger, 1998) or professional learning communities (DuFour, 2004, 2007). Use of these types of configurations for learning has been touted as the "most powerful professional development and change strategy available" (Huffman & Hipp, 2003, p. 4). And, while these communities can exist without a formal mentor or coach, having a learned other who takes the role of consultant and practices within the parameters of the language of collaboration and engages community members in dialogic processes helps to increase the power of teachers' voices as agents of change (Crafton & Kaiser, 2011).

There is no empirical research to promote IR as a school improvement model, but the anecdotal evidence is intriguing (City et al., 2009; Roberts, 2012). One of the most compelling reasons to engage in rounds is "that what distinguishes instructional rounds from virtually all other school improvement ideas is that it is intended to disrupt the typical patterns of interaction between adults in schools. Disrupting these patterns activates organizational problems that few school systems have any experience in solving" (Roberts, 2012, p. 10). We would also argue that disrupting these patterns is the very reason that a mentor experienced in the rounds process can serve initially as an expert in the process, then as a professional collaborator. This is why the district contracted with a university collaborator as its staff members began their journey into the use of instructional rounds.

MENTORING FOR SCHOOL CHANGE: SHAPING THE CONTEXT WITHIN GROUP DYNAMICS

In theory, university–school collaborations should be win-win situations. Unfortunately, that is often not the case (Goldenberg, 2004). There is often an inherently perceived relationship of teacher–learner/expert–novice, as "research faculty have tended to treat schools and teachers as *subjects of,* rather than *partners in,* their projects" (Salzman, 1999, p. 28). On the positive side, universities have resources to bring to schools, including specific expertise and, often, human resources with time to invest; time is often a luxury for teachers as they deal with the day-to-day demands of the classroom. Too often, however, university researchers are interested in testing out theory and use schools as their proving grounds, with the results often not addressing the real concerns that school personnel have about improving teaching and learning. Changing the role, however, changes the relationship. If the university consultant takes on the role of mentor rather than researcher, then he or she uses the skills of close observation and analysis to facilitate individual reflection and guide the group members' efforts at "analyzing [their] actions, decision, or products by focusing on [their] process of achieving them" (Killion & Todnem, 1991, p. 15).

Goldenberg posits four elements that shape the context of schools and are required of school cultures if they are to effect positive change: (1) goals that are set and shared, (2) indicators that measure success, (3) assistance by capable others, and (4) leadership that supports and pressures. Three of these—goals, indicators, and leadership—are generally present in most schools. Assistance by capable others often is not. Goldenberg (2004) describes it this way:

> Meaningful professional assistance must be long-term, substantive, and specifically focused on accomplishing generally understood and agreed-upon goals. Assistance involves many things, such as presenting new information, providing specific and concrete guidance in applying both new information and important understandings about a school site. All of these require creating settings that encourage learning

new information and skills, coupled with discussions and analysis of practice and
opportunities to attempt and reflect upon new behaviors. (p. 52)

This definition of a long-term, substantive, and mutually beneficial relationship
with specific outcome goals is precisely what successful mentoring relationships
entail. The specific characteristics that Eby and associates (2010) generalized,
especially in regard to the creation of relationships within a learning partnership
that exists with reciprocity among both school and university partners, are what
set apart the type of work in which the authors engaged at Wellston from a typical
university–school research project. In this case, the mentor became an ex officio
member of the DLT, first leading the professional development and the overall
process and then, in time, becoming a "guide on the side" as he coached and facilitated the DLT members' taking on the responsibilities of leading the process.

CREATING SETTINGS FOR SUCCESS

Unlike traditional university-to-K–12-educator relationships, mentoring relationships take shape in the K–12 educators' workplace. In Goldenberg's case study in
California, the school leadership had to create a setting, the Academic Expectations Committee; that already existed in Wellston. Settings are defined as "any
instance in which two or more people come together in new relationships over a
sustained period of time in order to achieve certain goals" (Sarason, 1972, p. 1).
One element needed for school change existed already within the setting of the
DLT. In this case, the district had created a structure to address leadership issues.
This structure included selected central office administrators, all building principals, and teachers, including union leadership, with the majority of the members
being teachers.

The primary role of Wellston's DLT is to promote a culture of common expectations or commitment by maintaining a district-wide focus on high achievement
for all students through the implementation and monitoring of the continuous improvement process. Staff in the district worked to put structures in place that supported the Ohio Improvement Process, including establishing collaborative structures, such as building leadership teams (BLT) and teacher-based teams (TBT).
Included in the DLT are members of the Race-to-the-Top (RttT) transformation
team, as it is part of the district's scope of work in relation to their RttT funding.

The DLT setting on its own, however, was not sufficient to engage members
in systematic exploration of the current state of instructional practice and student
learning within the district. To that end, the use of IR provides what is essentially
a setting within a setting, and it is the job of the mentor to collaborate with the
group to integrate IR into the current work of the committee, rather than have this
type of activity become an added responsibility. As described in the introduction,
as DLT members engage in rounds, the mentor provides them with a template of
a scope and sequence of activities that is placed upon the day and provides the
structure in which members interact. Within those parameters, the leadership team

members are trained in protocols that they use to interact with content and with each other. We would argue that protocols are especially important in a group mentoring relationship because of the danger of underregulated talking that often takes place in meetings called to address serious problems (White, 2006, as cited in McDonald, Mohr, Dichter, & McDonald, 2007). "Often those leading the meetings talk too much, and often they let others talk too much. Together the talkers choke off real listening and the kind of distributed and beyond-your-comfort-zone learning that solving serious problems usually requires" (McDonald et al., 2007, pp. 6–7). In order to be successful in this new setting, former, comfortable ways of interacting with each other need to change (City et al, 2009).

TRUST AND RAPPORT: KEYS TO A SUCCESSFUL MENTORING RELATIONSHIP

A prerequisite to altering groups' ways of interacting with each other, however, is that mentors possess strong interpersonal skills in order to establish empathic and trusting relationships (Costa & Garmston, 2002; Salzman, 1999, 2002). This is especially important, and much more challenging, when engaging with a community of professionals who bring with them their own concerns and anxieties about changes that are inevitably required for schools to improve. These anxieties were especially prevalent in the fall of 2010, when the subject of IR was first raised between Jim and Karen in discussing the district schools' professional development. Prior to this meeting, the previous curriculum director, with superintendent support, had instituted classroom walkthroughs (CWT); but a lack of training, support, and clear communications with staff had been a recipe for disaster. A lot of animosity and anxiety resulted from the CWT process. These feelings were more than likely due to the lack of training and common understandings among teachers who were observed, even though a team of teachers met to look at the forms, discuss the process, and so on. The process was also difficult because each building had a different level of engagement. In buildings where leadership didn't value the process or make it a priority, it didn't happen. In other buildings, implementation was such that teachers were doing CWT in colleagues' classrooms, which presented a challenge because the parameters and ground rules either had not been established or were not enforced.

Building Trust and Trusting the Building (Staff)

In that first meeting about IR in August 2010, Karen explained to Jim that teachers were distrustful of observations because they tended to be "gotcha" opportunities, and teachers felt ambushed by both administrators and fellow teachers, their colleagues. Jim and Karen decided that, for the IR process to be embraced in the current climate, DLT members needed to choose the process rather than have a new initiative foisted upon them. Jim prepared a presentation that explained what instructional rounds were, contrasted it with the CWT process that they had recently experienced, detailed the three-year plan to train and then guide members in its introduction and implementation, and described the intention to build capacity for DLT members to lead the process themselves as Jim mentored himself out of a job. At this meeting, Jim described his experiences with being a facilitator for one of the districts that implemented instructional rounds within the Ohio Leadership Collaborative (OLC) (City et al., 2009). DLT members were able to ask questions and express concerns; they were not asked for a commitment on the spot.

As the meeting ended, DLT members were told that they could have some time to think about whether they were interested in engaging in the process and that at the next meeting they would vote. Between meetings, some of the staff called people in other Ohio districts that were part of the OLC and asked them pointed questions about the process. Others spent time polling their peers and colleagues about their impressions of this new process. As one DLT member reflected recently about the initial presentation: "I think that we were able to build trust because we researched the pros and cons, brought in an expert in the process, committed to professional development (long term), and everyone had a voice. We also called the districts in the IR book to get their feedback on the process." In the end, DLT members voted unanimously to pursue IR as a school improvement tool. Given their previous experience with CWTs, this was a huge leap of faith, and mentors have an obligation to honor such trust.

Maintaining Trust: Establishing Norms

Once the DLT provided the go-ahead, it was essential to establish norms in order to maintain the trust that they showed in their vote. Consequently, at the first meeting of the full DLT after the vote, one of the first activities was to establish norms of behavior for the group. The group came up with six norms: (1) listen actively; (2) be on time for meetings; (3) respect others' ideas and opinions; (4) focus on ideas and actions, not individuals; (5) come prepared; and (6) maintain confidentiality. These norms became part of the agendas so that group members were reminded of them at each meeting. All of these norms allowed DLT members to work from the "premise that good teaching (and good leading) is a set of professional practices that can be learned by most people. In order to support improvement, [groups] need to learn to recognize, name, and describe these practices—without being distracted by personality, style or personal biases" (City et al, 2009, p. 77).

Because team members are going into classrooms and because the conversations that take place after these observations involve peers and colleagues, it is incumbent on members to be sure that the tenor and content of the discussions stay in the room in order to provide a safe place for discussing teaching, not teachers. Team members found out early in the process that teachers whose classes were observed wanted to have some feedback from them, and this became one of the challenges—how to maintain confidentiality while providing information.

In order to meet those sometimes conflicting goals, one of the action steps the DLT took was to provide time after school in each building to discuss the evidence the team saw in relation to the problem of practice. While the turnout was mixed at the different buildings, the feedback from the participants was similar and positive. Comments and discussions were consistent across buildings. Teachers felt they gained an understanding of the process and that confidentiality was respected. One DLT member reported, for example, a teacher's opinion that "The evidence collected was exactly what she was told [would be collected], 'What the teacher is saying/doing and what the students are saying/doing.'" Teachers were pleased with the responsiveness of DLT members, who discussed the process and talked about individual feedback when asked.

BUILDING SKILLS THROUGH HIGH-QUALITY PROFESSIONAL DEVELOPMENT

Throughout these three school years, DLT members participated in a minimum of three hours of job-embedded professional development per month, with most days being full-day sessions. The design adhered to standards of high-quality professional development, and each session used a common structure with learning activities that supported teacher learning (Ball & Cohen, 1999; Hawley & Valli, 1999; National Staff Development Council, 2001; Sparks & Hirsh, 1997). All professional development took place on site within the school district, with most sessions being staged in either the district office or the professional development room at the high school. The relationship of the university partner and DLT members was also ongoing, as the monthly meetings for three years would indicate. However, in order to successfully engage in instructional rounds, a great deal of initial training is required. The training can be broken into three major categories: (1) investigating the rounds process, (2) preparing for a problem of practice, and (3) learning how to observe in classrooms.

Investigating the Rounds Process

Unpacking the rounds process provided the bulk of the agendas over the first couple of meetings. All team members were provided with copies of the book, *Instructional Rounds in Education: A Network Approach to Improving Teaching and Learning* (City et al., 2009), and were assigned chapters to read in preparation for the meetings. As mentioned earlier, even prior to beginning rounds, DLT members explored the experiences of other districts that had participated in the pilot program called the Ohio Leadership Collaborative, a project that was cited within the book and provided some of the examples for the authors. Jim's own experiences as part of that original network also became part of the professional development presentations. Members gained insight into the process and came to understand the underlying principles that formed the theory for the practice.

Part of the responsibility of the mentor here was to explicitly teach the clear structure in which DLT members were to engage as they implemented the IR process. Participants used protocols to process the reading, identified significant problems of practice that they believed could improve teaching and learning, explored their beliefs on theories of action as to how these problems can be impacted to improve teaching and learning, and learned how to observe effectively in classrooms. Two issues, identifying and explicating a problem of practice and effectively observing in classrooms, are at the crux of an effective IR implementation.

Preparing for a Problem of Practice

Presentations on a process only go so far in helping to illuminate how rounds work on the ground. Concurrent with learning about the process, the team had to choose a problem of practice upon which they wanted to work as they implemented rounds in the district. To be meaningful, a problem of practice (PoP) must meet several criteria, such as: (1) "focusing on the instructional core"; (2) "being directly observable in classrooms"; (3) "being actionable within the district's (or school's) control"; (4) "connecting to a broader strategy of improvement"; and (5) "being *high-leverage*, i.e., if acted on, it will lead to significant improvements in student learning" (City et al., 2009, p. 102).

Problems of practice arise from the concerns that already exist in schools and should be related to an issue that teachers are already addressing. This could be a problem that is being addressed in professional development or one that has arisen organically from concerns that teachers and principals have raised. Since these problems situate themselves within the instructional core, which consists of the interrelationship of students, teachers, and content, the problem that IR teams investigate will create rich data from classroom observations for conversations on teaching and learning. Before the team engages in those observations, though, its members must articulate their understandings of what the problem is and what it will look like within classrooms. As participants sensitize themselves to their chosen PoP, mentors can help prepare them by identifying articles and facilitating discussions on the problem, both in general terms and as they manifest themselves in their schools. The National School Reform Faculty website (http://www.nsrfharmony.org/protocols.html) provides effective resources for facilitating readings.

In the case of Wellston, the DLT initially chose to work with the problem of student engagement, theorizing that if students are not engaged then no amount of good teaching or better content will help improve schools. They also discussed the need to choose a PoP that could be seen in any classroom and that did not involve content-specific strategies or require deep content knowledge on the part of DLT members. In order to investigate this issue, Jim chose to have DLT members read *Working on the Work: An Action Plan for Teachers, Principals, and Superintendents* (Schlechty, 2002). Schlechty provides a continuum of five qualitatively different levels of engagement, from rebellion to authentic academic engagement.

DLT members spent time in their professional development sessions discussing the work and identifying the kinds of behaviors that they would anticipate seeing from students who were engaged in any of the different levels. They spent a good deal of time distinguishing between the concepts of *strategic compliance* (where students weren't intrinsically motivated to engage with the content but they recognized that there were extrinsic rewards for doing the work—for example, when students read a book because they see that reading it is likely to lead to a better grade) and *ritual compliance* (the level at which students are willing to engage in work to avoid a negative consequence—for example, when they complete homework so that they remain eligible for an athletic team) in rich discussions that focused on whether and how one could truly tell the difference when observing in the classroom.

The team focused on this particular PoP for the first two years of their engagement in IR. One of the interesting things to happen in that time is that the team members discovered that students could be engaged in tasks but that the tasks themselves were not necessarily ones that would allow deep learning to take place. This led to a number of discussions toward the end of the second year about how this particular problem of practice was insufficient to really help the district move student achievement forward. While a mentor could have proactively cautioned team members that engagement was a necessary but not sufficient element of greater student achievement, the greater power lay in the DLT's discovering this through their own investigations and recognizing that, by following the processes, they could shift their attention to other problems of practice as teachers and staff engaged in a cycle of continuous improvement.

Learning How to Observe in Classrooms

To be able to determine, though, that a particular problem of practice will not yield the outcomes for which members hope, team members must become adept at observing classroom behaviors. To be effective at this, mentors themselves must be highly trained observers and must be able to design a training regimen that helps the individuals on a team learn to focus their attention on artifacts of the PoP within the classroom. This has several challenges. First, educators must recognize that each of them brings biases into classrooms. If one is engaging in rounds within his/her own school district, this is equally challenging for both administrators and classroom teachers. In the case of the former, principals and district office staff often have opinions about the effectiveness of teachers based upon district or building evaluations. While this has the advantage of data behind it, the data that have been gathered within those observations were not necessarily focused on this particular PoP, and any attempts to extrapolate from observations done for evaluations will miss the point of focusing on the teaching, not the teacher. In the case of the latter, classroom teachers have had little experience in observing other teachers and will need to learn a new set of skills. Additionally, they are now observing their peers, which is often uncomfortable for a variety of reasons. Teachers in the DLT often mentioned that they felt out of their comfort zones when being asked to observe in a grade level or academic subject far removed from their own.

The first thing the mentor must do then is to provide instruction in how to observe in classrooms. The principles that guide this work are description before analysis, analysis before prediction, prediction before evaluation. In order to describe, team members learn to take down only what teachers and students actually say (verbatim quotes and exchanges) or describe what teachers and students do. New observers, for instance, are often quick to summarize what happens in a classroom (e.g., "teacher used proximity to get a student to stop talking and redirect him back to task") rather than being descriptive (e.g., "student whispers in front of room to another student. Teacher moves near the desk and puts her finger on the student's desk. Student stops talking and looks back at book"). The former is much more efficient, but the latter is much richer. As teams find out when they actually do classroom observations, if they summarize when they are in classrooms, they lose too much information, and they may not remember exactly why they wrote that particular piece of evidence.

Once individuals have a set of notes, they analyze them. In the case of student engagement, for example, DLT members put single pieces of evidence (could be just one description of something observed or a piece of evidence could be an exchange between teacher and student or student and student) on post-it notes, then they discuss what type of engagement they believe that evidence represented. For example, there may be discussion as to whether the student who had to be redirected was indicating her rebelliousness toward the task or whether she was being ritually compliant by looking at the book after being discovered whispering. In fact, in a classroom situation where team members may be in different parts of the room, an observer close to that child may have more information about what she was whispering and believe that she was actually demonstrating engagement because she was excited about something she discovered in the reading. The power of this activity is in the discussion of the evidence, which is why observers must suspend judgments until they have gathered enough evidence to see the PoP through a number of lenses.

To practice these newly introduced skills, the mentor needs to find videos of teachers engaging in the PoP within classrooms so that participants can have ample opportunities to observe and process these exchanges. This is relatively easy when the problem is a generic one, like student engagement, but more challenging if the team takes on some content-specific strategies. It's also important to make sure that team members continue to build their observational skills. It is tempting to say, after a few videos, that the team understands the problem of practice and that there is no need to continue to practice it. The reality is that team members must continually refresh their skills. The time lapse between meetings for groups is often a month or more. Because of this, the use of videos, even when used to practice on the PoP prior to going into classrooms, is important to focus all team members on the problem. This is analogous to a basketball team's doing layup drills prior to playing a game as a way of getting into the mindset of the skills that will help them to be successful. In this sense, the mentor takes on the role of a coach for team members and is responsible for the drills that will help them when they perform this task *for real*. As the mentor fades into the background and the district team takes on full responsibility for facilitating the IR process, team members should hear the mentor's voice reminding them to suspend their judgments until they have their data gathered and analyzed.

DEVELOPING CAPACITY FOR SUSTAINABILITY

In the end, a successful mentoring relationship should have a built-in obsolescence that promotes the capacity of the entity, whether an individual or organization, to function independently and, thus, sustain the professional work in which the two have been engaged. As school staff members approach school reform, they plan, they implement, and, too often, only hope to sustain. The planning process often includes "good intentions" to sustain efforts, but the reality is less positive. Fullan (2001) points out that seldom are programs implemented with deliberate intent to sustain and continue. He states, "One last caution: we talk about continuation as the third phase in a planned change plan process, but it should be clear that the process is not simply linear and that all phases must be thought about from beginning and continually thereafter" (Fullan, 2001, p. 90). Generally, the focus for schools is the implementation of projects, most often grant funded and therefore operating within externally established timelines. Schools fall into the trap of believing that when the grant funding ends, the reform effort is complete or, if not complete, certainly over.

Facilitating one's own obsolescence creates responsibilities for the mentor. First, it needs to be part of the plan from the beginning, and all parties must prepare for it. While there was a great deal of collaborative planning done by the mentor and a subcommittee of the DLT, in the first year and the beginning of the second year, the mentor facilitated the professional development meetings for the DLT. Near the end of the second year, several DLT members stepped in and co-facilitated portions of sessions with the mentor. And in the third year, DLT members were to take on the responsibility of leading all of the meetings. Not all plans, however, go as designed, and the mentor needs to be flexible. Early in the third year, DLT members expressed some concerns about leading the rounds process in its entirety and requested that Jim model the entire process one last time. After that, the mentor reverted back to the role of consultant as DLT members took on all responsibilities for PD and used the mentor for guidance and feedback, both before and after the meetings they facilitated.

In order to scaffold the learning and provide resources that the additional responsibilities for leading PD required, Jim created a Dropbox folder and invited all members of the DLT into it. In it were subfolders that included all of his materials from the first two years of the project. These included PowerPoint slides;

reading protocols that had been used; and all of the agendas, articles, readings, and so on. These were provided so that DLT members had models from which they could build and extend the learning that had taken place in the first two years.

As of the writing of this chapter, the district was nearing the end of the third year of implementation. As described above, district leadership planned for sustainability from the outset and has seen some of the results already. In the introduction to the chapter, the narrative described the roles that individual members of the DLT took on in planning and delivering professional development within the rounds structures; most of those members taking on these professional development roles were classroom teachers, which we believe gives additional credibility to the claim of having an egalitarian learning organization. They also are taking on ownership of the process in other ways, as demonstrated through the comments of one leadership team member who stated, "It is apparent that we need to continue to *Wellston-ize* the process and take deeper ownership into the process. One of the challenges will be to delve deeper into the practices we have in place and develop protocols that explain what the PoP [problem of practice] looks like/ sounds like at Wellston City Schools."

Within the rounds process, City and associates (2009) cite numerous potential benefits to school improvement, many of which are already being experienced in Wellston. These include helping district and school leaders (1) develop a clearly articulated and widely held view of high quality teaching and learning, (2) build a collaborative learning culture, and (3) develop and implement a coherent system-wide strategy to support teaching and learning in all classrooms. They also suggest that these benefits become integrated into the work of districts when they involve the *right* people and provide them with explicit expectations for individual, group, and systemic learning, as well as follow-up applications. Finally, they echo the dynamic relationship of the mentoring process when they state,

> The experience creates a virtuous cycle: As people do the work, they learn the work and get better at it. They learn more about instruction and their role in improving it. As they and their colleagues begin to implement ideas generated by rounds, they see small gains that lead to continued learning, experimentation, and further commitment. (City et al., 2009, p. 181)

SUMMARY AND TAKEAWAYS

The educators in Wellston City Schools, in an effort to improve teaching and learning for their children, sought to incorporate instructional rounds into their school improvement process. In order to do so, the members of the DLT chose to enter into a group mentoring relationship to learn about IR and to be guided into its use in "assessing the health" of the instructional core in the district. When engaging in this type of mentoring relationship, there are a number of issues with which the mentor must be prepared to deal. First, as with any successful mentoring relationship, *it is imperative that the mentor build a trusting rapport with members of the team*. Second, because this type of relationship often requires the training of groups of learners, *groups will benefit if their mentors are skilled professional developers who can deliver high-quality trainings*. In this case, trainings included those necessary to understand and implement the rounds process, as well as training and practice in becoming competent classroom observers. After the trainings, though, *mentors also must be proficient facilitators of these newly learned skills and protocols* as members of the group implement rounds in their schools. Finally, the ultimate goal of any group mentoring process should be building the capacity of the protégés to do the work without the mentor's direct involvement. To do this effectively, *building a planned obsolescence into the relationship from the outset will help both the mentor and members of the organization to feel an appropriate sense of urgency in the gradual release of responsibility for turning over the planning and implementing of the program from the mentor to the group*.

Teachers and administrators in schools are under increasing pressure to be results-oriented. They also have a great many people outside of their organizations—legislators, pundits, for-profit marketers—who seem to think that they know better than those inside the districts how to improve teaching and learning. In the end, though, improvements in teaching and learning don't happen from the outside, and all the pressure from external forces often leads teachers and administrators to become defensive and protective of the status quo. To make real and substantive changes to instruction and learning, stakeholders in educational change may want to remind themselves of what Jim Collins (2001) has said about what makes good organizations great. Though he was talking about businesses, he maintained that organizations that become great are able to overcome resistance to change when the people *inside* the organization are the ones who monitor and document the results of new practices. Harkening to Collins's call, this adventure in collaboration enabled a group mentoring relationship that provided protocols and created settings that facilitated the educators in the district as they strove to overcome any resistance to change by generating the results themselves, rather than relying upon outside forces to determine their worth.

REFERENCES

Ball, D. L., & Cohen, D. K. (1999). Developing practice, developing practitioners. In L. Darling-Hammond & G. Sykes (Eds.), *Teaching as the learning profession: Handbook of policy and practice* (pp. 3–32). San Francisco, CA: Jossey-Bass.

City, E. A., Elmore, R. F., Fiarman, S. E., & Teitel, L. (2009). *Instructional rounds in education: A network approach to improving teaching and learning*. Cambridge, MA: Harvard Education Press.

Collins, J. (2001). *Good to great: Why some companies make the leap...and others don't*. New York, NY: HarperCollins.

Costa, A. L., & Garmston, R. J. (2002). *Cognitive coaching: A foundation for Renaissance schools* (2nd ed.). Norwood, MA: Christopher-Gordon.

Crafton, L., & Kaiser, E. (2011). The language of collaboration: Dialogue and identity in teacher professional development. *Improving Schools 14*(2), 104–116.

DuFour, R. (2004). What is a professional learning community? *Educational Leadership,* *61*(8), 6–11.

DuFour, R. (2007). Professional learning communities: A bandwagon, an idea worth considering, or our best hope for high levels of learning? *Middle School Journal, 39*(4), 1–8.

Eby, L. T., Rhodes, J. E., & Allen, T. D. (2010). Definition and evolution of mentoring. In L. T. Eby & T. D. Allen (Eds.), *The Blackwell handbook of mentoring: A multiple perspectives approach* (pp. 7–20). West Sussex, UK: Wiley & Sons.

Emelo, R. (2011). Group mentoring best practices. *Industrial and Commercial Training,* *43*(4), 221–227.

Fullan, M. (2001). *The new meaning of educational change* (3rd ed.). New York, NY: Teachers College Press.

Goldenberg, C. (2004). *Successful school change: Creating settings to improve teaching and learning.* New York, NY: Teachers College Press.

Hawley, W. D., & Valli, L. (1999). The essentials of effective professional development: A new consensus. In L. Darling-Hammond & G. Sykes (Eds.), *Teaching as the learning profession: Handbook of policy and practice* (pp. 127–150). San Francisco, CA: Jossey-Bass.

Huffman, J. B., & Hipp, K. K. (2003). *Reculturing schools as professional learning communities.* Lanham, MD: Rowman & Littlefield.

Jones, R. (2006). *Mentorship strategies: Group mentoring.* Cincinnati, OH: Human Capital Institute.

Killion, J. P., & Todnem, G. R. (1991). A process for personal theory building. *Educational Leadership, 48*(6), 14–16.

Kram, K. E. (1983). Phases of the mentor relationship. *Academy of Management Journal,* *26*(4), 608–625.

Kram, K. E. (1985). *Mentoring at work: Developmental relationships in organizational life.* Glenview, IL: Scott, Foresman.

Levinson, D. J., Darrow, C. N., Klein, E. B., Levinson, M. A., & McKee, B. (1978). *Seasons of a man's life.* New York, NY: Knopf.

McDonald, J. P., Mohr, N., Dichter, A., & McDonald, E. C. (2007). *The power of protocols: An educator's guide to better practice* (2nd ed.). New York, NY: Teachers College Press.

National Staff Development Council. (2001). *National Staff Development Council's standards for staff development.* Oxford, OH: Author.

Roberts, J. E. (2012). *Instructional rounds in action.* Cambridge, MA: Harvard Education Press.

Salzman, J. A. (1999). With a little help from my friends: A course designed for mentoring induction-year teachers. *Mid-Western Educational Researcher, 12*(4), 27–31.

Salzman, J. A. (2002). *Becoming a mentor: Are you the right one for the job?* Chicago, IL: Fogarty.

Sarason, S. (1972). *The creation of settings and the future societies.* San Francisco, CA: Jossey-Bass.

Schlechty, P. C. (2002). *Working on the work: An action plan for teachers, principals, and superintendents.* San Francisco, CA: Jossey-Bass.

Sparks, D., & Hirsh, S. (1997). *New vision for staff development.* Alexandria, VA: Association of Supervision and Curriculum Development.

Wenger, E. (1998). *Communities of practice: Learning, meaning, and identity.* Cambridge, UK: Cambridge University Press.

White, E. (2006). *Presentation in honor of Nancy Mohr.* Denver, CO: Winter meeting of the National School Reform Faculty.

CHAPTER 15

IMPROVING TEACHER PREPARATION, ENHANCING STEM EDUCATION AND CREATING A STEM PIPELINE THROUGH MENTOR-ASSISTED ENRICHMENT PROJECTS

William A. Gray and Marilynne Miles Gray

ABSTRACT

Two educators describe how they improved teacher preparation, enhanced STEM education, and created a STEM pipeline (youth–undergrads–professionals in science, technology, engineering, mathematics) by giving future teachers course credit for implementing mentor-assisted enrichment projects (MAEPs) with protégés in grades 4–12. One research and development (R&D) insight was foundational for what occurred over eight years: making well-meaning announcements to encourage "do-your-own-thing-mentoring" and partially planning an initiative do not produce intended benefits. Rather, benefits can come from a formalized mentoring program in which all essential components are defined, designed, aligned, and implemented. Another important discovery: Future teachers (as mentors) learn how to identify and respond to individuals within their small group of protégés and graduate as ef-

Mentoring for the Professions: Orienting Toward the Future, pages 277–292.

fective teachers who can use this same approach in the classroom. MAEPs enabled mentors to share STEM-related expertise and experience with their protégés over a semester. From this interaction they learned long-term planning and how to engage protégés in formal and informal learning that connects learning of STEM concepts with learning of how those concepts are applied in real-world settings by professionals. Training mentors to employ four mentoring styles in a flexible manner enabled them to equip protégés with the knowledge the mentor offers and empower protégés to pursue what they want to learn, do, and become.

A FOUNDATIONAL R&D DISCOVERY

Because this book addresses "mentoring in the professions," it is appropriate to describe how an announcement to encourage "do-your-own-thing-mentoring" and a partially planned mentoring initiative produce fewer intended benefits than a well-developed formalized mentoring program (Gray, 2007a). The program development expertise we gained via eight years of R&D has enabled us, for over 30 years as a vocation, to create more than 175 distinctive mentoring programs for different groups: (1) in education for youth, new teachers, new principals, college freshmen and interns, and faculty; (2) in corporations and government for new hires, career and leader development, talent and competency development; and (3) for other groups (entrepreneurs, parents). Every mentoring program has been different because every situation was different in purpose, goals to attain, protégés, mentors, what they worked on, for how long, and so on. Hence, every successful program required situational mentoring (Gray, 1986, 1989a, 1989b).

Avocation for mentoring began in the summer of 1978, when the author was a novice in the field of mentoring and a teacher/friend (Sheila Herman) asked a life-changing question: "I have so many students coming into my enrichment center from their grade 4–7 classrooms, to work on independent projects, that I cannot help each one. What would you suggest?" He replied, "My students can work with your students," because he wanted future teachers to apply the content from his educational psychology courses while working with younger students. So he began giving undergrads course credit for applying concepts and skills he was teaching while mentoring youth in an area of personal expertise and experience, which was usually related to science, technology, engineering, or mathematics (STEM). He discovered that making announcements that encouraged "do-your-own-thing-mentoring" created many problems (e.g., protégés stopped showing up, mentors needed another assignment to do). Because of a commitment to help Sheila Herman, he began doing R&D to find out what makes mentoring work and why. Initially, he identified some essential components, such as that mentors needed to create a mentoring action plan to provide needed structure, and he named this new approach mentor-directed enrichment project—until discovering that some mentors imposed their plan and overly directed everything protégés did, which caused them to walk away.

So the approach was changed and renamed, becoming mentor-assisted enrichment projects (MAEPs)—until discovering that many essential components were still missing. For example, we began training mentors, but this proved to be inadequate because no literature existed (in ERIC or elsewhere) on what kind of mentor training was needed. In sum, this partially planned initiative did not work.

Nearly everything written at that time (1978–1979) described informal mentoring that happens spontaneously without any training for anyone, without any oversight or formal evaluation of outcomes. We discovered this almost universal focus on informal mentoring in two ways. First, preparing *Mentoring: A Comprehensive Annotated Bibliography* that described 789 entries (Gray & Gray, 1986a) revealed that over 90% described informal mentoring. Second, we organized the First International Conference on Mentoring (held in Vancouver, BC, July 1986) and required each presenter to submit a paper for inclusion in two conference proceedings, which we edited and published (Gray & Gray, 1986b, 1986c). From this we realized that nearly all presenters but us (Gray, 1986) were either encouraging informal mentoring or implementing a partially planned mentoring initiative. (This same realization continued over the next eight years while publishing *The International Journal of Mentoring*, which became *Mentoring International*, because we initially reviewed all manuscripts before sending them out for peer review.)

TABLE 15.1. Main Characteristics of a Mentoring Program Expert

Level	
Expert	Has at least 10 dedicated years focusing on a field. In this case, developing distinctive formalized/planned/structured mentoring programs. Experience in field is broad and deep. Intuitively aware of irrelevant and important variables in any new situation. Able to use different paradigms from education and business to solve problems quickly and creatively. Reflective practitioner who self-assesses what works and what doesn't. Engages in "forward" reasoning to solve a problem. Able to define, design, align, deliver the right components in each situation to produce multiple outcomes (develop competencies/talent and reduce turnover while involving the diversified workforce). Typically, this person develops the Guiding Principles and the rules of engagement.
Proficient	Has at least 5 years in the field with varied experience. Can plan and implement several different types of mentoring programs, each of which produce a desired outcome (seldom multiple outcomes). Still "rule-bound" when solving problems, but becoming a reflective practitioner on defining, designing, aligning, delivering essential components.
Competent	Has repeated experience doing the same thing enough times that it becomes successful (e.g., can plan and implement one type of mentoring program—such as for youth—but not for developing leadership competencies). Can produce singular outcomes for this particular program.
Advanced Beginner	Knows "about" mentoring for specific circumstances, but not broadly, and has limited practical "know-how." Likely to announce/encourage simplistic "do-your-own-thing" mentoring (a "feel-good" approach) or implement a partially planned initiative. Does not know how to plan and implement a formalized mentoring program with structured components that produce intended outcomes. Doesn't feel responsible for producing outcomes.
Novice	Has little or no direct practical experience or know-how. May have gathered information, read books or articles, but has no practical understanding based on actual experience.

In marked contrast, our research surveying and interviewing protégés and mentors had enabled us to define, design, align, and then deliver the essential components that comprise a successful formalized mentoring program for youth (Gray, 1986). The multiple benefits this produced for everyone involved led us to combine our avocation for mentoring with over 30 years as a vocation developing over 175 successful formalized mentoring programs for different groups and situations (for some examples see: Gray, 1989a, 2007a, 2007b, 2011a; Gray & Gray, 1982b, 1987, 2002).

The U.S. Department of Labor's *Dictionary of Occupational Titles* (1991) claims mentoring is the most complex kind of human interaction. Developing successful mentoring programs is even more complex, since each individual in the participating group must benefit for success to result. Table 15.1 describes the main characteristics of a mentoring program expert who is best able to produce multiple benefits for everyone involved. The 5-level model in this table is based on several meta-analyses of research on what's required to become an expert in a dedicated field of focus (Dreyfus & Dreyfus, 2005; Gray, 2008b).

Keep in mind the importance of developing a formalized, structured, planned mentoring program, while we describe how mentor-assisted enrichment projects can rectify the three critical challenges mentioned in the title of this chapter.

IMPROVING TEACHER PREPARATION

At Columbia Teachers College on October 22, 2009, U.S. Secretary of Education Arne Duncan said:

> By almost any standard, many if not most of the nation's 1,450 schools, colleges, and departments of education are doing a mediocre job of preparing teachers for the realities of the 21st century classroom. America's university-based teacher preparation programs need revolutionary change—not evolutionary tinkering.... Nearly 30 percent of our students today drop out or fail to complete high school on time—that is 1.2 million kids a year. Barely 60 percent of African American and Latino students graduate on time—and in many cities, half or more of low-income teens drop out of school. (See Duncan, 2009, for the complete transcript)

In the 1980s, formalized mentoring programs began to be established in most states in the United States to induct beginning teachers into the teaching profession, by helping them become more effective in ensuring individual students were learning (Gray & Gray, 1985). Less time, effort, and money can be spent on this if preservice teachers graduate as effective teachers after learning how to plan and implement mentor-assisted enrichment projects (MAEPs) over a semester, with small groups of interested protégés (students in grades 4–12). MAEPs can be implemented as a course assignment that any professor can offer, or as a replacement for teaching entire classes or smaller groups on a conventional student teaching practicum.

HOW MAEPS IMPROVE TEACHER PREPARATION

During 16 semesters, more than 300 undergrads (future teachers) mentored more than 1,000 different kinds of protégé (gifted/talented, English as a second language, at-risk, native) in grades 4–12 (Gray, 1982, 1983a, 1983b; Gray & Gray, 1982a, 1982b). These mentors learned how to take responsibility for longer-term planning and implementation than is possible on a typical field experience or student teaching practicum, where student teachers are expected to maintain what is already established in order to earn a good grade. While providing group mentoring, our future teachers learned how to teach, motivate, discipline, and communicate with individuals in their small groups—so that they graduated with the competencies (knowledge/understanding, attitudes, skills) needed to be effective teachers who can maximize learning by individuals in the classroom (Gray & Gray, 1987).

Initially, these future teachers chose to carry out a MAEP as an alternative course assignment and to earn course credit for providing effective mentoring. Research on these mentors found that, by their third meeting with protégés, they were able to identify and respond appropriately to individuals within their small group of protégés. These mentors skipped Stage 1 below, and by their third meeting with protégés reached Stage 3 of Frances Fuller's "Concerns of Teachers" (Fuller, 1969):

- Stage 1: Concern for Self (Do I know my subject so I can teach it? Can I control my class so I can teach?)
- Stage 2: Concern for "Them" (the entire class or a smaller group)
- Stage 3: Concern for Individuals (maximize learning for each individual)

This finding is significant because Fuller found that preservice teachers do not reach Stage 3 on a practicum while teaching entire classes, but got stuck at Stage 2 as do many first-year teachers, which is one reason why first-year teachers have needed mentoring (Gray & Gray, 1985).

Our mentors reported that they learned more about working effectively with individual learners while carrying out a MAEP over a semester than they had learned over four or five years while doing coursework or student teaching to earn a B.Ed. degree. Future elementary teachers, who tend to be student-oriented, became more subject-oriented. Future secondary teachers, who tend to be subject-oriented, became more student-oriented. These and many other benefits motivated these 300 mentors to stay in university during the semester they carried out a MAEP.

MAEPs replaced the initial student teaching practicum for future secondary teachers when the dropout rate reached 40%. The traditional procedure required beginning student teachers to observe the regular classroom teacher for several hours and then teach the entire class or smaller groups, with little instruction in classroom management or in their academic major, and typically with no prior experience speaking in front of any group. It's a tribute to these idealistic student teachers that more did not drop out because of this sink-or-swim tradition.

After MAEPs became the initial practicum, we confirmed our earlier discovery: All student teachers reached the Stage 3—Concern for Individuals by the third meeting with small groups of interested protégés. Investigating these same student teachers when they taught entire classes on their next practicum revealed that 50% to 70% reached Stage 3, depending on the semester investigated (Gray, 1984a, 1984b; Gray & Gray, 1987). Our student teachers did not get stuck at the Stage 2—Concern for "Them" as Francis Fuller had found, but reached Stage 3—Concern for Individuals while teaching entire classes.

To understand what a mentor-assisted enrichment project is, below is an explanation for each word and how a MAEP differs from other approaches (teaching, coaching, collaboration).

WHY A MENTOR IS ESSENTIAL

Each mentor-assisted enrichment project is based on the particular expertise and experience a mentor already has and wants to share with protégés. Mentors provide many more types of assistance than teachers or coaches or collaboration facilitators by employing situational mentoring (Gray, 2011b; Gray & Gray, 1987), so they provide different kinds of assistance to equip and empower protégés. In contrast, teachers and coaches primarily focus on equipping learners with knowledge or new skills, not on empowering each learner's talents, creativity, diversity, and dreams to learn, do, and become what they desire. Collaboration facilitators primarily focus on empowering participants to contribute to problem solving that involves open inquiry, with less focus on equipping participants with what is known.

R&D revealed that effective mentors provide both equipping and empowering because both are essential during all phases of a mentor-assisted enrichment project. If a mentor gets stuck, only equipping protégés, they eventually perceive the mentor as being too dominating. If a mentor gets stuck, only empowering protégés, they must learn everything by discovery instead of benefiting from what the mentor knows.

After R&D revealed that flexibly employing four mentoring styles created better relationships and achieved desired outcomes, we trained mentors to employ situational mentoring (mentoring style flexibility) as depicted in Figure 15.1 (Gray, 1985, 2011a, 2011b).

To prevent getting stuck, we developed a mentoring style indicator for mentoring youth to identify 25 mentoring style behaviors a mentor prefers to provide and a protégé prefers to receive. We trained mentors to employ the informational and guiding styles to equip protégés with what mentors know and to employ the collaborative and confirming styles to empower what protégés want to learn, do and become. Teachers, coaches, and collaboration facilitators don't do this in the same way as effective mentors.

Because the mentoring style indicator (MSI) proved to be so beneficial in developing good mentor–protégé relationships and achieving desired goals, we developed eleven other versions (e.g., for new teachers and principals, for college

M ----------------Mp ------------------MP ----------------mP -------------- P

Informational Mentoring Style	Guiding Mentoring Style	Collaborative Mentoring Style	Confirming Mentoring Style	Protégé is Successful
Mentor uses 1-way communication to impart information	Mentor guides 2-way communication during interaction with protégé	Mentor & protégé jointly contribute to interactions with no one dominating	Protégé's ideas & feelings are acknowledged & confirmed by the mentor	Aware of what to do & able to do it [Consciously Competent]

FIGURE 15.1. Gray's Situational Mentoring Model

students and faculty). Over 20 years ago, the MSI was the first mentor assessment to be included in Buros Center's *Mental Measurements Yearbook* (Carlson, Geisinger, & Jonson, 2014).

Here is one example of how the mentoring style indicator is beneficial: The MSI for career development helped a vice president at Varian Associates Radiation Division equip a high-potential protégé with the competencies needed to become a project leader, instead of having to learn this by osmosis while participating on different projects. These mentoring partners realized that what was taught and learned could and should be converted into training courses to develop project leaders more effectively, so this high-level mentor empowered the protégé to work with the training department to create training courses. The result: Radiation moved from losing money to become a top money-maker among Varian's 23 divisions worldwide.

Below is a situation from the MSI for mentoring youth.

MSI Situation 4: Interviewing Professionals

Protégés look forward to interviewing professionals and other workers to find out what they do and how they chose their occupation. Busy professionals and workers give more time for interviews when protégés have prepared and rehearsed asking good interview questions. How might the mentor get protégés ready to interview busy professionals and workers?

- Mentor could describe interview questions that should be asked.
- Mentor could suggest interview questions that protégés decide they will ask.
- Mentor and protégés together decide which interview questions will be asked.
- Mentor could listen to interview questions protégés want to ask.

WHY ASSISTING IS BETTER THAN DIRECTING

Initially, projects were called mentor-directed enrichment projects (Gray, 1981a; Gray & Rogers, 1981) until important R&D discovers were made: (1) mentors were literally directing their protégés to carry out the mentor's project plan, and (2) many protégés dropped out because they saw project tasks being no different than what teachers or coaches direct them to do. In contrast, mentor assistance enabled protégés to perceive the project as theirs, even though it is based on the mentor's expertise and experience (Gray, 1982).

An essential component of every successful MAEP is the mentoring action plan (MAP) it is based on, because the MAP serves as a structured roadmap of diverse activities the mentoring team is going to do. It provides freedom within its structure so that each mentoring team can agree on what will be done. Such agreement is essential so that everyone psychologically buys in and commits to carrying out, completing, and presenting each MAEP. Thirty years ago, a study revealed just how essential the MAP is: Survey data indicated that 29 of 31 protégés in grades 5/6 said the mentoring action plan must be completed for them to view the project as worthwhile (p< .000). When interviewed, protégés said that, because they knew from the outset they were required to present a completed enrichment project, they were motivated to do homework and show up for scheduled meetings with mentors, prepared to do what was planned (Gray, 1982).

This same study revealed what happens when protégés carry out, complete, and present a self-directed enrichment project (SDEP) on their own, after carrying out a mentor-assisted enrichment project (MAEP). Although protégés want to carry out a SDEP to completion, and tried to, there were significant differences favoring MAEPs, such as: (1) more MAEPs were completed and they were better presented, (2) MAEPs were better planned and involved more professionals and other resources in the community, (3) MAEPs enabled protégés to learn how to take more responsibility for doing an enrichment project, and (4) protégés put more effort into MAEPs and were more satisfied with this type of project.

One major component missing from all SDEPs is didactic instruction provided by someone (e.g., the mentor) who knows more than the protégés. To maximize learning outcomes from MAEPs, trained mentors used both didactic instruction and open inquiry because most learners, most of the time, need both methods to maximize learning (Coleman, Livingston, Fennessey, Edwards, & Kidder, 1973). Trained mentors also learned how to involve STEM professionals (who were too busy to be mentors) so that protégés connect learning about STEM concepts with learning how they are applied in real-world situations. (This is part of the STEM pipeline discussed later.)

HOW ENRICHMENT ACTIVITIES ENGAGE LEARNERS

Each MAEP provides diverse enrichment experiences and activities not normally provided by teachers in the school curriculum nor by coaches who focus on skill mastery. Enrichment includes using Bloom's higher-level thinking skills (Bloom, Engelhart, Furst, Hill, & Krathwohl, 1956), preparing and then interviewing/job shadowing professionals in occupations of interest, doing activities on the college/university campus or in the community, creating an end product that illustrates what was done and learned, and presenting this to an audience so they also benefit from such enrichment.

Although professionals are often too busy to be the primary mentor for a semester-long project, they willingly spend time contributing enriching practical experiences to the overall mentor-assisted enrichment project (Gray, 1981b, 1983a; Gray & Gray, 1982a). Here is one example that had a life-changing impact on the protégés and their audience:

Shoplifting and the Law Project

The mentor assisted three protégés (who were starting to shoplift) to investigate how shoplifting by juveniles gets them arrested, taken to court, found guilty by the judge, taken to jail, fingerprinted, and locked up. The mentor arranged all of these enrichment experiences and transported protégés to them. Protégés reenacted these enrichment experiences during their presentation to classmates and described in vivid detail what they learned at each point (one protégé wore a police uniform, one wore a judge's gown and had a gavel, one was the arrested juvenile). Not only did this MAEP motivate all three protégés to immediately stop ripping off the corner store, but their classmates also stopped shoplifting (Gray, 1983a)!

WHY A STRUCTURED PROJECT IS NECESSARY FOR SUCCESS

What mentoring teams do in a MAEP over a period of time (usually a semester) requires a structured project, which has three distinctive phases: (1) A beginning based on the mentoring action plan proposed by the mentor, modified using protégé input, until it is an agreed-upon plan (their plan for their project); (2) a middle when protégés carry out planned activities such as incorporating practical applications demonstrated by professionals in the workplace, with mentors providing various types of assistance; (3) an end when protégés complete an end product that illustrates what was done and learned and present this to an audience. Trained mentors provide project management for their small group of protégés as they work together as a project team through all phases of the project—taking turns leading and following and making unique contributions via empowerment. Within the structure of a mentor-assisted enrichment project, mentors motivate protégé commitment to their project so it is not a list of prescribed tasks.

HOW MAEPS ENHANCE STEM EDUCATION

Many youth, especially minority youth and females, have an aversion to science and math, and hence do not take the courses needed to pursue an undergraduate major in these disciplines. Mortimer B. Zuckerman points out the severity of this challenge:

> The experts reported last year [2010] that among 29 wealthy countries, the United States ranked 27th in the proportion of college students with degrees in science and engineering. And among developed countries, the United States ranks 31st in math and 23rd in science, not to mention the achievement gap between low-income and minority students and their peers. American 12th graders were near the bottom of students from 20 nations assessed in advanced math and physics. Large parts of our student population are literally being deprived of a top-notch education.... Recent studies indicate that about 30 percent of high school math students and 60 percent of those in the physical sciences are taught by instructors who either did not major in the subject or are not certified to teach it. (Zuckerman, 2011, p. 3)

To address this deteriorating situation, STEM education kits are being purchased to heighten interest and increase understanding and skills of students at all levels (K–16). When used effectively, these kits produce several benefits: the kits (1) have produced a 64% improvement in math scores and 128% increase in technology scores; (2) promote project-based, student-driven, STEM directed activities for K–12 students; (3) build student self-esteem; (4) develop critical thinking and problem-solving skills; (5) introduce real-world applications of math and science; and (6) promote 21st century skills (called the 4 C's): critical thinking, communication, collaboration, and creativity (Gray & Albert, 2012a, 2012b).

At a recent combined conference on STEM education and problem-based learning (PBL), we gave two co-presentations (Gray & Albert, 2012a, 2012b) and asked attendees to raise their hands if they were teachers being introduced to STEM education or PBL for the first time; 80% of the hands went up. Attendees' enthusiasm went up even higher when they learned how utilizing undergrad mentors to facilitate student learning from STEM education kits would relieve them from the added pressure of having to do this themselves. Teachers' questions in other sessions we attended revealed how overwhelming was the prospect of adding STEM education or PBL to everything else they are expected to do, especially facilitating open inquiry outside the classroom.

This conference underscored the importance of implementing reality-based answers for these questions:

- How can classroom teachers take on added responsibility for STEM education and PBL when faced with diverse students, varied levels of achievement and learning gaps, and mandated requirements to meet state standards? Who can relieve the added burden of providing STEM education and PBL, especially in after-school programs?
- How effectively are STEM education kits being used to maximize both formal and informal learning? Or are kits being purchased and not being used properly, or not used at all? How can cost-effectiveness be ensured in the face of diminishing budgets?

One solution is to implement structured mentor-assisted enrichment projects that focus on properly using STEM education kits. To do this, trained mentors teach protégés how to (1) work on a team, (2) take turns being the leader and follower, (3) learn how to listen to each other's ideas and try ideas that seem promising of a problem solution, (4) complete a task they start by solving the problem posed by the kit, and (5) give a presentation where they describe what they did to solve each problem and what they learned from this.

Trained mentors can facilitate open inquiry to solve problems and provide didactic instruction to teach main concepts associated with doing the problem-solving activity. Protégés can be taught propositional thinking (If I do this, what might be the consequence?) and higher-level thinking skills based on Bloom's (Bloom et al., 1956) cognitive taxonomy (especially application, analysis, synthesis, evaluation) to enhance solving problems.

Most of our 300 MAEPs focused on some aspect of STEM. Some examples include building a robot, designing a model for a light rapid-transportation system, growing cells in the biochemical lab, developing software for a computer game, and building a wind tunnel to explore the aerodynamics of airplane wings.

HOW MAEPS COMPLETE A STEM PIPELINE

Nearly all of the STEM initiatives and research on enhancing STEM education has focused on singular challenges, such as (1) getting youth interested in STEM subjects (mainly science and math), (2) transforming undergraduate education to have a stronger STEM focus, and (3) utilizing STEM professionals in the workplace as mentors for these two groups.

Typically, only two of these three groups are involved in a STEM initiative, such as when undergrads assist youth with robotics or rocketry in after-school programs or when professionals mentor undergrads or youth to fulfill corporate social responsibility mandates. Notice what's missing? A linkage between all three required segments of a complete STEM pipeline.

These initiatives do not rectify the quantitative shortage of persons in each group nor qualitative shortcomings by developing needed competencies (knowledge/understanding, attitudes/motivation, and skills). These shortcomings include:

- Not enough students are taking the right courses to become STEM majors in college or university. These youth are not college- or career-ready enough to be successful.
- There are not enough undergrads graduating with the competencies and real-world experiences needed to perform capably in an occupation. This is a primary reason for starting mentoring programs for new hires (Gray, 2011b).
- America is falling behind other nations in the number of professionals in STEM occupations, including teachers of STEM subjects.

In contrast to these initiatives, mentor-assisted enrichment projects involve and link all three groups to create a STEM pipeline of youth, who become STEM majors, who become STEM professionals. MAEPs help younger protégés connect learning about STEM concepts with learning how they are applied in the real world. Undergrad mentors serve as the bridge that links all three groups and connects formal and informal learning (Gray & Albert, 2013).

Example

A small team of protégés wanted to learn about the relationship between architectural design and construction of buildings because they were considering architecture as a potential career. Their mentor took them to view and take photos of all the major buildings in Vancouver, Canada that Arthur Erikson had designed—and then helped the protégés formulate good questions to ask him, such as: "What design and construction problems had to be solved when you decided to let large trees grow through the roof of the underground library at the University of British Columbia?" "What challenges had to be resolved when you designed Simon Fraser University as a single construction to sit on top of Burnaby Mountain?" Even though Erikson was extremely busy (being Canada's top architect), he was so impressed by the protégés' preparation (the photos and rehearsed questions) that he gave these young architectural hopefuls several additional hours in his busy day (Gray, 1983a).

To Summarize

This involvement of youth, plus undergrad mentors, plus professionals is important because it enables young protégés to overcome their fear of science and math while talking candidly with a slightly older undergrad mentor and while gaining exposure to the possibilities and realities of STEM careers as they learn from professionals. Slightly younger protégés easily identify and talk with undergrads because there is a small age gap, and they learn about best-fit careers from busy professionals, so protégés can make informed decisions to pursue the right careers for themselves. Undergrad mentors provide the missing link between youth and professionals, as well as the bridge that connects youth with professionals who are too busy to be full-time mentors for semester-long projects.

HOW TO INCLUDE MORE PARTICIPANTS IN MAEPS

Including more participants in a formalized mentoring program requires more work on the part of the mentoring coordinator, because successful programs do not run themselves (this is what occurs when announcements or partially planned initiatives are launched). The program coordinator must fulfill key tasks, such as those indicated in Table 15.2. It takes more time to fulfill these tasks when they are paper-based, compared to when the right Web-based mentoring management

TABLE 15.2. Time Needed by Mentoring Program Coordinators to Fulfill Key Tasks Using Paper-based vs. Web-based Methods

Key Coordinator Tasks (Reported by 34 Coordinators of Mentoring Programs enrolling 12–25 pairs of matched partners)	Time Required Using Paper-Based Applications, Resumes, Surveys, Reports	Time Needed When Using CMSI's Web-based Mentoring Management Systems®
Enrolling/registering participants	1– 2 people spent 3– 5 hours	Participants spend 30– 60 minutes
Matching mentor-protégé partners	3– 6 people spent 10– 13 hours	1 Coordinator needs 1– 3 hours
Mentoring progress on goals	1– 2 people spent 11– 13 hours	1 Coordinator needs 1– 2 hr/month
Surveying protégé benefits	1– 2 people spent 9– 11 hours	1 Coordinator needs 2– 3 hours
Surveying mentor benefits	1– 2 people spent 5– 7 hours	1 Coordinator needs 2– 3 hours

system is used, according to a benchmark survey of 34 mentoring program co-ordinators overseeing 12–25 pairs of matched partners (M. M. Gray, 2002). For example, using written applications for matching mentoring partners takes much longer than using a Web-based system, and paper-based matches are guesstimates compared to the quicker and more precise partner matching a system can do.

If a Web-based system is used, it should provide online tools that mentors and protégés can easily access and that a coordinator can easily monitor online, such

TABLE 15.3.   How Online Tools Meet Mentoring Program Purposes (in Gray's Web-based Mentoring Management System ®)

Mentoring Style Indicator	• Identifies the style of mentoring mentor prefers to provide and protégé prefers to receive. • Enables mentors to provide varied assistance that protégés will accept and utilize. • The Informational and Guiding Styles equip protégés with what mentors know. • The Collaborative and Guiding Styles empower what protégés want to do and become.
Mentoring Action Plan	• Ensures mentors and protégés are prepared for meetings, complete and present MAEPs. • Trained Coordinators monitor progress on carrying out Plans to enhance results. • Completed Plans document what was done and learned (qualitative evaluation).
Mentor Report	• Describes what mentor is learning and any Coordinator help that is needed. • Enhances ultimate outcomes.
Mentor Concerns	• If mentors are pre-service teachers, tracks their progress through 3 Stages of Teacher Concerns for: 1) Self, 2) Them, 3) Individuals.
Online Surveys	• To targeted participants (mentors, protégés, others) for quantitative evaluation of benefits gained and suggested enhancements.

as a mentoring action plan, to ensure that it is being carried out to completion (completed plans provide evidence of what was done and learned). Online surveys should ensure there are no missing data and that all responses are returned automatically (electronically) to the coordinator, so time is not wasted chasing after data needed for statistical analysis. Table 15.3 describes key online tools that save time and money and provide a green infrastructure (in contrast to consumable paper methods). Online tools should also promote accountability, permit capacity building, and provide sustainability—because most funders of grants require this.

CONCLUDING COMMENTS

From 16 semesters of R&D on how to make mentor-assisted enrichment projects work for different kinds of protégés in grades 4–12, we discovered how to improve teacher preparation, how to enhance STEM education, and how to create a STEM pipeline of youth plus undergrad mentors plus professionals in science, technology, engineering, and mathematics. What we did, you also can do, by defining, designing, aligning, and then delivering the essential components for a successful formalized mentoring program so that intended benefits result.

REFERENCES

Bloom, B. S., Engelhart, N. D., Furst, E. J., Hill, W. H., & Krathwohl, D. R. (1956). *Taxonomy of educational objectives, Handbook I: The cognitive domain.* New York, NY: David McKay.

Carlson, J. F., Geisinger, K. F., & Jonson, J. L. (Eds.). (2014). *The nineteenth mental measurements yearbook.* Lincoln, NE: The Buros Center for Testing.

Coleman, J. S., Livingston, S. A., Fennessey, G. M., Edwards, K. T., & Kidder, S. J. (1973). The Hopkins Game Program: Conclusions from seven years of research. *Educational Researcher, 2*(8), 3–7.

Dreyfus, H., & Dreyfus, S. (2005). Expertise in real world contexts. *Organization Studies, 26*(5), 779–792.

Duncan, A. (2009). Teacher preparation: Reforming the uncertain profession. Retrieved from http://www2.ed.gov/news/speeches/2009/10/10222009.html

Fuller, F. (1969). Concerns of teachers. *Educational Research Journal, 6*(2), 207–226.

Gray, M. M. (2002, July–August). Benchmark 2000 survey: Part 6—The findings and conclusion. *Mentor Ink Newsletter, 16*(7), 4.

Gray, W. A. (1981a, September) *Mentor-directed enrichment projects for gifted and talented pupils: A concept whose time has come.* Paper presented at the Fourth World Conference on Gifted and Talented Children; Montreal, Canada.

Gray, W. A. (1981b). Utilizing mentors to provide community-based enrichment experiences in social studies for grades 5-7. *Intermediate Teacher, 20*(1), 69–76.

Gray, W. A. (1982). Mentor-assisted enrichment projects for the gifted and talented. *Educational Leadership, 40*(2), 16–21.

Gray, W. A. (1983a). *Challenging the gifted and talented through mentor-assisted enrichment projects.* Phi Delta Kappa Fastback #189. Bloomington IN: PDK Educational Foundation.

Gray, W. A. (1983b). Utilizing pre-service teachers as mentors to provide enrichment experiences for gifted/talented ESL pupils. *Educational Research Institute of BC Report, 82*(17), 1–28.

Gray, W. A. (1984a). Mentoring as an alternative approach to the student teaching practicum. *Journal of Educational Thought, 17*(1), 74–76.

Gray, W. A. (1984b). Mentoring gifted/talented/creative students on an initial student teaching practicum: Guidelines and benefits. *Gifted Education International, 2*(2), 121–128.

Gray, W. A. (1985). A helping relationship model for enabling mentors to work successfully with protégés: Guidelines and benefits. In F. L. Denmark (Ed.), *Social/economical psychology and the psychology of women.* (Proceedings of the XXIII International Congress of Psychology, Vol. 7, pp. 237–254.) Acapulco, Mexico.

Gray, W. A. (1986). Components for developing successful formalized mentoring programs in business, the professions and other settings. In W. A. Gray & M. M. Gray (Eds.), *Mentoring: Aid to excellence in career development, business and the professions* (Vol. I, pp. 15–22). Vancouver, BC: International Centre for Mentoring.

Gray, W.A. (1989a). Advice on planning mentoring programs for at-risk youth. *Mentoring International, 3*(3), 17–22.

Gray, W.A. (1989b) Situational mentoring: Custom designing planned mentoring programs, *Mentoring International, 3*(1), 19–28.

Gray, W. A. (2007a). *Mentoring is mentoring is mentoring is not true.* Unpublished white paper.

Gray, W. A. (2007b, January). *When and how to transfer knowledge, mentor and coach skills.* First Middle East e-TQM Conference, Dubai United Arab Emirates.

Gray, W. A. (2008a). Before knowledge exits. *Oil and Gas Investor, 28*(4), 83–85.

Gray, W. A. (2008b). Define, design, deliver for mentoring success. *E&P Magazine.* Retrieved from http://www.epmag.com/Technology-Equipment/Define-design-deliver-mentoring-success_23582

Gray, W. A. (2011a). *Mentoring relationships that work.* North Saanich, BC, Canada: Corporate Mentoring Solutions. (ebook available at www.amazon.com and http://www.smashwords.com)

Gray, W. A. (2011b). *Situational mentoring.* North Saanich, BC, Canada: Corporate Mentoring Solutions. (ebook at: http://www.smashwords.com and www.amazon.com)

Gray, W. A., & Albert, W. F. (2012a, April). *STEMulate K–12 students with mentor-assisted enrichment projects and STEMfinity kits.* Paper presented at the Scaling STEM Conference, Durham, NC.

Gray, W. A., & Albert, W. F. (2012b, April). *STEMulate K–12 students with PBL, didactic instruction and inquiry to maximize learning.* Paper presented at the Problem-Based Learning Conference, Durham, NC.

Gray, W. A., & Albert, W. F. (2013). Create a STEM pipeline for students who become engineering majors who become engineers. *Leadership and Management in Engineering, 13*(1), 42–46.

Gray, W. A., & Gray, M. M. (1982a). Utilizing pre-service teachers as mentors to provide enrichment experiences for gifted/talented ESL pupils. Vancouver, BC, Canada: Education Research Institute of British Columbia.

Gray, W. A., & Gray, M. M. (1982b). An enrichment model for gifted/talented ESL pupils. In M. Clarke & J. Hanscombe (Eds.), *ON TESOL 82: Pacific perspectives on language learning and teaching* (pp. 259–272). Washington DC: TESOL.

Gray, W. A., & Gray, M. M. (1985). Synthesis of research on mentoring beginning teachers. *Educational Leadership, 43*(3), 37–43.

Gray, W. A., & Gray, M. M. (1986a, July). *Mentoring: A comprehensive annotated bibliography.* Vancouver, BC, Canada: International Centre for Mentoring.

Gray, W., & Gray, M. M. (Eds.). (1986b). *Mentoring: Aid to excellence in education, the family and community.* Proceedings of the First International Conference on Mentoring, Vol. I. Vancouver, BC, Canada: International Centre for Mentoring.

Gray, W. A. & Gray, M. M. (Eds.). (1986c). *Mentoring: Aid to excellence in career development, business and the professions.* Proceedings of the First International Conference on Mentoring, Vol. II. Vancouver, BC, Canada: International Centre for Mentoring.

Gray, W. A. & Gray, M. M. (1987). Improving teacher preparation through formalized mentoring. *International Journal of Mentoring, 1*(2), 31-37.

Gray, W. A. & Gray, M. M. (2002). Mentoring for diversity. In R. Millar (Ed.), *International Executive Development Programmes* (7th ed., pp. 7–10). Bethesda, MD: Blue Ibex Publishers.

Gray, W. A., & Rogers, D. (1981). Mentor-directed enrichment projects for gifted elementary school pupils: Rationale, guidelines and benefits. *Association for Educators of Gifted/ Talented, Creative Children in BC, 3*(2), 45–55.

U. S. Department of Labor. (1991). *Dictionary of occupational titles* (4th ed.). Ann Arbor, MI: Author.

Zuckerman, M. B. (2011). Why math and science education means more jobs. Retrieved from http://www.usnews.com/opinion/articles/2011/09/27/why-math-and-science-education-means-more-jobs?page=3

CHAPTER 16

COACHING AND MENTORING IN ADULT BASIC EDUCATION

Sharon Reynolds, Cristine Smith, and Kimberly A. Johnson

ABSTRACT

Adult basic education teachers come to the profession with little formal training in working with adult learners, and many have no paid preparation time, limited instructional resources and access to professional development, and little contact with other ABE teachers. Multiple mentoring and coaching models have recently been developed to meet ABE practitioner needs. The authors describe three unique projects that took place in the Massachusetts, Ohio, and Minnesota adult basic education systems, utilizing mentoring and coaching for professional learning. Massachusetts teachers participated in mentor teacher groups and reported more change than teachers in other types of professional learning situations. They also valued opportunities for one-to-one observation and feedback from the mentor. The Ohio model of peer coaching emphasized a relationship between peers that is collaborative, nonevaluative, reciprocal, and grounded in the process of cognitive coaching and the idea of gradual release of responsibility. In Minnesota, the state professional development system and its university partner launched a peer coaching project for partner teachers that incorporates aspects of action research and multiple rounds of observations and reflection. The chapter includes suggestions for good practice and further research into the effectiveness of mentoring and coaching as an approach to providing adult basic education teachers with high-quality professional development.

Mentoring for the Professions: Orienting Toward the Future, pages 293–315.
293

INTRODUCTION

Imagine that you are a teacher who has been hired to teach a population of students with whom you've never worked, and that you did not receive any formal and/or preservice training in how to work with these students. Instead, you were given several student workbooks and told to use those as a guide. In addition, you are hired to teach part-time—usually several nights a week—with no paid preparation time; you have limited access to professional development or even to a supervisor who can come to observe your class, and have little contact with other teachers.

This is the situation in which many adult basic education (ABE) teachers find themselves. Under such conditions, having a mentor or a coach can be transformational. The advice, feedback, and support of a coach or mentor can offer the promise of validation that one is "doing the right thing." Such a guide can help a teacher understand the specific population of students and even challenge a novice teacher's unexamined assumptions about what works and does not work with adults who have low or less-than-functional basic literacy or English-speaking skills.

As a contribution to understanding the potential role of mentoring and coaching in a field very different from K–12 or postsecondary education, we describe three different initiatives to help adult basic education teachers learn their craft with the help of a mentor or coach. Our goal here is not to describe whether or how mentoring or coaching works for teachers with different needs (e.g., those who lack content vs. pedagogical skills), but to present the potential of mentoring/coaching as an alternative form of professional development for a diverse group of teachers, some of whom may not be well served by traditional workshops. We start by briefly describing the adult basic education system and the challenges it presents for providing teachers with evidence-based, effective professional development. We then provide brief profiles of projects in Massachusetts, Ohio, and Minnesota to organize mentoring and coaching for adult basic education teachers, each project with unique features tailored to the specific needs of this population of teachers. Finally, we summarize our suggestions for good practice and further research into the effectiveness of mentoring

CHALLENGES TO EFFECTIVE
PROFESSIONAL DEVELOPMENT IN THE ABE SYSTEM

The ABE system in the United States is designed to provide education to adults functioning below the 12th-grade level in any of the basic academic areas, including reading, mathematics, and writing. ABE English-language instruction is also provided for adult immigrants and refugees, sometimes in combination with basic skills instruction. ABE is delivered at a variety of sites, with variations across and within states: public schools, workforce centers, community/technical colleges, prisons, jails, libraries, learning centers, tribal centers, and community-based organizations. System structure within states is equally varied: ABE may be part of the K–12 education system, a postsecondary system, or even a state department of labor system, and certification and preservice preparation for teachers is not uniform (Smith & Gomez, 2011). Adult basic education, unlike K–12, is largely funded with federal or state year-to-year "soft money" funding that keeps the ABE system staffed by part-time or volunteer teachers with little background in teaching adults and working in poorly paid, non-benefitted jobs without preparation time. Unlike K–12 teachers, ABE teachers often work in isolation, teach part-time in evening or weekend programs, and receive no paid time to participate in professional development activities (Smith, 2006). Lacking stable funding from a tax or tuition base, ABE programs and state systems operate via annual allocations from federal and state legislatures, and thus lack resources to invest in extensive professional development. The overwhelmingly part-time workforce has limited time to attend the brief workshops or conferences that are offered. All of this presents unique challenges to providing high-quality professional development for ABE practitioners. These challenges result from the structural, policy, and funding constraints not typically faced by the K–12 or higher education system.

The need for professional development and learning opportunities is critical because teachers often come into ABE classrooms with limited experience, formal training, or theoretical background in working with adult learners (Smith & Hofer, 2003). Certification specifically in teaching adults is not required in many states (Smith & Gomez, 2011). In Minnesota, for example, while approximately 80% of ABE teachers hold current teaching licenses, only 20% of those licenses are in adult basic education; 22% of licensed ABE teachers hold elementary teaching licenses. In addition, Minnesota expects a turnover of approximately one-third of ABE teachers within the next few years (Marchwick, 2010). These statistics point to a critical and ongoing need for professional learning opportunities focused on how to teach adults.

Providing high-quality professional development is challenging with limited resources, particularly because research indicates that the best professional development takes time, careful design and follow-up, collective participation, and a strong link to program efforts to improve instruction. Reviewing both the K–12 and ABE research on features of effective professional development, Smith and Gillespie (2007) argue that both traditional and job-embedded[1] professional development should reflect the following characteristics:

- be of longer duration
- make a strong connection between what is learned in the professional development and the teacher's own work context
- focus on subject-matter knowledge
- encourage teachers from the same workplace to participate together
- focus on helping teachers to study their students' thinking, not just try new techniques

- include collaborative learning activities among teachers
- include activities in which teachers make use of student performance data
- enlist facilitators to organize job-embedded professional development
- link professional development to curriculum based on standards
- help program/school leaders to support instructional reform, not just accountability (Smith & Gillespie, 2007, pp. 216–221)

These best practices in professional development can be difficult to enact because of the specific constraints inherent in the ABE system. Attending professional development for multiple sessions over time is difficult when teachers/tutors are part-time or volunteer, without funding to attend professional development (Smith, 2006), factors that also lessen the possibility of teachers from the same program attending together. A focus on subject-matter knowledge in any single professional development activity is difficult to achieve when ABE teachers often teach multiple subjects, such as reading, writing, numeracy, science, and social studies, to low-level readers and to adults preparing for their General Educational Development (GED) test. In addition, working in jobs without benefits, without paid prep time, without a strong voice in program decision making, and without regular contact with colleagues (Smith & Hofer, 2003) results in higher attrition from the field (Smith, 2006). Lack of such resources is also a barrier in helping teachers to make a strong connection between the professional development and their workplace context.

How can the ABE field reconcile the need for professional learning with the realities of teacher isolation and limited access to extensive professional development activities? Research in K–12 education (Bush, 1984) indicates that when teachers participate in standard inservice models (e.g., part/single-day workshops or after-school professional development sessions), fewer than 20% apply their learning back in the classroom. However, when coaching is added to the professional development process, classroom implementation of learned strategies increases to 90% (Joyce & Showers, 1995; Showers, Joyce, & Bennett, 1987). Since the goal of professional development is to have a positive impact on teaching and learning, expanded opportunities for coaching or mentoring hold promise.

MODELS OF COACHING AND MENTORING IN ABE

Just as there are huge differences in state and program structures, facilities, and resources for training and professional development within ABE, multiple mentoring and coaching models have recently been developed to meet practitioner needs. In the field of ABE, interest in peer coaching and mentoring has been growing in the past decade. Sherman, Voight, Tibbetts, Dobbins, Evans, and Weidler (2000) created a guide for integration of mentoring programs that utilizes a "master/novice" model, designed to "nurture the growth of a less experienced instructor or administrator through counseling, coaching, and supporting reflective problem solving" (p. 1). The U.S. Department of State has produced videos that model a peer observation process for teachers of adult English language learners (Bureau of Educational and Cultural Affairs, Office of English Language Programs, n.d.). Additionally, some states, including Ohio (Reynolds, 2007) and Minnesota (Johnson, 2012), have begun integrating variations of coaching into work with ABE and adult English language teachers.

Typically, mentoring involves an intentional relationship for the purposes of learning and growth between a more experienced professional and one who is less experienced. In this chapter, we present three variations on this one-on-one expert/novice mentoring model and the modifications that have made them viable in different ABE contexts. One variation includes guidance by a more experienced practitioner but expands on this model by teaming a single "mentor teacher" with a small group of less-experienced teachers. Another variation is here referred to as *coaching*. While coaching, like most traditional mentoring models, can involve an expert/novice relationship, coaching, in this context, differs from mentoring in that coaching emphasizes a *mutual* learning opportunity with a focus on inquiry to guide reflection and changes in practice. Thus, *peer coaching* can facilitate reflection and change between even very experienced veteran teachers or administrators. There are many terms associated with *mentoring* or *coaching*, including *peer coaching* (Hutson & Weaver, 2008; Swafford, 1998), *peer mentoring* (Johnson, 2012; Parrish, 2004), and *reciprocal peer coaching* (Zwart, Wubbels, Bergen, & Bolhuis, 2007), and many are used interchangeably. We three authors operate within different contexts that use various terms. In this chapter, we use both terms, *mentoring* and *peer coaching*.

Peer coaching, as we define it here, is a mutual learning opportunity that builds on principles of self-directed learning and inquiry into teaching. Teachers benefit from the chance to ask questions about their own teaching, assess and critically reflect on their own strengths and weaknesses, and then experience and construct meaning from experiences within a particular context. Teachers set their own goals and plans to achieve those goals (Richards & Farrell, 2005). Peer coaching is a form of professional inquiry in which teachers work with colleagues to examine, reflect upon, and alter instructional practices. Robbins (1995, as cited in Rhodes & Beneicke, 2006) defined peer coaching as "a confidential process through which two or more professional colleagues work together to reflect upon current practices; expand, refine, and build new skills; share ideas; conduct action research; teach one another; or problem solve within the workplace" (p. 298).

Models of peer coaching and mentoring in ABE vary in structure, scope, and time span, although all incorporate what we know to be effective in teacher professional development: They take place over a period of time, focus on content that is relevant to participating teachers, and feature experiential and collaborative activities. The following section describes the structure and unique features of three models of coaching and mentoring in ABE: mentor teacher groups in New England and New Mexico, coaching models in Ohio, and peer coaching integrated into professional development for adult numeracy teachers in Minnesota.

Mentor Teacher Groups in New England and New Mexico

The benefits of teachers mentoring or peer coaching other teachers are well documented in the professional development literature (Danielson, 1999; Ingersoll & Strong, 2011). However, there are two limitations to mentoring as a professional development approach for those responsible for planning ABE professional development, who usually work at the state level (Belzer, Drennon, & Smith, 2001). First, mentoring requires an affinity between mentor and mentee that is difficult to set up deliberately as part of a professional development system; second, mentoring is usually a one-to-one relationship, which limits the numbers of teachers who can participate in mentoring, compared to other professional development approaches, such as workshops or teacher learning circles.

In the early 2000s, the National Center for the Study of Adult Learning and Literacy (NCSALL) sponsored a mixed-method study of how teachers change as a result of participating in one of three models of professional development. When we (Smith, Hofer, Solomon, Gillespie, & Rowe, 2003) initiated this four-year study, the aim was to compare three different approaches: (1) training workshops, (2) practitioner research groups, and (3) peer coaching. However, the limitations of one-on-one peer coaching or mentoring gave us pause. How could we organize peer coaching or mentoring from the "outside" in a manner that would be as effective as peers or mentors who find each other naturally; and could we justify researching an approach that promised to serve so few teachers, when the need for teacher preparation in adult basic education was so marked (Smith & Hofer, 2003)? After much thought, we came up with the idea of a *mentor teacher group*, an 18-hour professional development approach offering both the benefits of mentoring and the benefits of a number of teachers working together in a group. This approach combines the teacher study group with mentor observation and coaching for individual teachers. The list below outlines how a *mentor teacher group* works:

- The professional development organizers find an experienced ABE teacher and train her/him in how to facilitate a mentor teacher group (MTG) on a particular topic of need among teachers (e.g., working with learning disabled adults, teaching low-level math or reading, helping adults set goals for their learning, etc.).
- The organizers advertise the professional development opportunity and recruit five interested teachers to participate in the MTG.
- The group—one facilitator and five participant teachers—meet together for their first three-hour session, introducing themselves, discussing their current knowledge of the topic, and learning about what will happen during the MTG, including the readings they will do before the next session.
- Several weeks later, the group meets a second time in another three-hour session, discussing the readings and the topic, and preparing for the first mentor teacher observation.

- During the two months after the second group meeting, the mentor teacher visits and observes one class of each of the five teachers, as scheduled with the participants, and conducts with each teacher a one-hour pre-observation discussion ("What should I look for as I observe your class?"), the two-hour class observation, and then a one-hour post-observation discussion ("How did you feel the new technique or strategy worked?" and "Here are the data I collected about what you asked me to observe").
- After the mentor teacher has visited and observed a class session with each of the five teachers, the whole group meets for a third time for a two-hour session; the teachers talk about the experience of being observed, and they plan for their next observation with the mentor teacher.
- After the third meeting, there is a second round of mentor teacher observations in each teacher's class.
- Finally, the whole group meets for the fourth and final time for two hours, discussing what they have learned on the topic and making action plans for continuing to try new techniques or approaches in their classrooms.

In the study that tested these three models of professional development, each mentor teacher group met for 10 hours as a group; each participant teacher got eight contact hours one-on-one with the mentor, and the whole experience occurred over a four- to six-month time span. Thus, a MTG allows for a small group of teachers to learn about a topic and share plans about how to change their teaching. It also allows each teacher to be observed twice by the mentor teacher, receiving suggestions and advice about using new techniques related to the topic in their classrooms.

How effective is the mentor teacher group, as compared with other professional development approaches, in promoting teacher change? The NCSALL researchers followed 101 adult literacy teachers across New England who participated in 18 hours of professional development in either a three-day workshop, a mentor teacher group, or a practitioner research group. Teachers completed questionnaires before, immediately after, and one year after participating. They were questioned about their learning on and off the topic of professional development, and about the actions they took in their classrooms, programs, and in the field of adult literacy. Researchers also randomly selected six teachers from each of the three models, for a subsample of 18 teachers who were interviewed in depth at each of the same three points of time. Through these data, researchers were able to categorize the overall amount of change (thinking and acting) each teacher demonstrated, as well as the type of change: (1) more changes in thinking (i.e., learned new knowledge but took no or little action), (2) more changes in action (i.e., used a new technique in their classroom unrelated to the topic of the professional development and without a good explanation of why they were using the technique, other than that they thought it was an "interesting" technique), or (3) integrated change (i.e., a change in both thinking and acting where new learning was tied to using a new technique, and the practitioner could also reflect on the use and outcome of the technique related to the topic of the professional development). Types 1 and 2 (more thinking than acting, more acting than thinking change) were categorized as "nonintegrated" change, with integrated change being the preferred type of change.

While the findings showed no statistically significant differences between the three models in terms of the amount and type of change teachers reported immediately after and one year after participating in the professional development, teachers who participated in mentor teacher groups did demonstrate more overall change than their counterparts who participated in a multisession workshop of the same length and on the same topic. In addition, a slightly higher percentage of teachers who participated in the mentor teacher group model demonstrated integrated change: 29% of mentor teacher group completers ($n = 24$) versus 25% of practitioner research group completers ($n = 24$), as compared to 20% of workshop participants ($n = 35$), demonstrated integrated change. Again, these differences in change according to professional development model were not statistically significant but have implications for future research:

> The subtle differences we found among the models—that teachers completing practitioner research group professional development showed slightly higher overall change, and that teachers completing mentor teacher group professional development were slightly more likely to demonstrate integrated change—might have been stronger with a larger sample. (Smith et al., 2003, p. 32)

Feedback from teachers indicated that those who participated in mentor teacher groups particularly valued the two opportunities for one-to-one observation and feedback from the mentor. Teachers may appreciate such in-class observations and coaching from a mentor because many new teachers in ABE do not, as a rule, receive direct feedback and observation on their teaching, as the following two comments demonstrate.

One teacher expressed her feelings this way:

> I never feel confident in what I'm doing even though other people will say, "Oh, she's a great teacher." They've never seen me teach; no one's ever come in and watched. How do they know? (Smith & Hofer, 2003, p. 105)

Another teacher in Smith and Hofer's (2003) study explained the appeal of being observed and given feedback by a mentor: "We're on our own.... There's no support. Maybe that's why I gravitated towards mentoring. I was so desperate for some kind of feedback! Am I doing a good job?" (p. 105).

When asked what type of professional development they would most prefer, one out of five participants (21%) in the NCSALL professional development study ($n = 87$) said they would prefer to learn from or be coached or mentored by an experienced practitioner or professional developer who comes to their program to provide technical assistance (Smith & Hofer, 2003).

Based on these results and the relative success of the model, one of the research team members, research coordinator Judy Hofer, planned and organized five mentor teacher groups in 2002 in New Mexico on the topic of Gardner's theory of multiple intelligences, adapted for adult basic education classrooms. Hofer (2004) concluded that the model's nonhierarchical and flexible form contributes to its effectiveness:

> The strength of this model is that it offers participants the opportunity to learn not only from the mentor teacher during the classroom observations but also from one another during the group meetings.... The strength of the individualized mentoring process is that it supports teachers in integrating their learning directly and immediately into their own unique contexts. The group component supports teachers by giving them the opportunity to share ideas with their colleagues. (p. 6)

Peer Coaching in Ohio ABE

In 2006, as a response to increasing demand from teachers and program administrators for support in how to serve adults with (undiagnosed) learning disabilities, the Ohio ABE system[2] piloted a peer coaching model of professional development specific to providing support for teachers working with adults with special learning needs (Reynolds, 2007). As with the Minnesota model, the Ohio model of peer coaching emphasized a relationship between peers that is collaborative, nonevaluative, reciprocal, and focused on learners and learning (Johnson, 2012; Parrish, 2004). The Ohio model was grounded in the process of cognitive coaching and the idea of gradual release of responsibility (Pearson & Gallagher, 1983), which, as with scaffolded instruction, allows for increasing autonomy on the part of the mentee or individual being coached. Pearson and Gallagher's model includes four progressive steps: (1) "I do, you watch," in which the coach teaches, and the teacher observes, with the coach planning and leading the debriefing session after the observation; (2) "I do, you help," in which the coach teaches, the teacher assists, and both plan the debrief; (3) "You do, I help," in which the teacher teaches and the coach assists, both planning the debrief; and (4) "You do, I watch," in which the teacher teaches, the coach observes, and the teacher plans and leads the debrief session. The process we employed used three basic steps: a planning conference, observation, and reflecting conference (Costa & Garmston, 1994). During the planning conference, which occurs right before the lesson, coaches work with teachers to (1) build trust, (2) focus on the teacher's goals, (3) facilitate a mental rehearsal of the lesson, (4) set parameters for the reflecting conference, and (5) promote self-coaching. During observation, the coach collects the data (e.g., student interaction, level of questions asked) identified by the teacher. The coach can utilize a variety of means to gather data during observation, including videotaping, tallying student actions, and classroom mapping of teacher movement or teacher–student interactions. After the lesson, the coach and teacher meet for the reflecting conference. In the reflecting conference, the coach encourages the teacher to reflect on the lesson, giving his/her impression, supported with specific examples.

As the designers of this coaching model, we felt it important that participants understand the distinction between coaching, mentoring, and evaluation (see, e.g., Costa & Garmston, 1994, p. 14). The primary goal of coaching is—through reflective practice—to help teachers develop their craft. Evaluation and feedback play an important role in teacher professional development, and we felt it was necessary to make a clear distinction between them. Coaches restate, reflect, and question; they do not offer judgments (positive or negative). To do so would limit the ability of the teacher to reflect on her own practice and would detract from the trusting relationship that is required for deep reflection to occur.

Because peer coaching was a new model of professional learning in Ohio ABLE, the two state leadership professional development staff members assigned to coordinate the initiative developed a protocol and training resources to prepare participants to engage in the peer coaching process. This preparation included a two-day, face-to-face skills workshop on coaching, with extensive training in the questioning and reflection techniques applied in peer coaching relationships. The designers also developed and maintained a website with additional training and support materials, including an online tutorial designed to make clear the differences between coaching, mentoring, and evaluation. Overall, the training was intended to help participants to do the following:

- use coaching as a tool to enhance ongoing professional dialogue that develops self-efficacy and produces high-impact teaching and learning
- define the coaching process, roles, and ABLE coaching model (including the "gradual release of responsibility" model by Pearson & Gallagher, 1983)
- differentiate between peer coaching and mentoring and peer coaching and evaluating
- reflect on the Five States of Mind[3] (Costa & Garmston, 1994) to design questions that mediate thinking and behavior, then practice paraphrasing and questioning techniques
- create coaching framework maps to use with coaching conversations
- practice effective interpersonal communication skills (listening, trust and relationship-building strategies)
- reflect on personal coaching strengths and challenges
- network with the coordinator and other coaches regularly through website and electronic lists
- complete a practice coaching session

Twelve ABE instructors from across the state participated in this face-to-face and online training; this pool of coaches was then available to interested ABE teachers who might want a coach. Those who did participate in coaching provided very positive feedback; indeed, the experience was positive for both parties. Yet, over the course of the initiative and despite sustained promotion, few instructors

(n < 10) or administrators (n < 10) took advantage of the peer coaching program. Of note, we offered teachers and administrators a traditional workshop session on the techniques of coaching (e.g., questioning skills, such as probing and clarifying and using positive presuppositions) outside the peer coaching initiative as a way to educate program staff about peer coaching; the rooms were full and evaluations were positive. We were unable to determine the reasons for the general lack of participation, but lack of understanding of the peer coaching process and/or lack of time could have been factors. Establishing and sustaining a coaching program is challenging at the K–12 level (Neufeld & Roper, 2003), and perhaps even more so in the ABE system, where programs and teachers are isolated. As a result of the lack of participation after the first year, focus on this pilot peer coaching program was shifted as other initiatives took priority.

In 2011 through 2012, we implemented a modified version of this peer coaching model as part of a statewide professional development program in mathematics. Instead of having a pool of coaches for teachers to call upon, ABE program directors who wanted to participate in this new pilot were asked to select two or more instructors from their program. The teams of teachers selected from each participating program were expected to work together throughout the pilot program. We employed the same coaching process as in the earlier peer coaching pilot (i.e., planning conference, observation, reflecting conference) and provided training on observation techniques. Over the course of the year, each team of teachers was expected to complete two formal coaching sessions encompassing all three steps, including structured classroom observations of each other, using the following questions to guide pre- and post-observation conferencing:

Planning Conference Questions

1. What are your goals for the students?
   a. How will you know the students have reached these goals?
   b. What will you do to help your students reach the goals?
   c. What will you do for those students who do not reach the intended goals?
2. What data would you like me to collect about your students and/or yourself?
3. How has this conversation helped you?

Post-observation Questions

1. How do you feel your lesson went?
2. What went well? How do you know?
3. What did you see or hear that would indicate that the students achieved the goals?
4. What might you change or do differently?
5. How has this conversation helped you?

In addition, the participating program directors ($n = 6$) were required to participate in a study circle, designed to promote awareness of relevant research in math, so that the teachers participating in peer coaching would have administrative support within their program to try new instructional strategies in math.

Feedback from the pilot was mixed. Some teacher teams felt that the process, particularly the observations, was too highly structured. The questions, which were provided to protect the integrity of the coaching conversation, and the structured observation techniques seemed to limit the teachers in a way that made them uncomfortable. Teachers reported that they preferred to meet and talk informally about their teaching. As a result, many teams resisted the formal process and "just talked."

When reflecting on this feedback from participating teachers, we heard not only their desire for peer support but also a clear resistance to the formality and structure we had built into the process. We used this feedback to make some adjustments to our process the following year (2012–2013). In the second year of the statewide math professional development initiative, we again asked for teams of teachers who could provide support throughout the program year; this time, however, we focused more on the conferencing aspect of coaching, going back to the questioning and feedback techniques of cognitive coaching (Costa & Garmston, 1994). Thus, the design of this peer coaching professional development model continues to evolve, building on the desire of teachers to share their practice through conversation and coaching conferences that help teachers develop what Costa and Garmston (1994) referred to as *craftsmanship*: "The drive for elaboration, clarity, refinement, precision—craftsmanship—is the energy source from which persons ceaselessly learn and deepen their knowledge and skills" (p. 137).

Peer Coaching and the Minnesota Numeracy Initiative

In 2008, the Adult Basic Education Teaching and Learning Advancement System (ATLAS), the Minnesota professional development center housed at Hamline University, launched a peer coaching project for partner teachers that incorporates aspects of action research and multiple rounds of observations and reflection (termed "peer mentoring" and adapted from Parrish, 2004). This peer coaching model intentionally moves away from the master/novice pairing and emphasizes a relationship between colleagues that is collaborative, nonevaluative, reciprocal, and focused on learners and learning (Johnson, 2012; Parrish, 2004). To facilitate reflection on current practice, ATLAS peer coaching integrates a process of self-assessment with reflection on ideas about teaching and learning and encourages professional conversations with a colleague to facilitate teachers' insights into their own beliefs and classroom decision making and the impact those choices have on learning (Danielson, 2009; Joyce & Showers, 1996). We encourage peers to focus on student learning, based on the belief that, with such a focus, peer coaching can lead to changes in teacher practices and ultimately to improved student outcomes (Joyce & Showers, 2003; Zwart et al., 2007).

TABLE 16.1. The Structure of the Minnesota Numeracy Initiative

Phase 1 August–December	Phase 2 December–February	Phase 3 February–April
• full-day, face-to-face, kick-off meeting • online course 1 *(Foundations of Teaching Adult Numeracy)* • weekly partner meetings • webinar at the end of online course • ongoing participation in MNI Wiggio	• partner observations • ongoing participation in MNI Wiggio	• online course 2 *(Teaching Reasoning and Problem-Solving Strategies)* • weekly partner meetings • partner project • project presentation at final full-day, face-to-face meeting • ongoing participation in MNI Wiggio

Peer coaching through ATLAS is offered as a professional development option for practitioners who can now access an online training at any time to begin the process; unfortunately, this has had very limited success. Despite aggressive marketing and the very positive impact reported by past participants, few teachers seem willing or able to take the time required in this model, which includes training time, multiple observations, and pre- and post-observation meetings.

In 2010, we launched a new professional development project for teachers of math, called the Minnesota Numeracy Initiative (MNI), with the goal of improving numeracy instruction and implementation of new instructional practices for participating teachers. Fixsen, Naoom, Blasé, Friedman, and Wallace (2005) reviewed implementation practice studies and found that changes in practice are best facilitated through introduction of skills through training, followed by on-the-job learning with the support of a consultant or coach. Thus, we drew from our experiences with past peer coaching and this awareness of the power of support to integrate a new peer coaching model into MNI.

MNI is a professional development activity designed to meet the needs of a cohort of approximately 24 ABE or adult English-language teachers who teach numeracy at any level each year. MNI has multiple components: two face-to-face meetings, two online courses about adult numeracy instruction offered through World Education (professionalstudiesae.worlded.org), an electronic community of practice (using Wiggio; more at www.wiggio.com), and peer coaching activities. These components are organized into three phases, as outlined in Table 16.1.

The vision of MNI peer coaching is broad, and includes work and support with a colleague throughout the year. Peer activities during Phases 1 and 3 include the following:

1.   participation with the partner in training and support activities at the kick-off meeting

2. weekly partner meetings through fall and spring online courses to reflect on course content and course assignments, including implementation of instructional strategies
3. submission of weekly email "notecards" with questions or highlights of the partner meetings to a designated MNI project lead
4. the creation and presentation of culminating partner projects for the final meeting

However, the heart of MNI peer coaching is a partner observation process that occurs during Phase 2. This activity facilitates and promotes the use of newly learned strategies into instruction with peer support. We have identified six critical steps needed for the peer coaching experience to result in the reflection and instructional changes desired.

Preparation and Training

Teachers are encouraged to apply to MNI with a partner, although we have been mostly successful at pairing teachers who may not know each other at the start. Whether teachers apply together or not, like all adult learners, they benefit from a clear understanding of purpose and expectations, so training and team building are critical. We spend time emphasizing the nonevaluative nature of peer coaching and the process of using a structured protocol for observation and discussion. And, no matter how comfortable partners may be with each other, we integrate activities on communication styles and nonjudgmental listening and provide opportunities for partners to talk about how they feel about being observed. It has also been very helpful to do the observations after partners have worked together through an online course and weekly meetings, allowing them a chance to build rapport and a level of comfort with each other.

Teacher Self-Assessment and Identifying an Area for Exploration

A distinguishing feature of the MNI peer-coaching model is the use of a tool provided to teachers for self-assessment and reflection, added as an important step prior to a pre-observation discussion. Working with national numeracy colleagues, we created an *Effective Numeracy Teaching Self-Assessment* (http://atlasabe.org/_literature_112172/MNI_Overview_and_Design) that builds on the principles of effective numeracy instruction that MNI teachers have learned about in the first online course. The self-assessment tool includes places for teachers to assess the frequency with which they integrate key numeracy instructional practices in instruction ("0" as *never* to "5" as *always*), and also to list actual teaching activities they believe might exemplify that practice.

Use of the self-assessment tool gives teachers a rubric and destination (*What am I aiming for?*), as well as a chance to affirm what they are doing well and gain insight into what they may not be doing so well. After completing the self-assessment, teachers are asked to reflect on their responses, identify their own strengths and weaknesses, and select a particular area that they would like to explore more fully in their teaching. Once teachers have thought about their classroom and selected an area for exploration, the peers meet together for the pre-observation discussion.

Pre-observation Discussions and Observation Tasks

Partners set up a time to meet to share and discuss the self-assessment, specifically talking through what they would like to improve or modify in their teaching. Partners can brainstorm activities or practices to better integrate the instructional practice each has identified as a personal challenge or area to explore. In addition, individuals decide with their partner what the observing partner will look for in the class and what kind of notes would be most helpful. Preparation for this step should include practice with the structured process of narrowing from goal to observation task, which can be challenging for some. Observations like this are different from the evaluative checklist of teaching practices that many teachers may have experienced with supervisors, so this preparation should not be overlooked.

Observations

The purpose of the observations is key: *Keep the focus on learners and learning.* The purpose of observations for these peer coaches is not to judge teacher performance and give feedback on what the teacher is or is not doing well. Rather, the peer coach is there to observe the students' reactions, engagement with activities and strategies, and evidence of learning. During the observation, the peer coach collects evidence and insights for the teacher. Peers may observe for varying lengths of time, but most observations last from 30 to 60 minutes. Observers should take notes and can participate in the classroom activities or not, as determined by the partners. Either way, the focus of the observation should be on learners and connected to the teacher-defined goals from the pre-observation meeting.

Post-observation Discussion, Reflection, and Next Steps

Soon after the observation, teachers meet to talk together about what was observed, what it means for learning and teaching, and natural next steps. We recommend a process in which the teacher shares how s/he felt about what happened in class with the new strategy or activity, and then the observer shares what s/he observed, specifically, discussing the students' learning and reactions to the instructional strategies or activities tried. Together, partners consider such questions as these:

- What seemed to work well? When did learning seem to happen?
- How would you tweak this strategy or activity for next time?
- How do you want to continue integrating this instructional practice into your teaching?

If the teacher feels that her goal was not met, then the two can brainstorm strategies and additional ideas to meet goals. This process may lead back into a second cycle, when the peer once again observes the colleague. Although we only require one observation each for MNI, two to three cycles of feedback and observations with the peer coach would provide more opportunity for peers to refine and incorporate new ideas to meet their goals.

Final Reflection

At the end of the observation and reflection cycle, the teachers revisit their initial self-assessments and complete the self-assessment again. This allows teachers to chart their own growth and affirm what goals have been met and/or what else they would like to explore in their teaching. Following a process of observing and being observed, this final meeting can be a powerful reminder of the value of collaborative work and a reinvigorating affirmation of what is going well and what has had a positive impact on learners and learning.

MNI was piloted in 2010 through 2011 with 24 teachers and ran a second cohort of 22 teachers in 2011 through 2012. To determine whether we had met our project objectives, including teacher implementation of effective adult numeracy instructional strategies, we brought in an external evaluator during the pilot year to analyze data collected through pre- and post-MNI year questionnaires, weekly note cards, discussion posts in the courses and through the Wiggio, as well as teacher self-assessments and final reflections. The analysis by Waldron (2011) provided confirmation that MNI participants did indeed implement effective and more varied adult numeracy instructional strategies in their classrooms as a result of participation in MNI and that the peer coaching component was valuable because of the opportunities it provided for feedback on teaching in addition to the self-assessment of teaching strengths and needs.

A challenge has been the need to manage the logistics of required activities, such as the partner observations, for teachers who may not work in the same program and who may be spread across a wide geographic area, a situation common in ABE. This has required flexibility with the weekly meetings; if teachers cannot meet in person, we require them to speak to each other over the phone. For ABE teachers who may need to travel to do observations in a peer's classroom, state funds are available for mileage. Administrator support and encouragement also play an important role in peer coaching success (Swafford, 1998). Administrators must value this process and be willing to provide time needed for teachers to visit and observe a partner's classroom and to meet for professional conversations before and after observations. Administrators have sometimes struggled with the problem of teachers leaving class in order to participate in partner observations, so state resources were made available to fund substitute teachers as needed.

Another challenge to MNI partner observations is the need that this happen in an environment of mutual respect and trust that supports nonevaluation and a focus on learners and learning. For the MNI peer-coaching model, it is important that participants be willing to make changes and take the time to work through challenges with their peer coach and for observers to resist the impulse to evaluate the teaching. This wasn't always easy, perhaps because some teachers may have only experienced high-stakes observations by supervisors or master teachers:

> Keeping the focus of the post-observation to a nonevaluative description was tough. I kept wanting to tell her where things went right and what could be improved rather than the description of the students and their reactions to the activity of the room. My partner kept asking for what she could have done better, and I worked to keep the focus on the students. (MNI peer-teaching participant)

Overall, however, evaluation of comments following the peer coaching cycle from 2010–2011 and 2011–2012 indicated that most teachers valued the experience and found it beneficial to be both the observed teacher and the one observing. Most liked the *Effective Numeracy Teaching Self-Assessment*. Although not unanimously favored (four of 43 teachers reported that the tool was confusing or not helpful), the vast majority found it valuable to begin with the self-assessment to focus observations and set goals for instruction, as the following quotes from MNI participants in both cohorts attest:

- The self-assessment tool was helpful because it forced me to really evaluate not only what I teach, but how and also why I teach the way I do. It helped me to break out of my comfort zone, and start thinking outside the box. It made me realize that I have areas that I really am happy with the results, but also areas that I need to tweak and change.
- It helped me look into areas that I have not thought about before. It allowed me to get more specific about areas I wanted to improve on. It is nice to have something that makes you sit and reflect on the work you are doing.
- It made me look at what I'm already doing instead of only concentrating on in what ways I fall short. It was a simple, but thoughtful way to reflect on my teaching.
- I liked the idea of setting goals and something tangible for the other person to observe. I also enjoyed having someone come in to watch my teaching who had a similar background in numeracy.

Overall, comments about the partner observations echoed the conclusion of Bailey, Curtis, and Nunan (2001) that, with a voluntary process with clear guidelines and expectations, "the real educational power of peer observation is found in the sheer luxury of watching someone else teach for a time and discussing the teaching afterwards...the experience can be very rich indeed" (p. 167). Specifically, teachers commented on the value of observing, reflecting, and collaborating with a partner:

- I appreciated another set of eyes [in the classroom]. She could see the problem from a different lens. She also could see my students from a different perspective and offer other ways she would present the problem.
- Observing other teachers as they teach has been one of my favorite things to do because I get insights on what ideas work and how to present those ideas. What I found useful this time was the pre-planning and post-reflection activities. The method helps focus on both partners as observers and observed. The time to convene right after observation happened helps get ideas for improving the following lesson as well as future teaching of that particular lesson.
- Feedback based on a particular aspect of teaching was very helpful (rather than a general evaluation). It also helped that we had a shared language (from MNI) to discuss details about what was happening in both classes. It was also helpful to take time to see what is happening in other classes in general, just to widen my perspective.
- My partner was able to see small aspects of my teaching style and my students' learning style that I overlook on a day-to-day basis in the busy interaction of the classroom. It was helpful to have an objective pair of eyes to observe what approaches and interactions work and which ones don't and why. I am not always able to identify why something does not work, and my partner was able to provide some insight.

In our post-survey of MNI from both the first and second years, we asked participants to respond to the following question: *As part of MNI, you had the opportunity to observe and collaborate with a peer for teaching. How likely are you to collaborate with a peer in the future and in what way?* In both the 2011 and 2012 MNI cohorts, approximately 39 of 43 teachers, or 90%, indicated that the work with partners, including the observation, was something they would like to do again in the future. In fact, although we only require one observation each, feedback indicated that some would like for MNI to require multiple observations during the peer observation cycle. Given the success of peer coaching within MNI, we have been encouraged to integrate peer coaching into other professional development activities in the future.

LESSONS FOR SUPPORTING MENTORING AND COACHING IN PRACTICE

Although mentoring and peer coaching, regardless of the model, can be as challenging to implement as any other professional development, taken together, the experiences above lead us to several conclusions about the value of mentoring and peer coaching. First, particularly for ABE teachers, who are often isolated and rarely receive feedback about either their performance in the classroom or about how their students seem to be responding to their instruction, mentoring and peer coaching help to address teachers' need for direct feedback. Teachers appreciate the simple validation they can receive from mentors or coaches that they are "on the right track." Having another pair of trusted eyes in one's classroom seems to be a valuable component of helping teachers reflect on what is happening in the classroom with students.

Second, both the available research and our experiences support the conclusion that the processes and techniques applied in coaching provide opportunities for teachers to become more reflective educators. This appears to work for both mentor/coach and partner teacher; it is a *mutual* learning opportunity with a focus on inquiry to guide reflection and changes in practice. ABE teachers in these three models have indicated that they value the opportunity to learn with their peers through reflective discussions.

Third, specific components of these mentoring or peer coaching models have proved successful at guiding the professional development of ABE teachers. For example, ABE teachers in Minnesota who have experienced peer coaching within our professional development for numeracy instruction found the experience to be affirming, and we have seen changes in instructional practices as a result. The importance of training, structure, multiple opportunities to work and support one another, and a focus on student learning are important aspects of the experience. Perhaps the distinctive feature of the MNI peer coaching model is the use of a self-assessment tool that builds on what was learned in the online course and provides a platform for exploration and reflection for teachers, whatever their level of experience. For the MNI, the *Effective Numeracy Teaching Self-Assessment* has benefits as a tool to promote reflection and a focus on targeted instructional practices for both observer and observed, and it can be used for multiple cycles of peer observation and/or live beyond the experience for teachers seeking to improve practices on their own. A basic tool can be modified for many contexts, and, in Minnesota, we have created self-assessments around effective learner-centered instruction for English-language teaching, academic readiness, or volunteer teachers working in a community-based program.

Another example of a specific component of mentoring or peer coaching is the emphasis on the difference between coaching and evaluation. As discussed earlier, teacher reflection is an integral part of coaching. Trust between the two coaching participants is required to facilitate the reflective process. In Ohio, we found it important to make clear that the role of the coach was to mirror and ask, not to judge or evaluate. In a coaching relationship, any movement toward evaluation (positive or negative) may take away from the teacher's ability to reflect on and honestly evaluate his or her own teaching.

Over the course of several years of piloting peer coaching, we have also learned about the challenges in integrating coaching into professional development. Peer coaching can be challenging to implement, in part because of the level of trust that is required between the participants (Belzer et al., 2001). Relational issues (between participants) are perhaps less of a consideration in other models of professional development, such as workshops and study circles. It is possible that this foundational component of peer coaching was not well established in the 2006 model of peer coaching in Ohio; teachers did not know the cadre of coaches well enough to engage in the process. When peers *from the same program* were trained in coaching techniques, teachers seemed more willing to participate. Asking teams of teachers (as opposed to a single teacher) from the same program to participate in state-sponsored professional development initiatives, and providing training in the skills of coaching, can facilitate the application of peer coaching. The MNI paired teachers found success even with teachers who did not know each other at the outset, perhaps because numerous opportunities were built into the MNI model to develop trust and build the relationships between teachers. Professional developers and program leaders need to consider relationship building carefully when using these models of professional learning.

All professional development activities, including mentoring and peer coaching, require program leaders and professional development staff to consider elements such as audience and purpose/intended outcomes. The coaching model of shared learning can be applied between novice or expert teachers or between program administrators and support staff. Mentoring, as we have defined it here, is perhaps a more commonly implemented model of informal professional learning, perhaps because the expert/novice roles inherent in a mentoring relationship provide a familiar framework for mentors and mentees. The difficulty, then, is how to set up such mentoring on a more formal level, as part of a professional development system that can be organized intentionally; mentor teacher groups provide an example of how this might be done, since mentor teacher groups can work with teachers who do not initially know each other but have the opportunity, over the course of the group meetings, to build the types of relationships of trust that mentor/coaches and teachers need.

Thus, we argue that mentoring and coaching are promising forms of alternative professional development in the field of adult basic education, and possibly in other fields where teachers have differing levels of experience and training and who work in a wide range of teaching situations with a diverse population of students. Future research should investigate whether and how mentoring, as a form of professional development, works for teachers with different needs and questions, such as teachers who seek content, versus pedagogical, knowledge.

NOTES

1. School-based or job-embedded teacher learning circles (Webster-Wright, 2009; Ball & Cohen, 1999).
2. The Ohio ABE system is referred to as the ABLE (Adult Basic and Literacy Education) Program
3. Costa & Garmston's Five States of Mind are (1) efficacy, (2) flexibility, (3) craftsmanship, (4) consciousness, and (5) interdependence.

REFERENCES

Bailey, K. M., Curtis, A., & Nunan, D. (2001). *Pursuing professional development: The self as source*. Boston, MA: Heinle & Heinle.

Ball, D. L., & Cohen, D. K. (1999). Developing practice, developing practitioners: Toward a practice-based theory of professional education. In L. Darling-Hammond & G. Sykes (Eds.), *Teaching as the learning profession: Handbook of policy and practice* (pp. 3–323). San Francisco, CA: Jossey-Bass.

Belzer, A., Drennon, C., & Smith, C. (2001). Building professional development systems in adult basic education: Lessons from the field. In J. Comings, B. Garner, & C. Smith (Eds.), *Annual review of adult learning and literacy* (pp. 151–188). San Francisco, CA: Jossey-Bass.

Bureau of Educational and Cultural Affairs, Office of English Language Programs. (n.d.). *Shaping the way we teach English: Module 13, Peer observation in teaching practices*. Washington, DC: Author. Retrieved from http://www.youtube.com/watch?v=r-abWqXlkFY

Bush, R. N. (1984). *Effective staff development in making our schools more effective: Proceedings of three state conferences*. San Francisco, CA: Far West Laboratory.

Costa, A., & Garmston, R. (1994). *Cognitive coaching: A foundation for renaissance schools*. Norwood, CA: Christopher-Gordon.

Danielson, C. (1999). Mentoring beginning teachers: The case for mentoring. *Teaching and Change, 6*(3), 251–257.

Danielson, C. (2009). Revisiting teacher learning: A framework for learning to teach. *Educational Leadership, 66*(9). Retrieved from http://www.ascd.org/publications/educational-leadership/summer09/vol66/num09/A-Framework-for-Learning-to-Teach.aspx

Effective Numeracy Teaching Self-Assessment. (2011). Minnesota Numeracy Initiative Overview and Design. Retrieved from http://atlasabe.org/_literature_112172/MNI_Overview_and_Design

Fixsen, D. L., Naoom, S. F., Blasé, K. A., Friedman, R. M., & Wallace, F. (2005). *Implementation research: A synthesis of the literature* (FMHI Publication #231).Tampa, FL: University of South Florida, Louis de la Part Florida Mental Health Institute, The National Implementation Research Network.

Hofer, J. (2004). *Mentor teacher group guide: Adult multiple intelligences*. Boston, MA: National Center for the Study of Adult Learning and Literacy.

Hutson, T., & Weaver, C. L. (2008). Peer coaching: Professional development for experienced faculty. *Innovative Higher Education, 33*, 5–20.

Ingersoll, R., & Strong, M. (2011). The impact of induction and mentoring programs for beginning teachers: A critical review of the research. *Review of Educational Research, 81*(2), 201–223.

Johnson, K. A. (2012). *Improving student learning through teacher collaboration*. White paper for TESOL International Symposium: Facilitating Learning through Student Empowerment. TESOL International Association.

Joyce, B., & Showers, B. (1995). *Student achievement through staff development: Fundamentals of school renewal* (2nd ed.). White Plains, NY: Longman.

Joyce, B., & Showers, B. (1996). Evolution of peer coaching. *Educational Leadership, 53*(6), 12–16.

Joyce, B., & Showers, B. (2003). Student achievement through staff development. *National College for School Leadership*. Retrieved from http://literacy.kent.edu/coaching/information/Research/randd-engaged-joyce.pdf

Marchwick, K. (2010). *Charting the future— Minnesota's ABE workforce: Professional experience, challenges and needs*. Adult Basic Education Teaching and Learning Advancement System (ATLAS) report. Retrieved from http://www.atlasabe.org/pd-system/research-surveys/abe-practitioner-survey-2009

Neufeld, B., & Roper, D. (2003). *Coaching: A strategy for developing instructional capacity—Promises and practicalities*. Washington, DC: Aspen Institute Program on Education and the Annenberg Institute for School Reform.

Parrish, B. (2004). *Teaching adult ESL: A practical introduction*. New York, NY: McGraw-Hill.

Pearson, P. D., & Gallagher, M. (1983). The instruction of reading comprehension. *Contemporary Educational Psychology, 8*, 317–344.

Reynolds, S. (2007). Peer coaching: Building relationships and growing professionally. *FieldNotes for ABLE Staff*, 1–4. Retrieved from http://www.iu17.org/393910219133648980/lib/393910219133648980/_files/fn07peercoaching.pdf

Rhodes, C., & Beneicke, S. (2006). Coaching, mentoring and peer-networking: Challenges for the management of teacher professional development in schools. *Journal of In-Service Education, 28*(2), 297–310.

Richards, J., & Farrell, T. S. C. (2005). *Professional development for language teachers: Strategies for teacher learning* (pp. 165–195). Cambridge, UK: Cambridge University Press.

Robbins, P. (1995) Peer coaching: Quality through collaborative work. In J. Block, S. F. Everson, & T. R. Guskey (Eds.), *School improvement programs: A handbook for educational leaders*. New York, NY: Scholastic.

Sherman, R., Voight, J., Tibbetts, J., Dobbins, D., Evans, A., & Weidler, D. (2000). Adult educators' guide to designing instructor mentoring. Retrieved from http://www.calpro-online.org/pubs/Mentoring%20Guide.pdf

Showers, B., Joyce, B., & Bennett, B. (1987). Synthesis of research on staff development: A framework for future study and state of the art analysis. *Educational Leadership, 45*(3), 77–87.

Smith, C., & Gillespie, M. (2007). Research on professional development and teacher change: Implications for adult basic education. In J. Comings, B. Garner, & C. Smith (Eds.), *Review of adult learning and literacy* (pp. 205–244). Mahwah, NJ: Lawrence Erlbaum.

Smith, C., & Gomez, R. (2011). *Certifying adult education staff and faculty*. New York, NY: Council for Advancement of Adult Literacy.

Smith, C., & Hofer, J. (2003). *The characteristics and concerns of adult basic education teachers* (NCSALL Report No. 26). Boston, MA: National Center for the Study of Adult Learning and Literacy.

Smith, C., Hofer, J., Solomon, M., Gillespie, M., & Rowe, K. (2003). *How teachers change: A study of professional development in adult basic education* (NCSALL Report No. 25). Boston, MA: National Center for the Study of Adult Learning and Literacy.

Smith, M. C. (2006). The preparation and stability of the ABE teaching workforce: Current conditions and future prospects. In J. Comings, B. Garner, & C. Smith (Eds.),

Review of adult learning and literacy (Vol. 6, pp. 165–195). Mahwah, NJ: Lawrence Erlbaum.

Swafford, J. (1998). Teacher supporting teacher through peer coaching. *Support for Learning 13*(2), 54–58.

Waldron, S. (2011). *Final evaluation report: Minnesota Numeracy Initiative.* Boston, MA: World Education. Retrieved from http://www.atlasabe.org/_literature_110912/MNI_Evaluation_Report-FY11

Webster-Wright, A. (2009). Reframing professional development through understanding authentic professional learning. *Review of Educational Research, 79*(2), 702–739.

Zwart, R. C., Wubbels, T., Bergen, T. C. M., & Bolhuis, S. (2007). Experienced teacher learning within the context of reciprocal peer coaching. *Teachers and Teaching: Theory and Practice, 13*(2), 165–187.

CHAPTER 17

MENTORING FOR SCHOOL ADMINISTRATORS

Leadership Project

William K. Larson

ABSTRACT

This chapter provides an examination of mentoring for educational administrators, as it represents an aspect of their professional development. Professional development, in this context, pertains to induction, provided by mentors, often seasoned district and school administrators, of useful information and skills for mentees, frequently novice administrators, as they begin to address the challenges of their craft. Mentoring in this context includes a mentee-to-mentee approach, a form of peer mentoring, in the context of a university-based model for provision of ongoing development of administrators, whether beginners or seasoned professionals. The manifestations of formal and informal approaches, which constitute two ways of viewing mentoring, are explored in the chapter describing the Leadership Project (LP), a professional development program, in which mentoring of elementary principals, secondary principals, superintendents, and treasurers has occurred for 19 years. The LP has been operated as a grassroots initiative in which the input of its participants has been requested and used to provide direction regarding substantive matters, such as the topics of the professional development activities.

Mentoring for the Professions: Orienting Toward the Future, pages 317–335.

317

INTRODUCTION

The mentorship of educational administrators, particularly as a function of professional development, is the focus of this chapter. Mentoring, after all, is a form of professional development (Browne-Ferrigno & Muth, 2004; Daresh, 2004; Kennedy, 2005). Mentoring, in the context of this chapter, refers to a relationship in which the work of one person or a group of persons is developed by another person or an organization (Bozeman & Feeney, 2007; Glitz, Danzig, & Szecsy, 2004; Karcher, Nakkula, & Harris, 2005). This form of nurturing is often an active endeavor, such as with coaching and modeling, as opposed to a matter of simply giving advice (Davis, Darling-Hammond, LaPointe, & Meyerson, 2005). Mentoring, for these reasons, pertains largely to transformational (Bass, 2000; Geijsel, Sleegers, Leithwood, & Jantzi, 2003; Williams, Matthews, & Baugh, 2004) and servant (Barbuto & Wheeler, 2006; Crippen, 2005) forms of leadership, though some aspects of mentoring are transactional in nature. Both formal and informal structures of mentoring are considered in this chapter.

The objectives of the chapter are to provide (1) a review of the work-based challenges by which educational administrators can be served through mentoring, (2) an examination of mentoring programs that can help administrators deal successfully with the challenges and achieve positive outcomes with their work, and (3) an investigation of the work of an existing professional development program, titled the Leadership Project (LP). The LP's mentoring structure and delivery mechanism will be described. Particular attention will be given to suggested "takeaway" practices from the project. The intent of discussing the LP is to provide the reader with a "nuts and bolts" perspective of the provision of mentoring. The ultimate objective of the chapter is to enhance the reader's perspective of mentoring for school administrators.

Educational administrators, including business officials, principals, and superintendents, typically are served by being mentored to address their multifaceted and complex work (Kochan, Bredeson, & Riehl, 2002; O'Day, 2002). The primary function of administrators is to afford effective direction, including leadership and management, with the intent of providing the best possible educational experiences for the students in their schools. Pursuing this objective necessitates that administrators have the capacity to address a plethora of responsibilities, such as attending to the demands of state and federal legislatures (Fusarelli, 2002) and preparing students for adulthood in an ever-changing world in which they may be seeking employment in jobs that do not exist now (Levy & Murname, 2004). Administrators also need to be equipped to approach their work in the face of limited financial and human resources and in keeping with the provisions of collective bargaining contracts and other employee-related policies and laws. These challenges tend to intersect with another factor for which school administrators should be prepared, namely dealing with boards of education, which often are composed of elected or politically appointed officials, who can have reelection, reappointment, or the obtainment of higher offices, coupled with intentions to improve the operation of the districts, as their primary objectives (Bryer, 2006; Petersen, Fusarelli, & Kowalski, 2006).

Positive and negative outcomes can materialize from the challenges of administrative work, and the outcomes can be influenced by the nature of the mentoring administrators receive for their work-related challenges. After all, administrative work is a craft (Heck & Hallinger, 2005; Kowalski, 2009) that can be approached best with useful development (Hess & Kelly, 2007; Nelson, Colina, & Boone, 2008). Effective preparation tends to emerge from professional development programs, which help administrators obtain the knowledge, skills, and dispositions needed to attend to the work. Working through such stressful and difficult craft-related challenges can also contribute to the growth of administrators, particularly if they have been mentored to develop a strong sense of self-efficacy, coupled with problem-solving skills (Leithwood & Jantzi, 2008; Leithwood & Mascall, 2008; Tschannen-Moran & Woolfolk Hoy, 2007). Administrators can be mentored to engage in reflection, for example (Barnett & O'Mahony, 2006; Begley, 2006; Pedro, 2006), upon which strategies can be identified to solve the challenges of their work. For these reasons, the mentoring of administrators to address their craft is a substantive issue, which, if approached effectively, can contribute to the quality of the outcomes of their work.

A DISCUSSION OF MENTORING PROGRAMS

Preparation programs, particularly those involving mentoring, reflect an ancient practice in which the development of beginners is handed over to sage members of an organization, in much the same way that Odysseus, as described in Homerian legend, handed over his son's development to a knowledgeable elder, whose name was Mentor (Barker, 2006; Onchwari & Keengwe, 2008; Orland-Barak & Yinon, 2005; Smith, 2005). Mentoring programs have existed, in the interim, in various configurations and have become a typical practice in many organizations as a way for the wisdom of seasoned practitioners to be passed to those who would benefit from it, which would include but not be limited to beginners (Rockoff, 2008). Mentors, mentees, and organizations have, according to research, experienced both positive and negative outcomes from their efforts. However, more positive than negative results have surfaced (Fink & Brayman, 2006; Hall, 2008; Hansford & Ehrich, 2006; Hansford, Tennent, & Ehrich, 2003). For example, the mentee's development tends to be enhanced; the mentor typically grows from the experience of teaching the craft to the mentee; and the organization enjoys more effective and committed employees. On the other hand, the mentee and mentor, particularly in a formal structure in which the arrangement is assigned, can experience conflict. The mentor can become overwhelmed while attempting to address regular work demands, and both the mentorship and the organization can suffer if the mentee and mentor are disgruntled, feeling the organization has imposed the arrangement upon them (Ewing et al., 2008; Marable & Raimondi, 2007). Regardless, mentoring can be a useful enterprise if the potential positive and negative aspects are addressed in a reflective, thoughtful, and well-planned manner (Daresh, 2004; Flynn & Nolan, 2008).

Two of the more traditional ways in which current administrators can be prepared to meet the challenges of their work are induction programs and workshops (Daresh, 2004). Induction programs, typically offered by school districts and professional organizations during the first year that an individual is in an administrative position, frequently contain some form of formal mentoring (Browne-Ferrigno, 2004; Davis et al., 2005; Wong, 2002). The second approach, namely workshops, involves informal mentoring, at best. The remainder of this section describes the mentoring functions of induction programs and workshops, particularly as they relate to formal and informal mentoring.

Induction programs and their mentoring components (Bloom, Castagna, & Warren, 2003) are geared toward helping beginning administrators meet the challenges of the craft. One of the challenges, as previously mentioned, involves changing the "lenses" that the administrators have acquired in their graduate training or previous work, in order that they can gain accurate and useful perspectives of their new work. Plus, the mentorships can assist the administrators in interpreting the unexpected and the hurdles that are often experienced during the initial year or two of a new job (Daresh, 2004). Mentoring in induction programs tends to be formally structured, but it can also be based upon informal dynamics.

The formal structure (Ehrich, Hansford, & Tennent, 2004) tends to enhance the likelihood that mentoring, in some form, will occur as a mentee is assigned to a mentor. In fact, some authors report that this approach leads to more effective outcomes than the informal approach (Allen, Eby, & Lentz, 2006). Women reportedly benefit more from formal mentorship arrangements, as they appear to have more difficulty than men with the establishment of informal internships. Beginners purportedly are served more effectively with formalized programs (Daresh, 2004; Erich et al., 2004; Klug & Salzman, 1991). Mentees and mentors in formal programs have reported positive experiences, especially those associated with learning, personal support and gratification, and improved administrative skills (Eby & Lockwood, 2005). However, problems reportedly have occurred with formal mentorship relationships, such as mismatches emerging from top-down mentor and mentee assignments. In addition to the mismatches, mentors have reported feeling overwhelmed with the responsibility, and mentees have expressed experiencing a lack of commitment on the part of the mentors, which is the opposite of the reactions reported with informal mentoring relationships (Hansford et al., 2004).

With the informal structure (Sosik, 2005), a mentee can choose whether to seek out the assistance of a mentor or not. For this reason, informal mentoring could be considered less effective than formal mentoring, as it does not guarantee that mentoring will occur. While formal mentoring relationships certainly can be effective, the relationships that emerge from informal mentoring tend to be particularly authentic, as the participants have chosen to be mentored and have chosen by whom they want to be mentored, and the mentors have accepted the responsibility (Ehrich, Tennent, & Hansford, 2002). The opportunities to make choices are purported to contribute to the quality of mentoring (Browne-Ferrigno, 2004; Douglas, 1997). A mutually participative—as opposed to a top-down, forced relationship—exists. In addition, the opportunity to make these choices results in involvement, ownership, and commitment to the relationship. This potential for a negative relationship between a mentor and mentee in a formal arrangement has led to a proposed co-mentor approach, which has some of the traits of an informal approach, in which a mentee could seek out other mentors in order to obtain needed nurturing (McGuire & Reger, 2003; Mullen, 2000).

Studies have been conducted in which comparisons have been made of informal and formal mentorships. The participants in the informal mentorships have reported receiving more career mentoring and enjoying more of a long-term relationship with their mentors, as a result of being the beneficiaries of mentors who were committed to the endeavor (Chao, Walz, & Gardner, 1992; Ragins & Cotton, 1999). The mentees have also reported higher levels of compensation and overall satisfaction with their mentoring experience than have participants in formal mentorships (Chao et al., 1992; Ragins & Cotton, 1999). In addition, greater long-term organizational benefits have been reported by participants in informal mentoring programs (Singh, Bains, & Vinnicombe, 2002). However, these overall results may be skewed if the mentors in the informal approach have selected, as their mentees, the individuals who perform best (Chao et al., 1992).

The closest thing to mentoring that some administrators enjoy is workshop-based professional development. The workshops that school administrators understandably choose to attend in order to remain abreast of their respective crafts often pertain to current, though disparate, topics. Such workshops are frequently sponsored and conducted by state administrator associations, state departments of education, and private vendors. The workshops, which typically last for a day or two, are characteristically directed toward, and composed of, important but single-focus topics and information. The workshops regularly feature compelling speakers, capable of effectively communicating with and motivating their audiences. Sometimes the participating administrators are able to develop positive rapport with a speaker, which in turn can result in a form of informal mentoring.

However, professional development can be structured within another, more effective mentoring-based framework. School employees of some districts identify individual professional objectives that are in alignment with their own growth needs and their district's and school's goals. The identification occurs in a manner that is in sync with their mentors. Then the employees seek out ways to attain the objectives, which can include attendance at workshops. A follow-up to the workshop attendance can involve the employees' working with their mentors for the identification and implementation of strategies to address their previously identified objectives. The training that the employees receive can also be used to instruct other employees. For example, a principal who has attended a useful workshop can share the information learned at the session with the other principals.

The foci of the workshops and induction programs, particularly those approached in a formal manner, can be, and may even frequently be, identified and delivered in a top-down manner that reflects a rational system and closed structure, as opposed to a participant-infused manner (Fink, 2003). The potential importance of the input of the participating administrators is that it can contribute to the identification of meaningful seminars, ones that reflect the cultures and needs of the schools and districts in which the participants work. However, statewide workshops, which can be well constructed and delivered regarding such important matters as the ingredients of state and federal mandates, can fail to provide needed attention to ways in which the participants might go about implementing the mandates, given the unique aspects of the communities in which they work (Malen, 2003). As previously mentioned, the workshops may feature excellent speakers, but in a format that leads to "one-size fits all" messages. In addition, some of the workshop programs represent efforts by sponsoring organizations to obtain dearly needed sources of revenue, with less than desirable levels of attention being directed to the learning needs of the participants. Even programs that have authentic concern for the participants can fail to provide them with an opportunity for input and the resulting sense of involvement, commitment, and ownership.

With consideration of these concerns, a professional development program focused upon the learning needs of individuals, from the time they become administrators through their exit from the craft (Browne-Ferrigno & Muth, 2007; Crow & Matthews, 1998; Klinger, 2004) and particularly when they are striving to address difficult work situations (Browne-Ferrigno, 2004), can represent a useful endeavor. An important aspect of providing mentoring over the course of administrative careers, such as might occur in an ongoing professional development program, is that it would contribute to the continuity of the preparation of administrators for their work. In other words, the provision of mentoring and professional development that is attentive to a trajectory and that is mindful of the growth needs of the administrators has significant potential value. The contents of this form of professional development would reflect a career connectedness, as opposed to an isolated benefit for the participants.

Such a professional development program would provide a well-organized basis upon which the participants could grow and develop. Knowledge and skills would be approached in a manner that would build upon the administrators' existing conceptual and working framework. The program would also be focused on the specific, immediate, and long-term needs of the administrators, which would emerge from obtaining their input (Mullen, 2000). While such a mentoring program would need to address some of the same topics, utilize the services of powerful speakers, and be implemented in conjunction with the work of state administrator organizations and departments of education, the program would be approached in a manner that would help the administrators grow professionally from the perspectives of their own careers and the culture of the communities in which they work, as opposed to learning just about a specific workshop topic.

THE LEADERSHIP PROJECT

The remainder of this chapter is focused upon an existing professional development program, the Leadership Project, in which the participants, who are educational administrators, have been mentored. The Leadership Project (LP) is housed at a regional campus of a relatively large university located in a rural Appalachian portion of a Midwestern state. The project has been in existence for 19 years, a value of which is associated with the ongoing continuity that it has provided for the professional development and mentoring of the participants, an approach that is supported in the literature (Daresh, 2004; Stead, 2005; Van Velsor, McCauley, & Moxley, 1998). The continuity has been coupled with a singular focus, as the sole mission of the project is to provide professional development and mentoring for its participating administrators. In fact, participation in the project is limited to current administrators. Others can attend the project's seminars only by invitation.

Character and History of the Leadership Project

The participants share something of a homogeneous viewpoint, which reflects their type of work and Appalachian roots. However, some of the participants are from counties that are outside the officially designated Appalachian region, and for this reason they appear to have perspectives that are similar to, but not entirely in line with the perspectives of their Appalachian counterparts. Of course, the participants within Appalachia occasionally exhibit different points of view from each other, viewpoints that seem to reflect the dissimilarities in their counties. For example, some of the counties are primarily rural in nature and other counties have small cities, some of which signify a more urban outlook.

The LP began with a cohort of 15 superintendents. They responded to an invitation sent to superintendents throughout the region. In the interim, the LP has grown to four cohorts, one each for elementary principals, secondary principals, superintendents, and treasurers. Each of the cohorts has approximately 80 active participants, of which approximately half are in attendance at a given seminar. Some of the participants typically attend all of the seminars during a school year, while others attend on a more sporadic basis. Penalties do not exist for failing to attend the seminars, and the primary reward for attendance is the opportunity to engage in a meaningful learning experience. Attendees do receive a certificate, which hypothetically could be used for the renewal of a state administrative license. However, the number of certificates that could be obtained during the life of a license would only contribute to a portion of its renewal.

The seminars, during the first 12 years of the project, were scheduled from 9:00 a.m. through the early afternoon. Lunch was included. The initial portion of the seminars, that is the period prior to the lunch hour, typically included a speaker or speakers on topics chosen by the participants. The lunch hour generally involved informal discussions that were based upon the content of the remarks that had been offered by the speakers. Roundtable discussions occurred after lunch. During these discussions, the participants had the opportunity to request the input of the other participants regarding challenging issues.

The primary source of funding for the LP during this beginning stage of its existence was in the form of grants from the state of Ohio. In-kind support, such as office space, was provided by the university. The state grants paid for the speakers, lunches, and room rentals, and even helped with compensation of the LP's director and administrative assistant. The level of state support was, unfortunately, reduced on two occasions; on both of these occasions the state had experienced a serious revenue downfall. In fact, the level of state support was totally eliminated, effective the second occasion, as it was for other similar state-funded programs. The participants in the superintendents' cohort voted to initiate a district stipend to help compensate for the loss of the state funding. The revenue from the districts' payment of the stipend, along with an increase of in-kind support by the university, has helped to sustain the project. However, these initiatives have made up for only a portion of the lost state funding. For this reason, the number of seminars per year for each cohort has been reduced from approximately five to four; the provision of lunches for the participants has been eliminated, which has led to the seminars' ending at noon; and the manner in which the director and administrative assistant are compensated has been modified.

The LP is operated by a director and administrative assistant. As mentioned above, a significant portion of their compensation was provided, during the beginning years of the project, by revenues from state grants. This arrangement had to end with the reduction of state funding. Fortunately, the reduction of the LP's resources was accompanied by a growth in the other university responsibilities of the director and the administrative assistant. The director, who initially was an adjunct member of the faculty, is now a full-time member of the faculty and the coordinator of the university's educational administration program, the functions upon which his compensation is now totally based. The director, as part of his faculty responsibilities, is expected to provide teaching, scholarship, and service. The director's faculty colleagues have been willing to recognize his work with the project as representing a significant portion of his responsibility for service, which has allowed him to continue to serve the project. The project's administrative assistant is also responsible for the clerical functions of the educational administration program. Fifty-five percent of her time is devoted to these responsibilities, with 45% being devoted to the project. Her compensation is arranged accordingly. The changes have resulted in reallocation of the LP responsibilities of the director and administrative assistant. The director has continued to work with the participants to obtain their input regarding the seminar topics and to identify and arrange for the presence of speakers to address these topics. In addition, the director still attends and coordinates the seminars. However, the administrative assistant addresses most of the other responsibilities of the LP, several of which had previously been addressed by the director.

Regardless, the LP has continued to operate, with seminar participation equal to the levels experienced before these changes. For example, the seminar attendance levels, during the 2010 through 2012 period, have ranged from 24 to 77, with a mean and a median attendance of 46 attendees. The average attendance level prior to the changes had been slightly smaller, approximately 40. Also contributing evidence to the sustainability of the LP is the decision of the participants in the superintendents' cohort, as reported above, to initiate an annual district stipend. Most of the districts in which the LP's participants work have few or no discretionary revenues. The districts have paid the stipends only because the superintendents have been able to convince their school boards of the importance for the administrators in their districts to attend the seminars. A third factor, adding to the sustainability of the LP, is found in the comments made on the anonymous evaluations that are conducted with each seminar. The comments are almost always positive in nature, which may reflect the involvement of the participants in the identification of the seminar topics, a function explained in greater detail later in this section.

A significance of the attendance levels, district stipends, and continuation of the LP is that they have occurred in the face of the ongoing and even increasing constraints on the time of the participating administrators. After all, the time of educational administrators is greatly encumbered by district expectations and state and federal mandates. For this reason, the administrators typically spend their time on non-mandated activities, such as the LP's seminars, only if they are perceived as being extremely useful. The administrators do not have the luxury of spending their time on less than worthwhile endeavors.

Mentorship Endeavors

The remainder of this section of the chapter describes and analyzes the mentoring that has emerged from the work of the LP. The mentoring endeavors of the project are described, as is the manner in which they have been organized and sustained. The significance of the former is that it pertains to actual mentoring, and the relevance of the latter is that the mentoring would have been hypothetical without the strategies that have been used to support it. The mentoring activities include those provided by the project's director and administrative assistant; the mentoring that occurs between project participants, which can be labeled as mentee-to-mentee, participant-to-participant, or peer mentoring; and the mentoring that occurs in the learning community that has emerged from the project.

Also included are suggestions, each of which has been labeled as a "takeaway," that have grown out of the project's endeavors. The first takeaway is based upon the meaningfulness of the levels of attendance at the LP's seminars, the annual stipends that are paid by the districts of the participating superintendents, and the choice of administrators to continue to support and attend the LP's seminars.

A takeaway, which is at the "heart" of the other suggestions found in this section of the chapter, is that the perceived effectiveness of an informal mentoring program, such as the LP, can be measured by the willingness of the participating administrators to expend their precious, highly encumbered time and their district's funds to attend voluntarily the program's seminars and to support the program's activities.

Project's Director and Administrative Assistant

The primary focus of the LP's director and administrative assistant has been the provision, in a transformational and servant manner, of meaningful learning experiences and professional growth for the project's participants. Nearly all of the project's 300 participants are known by name to the director and assistant. This is indicative of the manner in which the participants are treated by the director and administrative assistant and the importance of the approach. They have, in effect, become mentors to the participants. The project represents a mission, as opposed to a job, in which the director and administrative assistant have aspired to help the participants grow and thrive in the craft of administration. The significance of this form of approach is described in Boverie and Kroth (2001). Evidence of the mission-based approach of the director and administrative assistant has emerged from an examination of the project conducted by an external investigator and the evaluations, which are addressed in an anonymous manner at the time of each project seminar. Also contributing evidence to the effectiveness of the mission approach is that the project had been predicted not to survive its first few years. However, the project's tenure of 19 years and the positive reactions that have emerged from the evaluations confirm the importance of the director and administrative assistant's commitment to the mentoring of the professional growth of the participants.

The participants expressed to the external investigator the importance of the caring and nurturing behaviors of the director and administrative assistant in the development and provision of the LP's professional development and mentoring activities. For example, the administrative assistant regularly exhibits authentic client care when addressing the project's participants. Proof of the positive manner in which her approach is viewed is reflected in the attempts that have been made by participants to hire her to work in their schools and districts. The importance and influence of the relationships that the director and administrative assistant have developed with the LP's participants resonate with the experiences of others described in the literature (Allen, Day, & Lentz, 2005; Allen & Poteet, 1999).

The director and administrative assistant also enjoy the opportunity to work with many of the future participants of the LP during the time that these students are involved in the university's preservice programs for principal and superintendent preparation and the obtainment of state licenses. The director has been the advisor and instructor for most of these participants. The work of the administrative assistant tends to be at the intersection of the procedural matters associated with the students' studies in the university. For this reason, the administrative assistant is often the person that the students go to first for solutions to their problems. An outcome is that the director and assistant have formed a bond with many of the students in the preservice programs. This bond reflects an understanding of the students, including their dispositions and professional needs; such insights can be very useful when attempting to mentor students once they become administrators and begin participating in the LP. The importance of this bond is supported by Galbraith (2003).

The work of the director has been augmented by the perceived credibility that he has brought to the project. More specifically, the director was a school administrator for over 20 years, the last 14 of which were as the superintendent of one of the largest city districts in the region. The district is known for being challenging to superintendents, as there has been a relatively high rate of turnover among them since the early 1900s. In addition, comments that were made to the external investigator about the director included indications that "you can talk to him," "he's been there," and "he knows the things we are facing." In addition, remarks were made by the participants that the director and administrative assistant "treat us with respect." However, another participant commented that he would not have kept participating in the project; regardless of how much he liked the director, if he did not see value in the content and format of the seminars.

A takeaway is that the provision of authentic understanding and caring by mentors can contribute to a perception among mentees that they are engaged in a meaningful learning experience, particularly if the experience is supported by effective professional development activities.

Mentoring Between Mentees (an Informal Approach)

The initial LP seminars, as noted above, involved approximately 15 superintendents from multiple counties in the region. While relatively small in size, the cohort of superintendents engaged in rich discussions. The discussions were focused primarily upon presentations that had been made by guest speakers and the issues that were on the minds of the superintendents. The discussions led to closeness among the participants. Mentoring began at this juncture. The more experienced superintendents, particularly those who had earned referent and expert respect for their work, forms of respect described in Adams and Waghid (2005) and Gronn (2009), became unofficial mentors to the other superintendents. When these senior superintendents explained strategies to operate a district, it was as if "Solomon had issued a decree," or "E. F. Hutton had spoken."

As friendships and camaraderie emerged among the superintendents, beginning and seasoned administrators began to pair off, of their own volition, for discussions of challenging administrative matters. This phenomenon has provided the beginners with the opportunity to seek the advice of the seasoned superintendents, if and when needed. They commonly have communicated, between seminars, both by phone and by meeting at mutually conducive locations. Seminar topics, such as dealing with difficult board members, addressing financial problems, and resolving challenging collective bargaining issues have often been the focus of the communications. Interestingly, the pairing off has not resulted in cliques and other such undesirable outcomes.

The favorable perceptions of the LP's superintendent participants to informal, participant-to-participant mentoring has been confirmed in their reactions to the external investigator. The superintendents indicated that this form of informal mentoring has contributed to their effectiveness as superintendents. Similar reactions to informal, mentee-to-mentee mentoring have been reported by Smith (2007) as having been experienced by New Zealand principals. Smith references the practice as peer mentoring, as opposed to mentee-to-mentee mentoring, and suggests that it represents a "community of practice."

A takeaway is that informal mentoring, including participant-to-participant, mentee-to-mentee, and peer-to-peer mentoring, among a group of school administrators such as superintendents, can contribute to the development of the capacity that they need to address their responsibilities.

Mentoring and the Emergence of a Learning Community

A similar "community of practice" outcome, as reported by Smith (2007), has occurred with the LP. The mentoring, which was initiated with superintendents at the outset of the LP, has continued in the superintendents' cohort and has become evident with the initiation and implementation of the other three cohorts—an approach also relevant to other administrators, such as principals. As Daresh (2004, p. 513) proposes, "Principals themselves need to become more active players in the development and maintenance of mentoring programs for inexperienced colleagues."

A cohort structure has been used, as it reportedly contributes to learning (Browne-Ferrigno & Muth, 2004) and has been expressly preferred by the participants. The mentoring is occurring on a multicounty basis. Participation in the LP's seminars is open to all administrators, regardless of whether they have attended the university's preservice preparation programs. The practice has resulted in participants from 81 districts in 16 of the 88 counties of the state.

Administrators tend, out of expediency, to meet with their peers in the counties in which they work in order to make plans and address issues. For this reason, attendance at an LP seminar typically provides the participants with an opportunity to engage with a broader group of administrators than would be found in the county-based meetings. The value of this LP form of engagement is that the participants are likely to be exposed to a more diverse array of useful and creative ideas, practices, and solutions than they would be in a county meeting. The participants have exhibited appreciation for the opportunities to get together with others from the multicounty regions in order to discuss and address the rigors of their work, in a secure and well-focused environment. For example, participants have shared with the project director that their attendance at the seminars often represents a desire to discuss with the other participants ways in which to initiate new mandates, as much as their attendance reflects the opportunity to listen to and engage with the speakers, who typically are acknowledged experts on topics of significance to the work of the administrators. This outcome has a broad appeal, outside the LP, as Baron (2008) reports that such seminars are useful to the development of principals who then are prepared to "identify practical ways to help teachers improve the quality of student work; critique one another's school improvement efforts; and practice such important skills as data analysis, strategic planning, and providing helpful feedback to teachers" (p. 58).

The rapport that has been established in the LP's seminars is frequently continued thereafter, as the participants often communicate with each other between sessions. A participant-to-participant informal mentoring network has been occurring in the 16 counties represented. In fact, the participants have developed an 81-district, 16-county administratively focused learning community. While unique to the region served by the LP, this is a similar form of learning community to that described by Dufour (2004).

A takeaway is that the provision of an opportunity for administrators from districts in several relatively homogenous, but somewhat diverse counties to meet on a regular basis and to interact with each other represents a form of informal mentoring that can contribute to their professional development.

Seeking the Input and Nurturing the Growth and Efficacy of the Participants

The input of the participants, which represents an important communication in the development of the mentoring process, is regularly sought regarding the manner in which the LP is operated. The importance of seeking input pertains to creating an environment in which mentoring will be effective. After all, mentoring is more likely to occur when the mentees perceive that they are being respected, as suggested in Fletcher (2007).

Input regarding the number of seminars, the dates of the seminars, and the topics and speakers for the seminars is obtained from the LP's participants, an overall involvement practice that is purported to be useful (Daresh & Playko, 1992). Planning sessions are conducted at least annually to seek the input of the participants. Email and phone conversations related to planning occur between the planning sessions themselves. In addition, seminar topic input is solicited on the evaluations that the participants are asked to complete at each session. The input is collected and reported at each of the planning sessions for utilization in the identification of future seminar topics. The approach reflects a belief that the participants have useful insights regarding their developmental needs. It also demonstrates authentic respect for the participants and contributes to a meaningful relationship in which to foster mentoring.

The approach is also used to mentor the planning skills of the participants and to encourage them to develop a thoroughly grounded sense of self-efficacy and self-esteem, the influence of which is significant to the quality of their growth and effectiveness as administrators. For example, the creation of a sense of self-efficacy contributes to a sense of internal attribution, which is useful to administrators as they attempt to forge solutions to the ongoing challenges of their work.

The solicitation of input from the LP's participants is in alignment with the precepts of andragogy, the theory of adult learning, as postulated by Knowles (1984). This theory indicates that adults are served by being involved in the planning and evaluation of their own learning, both of which are constructivist practices (Watry, 2008) that are at the foundation of the work of the LP. For that matter, other practices of adult learning, such as addressing topics that are of direct relevance to the work of the participants and approaching them in a reflective and problem-solving manner, also are used by the LP. This approach to learning seems to synchronize well with the notions of critical theory and critical dialogue.

The opportunity to provide input and to have it considered and embraced has been reported by the external investigator as being one of the most prominent reasons that the administrators participate in the LP's seminars. The administrators have told the investigator that the LP's seminars address their needs and, for this reason, the seminars are given the highest prominence on their calendars. For example, meetings that have been scheduled for superintendents by other organizations on the same dates as LP seminars have been cancelled because the superintendents have strongly expressed a desire to attend the seminars of the LP.

A takeaway is that efforts to mentor the professional growth and self-efficacy of school administrators can be enhanced by seeking and embracing, in an authentic and candid manner, their input regarding the dimensions of the developmental initiatives.

SUMMARY

The Leadership Project, described in this chapter, is located in the Appalachian region of a Midwestern state and has been providing professional development and mentoring to school administrators for 19 years. Many of the participants have engaged in the project from the time that they became administrators to the time of their retirement. The project represents an initiative in which seasoned and beginning administrators interact and grow together over an extended period of time.

The delivery of the project has been approached through cohorts. The project has experienced hurdles with the obtainment of funding. However, the participants of the superintendents' cohort have committed district stipends to counter the funding problems. In addition, the level of participation in the project's seminars has been maintained and has grown slightly, even in the face of the manifestations that have created the funding problems. While the outcomes of the project are not necessarily directly applicable to other situations, they appear to warrant consideration as representing the benefits of a model that has survived and flourished, having grown from 15 to approximately 300 participants. The practices of the project that have particularly received the plaudits of its participants include the following:

- An exhibition by the leaders of the project of care for the professional growth of the participants
- The use of an informal mentoring structure that exhibits respect for the manner in which the participants wish to participate in and receive mentoring
- An invitation to all administrators to participate in the seminars of the project's four cohorts: The approach has resulted in an 81-district, 16-county learning community.
- The provision of ongoing opportunities for the participants to provide input regarding the operation of the project: The outcome of this practice has been a sense of ownership and commitment by the participants to the project.
- An exhibition of recognition that the work of the project is always subject to revision and improvement

REFERENCES

Adams, F., & Waghid, Y. (2005). In defense of deliberative democracy: Challenging less democratic school governing body practices. *South African Journal of Education, 25*(1), 26–33.

Allen, T. D., Day, R., & Lentz, E. (2005). The role of interpersonal comfort in mentoring relationships. *Journal of Career Development, 31*(3), 155–169. doi: 10.1007/s10871-004-2224-3

Allen, T. D., Eby, L. T., & Lentz, E. (2006). The relationship between formal mentoring program characteristics and perceived program effectiveness. *Personnel Psychology, 59*(1), 125–153. doi: 10.1111/j.1744-6570.2006.00747.x

Allen, T. D., & Poteet, M. L. (1999). Developing effective relationships: Strategies from the mentor's point of view. *The Career Development Quarterly, 48*(1), 59–73. doi:10.1002/j.2161-0045.1999.tb00275.x

Barbuto, J. E., & Wheeler, D. W. (2006). Scale development and construct clarification of servant leadership. *Group & Organization Management, 31*(3), 300–326.

Barker, E. R. (2006). Mentoring: A complex relationship. *Journal of American Academy of Nurse Practitioners, 18*(2), 56–61.

Barnett, B. G., & O'Mahony, G. R. (2006). Developing a culture of reflection: Implications for school improvement. *Reflective Practice: International and Multidisciplinary Perspectives, 7*(4), 499–523.

Baron, D. (2008). Imagine professional development that changes practice. *Principal Leadership, 8*(5), 56–58.

Bass, B. M. (2000). The future of leadership in learning organizations. *Journal of Leadership & Organizational Studies, 7*(3), 18–40.

Begley, P. T. (2006). Self-knowledge, capacity, and sensitivity: Prerequisites to authentic leadership by school principals. *Journal of Educational Administration, 44*(6), 570–589.

Bloom, G., Castagna, C., & Warren, B. (2003). More than mentors: Principal coaching. *Leadership, 32*(5), 20–23.

Boverie, P. E., & Kroth, M. (2001). *Transforming work: The five keys to achieving trust, commitment, and passion in the workplace.* Cambridge, MA: Perseus Books Group.

Bozeman, B., & Feeney, M. K. (2007). Toward a useful theory of mentoring: A conceptual analysis and critique. *Administration and Society, 39*(6), 719–739.

Browne-Ferrigno, T. (2004). Leadership mentoring in clinical practice: Role socialization, professional development, and capacity building. *Educational Administration Quarterly, 40*(4), 468–494.

Brown-Ferrigno, T., & Muth, R. (2004). Leadership mentoring in clinical practice: Role socialization, professional development, and capacity building. *Educational Administration Quarterly, 40*(4), 468–494.

Browne-Ferrigno, T., & Muth, R. (2007). Leadership mentoring and situated learning: Catalysts for principalship readiness and lifelong mentoring. *Mentoring & Tutoring: Partnership in Learning, 14*(3), 275–295.

Bryer, T. A. (2006). Toward a relevant agenda for a responsive public administration. *Journal of Public Administration Research and Theory, 17*(3), 479–500.

Chao, G. T., Walz, P. M., & Gardner, P. D. (1992). Formal and informal mentorships: A comparison on mentoring functions and contrast with non-mentored counterparts. *Personnel Psychology, 45,* 619–636.

Crippen, C. (2005). The democratic school: First to serve, then to lead. *Canadian Journal of Educational Administration and Policy, 47,* 116–125. Retrieved from http://www.umanitoba.ca/publications/cjeap/articles/crippen.html

Crow, G. M., & Matthews, L. J. (1998). *Finding one's way: How mentoring can lead to dynamic leadership.* Thousand Oaks, CA: Corwin Press.

Daresh, J. C. (2004). Mentoring school leaders: Professional promise or predictable problems. *Educational Administration Quarterly, 40*(4), 495–517.

Daresh, J. C., & Playko, M. A. (1992). *The professional development of school administrators: Pre-service, induction, and in-service applications.* Boston, MA: Allyn and Bacon.

Davis, S., Darling-Hammond, L., LaPointe, M., & Meyerson, D. (2005). *School leadership study: Developing successful principals.* Stanford, CA: Stanford University, Stanford Educational Leadership Institute.

Douglas, C. A. (1997). *Formal mentoring programs in organizations.* Greensboro, NC: Center for Creative Leadership.

Dufour, R. (2004). What is a professional learning community? *Educational Leadership, 61*(8), 6–11.

Eby, L. T., & Lockwood, A. (2005). Protégés' and mentors' reactions to participating in formal mentoring programs: A qualitative investigation. *Journal of Vocational Behavior, 67*(3), 441–458.

Ehrich, L. C., Hansford, B. C., & Tennent, L. (2004). Formal mentoring programs in education: A review of the literature. *Educational Administration Quarterly, 40*(4), 518–580.

Ehrich, L. C., Tennent, L., & Hansford, B. C. (2002). A review of mentoring in education: Some lessons for nursing. *Contemporary Nurse, 12*(3), 253–264.

Ewing, R., Freeman, M., Barrie, S., Bell, A., O'Connor, D., Waugh, F., & Sykes, C. (2008). Building community in academic settings: The importance of flexibility in a structured mentoring program. *Mentoring and Tutoring: Partnership in Learning, 16*(3), 294–310. doi:10.1080/13611260802231690

Fink, D. (2003). The law of unintended consequences: The "real" cost of top-down reform. *Journal of Educational Change, 4*(2), 105–128. doi:10.1023/A:1024783324566

Fink, D., & Brayman, C. (2006). School leadership succession and the challenges of change. *Educational Administration Quarterly, 42*(1), 62–89.

Fletcher, S. (2007). Mentoring adult learners: Realizing possible selves. *New Directions for Adult and Continuing Education, 114,* 75–86. doi:10.1002/ace.258.

Flynn, G. V. & Nolan, B. (2008). The rise and fall of a successful mentor program: What lessons can be learned? *The Clearing House, 81*(4), 173–179.

Fusarelli, L. D. (2002). Tightly coupled policy in loosely coupled systems: Institutional capacity and organization change. *Journal of Educational Administration, 40*(6), 561–575.

Galbraith, M. W. (2003). The adult education teacher as mentor: A means to enhance teaching and learning. *Perspectives: The New York Journal of Adult Learning, 1*(1), 9–20.

Geijsel, F., Sleegers, P., Leithwood, K. A., & Jantzi, D. (2003). Transformational leadership effects on teachers' commitment and effort toward school reform. *Journal of Educational Administration, 41*(3), 228–256. doi:10.1108/09578230310474403

Glitz, G., Danzig, A., & Szecsy, E. (2004). Learner-centered leadership: A mentoring model for the professional development of school administrators. *Mentoring and Tutoring: Partnership in Learning, 12*(2), 135–153. doi:10.1080.1361126042000239901

Gronn, P. (2009). Leadership configurations. *Leadership, 5*(3), 381–394. doi:10.1177/1742715009337770

Hall, P. (2008). Building bridges: Strengthening the principal induction process through intentional mentoring. *Phi Delta Kappan, 89*(6), 449–452.

Hansford, B. C., & Ehrich, L. C. (2006). The principalship: How significant is mentoring? *Journal of Educational Leadership, 44*(1), 36–52.

Hansford, B. C., Ehrich, L. C., & Tennent, L. (2004). Formal mentoring programs in education and other professions: A review of the literature. *Educational Administration Quarterly, 40*(4), 518–540.

Hansford, B. C., Tennent, L. C., & Ehrich, L. C. (2003). Educational mentoring: Is it worth the effort? *Education, Research and Perspectives, 30*(1), 47–75.

Heck, R. H., & Hallinger, P. (2005). The study of educational administration and management: Where does the field stand today? *Educational Management Administration and Leadership, 33*(2), 229–244

Hess, F. M., & Kelly, A. P. (2007). Learning to lead: What gets taught in principal preparation programs. *Teachers College Record, 109*(1), 221–243.

Karcher, M. J., Nakkula, M. J., & Harris, J. (2005). Developmental mentoring match characteristics: Correspondence between mentors' and mentees' assessments of relationship quality. *Journal of Primary Prevention, 26*(2), 93–100. doi: 10.1007/s10935-005-1847-x

Kennedy, A. (2005). Models of continuing professional development: A framework for analysis. *Journal of Inservice Education, 31*(2), 235–250.

Klinger, J. K. (2004). The science of professional development. *Journal of Learning Disabilities, 37*(3), 248–255.

Klug, B. J., & Salzman, S. A. (1991). Formal induction vs. informal mentoring: Comparative effects and outcomes. *Teaching & Teacher Education, 7*(3), 241–251.

Kochan, F. K., Bredeson, P., & Riehl, C. (2002). Rethinking the professional development of school. *Yearbook of the National Society for the Study of Education, 101*(1), 289–306.

Knowles, M. (1984). *Andragogy in action.* San Francisco, CA: Jossey-Bass.

Kowalski, T. (2009). Need to address evidence-based practice in educational administration. *Educational Administration Quarterly, 45*(3), 351–374.

Leithwood, K. A., & Jantzi, D. (2008). Linking leadership to student learning: The contributions of leadership efficacy. *Educational Administration Quarterly, 44*(4), 496–528.

Leithwood, K. A., & Mascall, B. (2008). Collective leadership effects on student achievement. *Educational Administration Quarterly, 44*(4), 529–561.

Levy, F., & Murnane, R. J. (2004). Education and the changing job market. *Educational Leadership, 62*(2), 1–4.

Malen, B. (2003). Tightening the grip: The impact of state activism on local school systems. *Educational Policy, 17*(2), 195–216.

Marable, M. A., & Raimondi, S. L. (2007). Teachers' perceptions of what was most (and least) supportive during their first year of teaching. *Mentoring & Tutoring: Partnership in Learning, 15*(1), 25–37. doi:10.1080/13611260601037355

McGuire, G. M., & Reger, J. (2003). Feminist co-mentoring: A model for academic professional development. *NWSA Journal, 15*(1), 54–72.

Mullen, C. A. (2000). Constructing co-mentoring partnerships: Walkways we must travel. *Theory into Practice, 39*(1), 4–11.

Nelson, S. W., Colina, M. G., & Boone, M. D. (2008). Lifeworld or systemsworld: What guides novice principals. *Journal of Educational Administration, 46*(6), 690–701.

O'Day, J. A. (2002). Complexity, accountability, and school improvement. *Harvard Educational Review, 72*(3), 293–329.

Onchwari, G., & Keengwe, J. (2008). The impact of a mentor-coaching model on teacher professional development. *Early Childhood Education Journal, 36*(1), 19–24.

Orland-Barak, L., & Yinon, H. (2005). Sometimes a novice and sometimes an expert: Mentor's professional expertise as revealed through their stories of critical incidents. *Oxford Review of Education, 31*(4), 557–578.

Pedro, J. (2006). Taking reflection into the real world of teaching. *Kappa Delta Pi Record, 42*(3), 129–132.

Petersen, G. J., Fusarelli, L. D., & Kowalski, T. J. (2006). Novice superintendent perceptions of preparation adequacy and problems of practice. *Journal of Research on Leadership Education, 3*(2), 1–22. doi:10.1177/194277510800300204

Ragins, B. R. & Cotton, J. L. (1999). Mentor functions and outcomes: A comparison of men and women in formal and informal mentoring relationships. *Journal of Applied Psychology, 84*(4), 529–550. doi: 10.1037/00219010844529

Rockoff, J. E. (2008). Does mentoring reduce turnover and improve skills of new employees? Evidence from teachers in New York City. *National Bureau of Economic Research, Working Paper 13868.* Retrieved from http://www.nber.org/papers/w13868

Singh, V., Bains, B., & Vinnicombe, S. (2002). Informal mentoring as an organizational resource. *Long Range Planning, 35,* 389–405.

Smith, A. A. (2007). Mentoring for experienced school principals: Professional learning in a safe place. *Mentoring & Tutoring: Partnership in Learning, 15*(3), 277–291.

Smith, M. V. (2005). Modern mentoring: Ancient lessons for today. *Music Educators Journal, 92*(2), 62–67.

Sosik, J. (2005). Context and mentoring: Examining informal and formal relationships in high tech firms and K–12 schools. *Journal of Leadership and Organizational Studies, 12*(2), 94–108.

Stead, V. (2005). Mentoring: A model for leadership development. *International Journal of Training and Development, 9*(3), 170–184.

Tschannen-Moran, M., & Woolfolk Hoy, A. (2007). The differential antecedents of self-efficacy beliefs of novice and experienced teachers. *Teaching and Teacher Education, 23,* 944–956.

Van Velsor, E., McCauley, C. D., & Moxley, R. S. (1998). Our view of leadership development. In C. D. McCauley, R. S. Moxley, & E. Van Velsor (Eds.), *The center for creative leadership handbook of leadership development* (pp. 1–25). San Francisco, CA: Jossey-Bass Publishers.

Watry, D. N. (2008). *Leave no administrator behind: Mentoring administrators in small and rural school districts in Wisconsin.* (Doctoral dissertation). Retrieved from ProQuestLLC, 2009. (UMI Microform. 3329777)

Williams, E. J., Matthews, J., & Baugh, S. (2004). Developing a mentoring model for school leadership: Using legitimate peripheral participation. *Mentoring and Tutoring: Partnership in Learning, 12*(1), 53–70. doi:10.1080/1361126042000183048

Wong, H. K. (2002). Induction: The best form of professional development. *Educational Leadership, 59*(6), 52–55.

CHAPTER 18

THE ROLE OF THE MEGA-INSTITUTION IN ADVANCING MENTORSHIP THROUGH AN EARLY CAREER SYMPOSIUM

David Richard Moore and Jozenia Torres Colorado

ABSTRACT

The Early Career Symposium, an ongoing National Science Foundation-funded career development forum offered in collaboration with the Association for Educational Communications and Technology (AECT) at the annual international AECT convention, provides mentorship opportunities to new faculty and graduate students nearing completion of a doctoral program. The authors, project facilitators for the symposia, present this mentorship effort as an example of a successful professional development collaboration between mega-institutions. They identify roles and benefits of mega-institutions in relation to (1) the need for field-specific career development and mentorship, (2) differences between field-specific career development and institution-specific career development, (3) the nature of a collaborative partnership with a government agency and a professional organization committed to innovation and growth in instructional technology and learning science fields, and (4) strategies for effective mentorship based upon Early Career Symposium participants' experiences and comments.

Mentoring for the Professions: Orienting Toward the Future, pages 337–351.
Copyright © 2015 by Information Age Publishing

INTRODUCTION

Mentoring relationships often develop organically, beginning informally and locally. We live in a complex society with interlocking institutions at various levels, however, and this complexity often requires a formalization of mentoring relationships. The smooth and successful transition from an informal process to a formal one requires an intimate understanding of organizations and institutions. Increasingly recognized as part of the complexity is that institutions, like individuals, are often siloed and intellectually isolated from a larger context. One response to intellectual isolation is what we call the "mega-institution." Mega-institutions build cooperation among multiple individual institutions, facilitating their missions and serving their members in ways that cannot be accomplished by individual institutions on their own. Mega-institutions consist of such entities as government agencies, private foundations, and trade councils and unions, as well as professional organizations. These mega-institutions' missions are generally to promote the betterment of their constituents as a whole without regard to localized parochial interests. A mega-institution's scope of responsibility is, by necessity, neither informal nor ad hoc. Mega-institutions operate in a bureaucratic environment removed from the quotidian concerns of their members. This environment is vastly different from one in which personal relationships are generally formed. Yet, as our chapter reveals, mega-institutions can be important catalysts for nurturing mentoring alliances.

INSTITUTIONAL FRAMEWORKS

Higher education is a universe of unique expectations and opportunities. Colleges and universities have tasks, goals, and standards of work different from those of other communities of practice. Scholarship, teaching, and service are the primary domains of praxis in higher education, and successfully navigating each determines faculty members' career success. Higher education institutions tie tenure, promotion, and salary increments to activities in these domains. A novice scholar's career depends on mastering the major tasks associated with them.

There are approximately 4,000 institutions of higher education in the United States. Each institution has a unique mission, purpose, and value system, and each institution has access to different resources and has somewhat different responsibilities. These differences result in disparities of opportunities for faculty as well as for students, but disparity is apparent at many levels of higher education, both between and within institutions. Stratification can occur within a program, department, or college, as well as between colleges and universities, and it can occur in the macrosystem connecting professional organizations, government panels, and funding agencies (Fulton & Trow, 1974). Stratification results in unequal mentorship opportunities. Addressing these inequalities can promote scholarly activity at the periphery of such activity and energize the center with new ideas.

Evidence suggests that social connections are often made between similar universities and colleges, and that long-term, extended mentorship is more likely between scholars at similar institutions (Blackburn, Chapman, & Cameron, 1981). Mentors, to some extent, believe that placing their students in institutions similar to their own tends to reinforce and reestablish their networks (Blackburn et al., 1981). The culture of an organization influences the specifics of a mentoring relationship. An organization with a culture of mentorship may provide more support than one in which mentorship is not the norm. Moreover, the cycle of mentorship tends to perpetuate itself. Researchers have found that former mentees tend to take on roles as mentors themselves when the opportunity arises (Hunt & Michael, 1983).

There are benefits to becoming a successful scholar, and there are benefits to the institution for the development of scholars. Institutions make a substantial investment in recruiting, developing, and resourcing scholars. An institution's reputation, prominence, and standing are dependent, in large part, upon the success of its scholars; its mission can only be served by the quality of its human capital. Institutions have an obvious stake in developing scholars' abilities.

Human resource development is a probabilistic activity. There are few opportunities for inputs to be transformed directly into outputs. The knowledge required to develop scholars is not codified, algorithmic, or even heuristically oriented. Scholars develop their abilities from undergoing experiences, by trial and error, and, hopefully, from forming relationships with mature faculty who have mastered higher education's often ambiguous landscape. Institutions that value their human resources often support mentorship because it is one of the few effective tools at their disposal to nurture their faculty. Hunt and Michael (1983) suggest that former mentees "are better educated, better paid, less mobile, and more satisfied with their work and career progress" (p. 478). Dansky (1996) finds that the role modeling so often associated with mentoring predicts higher salaries for former protégés.

Many believe that transformative learning experiences primarily occur one-on-one as mentors advise, guide, and provide network support to the mentored. It is through social relationships that beliefs and values are shaped. Productivity depends not only upon the knowledge and skills of scholars but on their ability to maneuver the peculiarities of academic life. Mentoring readily provides insight into knowledge that is hidden, obscured, and opaque. Other educational experiences can better facilitate cognitive knowledge attainment or manual skill development; however, these methods may be less likely to provide the insight, tacit knowledge, and experience so necessary for career success in the academy.

Institutional partnerships can be useful tools for creating a culture of mentorship. One organization can influence another through informal contacts. For example, the Potential Administrator Development Program (PADP) demonstrated that a partnership between a K–12 school system, a local university, and a national organization for school principals was able to improve administrator preparation

(Peel, Wallace, Buckner, Wrenn, & Evans, 1998). Tucker and Adams-Price (2001) describe how a professional organization can encourage mentoring by establishing standards and guidelines for these relationships. Affiliated members often desire and demand that their professional organizations take an active role in building mentoring programs (Furgeson, George, Nesbit, Peterson, Peterson, & Wilder, 2008).

Institutions often assign mentees to mentors. Supplying time, resources, and a set of expectations may encourage professional relationships. Although somewhat artificial, these schemes have been successful in developing scholarly capacity (Boyle & Boice, 1998; DeNeef, 2002). Bureaucracy is often antithetical to organically developed processes, yet many institutions have found methods for formalizing such relationships. The robustness of a mentorship relationship is often dependent upon the local organizational ecosystem. The organization can create conditions that stimulate the development and nurturing of mentorship. Companies, schools, and universities have all found ways to sponsor and promote this type of apprenticeship.

Organizations have their limitations, though. Any institution is limited in the scope of support it can provide to mentoring relationships. Institutions rarely have an incentive to sponsor participants outside of their organizations, for example. We are living in a time of unprecedented occupational mobility. Employees are continually in transition. Seeking and finding new employment opportunities is standard working practice.

Mentor relationships clearly benefit the mentees and their affiliated institutions. However, accrued benefits from these relationships extend beyond the self-interest of individuals and individual institutions. Society in general, and a given academic field in particular, have an interest in developing scholars. Scholars are found at institutions of all types. Some of these institutions are better resourced than others, some have more collaborative cultures, and some have faculty better connected than others. An innovative civilization recognizes that institutions at the periphery have creative scholars and that invention is not exclusively the property of institutions at the center.

Mega-institutions with broader missions and purposes than individual organizations can encourage scholarly development. A universal, society-wide actor can overcome parochial limitations. Obvious entities for building society-wide human capacity are mega-institutions, such as professional organizations. Professional organizations service their members throughout the members' working lives, regardless of their career status or place of employment. Professional organizations have a unique role to play in encouraging mentoring relationships because their membership derives from virtually every geographical locale and every institution, regardless of size, scope, and mission. These organizations disseminate information, critique scholarship, and provide networking services. While scholars may move from one institution to another, they often remain affiliated with their professional organizations. Thus, professional organizations provide a stable anchor to the development of scholars.

Government institutions are similar to professional organizations; they, too, have society-wide missions and responsibilities. Professional organizations and government entities are mega-institutions with long-term goals and broad enduring mandates. The interplay between the individual and institutions of higher education, professional organizations, and government foundations represents an ecosystem of scholarship support and advancement. We suggest that mentoring relationships can benefit from the involvement of all levels of this ecosystem. An individual academic department is often primarily interested in the success of its own faculty and students. The departments often do not have the authority, or the mission, to consider the well-being of the field at large. Mega-institutions often have resources, both financial and human, that can foster mentoring relationships beyond the scope possible for a person or single institution of higher learning (e.g., Foote & Solem, 2009; Hardwick, 2005).

THE EARLY CAREER SYMPOSIUM

Government agency and professional organization involvement in the mentoring process is often neglected. In this chapter we report on a unique type of mentorship facilitation sponsored by two mega-institutions, the National Science Foundation (NSF), a U.S. government foundation charged with promoting and funding scientific research, and the Association for Educational Communications and Technology (AECT), a professional organization of instructional technologists and instructional designers. NSF and AECT have collaborated on the Early Career Symposium from 2009 to the present.

The symposium has been held in conjunction with the annual AECT international conference. Participants arrive two days before the conference for the intensive two-day event. The intended outcomes of the Early Career Symposium are as follows:

- mentoring early career faculty and advanced doctoral students into the social/professional network as partners in idea-making
- supporting early-career faculty and advanced doctoral students in developing viable technology-oriented research agendas
- providing specific feedback and guidance to early-career faculty and advanced doctoral students about their research agendas
- providing information about building a research agenda, pursuing funding, and building collaborations, developing a community of researchers interested in ways technology can transform teaching and learning

This symposium is one example of how mega-institutions can collaborate and lead mentoring efforts. By leveraging each organization's broad mission and mandate, the two mega-institutions and the participating higher-education institutions were able to support a mentorship model that could not have emerged from an institution in isolation.

NSF, CISE, and the Cyberlearning Initiative

The NSF is a government agency charged with supporting and facilitating fundamental research in the fields of science and engineering. The NSF organizes its research and education support through seven directorates, each encompassing several disciplines. The AECT/NSF symposia were funded by the Computer & Information Science & Engineering (CISE) directorate. The CISE's division of information and intelligent systems' recently established Cyberlearning: Transforming Education Initiative was the primary NSF sponsor for these symposia.

The Cyberlearning Initiative seeks to advance the science of cyberlearning—learning that is mediated by networked computing and communications technologies, through the "imaging, developing, and promoting of prototypes of next-generation technologies for stimulating learning," as well as "learning how to use those technologies effectively" (Kolodner, 2012). NSF's Cyberlearning Initiative focuses on technical and instructional design solutions, with a substantial emphasis on developing human capacity. The initiative actively seeks to "advance the science of learning, which entails building the scholars to do that work" (Kolodner, 2012). In other words, NSF recognizes that scholars pursuing these topics need a supportive ecosystem for their work to prosper—thus their interest in mentorship. Not every program in NSF goes out of its way to support building professional or "people" capacity; however, the Cyberlearning Initiative does because of its unique mission encouraging innovation (J. Kolodner, personal communication, February 1, 2013). The Cyberlearning Initiative has taken the position that our nation's system of graduate-level higher education has institutional inequities that may cloister students away from the centers of power, privilege, and prestige. In creating this initiative, NSF wanted to ensure that all of the next generation of scholars have opportunities to participate in the larger professional community, regardless of the circumstances of their institutional affiliation. Institutions of all types, in all geographic locations, generate meaningful scholarship facilitated by digital innovation, according to Kolodner (2012), who also explained that innovation in the cyberlearning space was to be encouraged wherever it could be found.

These emerging scholars are generating applications, models, and theories that can have a major impact on their fields of study. Supporting these scholars and integrating them into the larger academic community may keep their perspectives from being lost. NSF's Cyberlearning Initiative was designed to build national communities so that promising graduate students could gain from the perspectives of those outside their own institutions. From NSF's point of view, supporting activities that would help students build these relationships was a small investment that could have large, long-term results (J. Kolodner, personal communication, February 1, 2013).

To date, the Cyberlearning Initiative has sponsored three symposia with AECT. Initially, NSF allowed AECT to pair up mentors from within the organization with participants from without. However, after the first year, NSF actively encouraged organizers to invite mentors from other professional organizations and associated fields. Likewise, NSF recommended a formal grant to fund the symposium. These suggestions helped NSF reach its goal of bringing many different communities together to think more creatively (J. Kolodner, personal communication, February 1, 2013).

The NSF also encouraged organizers to invite mentors and participants from universities and colleges of different types and with different missions. Often, schools with large numbers of students and faculty dominate conference and professional activity. Large, well-resourced schools have implicit advantages in the size, depth, and breadth of their social networks. Their influence is substantial. Their size and scope can create a monolithic academic culture that reinforces scholarly orthodoxy. Divergent and marginalized voices from the periphery can encourage creativity and innovation simply as a function of their intellectual distance from the center. Many nondominant institutions have smaller faculties, and their students do not have access to an array of professional opinions and perspectives. Likewise, some programs with a larger faculty may not be able to provide intimate experiences as readily as can smaller institutions. Students and faculty, regardless of their organization, rarely have opportunities to collaborate with one another; the symposium created space for those relationships and partnerships to develop. Dominant academic programs might be infused with energy from outside the inner circle, and smaller programs might be given access to the larger community of scholars.

Based on initial feedback, NSF representatives believe that the AECT symposium has provided positive experiences for participants and has created a mechanism to generate intergenerational (professionally speaking) collaborations that build support for novice faculty and those ready to begin their professional lives and, simultaneously, reinvigorate and reintroduce established faculty into the field. AECT negotiated with NSF on the initial proposal parameters and was able to create a feedback loop, year after year, to improve the experience for participants as well as meet the broader goals of both mega-institutions. Funding for mentoring activities, such as the Early Career Symposium, is now part of the Cyberlearning Initiative's formal solicitation process and will continue as part of their ongoing activities and mission.

NSF and AECT were interested in mentorship because of its potential for transformative professional development. They recognized that entirely new partnerships and collaborations between scholars could be encouraged and fertilized at this macro level of intervention. While mentoring relationships primarily occur informally, locally, and organically, an intentional effort to bring together scholars from different colleges and universities could grow the field in ways that would be improbable within a single institution. Mega-institutions are uniquely positioned to create formal mentoring arrangements that mirror informal ones. Using their authority and prestige, mega-institutions can take a broad view of relationship development. Although it is somewhat unusual for mega-institutions to collaborate, the AECT/NSF Symposium demonstrates that these large mega-institutions can collaborate to achieve unique outcomes. Government organizations usually work directly with individual colleges and universities, while professional organizations work directly with individual scholars. By working together, mega-institutions such as these can influence the entire field of practice with greater efficiency and effectiveness than either could alone.

NSF Role and Expectations

NSF has supported the last three AECT Early Career Symposia. As part of a capacity-building grant, the role of NSF is to support the next generation of academics in the field of learning sciences and cyberlearning. According to Janet Kolodner, the investment is small compared to its large benefits (personal communication, February 1, 2013). The funding provided by NSF supports the symposium with travel stipends for mentors and participants, as well as funds to provide refreshments during the symposium. Mentors and participants are reimbursed for their conference registration and travel expenses. Both the stipend and provision of refreshments serve as incentives for mentors and participants. With this support, NSF expects participants to become the next generation of academics to (1) work collaboratively with professionals in other areas, such as learning sciences, artificial intelligence, and education; (2) create the next generation of learning technologies; (3) integrate current learning technologies in ways that will get them used; and (4) advance the science of learning with technology (J. Kolodner, personal communication, February 1, 2013).

AECT Role and Expectations

AECT is a professional association of members whose activities are directed toward improving instruction through technology. The association is for those scholars and practitioners actively involved in the designing of instruction and a systematic approach to learning (Association for Educational Communications and Technology, n.d.). The AECT international conference, held annually, supports professional development for its members by bringing together participants from around the world who offer practical applications, high-quality research, hands-on workshops, demonstrations of innovative instructional approaches, and developments in learning and performance. This conference venue serves as an ideal location for graduate students and early-career faculty to network with senior scholars and colleagues in the field.

In particular, AECT supports and cultivates high-quality research and scholarly activity. The conference offers a way to showcase member research and accomplishments. In particular, the research and theory division of AECT encourages professional development in this area. The Early Career Symposium was an attempt to cultivate and mentor the next generation of academics working in the field of educational communications and technology. Through the symposium, AECT expects to help early-career members not only succeed in academia, but also cultivate future leaders of the association. AECT and NSF share similar goals in this respect. AECT provides the venue and volunteer personnel to host this mentoring program, while NSF provides funding, advice, and expertise.

The Symposium

The AECT/NSF symposium was designed through a negotiated process. Initially, AECT approached NSF's Cyberlearning Initiative with the idea to host a weekend symposium connected to the organization's annual conference. A call for participants would be made to the organization's membership. Eighteen participants would be invited (nine graduate students readying themselves for the workforce and nine newly hired early-career faculty).

The symposium organizers recruited a board of application reviewers from AECT's research and theory division to evaluate applicants. Eligibility for participation in the symposium included that applicants (1) must be AECT members in good standing, (2) must be current faculty (within the first five years of career) or graduate students (within one year of finishing the doctoral degree), and (3) must make a strong argument for participation. Using these criteria, the review board sought a diverse group of scholars representing the entirety of the membership of AECT. Three professionals, chosen from AECT's senior membership, were invited to participate as mentors to the early-career faculty and graduate students who were accepted. NSF was asked to fund participants' and mentors' conference fees, lodging, and transportation to the conference.

Growth and Change

This funding request was modest relative to the size and scope of Cyberlearning's other projects, and the request was favorably considered. However, to get to the point of commitment, a number of bureaucratic hurdles needed to be cleared. NSF is designed to allocate funding to colleges and universities directly, not through a professional organization intermediary. The research and theory division of AECT identified a proposal organizer to submit the request through the organizer's own university grant office. In other words, the proposal organizer's university served as a proxy for the professional organization.

As the request for participants was extended to AECT's membership, the proposal organizer then began generating the mentoring plan in consultation with the three mentors. The symposium would take place over a two-day period and would include the following activities:

- Networking and introductions

- Mentor assignment
- Expectations for collaboration
- Success in the classroom
- Publication/Tenure/Promotion
- Creating a research agenda
- Interviewing skills and etiquette
- Service expectations of the professorate
- Plan for productivity
- NSF organization/Engaging in grants
- Funding/Proposal writing
- Project planning contract
- Evaluations and recommendations

The mentors chose these topics to provide essential success skills that early-career faculty would need, as well as skills needed to build mentoring relationships with colleagues and formal mentors. Each participant was assigned a single mentor and asked to create a mentoring contract, which included specific tasks to complete and milestones for the mentors and mentees to reach throughout the following year. The program organizer required mentors and mentees to attend a video conference in the spring following the conference to describe their progress on their projects and to report on their mentoring relationship.

Evolving Structure

In the first year of the symposium, mentors were specifically chosen from AECT's senior membership. In subsequent years NSF encouraged the symposium board to invite mentors from outside the organization, and mentors from the learning sciences were invited to participate. NSF's vision for the symposium was a forum for cross-field collaboration. Their rationale was that the professional domain designated by NSF as instructional technology/instructional design is split into camps that have limited contact with one another. The symposium was a method to create cross-pollination opportunities. Additionally, in subsequent years, the emphasis on research collaborations has become greater. Over the last three years, mentors' backgrounds have been varied, ranging from senior faculty from AECT's membership to scholars with experience from the learning sciences.

According to the symposium's past mentors, the Early Career Symposium is a different experience than traditional mentoring that occurs among faculty and graduate students on campus. Lasting over a two-day period, the Early Career Symposium provides an in-depth experience. The programming of the symposium during the past three years has included only a few prepared presentations, with more attention on building relationships and addressing participants' questions and concerns related to research, job search issues, and obtaining grants, but participants also had the opportunity to ask questions that were specific and unique to their research interests and situations. Perhaps equally important, mentees had the opportunity to build a supportive community with participants who had similar research interests.

Participant Benefits and Comments

Over the last three years, participants have reported being satisfied with their experiences in the symposium. In particular, participants were highly satisfied with their mentors' expertise, the small-group discussions with mentors, and the community-building and networking. Feedback regarding the 2010 and 2011 symposia showed that participants valued most the discussions regarding forming and working on a research agenda, publishing, and grant proposal writing. Advanced doctoral students also found discussions regarding finding a job to be beneficial. One participant commented,

> As a grad student, I found it very helpful to be in the same group with those going through the tenure process. During and after the Symposium I put much thought into how I would approach a new tenure-track faculty position over my first few years. Also, I appreciated each of the mentors.... [S]eeing their viewpoint on various topics was helpful. The personalities of all the mentors made me feel comfortable with contacting them in the future.

This comment demonstrates participant satisfaction in the community building as well as in the discussions surrounding research agendas and scholarly activity. Despite their varied areas of expertise, mentors reported that they derived tremendous benefit from working with early-career participants during the symposium. According to one mentor, the Early Career Symposium was the highlight of her year. She said that learning the concerns of the symposium participants helped her become a better mentor to the young faculty members on her campus. Another mentor said his experience refreshed his confidence in how he could help doctoral students. In addition, this mentor observed that the questions early-career faculty had were simple and focused, whereas, as a senior faculty member, he forgets how important these questions are.

Some participant-suggested topics to be added to the Early Career Symposium included course development, how to create a vita or professional portfolio, and time management or balancing work and personal life, as well as perhaps showing examples of grant proposals during the grant proposal writing discussion. One participant suggested separating the advanced doctoral students and early-career faculty for a portion of the symposium to allow for more focused discussion; however, most participants expressed satisfaction with the given topics. According to one participant, "Since the time is filled with very useful information and idea exchange, unless there were more time allocated for the Symposium, I do not have any suggestions for additional topics." Another participant commented, "[T]he AECT/NSF Early Career Symposium is the finest opportunity a graduate student, aspiring to pursue an academic career, can obtain. I really appreciate the opportunity to have one-on-one communication possibilities with the mentors who are willing to share their professional experiences and guide us in our job search process."

In 2012, the evaluation questions were changed to seek more focused answers regarding the role of the mentorship program and the mentees' contribution to the field. Questions revolved around how the symposium prepared the participants to (1) collaborate effectively with professionals in other areas, such as learning sciences, artificial intelligence, and education, to create the next generation of learning technologies; (2) integrate current learning technologies in ways that will get them used; and (3) advance the science of learning with technology. Participants realized that in order to work collaboratively with professionals in other areas to create the next generation of learning technologies, they would have to network with other professionals and build relationships to allow for collaborative projects. They also noted that some ways to do this include building a group of professionals committed to attending and networking at conferences and workshops related to the learning sciences, artificial intelligence, and education, as well as publicizing research online and creating an online identity to attract the attention of those interested in related research.

When asked what they needed to do to be able to integrate current learning technologies in ways that will get them used, one participant stated, "We need to design our research studies to solve practical problems in an efficient manner so that people in the field can get benefit from the results of our studies." In addition, other participants expressed the need to think about adoption when designing the technologies. One participant commented, for example, "As researchers, we need to consider what contributes to the wide adoption of those successful programs and be more responsive to the changing needs of learners." Other participants also agreed that blending research opportunities with instructional opportunities would be a way to use, test, review, and reuse such technologies.

When addressing the question of how they can advance the science of learning with technology, participants reported that all discussions during the symposium addressed this topic. One participant said, "This question is spot on. All three talks speak to this idea. Advancing the science is what we do in sum." This participant went on to describe how, as professionals, focusing their research agenda regarding learning with technology, seeking grant funding to work on their research, and ultimately publishing and presenting their findings, lead to this result. Other comments on ways the participants thought they could advance the science of learning with technology suggested creating interdisciplinary research studies, working collaboratively with professionals in other fields with a similar goal of advancing the science of learning with technology, and disseminating research results by publishing and presenting through a variety of communication venues.

Advice and Support

The collaboration between mega-institutions resulted in a number of long-term mentoring relationships within and across the instructional technology and learn-

TABLE 18.1.   Mentoring Advice

1.   Develop a Clear Research Agenda

Be able to relate your research to one umbrella theme. Be able to describe your research agenda briefly and clearly.

2.   Conduct Research that has a Broader Impact on the World

When deciding upon a research agenda, think about how you want to change the world. Be passionate about your research and think about how it can be meaningful to society.

3.   Network and Collaborate with Established Scholars

Working with established scholars will allow new scholars to learn how to write grant proposals that get accepted. This will also help the researcher establish experience working on grant funded research projects.

4.   Publicize Research Agenda and Ideas

Using blogs and other social media, researchers can publicize their research agenda and ideas. This is an opportunity to get feedback on research and find possible collaborators. Getting feedback will strengthen researchers' confidence in their topic.

5.   Design Interdisciplinary Research Projects

Work toward engaging professionals in other disciplines by designing interdisciplinary research projects. Work with practitioners to see how your research can be applied in the field. This increases collaborative opportunities.

6.   Be Consistent about Writing.

Set aside a regular time of the day to write and dedicate that time to writing on a consistent basis. Being consistent allows one to practice writing. This makes the writing process easier and accessible.

7.   Resubmit!

If a paper you submit for publication is rejected, review feedback, revise, and resubmit. If the publication you resubmit to still does not accept the paper, submit to a different publication. Do not take rejection personally.

8.   Set Priorities

Each university has different expectations of scholarly activity, teaching, and service. Depending on the culture of your university, set priorities for your activities. Learn to say no to the activities that do not align with these priorities.

9.   Find Balance

Learn to balance work life with personal life. Find ways to deal with stress and keep your health as a priority. Suggestions include going for a walk on campus with students for discussions as an alternative to meeting in your office during office hours.

ing sciences community. Many student attendees have subsequently moved to faculty roles. The nature of mentor relationships is difficult to quantify; nonetheless, there are many specific advice artifacts that emerged from the symposium. We have compiled, as a takeaway, a selection of such advice and suggestions (see Table 18.1). These statements may be of use to our readers; however, it should be remembered that the participants encountered this advice in the context of an ongoing mentoring relationship and the larger mega-institutional context. Participants were sure to have developed a more nuanced understanding than the mere factual advice.

The Early Career Symposium demonstrates that mega-institutions can collaborate effectively to build mentoring relationships. Those interested in mentorship will want to encourage relationships by drawing up plans to utilize organic personal relationships, encouraged and perhaps organized by the local institution. However, to encourage development of career scholars, the capabilities of mega-institutions should not be ignored. Professional organizations and governmental foundations can bring expertise, organization, and funding to ensure that mentoring relationships develop, grow, and prosper. A symposium that draws on the talent and resources of every level of mentorship cannot only support an individual scholar's career, but advance a field of study as well.

REFERENCES

Association for Educational Communications and Technology. (n.d.) *What is AECT?* doi:10.1080/03601270151075606.Retrieved from http://www.aect.org

Blackburn, R. T., Chapman, D. W., & Cameron, S. M. (1981). "Cloning" in academe: Mentorship and academic careers. *Research in Higher Education, 15*(4), 315–327.

Boyle, P., & Boice, B. (1998). Systemic mentoring for new faculty teachers and graduate teaching assistants. Innovative *Higher Education, 22,* 157–179.

Dansky, K. H. (1996). The effect of group mentoring on career outcomes. *Group and Organization Management, 21*(1), 5–21.

DeNeef, A. L. (2002). *The preparing future faculty program: What difference does it make?* Washington, DC: Association of American Colleges and Universities.

Foote, K. E., & Solem, M. N. (2009). Toward better mentoring for early career faculty: results of a study of U.S. geographers. *International Journal for Academic Development, 14*(1), 47–58.

Fulton, O., & Trow, M. (1974). Research activity in American higher education. *Sociology of Education, 47*(1), 29–73.

Furgeson, D., George, M., Nesbit, S., Peterson, C., Peterson, D., & Wilder, R. (2008). Role of the student professional association in mentoring dental hygiene students for the future. *Journal of Dental Hygiene, 82*(1), 1–14.

Hardwick, S. (2005). Mentoring early career faculty in geography: Issues and strategies, *Professional Geographer, 57*(1), 21–27.

Hunt, D. M., & Michael, C. (1983). Mentorship: A career training and development tool. *Academy of Management Review, 8*(3), 475–485.

Kolodner, J. (2012, February 14). *The NSF Cyberlearning: Transforming education programs* [Video file]. Retrieved from http://www.youtube.com/watch?v=rBknau3GdQQa

Peel, H. A., Wallace, C., Buckner, K. G., Wrenn, S. L., & Evans, R. (1998). Improving leadership preparation programs through a school, university, and professional organization partnership. *NASSP Bulletin, 82*(602), 26–34. doi:10.1177/019263659808260205

Tucker, R. C., & Adams-Price, C. E. (2001). Ethics in the mentoring of gerontologists: Rights and responsibilities. *Educational Gerontology, 27*(2), 185–197.

CHAPTER 19

A CONCEPTUAL FRAMEWORK FOR INCORPORATING MENTORING IN THE CLINICAL SUPERVISION OF MENTAL HEALTH PROFESSIONALS

Yegan Pillay, Bethany Fulton, and Timothy Robertson

ABSTRACT

The hierarchical relationship and the associated distributions of power distinguish mental health supervision from mentoring. A perusal of the professional counseling literature reveals that little or no attention has been devoted to the common thread that runs through both. The authors of this chapter highlight the similarities and differences between mental health supervision and mentoring. They identify Bernard's discrimination model of supervision as a process model that lends itself readily to accommodating three additional functions associated with mentoring and recommended for incorporation, namely, sponsoring, encouraging, and befriending. Because of its adaptability, the discrimination model of supervision—which initially served as a teaching tool for counselor educators as a means to organize supervisory activities, and has been adapted and used in many different supervisory relationships such as university settings, clinical settings, residential settings and

Mentoring for the Professions: Orienting Toward the Future, pages 353–362.

public schools—is discussed and presented as a model for integrating supervision with mentoring.

INTRODUCTION

The term "mentoring" has its roots in Greek mythology. Mentor, a character in Homer's *Odyssey*, was asked by Odysseus, who had to depart to fight in the Trojan War, to take care of his infant son Telemachos. The relationship between Mentor and Telemachos can be seen as one of the earliest documentations of what has become known as the mentor–mentee relationship (Tharp, 1992). The present-day role of a mentor has been revised and expanded and can be described as "a person who oversees the career and development of another person, usually junior, through teaching, counseling, providing psychological support, protecting, and at times promoting or sponsoring" (Zey, 1984, p. 7). Bozeman and Feeney (2007) add the following:

> Mentoring is a process for the informal transmission of knowledge, social capital, and psychosocial support perceived by the recipient as relevant to work, career, or professional development. Mentoring entails informal communication, usually face-to-face over a sustained period of time, between a person who is perceived to have greater relevant knowledge, wisdom, or experience (the mentor) and a person who is perceived to have less (the protégé). (p. 731)

In a similar vein, the supervision of the work of professionals also has its roots in Greek traditions and is estimated to have its beginnings circa 400 BC, when Hippocrates made reference to a teacher or a supervisor in what has become commonly known as the Hippocratic Oath (Bernard & Goodyear, 2014). The roots of work supervision can also be traced to the feudal societies of ancient Africa, China, and Europe with the establishment of the master/mistress–apprentice relationship whereby novices who were new to a craft or activity had to reveal and explore their work with those who were considered to be experts in a given profession or trade (Smith, 2012). Based on the nature of the relationship, "supervision"—which has its etymology in the Latin for *super* (over) and *vidêre* (to see or watch)— has become the *de jure* term used when a senior member of a profession or trade who is considered to be the expert oversees the work of a junior member.

MENTAL HEALTH WORK SUPERVISION: BEGINNINGS

The history of mental health work supervision in the United States is relatively new in its conceptualization and can be traced back to the evolution of social work as a *bona fide* discipline around the turn of the twentieth century. This new role formed in response to the themes that emerged from the National Conference of Charities and Correction in 1879 to develop practical methods to address social issues such as "dealing with the insane, paupers, dependent and neglected children, and criminals" (Dubois & Krogsrud, 2011, p. 29). The casework—as it became known—was initially provided by volunteers. As the cases became complex, the demand for paid personnel increased, and closer oversight became necessary. This can be viewed as the beginnings of modern day mental health work supervision.

Bernard and Goodyear (2014) assert that oversight is a necessary component of supervision in any profession, but oversight alone is not sufficient for mental health work supervision. They add that supervision has to be provided by a senior member to a junior member of a profession, and the relationship is evaluative, hierarchical, and extended over time. Moreover, the supervisor has the responsibility of "monitoring the quality of professional services offered to clients...and serving as a gatekeeper for those who are to enter a particular profession" (Bernard & Goodyear, 2014, p. 7).

An examination of the subject index for the most recent edition of *Fundamentals of Clinical Supervision* (Bernard & Goodyear, 2014), which has been the resource for mental health counselors, family and marriage therapists, psychiatrists, psychologists, psychiatric nurses, and social workers since it was first published more than two decades ago, reveals that the term "mentoring" is not listed. This omission is striking, given that there are some conceptual similarities between mental health work supervision and mentoring when the definitions are juxtaposed.

MENTAL HEALTH SUPERVISION AND MENTORING

The hierarchical relationship and the accompanying distributions of power distinguish mental health supervision from mentoring. The supervisor occupies a more powerful position in the supervisor/supervisee relationship primarily because of the "gatekeeping" role that a mental health supervisor performs. Mental health supervisors determine whether their supervisees, from the beginning of their academic training until they are independently licensed, have fulfilled the standards for practice as delineated by the license-granting authorities.

The evaluative role of mental health supervisors sets the stage for a formalized relationship during which the supervisor monitors the clinical and administrative responsibilities of the supervisee. The nature of the monitoring is initially guided by a contract, signed at the beginning of the relationship, that outlines the responsibilities of the supervisor and supervisee, the frequency of meetings between the supervisor and the supervisee, and the criteria by which the supervisee is evaluated.

The relationship in many mentor–mentee relationships, on the other hand, is neither formal nor hierarchical, in part because the mentor–mentee relationship is formed voluntarily and the mentor does not play the role of a gatekeeper or evaluator. Rather, the relationship may result in the mentor and mentee's forming a friendship, which typically does not occur in a supervisor–supervisee relationship.

Even though the roles of mental health work supervisor and mentor may be distinct, the common threads that run through both are the facilitation of encouragement, enhancement of professional development, provision of psychological support, and assumption of the roles of teacher and consultant. A perusal of the literature specific to mental health work supervision shows that not much attention by researchers has been given to the intersection between mental health supervision and mentoring.

House, Martin, and Ward (2002) assert that mentoring serves to eliminate some of the barriers to academic, career, and personal/social development, while mental health supervision, on the other hand, emphasizes gatekeeping, evaluation, and monitoring of client care as essential functions. Though these perspectives on mentoring and supervision may imply that mentoring and clinical work supervision are divergent activities, the authors of this chapter propose that mentoring and mental health work supervision ought not to be viewed as mutually exclusive activities. To this end, we offer a reconceptualization of the widely used and adapted model of mental health supervision, the discrimination model of supervision, by Janine Bernard (1979). This model of supervision was selected because it is adaptable and flexible for use in various settings, such as universities, clinical and residential agencies, and in public schools (Byrne & Sias, 2010). Because of its adaptability, it lends itself to the discussion within this chapter as a model that can be integrated with mentoring.

In the sections that follow, the authors provide an overview of Bernard's discrimination model and the reconceptualized iteration that will include pertinent aspects of mentoring. This is followed by identification of the advantages and limitations of the reconceptualized discrimination model. Within the reconceptualized model, the various components of supervision skills are reconfigured to incorporate mentoring.

BERNARD'S DISCRIMINATION MODEL (DM)

The discrimination model of supervision was developed in the mid-1970s by Janine Bernard, initially as a teaching tool for counselor educators and as a means to organize supervisory activities (Bernard & Goodyear, 2014). The model focuses on three areas: intervention skills, conceptualization skills, and personalization skills of the supervisee.

Three Skill Areas of Supervision Focus

1. *Intervention skills* are those skills most clinicians learn early in the training process (Bernard, 1979). They include, for example, opening, reflection, summarizing, restating, the use of nonverbal communication, implementing intervention strategies, and closing skills (Bernard, 1979). Attention is given to what the supervisor observes the supervisee *doing* in the counseling session (Bernard & Goodyear, 2014).

2. *Conceptualization skills* can be those that are "covert behaviors," or the ability to recognize underlying messages and meanings that are not clearly stated by the client (Bernard & Goodyear, 2014, p. 52). Conceptualization includes understanding client themes, recognizing goals, and recognizing subtle improvement (Bernard, 1979). The supervisor in this instance responds to the supervisee's understanding of what is going on

in the session, identifies themes, and considers the choice of intervention (Bernard & Goodyear, 2014).

3. *Personalization skills* are "overt and readily observable" behaviors, but can also include some that are more "subtle and more difficult to identify" (Bernard & Goodyear, 2014, p. 52). The personalization skills include how the supervisee incorporates a personal style with therapy but "keeps therapy uncontaminated by personal issues" (Bernard & Goodyear, 2014, p. 52).

The three areas of foci are also woven into the various roles performed by the supervisor in the discrimination model: the roles of teacher, counselor, and consultant. As the supervisee presents concerns or questions regarding aspects of client care, the supervisor can take on whichever role best meets the need of the supervisee.

Supervisor Roles

1. *Teacher*—a supervisee may be struggling with a specific intervention strategy to use with a client. In this case the supervisor may take on the role of teacher to teach the supervisee specific intervention skills as way to enhance the supervisee's ability to work with a client.
2. *Counselor*—in this role the supervisor may provide role-playing exercises to help the supervisee experience a situation from another perspective or explore how certain events in the life of a client may be over-identified by the supervisee, thus affecting or limiting the supervisee's ability to help the client. It must be clear that, in the counselor role, the supervisor is merely taking a counseling stance and not engaging in a therapeutic counseling relationship with the supervisee.
3. *Consultant*—in this role, the supervisor maintains an egalitarian relationship with the supervisee in order to consider client concerns and issues. In the consultant role, the supervisor's position is to work alongside the supervisee in developing approaches to such topics as intervention strategies, case conceptualizations, and specific populations the supervisee can work with.

DISCRIMINATION MODEL RECONCEPTUALIZED (DM-R)

Mentoring can be a natural extension of the supervisory relationship. Tentoni (1995) suggests that using mentoring in mental health supervision "allows students to assume and experience the role of a professional practitioner, under supervision, to determine how well the role fits the student rather than making the student fit the role" (p. 1). Anderson and Shannon (1988) identified five components of mentoring: (1) teaching, (2) sponsoring, (3) encouraging, (4) counseling, and (5) befriending.

Within the discrimination model of supervision, there is a clear overlap of two of the components with mentoring: teaching and counseling. Both components share similar functions with supervision. The supervisor, similar to the mentor, may take on a teaching role in order to teach the supervisee to learn new intervention techniques or to engage in a deeper understanding of client behavior. Likewise, in the counseling role—even though the relationship is not strictly a therapist–client interaction—there are some common features in both the mentoring and supervision roles to engage the supervisee in self-discovery of previously unknown or out-of-awareness behaviors that may reduce the effectiveness of the mentee or supervisee's effectiveness.

However, there are three additional roles in the mentoring relationship that are not addressed in the discrimination model: sponsoring, encouraging, and befriending. Sponsoring is uniquely a part of the mentoring role. One definition of the sponsoring role is to promote, support, and protect the mentee (Tentoni, 1995). The role of the supervisor in a sponsoring function may include a supportive role when the supervisee is faced with a difficult client or a difficult situation with a client. For example, a mentee working with a family who lost a child unexpectedly may have a child of a similar age and may have difficulty processing her or his feelings related to the death of the child. Here, the mentor may act in the sponsoring (supportive) role in order to provide support for the mentee, by just listening to the mentee and not actively engaging in therapeutic counseling.

A secondary component to sponsoring includes promoting. Here the supervisor may serve to promote the supervisee's abilities by encouraging him or her to present at a conference or workshop, either individually or as a co-presenter with the supervisor. A third component to sponsoring that can be integrated into supervision is the protective role for the supervisee. In this case, the supervisor can serve to protect the supervisee from getting involved in cases that are beyond the supervisee's training or unknowingly getting caught in an ethical dilemma (due to the supervisee's inexperience). This may occur in agencies where an administrative supervisor, who is pushing for billing units, tells a new clinician; "We need a diagnosis we can bill for." The new clinician, who wants to please the administrative supervisor, acquiesces to the demand. In this scenario, the clinical supervisor/mentor can intervene and *protect* the supervisee from potential long-term problems by serving as a liaison between the administrative supervisor and the mentee.

Encouraging and encouragement play a vital role in the mentoring relationship. Rudolph Dreikurs (1987) said, "A child needs continuous encouragement like a plant needs water" (p. 36). Recognizing that he is discussing children, the adage nevertheless holds true for both supervision and the mentoring relationship. Encouragement is more than just a series of "atta boy" comments by the mentor (supervisor); it also includes allowing the mentee (supervisee) to struggle with issues in order to experience a sense of accomplishment and resiliency. The role of encouragement gives the mentee a sense of empowerment to test his or her

TABLE 19.1. Reconceptualized Integrated Development Model Incorporating Mentoring (DM-R)

	Teacher	Counselor	Consultant	Mentor
Intervention	The supervisee struggles with confronting the client regarding her poor lifestyle choices. *Supervisor discusses strategies that the supervisee can use and models confrontation in the supervisory session.*	The supervisee is unable to confront the client because of the age, gender, and racial differences. *The supervisor encourages the supervisee to examine how this stance may impede the client's working toward her goals in therapy.*	The supervisee wants to explore narrative therapy with the client. *Supervisor provides resources for narrative therapy and explores ways in which narrative therapy can be incorporated into the supervisee's skill set.*	The supervisor determines that lack of knowledge about the "new" culture is impacting skills used by the therapist. *The supervisor invites the supervisee to community events and other social gatherings and offers to be the sounding board related to racial, age, and cultural issues (befriending).*
Conceptualization	Supervisee does not identify themes and patterns in the client's presenting issues. *Supervisor reviews a video session of counseling and teaches the supervisee to see common threads—e.g., how depression is contributing to the cycle of poor lifestyle choices.*	Supervisee assesses the client as being resistant because of his age, gender, and race. *Supervisor reflects on the supervisee's cultural values and how they may be contributing to the supervisee's perceptions of the client.*	Supervisee indicates that he would like to explore racial identity models with the client. *Supervisor assists the supervisee in identifying resources and discusses the various racial identity models including White and Black racial identity development.*	The supervisor observes that the agency "encourages" certain diagnoses for billing purposes. *Supervisor assists the supervisee in navigating the agency policies and may advocate on behalf of the supervisee with the administrators regarding the supervisees areas of competence and scope of practice (protecting).*
Personalization	Supervisee is unaware of his body language with this client. *Supervisor reviews videotape of session with supervisee, pointing out how his body language with this client is different from his body language with his other clients.*	Supervisee is unaware that his respect for the older female client results in not confronting the client's unhealthy lifestyle. *Supervisor assists the supervisee in seeing how he may be associating some of his personal cultural experiences with the client (transference) that results in his reluctance to confront the client because of the concern that he will be seen as being disrespectful.*	Supervisee shares that he wants to be comfortable working with older female clients who may be racially different. *Supervisor and supervisee discuss development concerns of older Caucasian women in the Appalachian region.*	The supervisor recognizes that the supervisee may benefit from professional development and scholarly advancement. *The supervisor assists the supervisee to write a presentation proposal and offers to co-present on the newly acquired skills. The supervisor identifies conferences that focus on some of the mental health issues of clients in southeast Ohio and shares this with the supervisee (sponsoring).*

development in the profession. Here the mentor or supervisor takes an observer stance but is available to *encourage* the mentee when needed. Encouragement also includes presenting the mentee with challenges that may serve to stretch the mentee's comfort zone. Encouraging the mentee to go beyond previous experiences in order to find other skills or interests serves to broaden the mentee's growth and developmental process throughout life.

The fifth tenet of mentoring as described by Anderson and Shannon (1988) is that of *befriending*. Befriending would suggest a relationship that goes beyond the supervisory relationship. As many ethical codes of professional organizations, such as the American Counseling Association (ACA), caution against relationships that could be deemed as dual or multiple, this element of mentoring may seem problematic for supervisors. However, in Tentoni's (1995) terms, "Befriending consists of two critical behaviors: accepting and relating" (p. 4). The terms essentially mean that the person is accepted without attaching any form of judgment. This level of acceptance is fundamental to both the supervisory relationship and the mentoring relationship.

It is evident from the aforementioned that the supervisor's role as teacher, counselor, and consultant can be enriched by including the elements of mentoring (sponsoring, encouraging, and befriending). The following case study illustrates how the role of mentor provides a more comprehensive approach to mental health supervision.

Case Study

Trevonne is a 29-year-old recently qualified African American mental health professional who has moved from a large city in northern Ohio to a small rural town in southeast Ohio.

Trevonne is not independently licensed, and the mental health agency provides clinical supervision as he works toward independent licensure. Trevonne has been assigned to John, who is Caucasian and a seasoned supervisor with more than 20 years of experience as a mental health professional. One of the clients that Trevonne is working with is a 59-year-old overweight Caucasian female who has been diagnosed with major depression and type II diabetes. The client's goal is to work on poor lifestyle choices that have contributed to her poor health. Trevonne reports that he leaves each session with the client feeling inadequate, stressed, and frustrated.

Table 19.1 identifies supervision issues related to intervention, conceptualization, and personalization from the supervisee's (Trevonne's, in this case) perspective and the roles of teacher, counselor, consultant, and mentor that the supervisor may take to address the presenting issues.

CONCLUSIONS

Clearly, mental health supervision and mentoring have a long history, and there are intersecting points that mental health supervision and mentoring share, the obvious intersection being the teaching role and the counseling role. However, a perusal of the literature reveals that little attention has been devoted to the common thread that runs through both. The authors of this chapter highlight the essential similarities and differences between mental health supervision and mentoring. Bernard's (1979) discrimination model has been identified as the process model that lends itself readily to accommodating the additional three functions of mentoring: namely, sponsoring, encouraging, and befriending. The use of a case study illustrates the benefits of incorporating mentoring into the already well-established paradigm of mental health supervision: improved client care, reduced supervisee defensiveness, increased scholarly development and research contribution, and enhanced trust and rapport. Following are takeaways implied by this discussion and illustration. The takeaways include both benefits of the DM-R and cautionary notes related to the inclusion of mentoring tenets in the role of mental healthcare supervision.

TAKEAWAYS

Benefits of the DM-R

- Professional development of the supervisee can be enhanced.
- The informal components of supervision using the DM-R can serve to reduce defensiveness in the supervisee—for example, the development of multicultural counseling awareness through informal social interaction facilitated by the supervisor.
- Scholarly development, such as co-presentation or co-publication with the supervisor, can serve to enhance the confidence of the supervisee and enhance contributions from practitioners in the field to the corpus of counseling research.
- Inclusion of mentoring in the supervisor's role can enhance the other domains, such as the role of a teacher, counselor, and consultant. The establishment of rapport and trust as a result of the mentoring relationship could contribute to the supervisee's seeing the supervisor as part of the support structure for professional development rather than seeing the supervisor as an evaluator or gatekeeper.

Cautionary Notes

- The number of supervisors is fewer than that of mentors by virtue of the fact that mentors do not need specialized education. Mentors are often self-selected by mentees based on a fit with the mentee and the value that the mentee perceives in pairing up with a specific mentor. Beginning supervisees typically do not have a choice in selecting a supervisor. The assigned supervisor may be a good fit as a supervisor but may not meet the supervisee's criteria for the mentoring aspects of the DM-R.

- The concept of *befriending* may lead to problems in the supervisory relationship. *Befriending*, as used in the DM-R, occurs within appropriate ethical boundaries through acceptance and relating. However, unless one is diligent in maintaining these boundaries, the supervisor/mentor–supervisee/mentee relationship can become a relationship that lacks professional etiquette.
- Not all supervisors may be interested in taking on the added role of being a mentor, for which they may not be compensated—for example, meeting with the supervisee over the weekend to enhance cultural competence.
- Philosophically, some supervisors may not be comfortable combining the role of being a gatekeeper, an evaluative role, with an informal mentoring role, such as in discussions about career goals or sponsoring and advocating on behalf of the supervisee.

REFERENCES

Anderson, E. M., & Shannon, A. L. (1988). Toward a conceptualization of mentoring. *Journal of Teacher Education, 39*, 38–42.

Bernard, J. M. (1979). Supervisor training: A discrimination model. *Counselor Education and Supervision, 19*(1), 60–68.

Bernard, J. M., & Goodyear, D. (2014). *Fundamentals of clinical supervision* (5ᵗʰ ed.). Boston, MA: Allyn & Bacon.

Byrne, A. M., & Sias, S. M., (2010). Conceptual application of the discrimination model of clinical supervision for direct care workers in adolescent residential treatment settings. *Child Youth Care Forum, 39*, 201–209 DOI 10.1007/s10566-010-9100-z.

Bozeman, B., & Feeney, M. K., (2007). Toward a useful theory of mentoring: A conceptual analysis and critique. *Administration and Society, 39*, 719–739. doi: 10.1177/0095399707304119.

Dreikurs, R. (1987). *Children: The challenge*. New York, NY: E. P. Dutton. (Original work published 1964.)

Dubois, B., & Krogsrud, K. M. (2011). *Social work: An empowering profession*. Boston, MA: Allyn & Bacon.

House, R., Martin, P. J., & Ward, C. (2002). Changing school counselor preparation: A critical need. In C. D. Johnson & S. K. Johnson (Eds.), *Building stronger school counseling programs. Bringing futuristic approaches into the present* (pp. 185–207). Greensboro, NC: CAPS.

Smith, M. K. (2012). The functions of supervision. In *The encyclopedia of informal education*. Retrieved from www.infed.org/mobi/the-functions-of-supervision/

Tentoni, S. C. (1995). The mentoring of counseling students: A concept in search of a paradigm. *Counselor Education and Supervision, 35*(1), 32–43.

Tharp, R. G. (1992). The developmental and psychological foundations of mentoring. Retrieved from http://www.academia.edu/2679167/The_Development_and_Psychologicl_Foundations_of_Mentoring

Zey, M. G. (1984). *The mentor connection*. Homewood, IL: Dow Jones-Irwin.

CHAPTER 20

MENTORING THROUGH SERVICE LEARNING

Peter C. Mather, Diana L. Marvel, and Lisa V. Nelson

ABSTRACT

This chapter explores the potential of service learning pedagogy as a mentoring modality, illustrated through the experiences of graduate student participants in a short-term study abroad program in Honduras. The student experiences are analyzed using Baxter Magolda's (2001) self-authorship theory and the service learning course construction is described using Strange and Banning's (2001) environment model and Parks's (2000) concept of a mentoring environment. The goal of mentoring is described as transformational, borrowing from Kegan's (1994) idea that development is holistic and that contemporary adult roles are complex and daunting, requiring structural complexity (as opposed to simply advanced skills) on the part of adults inhabiting those roles.

The chapter also includes the "Service Learning Mentoring Assessment," a 37-item tool designed to measure the mentoring strength of service-learning programs. The assessment can be used as both a planning tool and a mechanism for conducting formative evaluations of service learning programs.

Mentoring for the Professions: Orienting Toward the Future, pages 363–379.
Copyright © 2015 by Information Age Publishing
All rights of reproduction in any form reserved.

MENTORING THROUGH SERVICE LEARNING

As traditional-age students transition from higher education, the complex worlds of career and family often demand more advanced skills and maturity levels than are required to successfully navigate traditional college life (Baxter Magolda, 2001; Baxter Magolda & King, 2004; Kegan, 1994). Kegan described the developmental requirements for young adults as summed up in the concept of "self-authorship," highlighting the importance of the capacity in both career and personal domains to deal with life's complex challenges with agency and relative independence.

Acquiring self-authorship entails more than developing skills; it signals a holistic process of meaning-making that includes cognitive, intrapersonal, and interpersonal dimensions (Baxter Magolda, 1998, 2001; Kegan, 1994; Kegan & Lahey, 2009). Due to the complex processes of development for young adults, mentoring extends beyond traditional apprenticeship, in which a senior craftsperson who demonstrates some task-related accomplishment guides the protégé to acquire proficiency. Rather, mentoring to prepare students for today's complex world should be targeted at personal transformation. Kegan (2000) distinguishes between informative and transformative learning. The former occurs through traditional pedagogy (e.g., lecture) and apprenticeship, while the latter occurs through artful guidance, based on an understanding of the complex and daunting demands of adult life. In this chapter, we explore mentoring as an art of guiding students into transformation.

Parks (2000) describes the transformative process for young adults as a matter of faith. By faith, she means, "the capacity and demand for meaning." She elaborates:

> We human beings seem unable to survive, and certainly cannot thrive, unless we can make meaning. We need to be able to make some sort of sense out of things; we seek pattern, order, coherence, and relation in the disparate elements of our experience. If life is perceived as only fragmented and chaotic, we suffer confusion, distress, stagnation, and finally despair. (p. 7)

McAdams (1993) echoes Parks's notion of the importance of meaning-making in young adults, and describes adulthood as a process of mythmaking. For McAdams, mythmaking refers to the process of ascribing meaning, through a personal story or narrative, and to one's own personal and cultural history, as well as to the construction of a dream for the future.

Both Parks (2000) and McAdams (1993) note that young adulthood signals a transition from provisional commitments of late adolescence to a time of deeper commitments. They agree that this important transition is aided by providing unique types of support, or mentoring. Parks asserts that the term "mentor" is overused and "is best reserved for a distinctive role in the story of human becoming" (2000, p. 128). For McAdams, mythmaking refers to the process of ascribing meaning, through a personal story or narrative, as well as to the construction of a dream for the future..

The importance of a mentoring environment or community rests on the reality that we are social beings and our individual and collective futures rest on vital social networks. Parks (2000) states,

> [I]f each new generation is to contribute to the ongoing creation and renewal of life and culture, young adults need more than to be challenged individually to realize their full potential. They need to know they will not be alone—or alone with "just my mentor." If they are going to have the courage to take the road less traveled because it represents a more worthy truth, then they must discover that in doing so they will encounter a new sociality: a trustworthy network of belonging. Ideas and possibilities take hold in the imagination of the young adult in the most profound ways when he or she is met by more than a mentor alone—by a mentoring community. (p. 134)

So the idea of mentoring community or mentoring environment recognizes both the capacity of the environment for fostering maturity in individuals and the reality that adults can be most effective and successful in adult life when they recognize and honor the social context in which they operate.

We consider the environment to be a complex and multidimensional construct. Strange and Banning (2001) identify four frameworks of the environment: physical, human aggregate, organizational, and constructed. The physical environment refers to both natural and synthetic (e.g., architectural) aspects of one's surroundings. The physical environment includes artifacts such as displays of identity and other symbols and material evidence of a community's behaviors and values. Human aggregate encompasses the collective characteristics of the people who inhabit the place. This dimension can be experienced and described in terms of personality, behavior, and culture. For example, the degree of heterogeneity of cultural characteristics has relevance to an environment's educational potential. Organizational constructs refer to the structural dimensions, such as the formality of rules, hierarchical structure, and locus of decision making. Physical, human aggregate, and organizational characteristics can all shape an environment's conduciveness to healthy community engagement. Strange and Banning's fourth framework, the constructed environment, refers to the community members' (often subconscious) perceptions of reality that underlie and support the values and behaviors within an organization or environment. In the context of an educational environment, underlying assumptions about the meaning of truth and conceptions of how students learn are important to the learning practices that are employed. Strange and Banning's broad construction of what constitutes an environment recognizes the many dimensions that can make a difference in the education and transformation of young adults.

Parks (2000) describes certain gifts or attributes of the mentoring environment—in other words, modes by which mentoring is practiced. They are recognition, support, challenge, and inspiration. Recognition refers to the human need to be acknowledged or seen. It can come in the form of validation, where someone other than a parent recognizes the gifts, talents, and promise of a young adult. The mentor who provides this gift also recognizes the vulnerability of the person as she is in the process of recognizing her own strengths. It often moves young people to see something about themselves that they had not previously recognized. Support is the second mentoring gift. In this case, the mentor walks a delicate balance between recognizing the needs of the protégé for external approval and support while, at the same time, "champion[ing] the competence and potential the young life represents" (Parks, 2000, p. 129). Support is counterbalanced by an appropriate degree of challenge. Challenge is driven by the mentor's understanding that the world after formal education or professional preparation can be daunting. It is important to recognize that challenge should not be unidirectional. Although the mentor brings greater experience into the relationship, the mentor can still learn from the protégé. So this is not a traditional, hierarchical relationship, but a relationship that is steeped in mutual benefit. The final mentoring gift is that of inspiration. In Parks's notion that development is about the maturity of one's faith, inspiration is essential. As students learn to apply critical lenses to daunting problems, inspiration can ensure that criticism does not turn into cynicism.

In the context of service learning, the gifts of mentoring can be offered by a faculty member or adult administrator, or even by peers (Parks, 2000). We believe that it is important to highlight Parks's suggestion about the potential for peers to share in the responsibility of providing mentorship; that is, students who work together on meaningful projects can offer these gifts to one another.

In this chapter, we examine the potential for service learning as a modality or structure for mentoring. We have chosen service learning as a vehicle to describe a mentoring environment because it is a pedagogical process that synthesizes many of the components of a mentoring environment described by Parks (2000). However, we believe that the descriptions we provide in regard to mentoring can be translated into other educational settings—both traditional (e.g., classrooms) and innovative (e.g., virtual classrooms). Our collaboration for this chapter grew out of a service learning experience with Pete, the first author of this chapter, as an instructor, and co-authors Diana and Lisa, as participants. Each of us has a unique perspective regarding the nature of the mentoring environment. In describing this mentoring model, we also draw from the experiences of other participants and include their voices in our discussion of dimensions of the environment that seem to provide particularly effective mentoring modalities. Before discussing the environmental dimensions, however, we present a particular program that provides an illustrative context for mentoring environments.

SERVICE LEARNING IN HONDURAS

Ohio University has offered a service learning program in Honduras through the department of higher education and counseling for five years. This is a two-week, faculty-led, credit-bearing study abroad program for graduate students that combines service learning pedagogy and service work in rural Honduras. Service learning is a pedagogy focused on experiential learning. Rather than being bound by the classroom pedagogies of lecture and reading, service learning promotes learning through a cycle of action and reflection (Eyler & Giles, 1999). As with most community service or volunteering, it is common practice for service learners to devote their time and energy to a humanitarian or direct service-based project. However, service learning necessarily includes a reflection component, such as facilitated discussion with peers and mentors or journaling throughout the service experience. A broad range of student learning outcomes from participation in service learning programs is documented throughout service learning literature and scholarship. In particular, identity development (Eyler & Giles, 1999) and perspective transformation (Crabtree, 2008; Kiley, 2004) among participants are outcomes that are frequently discussed in service learning research. The particular goals of the program described in this chapter are congruent with Eyler and Giles's (1999) objectives of service learning outcomes in that, by putting students in environments where their assumptions, experiences, and biases are challenged, educators can increase students' opportunities for transformative learning.

The Ohio University service learning in Honduras program attracts a diverse community of learners. Students come from varied cultural backgrounds and nationalities as well as from universities across the country. Program participants in the summer of 2009, the service learning trip on which this chapter is focused, were graduate students hailing primarily, but not exclusively, from higher education and student affairs backgrounds. Students' academic disciplines included recreation and sports pedagogy, nutrition, intercultural relations, secondary education, and counseling. There was no language requirement to participate in the program, but a small percentage of students possessed Spanish language skills. This freedom from a language requirement was made possible in large part because of support from bilingual staff from the partnering organization in Honduras.

Honduras Outreach, Inc. (HOI), a nonprofit, faith-based group, handled the logistics of organizing the program and service work for Ohio University. HOI regularly hosted service groups at their ranch in the Agalta Valley and organized ongoing service projects based on needs in the communities it serves. In Honduras, HOI is staffed by local Hondurans who act as program coordinators, interpreters, and cultural consultants. As a community-development organization, HOI brokers service projects funded by service groups, creating opportunities for Ohio University students to engage in construction work alongside community members. Collaborative involvement in the project by both community members and service learners, such as in HOI projects, is an important dimension of a well designed service learning program. In this way, community members and students experience a sense of empowerment as citizens, and both groups benefit from the collaborative relationship (Crabtree, 2008). Community involvement also positively impacts learning outcomes for students (Crabtree, 2008; Keith, 2005), as reflected in the words of a service learner in Honduras:

> Within the first day or two of us being in the village we realized that the people
> in the village did want us there and that they were grateful for us being there, and

while they didn't necessarily need us to do the work for them because they were able-bodied and a lot harder workers than most of us were, it was nice to know that they were appreciative of the community that we were building with them while we were there, and that they knew that we cared about them and were trying to help.

In addition to building latrines and pouring cement floors, students also spent time in the local one-room school leading arts-and-crafts activities and playing outdoor sports with children ages four to twelve. The semi-structured classroom activities and time for play created opportunities for meaningful relationships to form between program participants and the children in the school, despite the short duration of the service learning program. Reflecting on her time spent in the school and a new understanding of the value of short-term relationships, Diana wrote:

> The children in the village invested in me as if I might see them next week—all the while knowing that we would soon be saying goodbye. It made me want to take more interpersonal risks—to risk getting attached to someone, even if only for the present moment, but enjoying how we make ourselves matter in being known to one another for the time we share.

During the week at the ranch, most program participants spent some time in each service environment (construction or school), which contributed to the variety of experiences and unique learning of each participant. The second week of the service learning program was focused on the educational system in Honduras. Students spent most days visiting Honduran universities in and around Tegucigalpa and interviewing students and administrators on research topics the Ohio University students had chosen in preparation for the service learning experience. Conducting this research had a lasting impact on students like Katie:

> I think one of the most valuable things was having the chance to do research while we were there. Particularly because it had me continually thinking about what we did and why we were there and what the people in Santa Rita thought and what they told us. So since I've been forced to work on that research for the last few months, it's forced me to keep thinking about it and keep evaluating. So that was good. And you wouldn't keep doing that after a two-week trip. You wouldn't keep thinking about it for six or eight months.

During this second phase of the program, nights were spent primarily with home-stay families, which increased students' level of cultural immersion and also provided a productive disorientation. Living, even for a short period, with Honduran families was an important passage for many students. It was particularly during this stage that, without their program companions at their sides for support or buffer, they faced the emotional and psychological challenges of a cross-cultural encounter on their own.

Critical reflection about service learning began on campus weeks before students started packing their bags for Honduras. Pre-departure meetings provided platforms for students to start reflecting on themes of poverty, power, and privilege. Students were asked to research and present a topic related to both their discipline and the service learning program. Lists of craft supplies and sports equipment to bring to the schools were made and funds allocated for their acquisition. Students were also asked to read *Enrique's Journey* (Nazario, 2006), a novel about the plight of a young boy from Central America trying to reunite with his mother working in the United States. All of these activities were combined with faculty-led discussion to prime students' thinking about their roles as service learners, as well as about the complex and varied cultural landscape of Honduras.

FEATURES OF A MENTORING
ENVIRONMENT IN SERVICE LEARNING

Mentoring gifts—recognition, support, challenge, and inspiration—are delivered through environments that possess the following features: a network of belonging, big enough questions, encounters with otherness, and habits of mind (Parks, 2000). As seen in Figure 20.1, service learning provides the context for the mentoring gifts through which the features of the mentoring environment are expressed.

With the help of student-participant voices, we discuss and illustrate the ways in which these features were presented in our Latin American service learning program.

FIGURE 20.1. Features and gifts of the service learning mentoring environment

A Network of Belonging

In order for service learning to work effectively as a mentoring modality, a network of belonging must be fostered among participants. Whether short-term or long-term, service learning programs can only realize their potential if participants are invited to become fully engaged members of the community of exploration and service. A sense of belonging extends beyond feeling welcome. Schlossberg (1989) notes the importance of a sense of mattering. In this case, "mattering" refers to students' sense that their presence in the community makes a positive difference. There is considerable evidence that personal and professional developmental changes are most likely to result when students are deeply engaged in educational and social experiences (e.g., Kuh, Cruce, & Shoup, 2008). This deep engagement can best occur when there is a sense of belonging and mattering.

Short-term programs like the Honduras program typically involve intensive group engagement. In the Honduras service learning program in which we participated, members of the class stayed in the same dormitory, ate together, travelled together in a small bus, and worked side by side in a village. This kind of intensive engagement presents certain challenges, but it also creates a common experience and fosters a sense of community among participants. This sense of community is aided by planned activities, including identification and employment of participants' strengths and areas of expertise and collective reflections that honor different voices and perspectives.

In the service-learning in Honduras program, student strengths were identified using the True Colors strengths assessment (http://truecolorsintl.com/), which, according to the professional materials, "distills the elaborate concepts of personality theory into a user-friendly, practical tool used to foster healthy productive relationships" (n.p.). A trained facilitator led us in a session in which we made sense of the different strengths in respect to the work we would do together. As part of this process, we discussed how various strengths could be useful to the program. Based on the strengths identification as well as participants' particular interests, leadership roles were assigned to students. For example, some students were assigned investigative roles (e.g., interviewing members of the community); others were assigned to lead children in craft activities; others presented on an area of their expertise to the rest of the class. The process helped members of the group understand their value in relationship to the work we were doing, as well as being exposed to the strengths of others.

Recognizing the cultural assets of class members is also important in fostering a sense of belonging. The service learning in Honduras program typically has included international students. In summer, 2009, the program included a total of 15 students, with 12 from the United States and one each from Japan, Sudan, and Kenya. During a closing celebration with members of the Honduran community, our service learning team witnessed the community singing the national anthem. This was followed by the U.S. students singing their anthem and then the Japanese, Kenyan, and Sudanese students each singing theirs. Baboo, who was from Sudan, noted the following in his journal after the program:

> It was an historic moment when they asked me to sing my national anthem. At that moment I felt I was making history. For sure, I am the sole Sudanese who ever sang that anthem in that part of the world and I don't think that anybody from Sudan will ever do that again in that same place.

This type of cultural sharing provided additional connection within the class and from the class to the community we were serving. When students feel connected to others based on the recognition of and appreciation for different gifts and experiences, a foundation is set for deep exploration and learning—for asking big enough questions.

Big Enough Questions

As students develop the capacity to think critically, it is important to facilitate the application of this emerging skill to deep questions of significance. The instabilities presented in the transitions into and out of undergraduate and graduate education tend to foster searches for meaning (Strange, 2001). The same holds true for experiences of immersion in a culture that is different from what students have previously experienced. Parks (2000) lists questions that she considers to be meaningful, such as, "Who do I really want to become?"; "Am I lovable?"; "How do I work toward something when I don't even know what it is?"; "Who will be there for me?"; "Do my actions make any real difference in the grand scheme of things?"; "How have I been wounded?"; and "Will I ever really heal?" (pp. 137–138).

Deep questions of significance surfaced repeatedly among participants of the service learning program in Honduras. Such questions are raised through a series of specific approaches. First, big questions are triggered when students have significant access to the people in the communities we serve. This kind of access occurs in the Honduras program because community members and students work side by side on projects. Both parties are encouraged to be open and to ask questions about one another's experiences. Assigning students research projects that involve interviewing community members gives service learning students further opportunity for rich interactions. Research projects are conducted by small groups of three or four students each. The projects have included topics such as community members' experiences with service groups, educational expectations of late adolescents, resources for and approaches to dealing with mental health concerns, and sources of happiness in high-poverty communities.

The article "Listening to Santa Rita" (Mather, Givens, Hendrickson, & Lash, 2010) resulted from one of the research projects and highlights questions about the meaning and significance of service. The article presents personal and rich critiques by student participants of the very purpose of conducting service work, as, for example, in Angela's reflection:

If all our work in Honduras did was to leave the people of Santa Rita desperately waiting for our heroic return, I had a hard time believing that we did much good there. It seemed as though instead I had helped them to create a dependence upon me, or others like me. Although the room additions I helped to fund and build were much needed, what was a resident of Santa Rita to do in a few years when another addition was needed? My feeling was that our ultimate goal should be to help others become self-sufficient, perhaps by creating jobs, improving education, or installing an irrigation system to enable year-round farming. It was unclear whether they or I took away more from these shared experiences. My experiences in Honduras forever changed me, but what was to become of the Hondurans? (p. 4)

The issues raised by Angela are illustrative of what Mezirow (2000) calls disorienting dilemmas, which he suggests are important catalysts for transformative learning. He contends that disorienting dilemmas result in adopting frames of reference that are more "inclusive, discriminating, open, emotionally capable of change, and reflective" (pp. 7–8). Service learning experiences present novel settings that serve as natural triggers for disorienting dilemmas that lead to the emergence of big questions and transformation. These confrontations with novel experiences can be supplemented by intentionally including provocative ideas, particularly through supplemental readings, including readings that problematize service work. One of the most provocative readings used in the program is Ivan Illich's (1968) essay, "To Hell With Good Intentions," in which Illich states:

I am here to suggest that you voluntarily renounce exercising the power which being an American gives you. I am here to entreat you to freely, consciously and humbly give up the legal right you have to impose your benevolence on Mexico. I am here to challenge you to recognize your inability, your powerlessness and your incapacity to do the "good" which you intended to do. (n.p.)

The questions implied by Illich, and other questions like them, are significant in speaking to the fundamental issues of self and relationships with others that reflect Baxter Magolda's self-authorship theme. In order to function ably in the world of post-college work and relationships, adults need to be able to manage themselves in the context of ambiguity—the mentoring environment helps participants learn self-management as they deal with the vexing problems that are part of a meaningful service learning experience.

Provocations described here are representative of the mentoring gift of challenge. The degree of tolerance for challenge varies by individual student and, particularly, by level of maturity. Several scholars (e.g., Baxter Magolda, 1992; Kitchener & King, 1994; Perry, 1999) have noted that the degree to which students can manage and respond favorably to challenge increases throughout the college years for traditional-age students. Since the service learning in Honduras program is for graduate students in the professions, the challenges that are presented are not beyond the capacity of most of these students. However, for all students, and especially those who are younger, the gift of challenges needs to be complemented with an appropriate degree of the support gift.

The mentoring gift of support is offered in part by naming and valuing the strengths of group members. Participants in the Honduras program also find considerable support from one another, as illustrated by Ardy: "Sitting on the porch in the evenings at the ranch it was really nice just to hear what people were thinking and feeling and to be able to support one another in their struggles and have them support me in mine." It is also important for leaders, teachers, and facilitators to be conscious of the disequilibrium that can be presented by service learning programs and to personally provide additional support.

One of the primary characteristics of discomfort in this type of intensive cross-cultural exercise manifests as resistance to learning. Jones, Gilbride-Brown, and Gasiorski (2005) have noted that resistance to cross-cultural learning is common. They recommend that service learning leaders do not react to resistance as failure. Rather, it is important to continue to support students where they are in their making of meaning. A two-week service learning experience can place students in a state of disequilibrium but may not provide the time and space for students to adequately process their experience. Opportunities to follow this experience with discussion and reflection can be important.

An article by Mather, Karbley, and Yamamoto (2012) illustrates the profound challenge to one's conception of identity that can occur as a result of a service learning experience. One of the participants, Megan, dealt with intense disorientation as she was confronted with the tension between her previous self-conception as a member of an oppressed population, while also facing aspects of her privilege. Becoming aware of tension or ambiguity in one's securely held view of identity is both challenging and important to maturity (McAdams, 1993). Megan's experience of dealing with ambiguity was aided by the extended process of working with a faculty member and a peer in making meaning of her experience, following the completion of the in-country component of the course.

Encounters with Otherness

Parks (2000) stated, "Encounters with otherness are the most powerful sources of vital, transforming questions that open into new ways of making meaning that can form and sustain commitment to the common good" (p. 139). Students participating in service learning programs may encounter otherness, both through their work with members of the recipient community and within their community of peers. The big questions that are raised during the service learning program are shared informally as participants interact with one another during the course of the two-week experience. The instructor also facilitates a nightly discussion, which takes the form of a semi-structured conversation focusing on events from the day and from the readings that students do as part of the course. These facilitated discussions ensure that students are exposed to the big questions emerging out of their peers' experiences and insights. In our experience, these discussions are enriched when the peer group represents diverse social identities. This has been a reality in the service learning in Honduras program in that some North American participants find the conditions of the Latin American communities where we work hard to believe, and yet some African students suggest that the communities in Honduras appear to be just on the border of poverty compared to what they sometimes see in their own home communities.

When encountering otherness in the communities where we work, the participants are often struck and even moved by the commonalities they recognize between their lives and the lives of those in these high poverty communities. The students who come from White, middle-class families in the United States rarely predict the level of personal connections they make with our counterparts in the community. However, they often develop rich connections, as described by Parks (2000): "An empathic bond arises from recognizing that the other suffers in the same way as we, having the same capacity for hope, longing, love, joy, and pain" (p. 140). Discovering these connections often inspires students in significant ways. This is illustrated by Angela's passionate reflection on her time in Honduras:

> New feelings began to creep in. Playing simple games with the children and building walls out of mud with the other women, I began to feel like I was a part of something larger, beyond the brief time I was going to be in Santa Rita. The real kicker was the fiesta at the end of the project. I will never forget those few hours: the children singing and dancing, the many hugs I received and the exchange of gifts.

While students have poignant experiences of shared humanity, they also are aware of privileges that allow them to travel across the Western hemisphere to expose themselves to a place that is profoundly different from what they see in their customary surroundings. When we first arrive in the country, it is difficult for participants to recognize similarities. From the window of a bus on which we travel for approximately seven hours before arriving at our rural destination, participants notice the many things that are different—levels of poverty, landscape, and so on. So, by the time we enter the community where the work is done, participants often experience some uncertainty about how they might connect with a place and people that seem so different. For this reason, we begin our interactions with a celebration of the opportunity to be together. This often involves a collection of songs, dances, and even jokes shared between the groups. Sometimes there are recreational games like a three-legged race and "pato, pato, ganso" ("duck, duck, goose"). The laughter that emerges from these lighthearted experiences helps to dissipate the anxiety and remind individuals from both groups that, in the midst of the differences, there are shared emotions and other commonalities.

Habits of Mind

Parks (2000) names four habits of mind that are important for cultivating "adult faith": dialogue, critical thought, connective-systemic-holistic thought, and a contemplative mind. In Parks's model, dialogue is as much about listening as it is about talking. At a foundational level, it involves a willingness to be affected by another person. This discipline of dialogue should be practiced by the leader of a service learning program and encouraged among peers. Group processing, a common pedagogical modality used in service learning programs, is a valuable forum for fostering healthy dialogue. The discipline is promoted by establishing ground rules in discussion. In a service learning program where cognitive dissonance is often a reality, it is important that students feel safe in expressing themselves openly and honestly. This is not to say that disagreement is discouraged. The basic principle is to respect and genuinely attempt to understand others' points of view.

This type of dialogue provides an openness for critical thought, which Parks (2000) defines as "the capacity to step outside of one's own thought and reflect upon it as object, to recognize multiple perspectives and the relativized character of one's own experiences and assumptions" (p. 143). Being in novel environments, like those presented by service learning programs, promotes curiosity; and the engagement of curiosity promotes critical thought (Kashdan, 2009; Mather, 2008). Curiosity that is nurtured by the novel experiences presented in service learning also provides a rich foundation for connective-systemic-holistic thought. As important as critical thought is for the young adult, so is the capacity to perceive the connections among seemingly disparate ideas and phenomena. A constructivist educational approach in which an instructor values the previous experiences of the student and respects the student as a legitimate knower can foster mature, holistic thought.

Baxter Magolda (2001) proposed that establishing a strong internal foundation is an important step in the road to self-authorship. Similarly, Parks (2000) points to the importance of growing a strong inner life; one strategy for fostering a strong inner life is to develop a contemplative mind. The contemplative mind is important in a world that is full of distractions that crowd out thought. Contemplation occurs naturally with the Honduras program due to the rural setting, where the Internet is unavailable, but hammocks and clean air are prevalent. Particularly due to the intensity of short-term service learning programs, space for quiet reflection is essential to promoting transformative learning. The deliberate pedagogical service learning practice of personal reflection through journaling is a powerful tool for fostering a contemplative mind.

ASSESSING SERVICE LEARNING AS A MENTORING ENVIRONMENT

We have illustrated the possibilities of service learning as a mentoring modality through describing a particular service learning program. However, other service learning and other engaging learning practices can also provide rich learning toward self-authorship, in the words of Baxter Magolda (2001), or a mature faith, as described by Parks (2000). The assessment offered as a takeaway in the appendix at the end of this chapter is designed to assist educators with constructing a rich and powerful mentoring environment.

The assessment is based on Parks's mentoring environment model and Baxter Magolda's theory of self-authorship, as both constructs are related to the developmental process for young adults. More specifically, self-authorship theory provides a means for understanding the developmental goals, while Parks's mentoring environment relates to the programmatic features of the service-learning program. Domains 1 through 8 of the assessment represent subscales of the mentoring environment; Domain 9 is a self-authorship scale. We recommend that service learning leaders use this mentoring assessment as a guide for planning programs and for assessing programming effectiveness.

Specific tools for enhancing mentoring capacity are discussed in a variety of service learning resources. Books by Butin (2005), Eyler and Giles (1999), Jacoby (2009), and Rhoads (1997) are among the many valuable resources that can assist service learning educators to develop programs that possess mentoring capacities.

CONCLUSION

A mentor–protégé relationship can be a powerful asset for educating young adults. Parks (2000) has pointed out the importance of conceiving of environments and communities as mentoring agents that can provide young adults with much-needed support in acquiring the capacities for successful adult life. In this chapter, we have presented service learning as a mentoring environment. We chose service learning because of our familiarity with the educational potential of this particular educational modality. While service learning is a unique and proven developmental approach, the applications we have described can be adapted to other educational modalities. As pointed out by Parks (2000) and Kegan (1994), today's complex world demands much of the adults who live in it. From partnering and parenting to working and neighboring, success in all these areas requires technical, interpersonal, and emotional competence and maturity. The educational environments that play a role in preparing these adults must provide recognition and inspiration and an appropriate blend of challenge and support in order to establish a foundation for lives of significance and thriving.

APPENDIX: SERVICE LEARNING MENTORING ASSESSMENT

Please respond to the following questions on the scale: 1 = Not at all; 2 = Seldom; 3 = Occasionally; 4 = Often; 5 = Almost Always True

Domain 1: Recognition

1. Program leaders acknowledged my personal strengths.
2. Some of my peers acknowledged my personal strengths.
3. Community members (i.e., service recipients) acknowledged my personal strengths.
4. I had opportunities to use my skills and talents in this program.

Domain 2: Support

5. I felt personal support from leaders when I encountered challenges.
6. I felt personal support from peers when I encountered challenges.
7. I felt personal support from community members when I encountered challenges.

Domain 3: Challenge

8. The program provided appropriate academic challenge.
9. I sometimes felt emotionally challenged in this program.
10. This program provided physical challenges.
11. The balance of challenge and support in this program were appropriate to help me learn.

Domain 4: Inspiration

12. This program inspired me to see the world in a new way.
13. This program inspired me to learn new things about myself.
14. This program inspired me to engage in future community service activities.

Domain 5: Network of Belonging

15. I experienced a sense of belonging in this program.
16. I felt that my presence mattered within my service group.
17. I felt that my presence mattered to the community where I was working.

Domain 6: Big Enough Questions

18. I was faced with large questions of meaning and purpose in this program.
19. I was faced with large questions about poverty or oppression in this program.
20. Many of the problems I faced as part of this program don't seem to have easy answers.

Domain 7: Encounters with Otherness

21. I often interacted with people culturally different from me while participating in this program.
22. I learned from the different perspectives offered by my peers.
23. I learned from different perspectives offered by my program's leaders.

Domain 8: Habits of Mind

24. There were formal opportunities for group reflection during this program.
25. There were informal opportunities for rich dialogue with my peers or leaders.
26. Conversations that occurred among group members dealt with important issues.
27. There were structured opportunities to reflect individually on this service experience.
28. I saw connections between the service project and my academic experiences.
29. I saw connections between the service project and the way I live my life.
30. This experience has improved my attitude about the goodness of people.

Domain 9: Self-Authorship

31. This experience has highlighted important decisions I want to make in my life.
32. This experience provoked me to question my life goals.
33. This experience has helped me clarify important goals in my life.
34. This experience has helped me understand myself better.
35. I am leaving this experience with new commitments related to my career.
36. I am leaving this experience with new commitments related to my lifestyle.
37. I believe that this experience will help me live a more fulfilling life.

REFERENCES

Baxter Magolda, M. (1992). Knowing and reasoning in college: Gender-related patterns in students' intellectual development. San Francisco, CA: Jossey-Bass.

Baxter Magolda, M. B. (1998). Developing self- authorship in young adult life. *Journal of College Student Development, 39*(2), 143–156.

Baxter Magolda, M. (2001). Making their own way: Narratives for transforming higher education to promote self-development. Sterling, VA: Stylus.

Baxter Magolda, M., & King, P. M. (Eds.) (2004). Learning partnerships: Theory and models of practice to education for self-authorship. Sterling, VA: Stylus.

Butin, D. (2005). Service-learning in higher education: Critical issues and directions. New York, NY: Palgrave Macmillan.

Crabtree, R. D. (2008). Theoretical foundations for international service-learning. Michigan Journal of Community Service Learning, *15*(1), 18–36.

Eyler, J., & Giles, D. E., Jr. (1999). Where's the learning in service learning? San Francisco, CA: Jossey-Bass.

Illich, I. (1968). To hell with good intentions. Retrieved from http://www.swaraj.org/illich_hell.htm

Jacoby, B. (2009). Community engagement in higher education: Concepts and practices. San Francisco, CA: Jossey-Bass.

Jones, S. R., Gilbride-Brown, J., & Gasiorski, A. (2005). Getting inside the "underside" of service-learning: Student resistance and possibilities. In D. W. Butin (Ed.), Service-learning in higher education: Critical issues and directions (pp. 3–24). New York, NY: Palgrave.

Kashdan, T. (2009). Curious? Discover the missing ingredient to a fulfilling life. New York, NY: HarperCollins.

Kegan, R. (1994). In over our heads: The mental demands of modern life. Cambridge, MA: Harvard Press.

Kegan, R. (2000).What form transforms? A cognitive-developmental approach to transformative learning. In J. Mezirow & Associates (Eds.), *Learning as transformation: Critical perspectives on a theory in progress* (pp. 35–70). San Francisco, CA: Jossey-Bass.

Kegan, R., & Lahey, L. (2009). Immunity to change: How to overcome it and unlock the potential in yourself and your organization. Boston, MA: Harvard Press.

Keith, N. Z. (2005). Community service learning in the face of globalization: Rethinking theory and practice. Michigan Journal of Community Service Learning, *11*(2), 5–24.

Kiley, R. (2004). A chameleon with a complex: Searching for transformation in international service-learning. Michigan Journal of Community Service Leaning, 10(2), 5–20.

Kitchener, K. S., & King, P. M. (1994). *Developing reflective judgment*. San Francisco, CA: Jossey-Bass.

Kuh, G. D., Cruce, T. M., & Shoup, R. (2008). Unmasking the effects of student engagement on first-year college grades and persistence. *Journal of Higher Education, 79*, 540–563.

Mather, P. C. (2008). Interns at an international, humanitarian organization: Career pathways and meaning making. Journal of College Student Development 49, 182–198.

Mather, P. C., Givens, B., Hendrickson, K., & Lash, A. (2010). Listening to Santa Rita: A critical examination of service-learning practice. Journal of College and Character, 11, 1–12.

Mather, P. C., Karbley, M., & Yamamoto, M. (2012). Identity matters in a short-term, international service-learning program. Journal of College and Character, 13(1), 1–14.

McAdams, D. P. (1993). The stories we live by: Personal myths and the making of the self. New York, NY: Morrow.

Mezirow, J. (2000). Learning as transformation. San Francisco, CA: Jossey-Bass.

Nazario, S. (2006). *Enrique's journey: The story of a boy's odyssey to reunite with his mother*. New York, NY: Random House.

Parks, S. D. (2000). Big questions, worthy dreams: Mentoring young adults in their search for meaning, purpose, and faith. San Francisco, CA: Jossey-Bass.

Perry, W. G., Jr. (1999). *Forms of ethical and intellectual development in the college years: A scheme.* San Francisco, CA: Jossey-Bass.

Rhoads, R. (1997). Community service and higher learning: Explorations of the caring self. Albany, NY: State University of New York Press.

Schlossberg, N. K. (1989). Marginality and mattering: Key issues in building community. In D. C. Roberta (Ed.), Designing campus activities to foster a sense of community (pp. 5–15). San Francisco, CA: Jossey-Bass.

Strange, C. C. (2001). Spiritual dimensions of graduate preparation in student affairs. In M. A. Jablonski (Ed.), New Directions for Student Services (no. 95, pp. 57–66). New York, NY: John Wiley & Sons.

Strange, C. C., & Banning, J. H. (2001). Educating by design: Creating campus learning environments that work. San Francisco, CA: Jossey-Bass.

AUTHOR BIOGRAPHIES

Pamela C. Beam is a lecturer in curriculum and instruction and secondary education courses in the Patton College of Education at Ohio University. Dr. Beam received her PhD from Ohio University in curriculum and instruction and teaches graduate and undergraduate courses. Her research agenda encompasses mentoring at multiple levels and the revisioning of the clinical model.

Karen Boch is superintendent at Wellston City School District located in Wellston, OH. Hers is the only rural school district in Ohio to engage in the use of instructional rounds (IR) to improve learning, and she is co-author of a chapter on IR in a forthcoming book. Dr. Boch has taught special education and has served as an elementary principal and a director of curriculum and instruction. In her previous leadership position for the Alexander Local Schools, she also coordinated the *Reading First* Ohio grant, the largest undertaking to improve K–3 reading instruction in the country's history. Her leadership skills have led to improved ratings in both districts.

Jozenia Colorado is an associate professor in the department of instructional design and technology at Emporia State University. Dr. Colorado's research interests include influences on student achievement and behavior in educational environments, including self-regulated learning, social community, self-awareness,

Mentoring for the Professions: Orienting Toward the Future, pages 381–386.
Copyright © 2015 by Information Age Publishing

and motivation. In addition, she is interested in new and emerging technologies in education, issues in distance education, and integrating technology into the K–12 learning environment.

Valerie Martin Conley holds a BA and MA in sociology from the University of Virginia and a PhD in educational leadership and policy studies from Virginia Tech. She is professor and chair of the department of counseling and higher education in the Gladys W. and David H. Patton College of Education at Ohio University. Dr. Conley received the Ohio University Outstanding Graduate Faculty Award in June 2007.

Maureen Doyle-Scharff is senior director for the office of independent grants for learning and change at Pfizer, Inc. She has worked in the field of medical education, quality improvement, and behavior change for over 20 years. She is currently a doctoral candidate in higher education administration at Ohio University, Athens.

Marged Dudek (née Howley), MEd, teaches middle and high school English in a rural Texas district and works as consultant with Oz Educational Consulting. In her consulting role, she conducts research and evaluations as well as develops curriculum, assessment instruments, and professional development tools. In the field of teaching she attends to sustainable implementation of liberating, differentiated instruction.

Bethany Fulton is a counselor in Ohio with a specialization in community mental health and the director of a mental health drop-in center. A graduate of Ohio University, Pittsburgh Seminary, and Chatham University, her research interests include auditory hallucinations in schizophrenia, grief counseling, and dialectical behavior therapy.

Marilynne Miles Gray holds an honours BA and MA in English literature from the University of British Columbia, where she taught courses and served as a teacher trainee supervisor. She holds the MEd in educational administration with a minor in English as a second language. In addition to developing mentoring programs and training participants, she served as editor for the journal, *Mentoring International*, produced *MentorInk Newsletter* for 20 years, and wrote articles and an eBook (*Mentoring: A to Z*) to help professionals implement effective mentoring programs.

William A. Gray developed distinctive mentoring programs for over 150 organizations. He holds the BA and MEd from the University of Virginia and the PhD from the University of Texas. Dr. Gray immigrated to Canada in 1970 to teach at the University of British Columbia, where he began developing formalized mentoring programs in 1978. He left academia in 1986 to devote himself full-time to developing mentoring programs. He has trained over 20,000 mentor–protégé partners, using Gray's Situational Mentoring Model and specially developed tools.

Dianne M. Gut is an associate professor of special education in the Patton College of Education at Ohio University. Dr. Gut received her PhD from the University of North Carolina at Chapel Hill and teaches graduate and undergraduate courses in special education and curriculum and instruction. Her major research interests include mentoring, interventions for students with disabilities, and integrating 21st-century skills into the curriculum.

Vikki F. Howard is professor of special education, University of Montana Western, director of a special education program, and co-author of *Very Young Children with Special Needs*, as well as numerous articles and chapters. Dr. Howard works with mentors in schools who serve as an integral part of teacher preparation and induction.

Aimee Howley, professor emerita from Ohio University's Patton College of Education and former teacher and administrator with the Jackson County (WV) schools now leads the consulting firm, WordFarmers Associates. Her current research and evaluation efforts include work on inclusive school leadership, instructional and process coaching, and rural education. Dr. Howley holds degrees from Barnard College, Marshall University (formerly the West Virginia College of Graduate Studies), and West Virginia University.

Kimberly A. Johnson, PhD, is the director of adult learning at St. Catherine University in St. Paul, Minnesota where she coordinates programs and advises on effective teaching and learning for adult students. Prior to this position, she directed the ATLAS center at Hamline University and designed, delivered, and evaluated professional development for adult basic education teachers and administrators across Minnesota.

William Larson is an assistant professor in the educational studies department of the Patton College of Education at Ohio University. Dr. Larson, who is the coordinator of the educational administration program, holds the PhD in educational administration and communications theory from Bowling Green State University. Dr. Larson's research focuses on the preparation of aspiring and current school leaders.

Barbara A. Mahaffey has a PhD in education from the Ohio State University and is a licensed professional clinical counselor with supervision credential. She is the regional program coordinator and associate professor of human services technology at Ohio University–Chillicothe. She is completing a study entitled, "Peer

Mentoring: A Project to Increase Retention among Human Services Technology Students."

Alvin Mares, PhD, is a faculty researcher in the College of Social Work at the Ohio State University. With over two decades of experience in the field of homelessness research, Dr. Mares has examined faith-based housing projects, managed two national evaluations of Veterans Administration's homelessness treatment programs, and examined numerous homelessness prevention programs for at-risk transition-aged youth. He has published 30 journal articles.

Diana L. Marvel holds an MA in intercultural relations from Lesley University, and her interest in international service learning has led her to pursue a PhD at Ohio University with concentrations in higher education and international development. Diana co-leads a graduate service-learning program in Ecuador and is contributing to global service-learning curriculum development at Ohio University.

Peter C. Mather is associate professor of higher education and student affairs and secretary to the board of trustees at Ohio University. He leads an annual service-learning-based program for graduate students to Latin America. Prior to his work at Ohio University, Peter was director of educational programs at the Carter Center, the headquarters of President Jimmy Carter's post-presidential, humanitarian work.

Renée A. Middleton, professor of counselor education, currently serves as dean of Ohio University's Gladys W. and David H. Patton College of Education and Human Services. In this capacity, she oversees the college's five departments and nine centers, numerous community partnerships, and the professional development schools that shape the education experience of approximately 1,300 undergraduate and 900 graduate students. Dean Middleton received the BS in speech and hearing from Andrews University, the MA in clinical audiology from the University of Tennessee, and the PhD in rehabilitation administration from Auburn University.

David Richard Moore, associate professor and chair of the department of educational studies at Ohio University, received a PhD in instructional systems design from Virginia Polytechnic Institute and State University (Virginia Tech) in 1995. His research focuses on instructional design for practice, visual learning, and instructional rhetoric. Much of this research is conducted through specially designed computer-based interactive systems (often using Flash™). David's latest book, *Designing Online Learning with Flash*, was published by Pfeiffer in January, 2009. David is an active speaker and consultant, most often on topics related to interactive computer-based training.

Lisa Nelson is a PhD candidate at Ohio University. She holds a JD and is a state-certified mediator. She founded San Francisco Area Mediation (SFAM) and previously ran a law and mediation practice in Ohio with a focus on juvenile and family law. Lisa has led service and adventure programs domestically and internationally with high school and university students.

Andrean Oliver is an associate professor in the department of school and community counseling at Virginia State University. Dr. Oliver has more than 15 years of experience in higher education and school counseling. Her research has focused on various counseling professional development topics. She has also facilitated professional workshops, presented at professional conferences, and published in areas relating to her professional interests.

Justina O. Osa is a professor and chair at Virginia State University. She has more than 30 years' experiences in higher education and P–12 teaching and administration. Dr. Osa is an avid researcher, a national and international presenter, author, and editor. Her research interests include student achievement, leadership, and mentoring. Dr. Osa serves as a reviewer/examiner for NCATE, ELCC, and SACSCOC.

Martha N. Ovando, PhD, is professor emeritus at the University of Texas at Austin. She served as professor for 24 years and as graduate advisor for 15 years in the educational administration department. She was selected as the 2010 J. Scribner Mentor of the Year by the University Council of Educational Administration. She has extensive experience in mentoring graduate students, and in 2012, the Martha N. Ovando Award was created in recognition of outstanding student leadership.

V. Ann Paulins holds bachelor's and master's degrees from Ohio University and earned the PhD from the Ohio State University. Her academic preparation focused on fashion and apparel. She is currently professor in the department of human and consumer sciences and senior associate dean in The Gladys W. and David H. Patton College of Education, Ohio University. Her scholarly interests focus on professional career development, ethical decision making, and women in leadership.

Sharon Reynolds, EdD, is an assistant professor in the department of family medicine and educational specialist for the Office of Rural and Underserved Programs at the Ohio University Heritage College of Osteopathic Medicine. Prior to this position, Sharon directed the Central/Southeast Adult Basic and Literacy Education (ABLE) Resource Center at Ohio University offering professional development for ABLE teachers and administrators across Ohio.

Cristine Smith is an associate professor at University of Massachusetts, Amherst. She specializes in literacy education in the U.S. and in developing countries. Prior to her appointment at the University of Massachusetts, she served as deputy director of the National Center for the Study of Adult Learning and Literacy, where she directed a study on adult literacy teacher professional development.

Mary Barbara Trube is a professor of early childhood education at Ohio University–Chillicothe. Dr. Trube received an EdD in educational administration with a concentration in special education from the University of Texas at Austin and an adult international English as a second language certificate from the University of Cincinnati. Her research interests include mentoring in diverse contexts.

Beth J. VanDerveer, associate professor, Ohio University, is department chair of recreation and sport pedagogy, and interim chair of the department of human and consumer sciences. She currently facilitates mentoring opportunities at the collegiate level and is involved in collaborative research projects with university faculty and coaches.

Tara A. VanDerveer is Setsuko Ishiyama Director of Women's Basketball at Stanford University and Naismith Memorial Basketball Hall of Fame Class of 2011. She is architect of over 900 career wins, two national championships, and an Olympic Gold Medal team in 1996. She is the author of *Shooting from the Outside* and currently is developing instructional videos for youth coaches aligned with the principles of positive coaching.

Tracy Walker is an associate professor in the College of Education at Virginia State University. Dr. Walker's areas of research interest include STEM, research methods, mentoring, and survey design. Recent publications focus on the inclusion of STEM-related activities in elementary schools and in the preparation of preservice elementary science teachers.

Guofang Wan, PhD, is a professor of teacher education who serves as director for graduate studies at the School of Education, Virginia Commonwealth University. Dr. Wan's research focuses on language and literacy education, mentoring preservice teachers, and curriculum studies. She has received several national awards including the 2010 Margaret Lindsey Distinguished Research in Teacher Education Award from the American Association of Colleges for Teacher Education.

Natalie F. Williams, PhD, is a clinical director for Autism Concepts, Inc. She has extensive experience providing ABA services (applied behavior analysis) and working in the field of early childhood mental health. As a graduate student at Ohio University, she served as the graduate research assistant for Dr. Middleton, Dean of The Patton College of Education.

CPSIA information can be obtained at www.ICGtesting.com
Printed in the USA
BVOW03s1228050515

398924BV00003B/9/P

9 781623 968359